Learning PHP, MySQL, and JavaScript

Robin Nixon

Beijing · Cambridge · Farnham · Köln · Sebastopol · Taipei · Tokyo

Learning PHP, MySQL, and JavaScript
by Robin Nixon

Published by O'Reilly Media, Inc., 1005 Gravenstein Highway North, Sebastopol, CA 95472.

O'Reilly books may be purchased for educational, business, or sales promotional use. Online editions are also available for most titles (*http://my.safaribooksonline.com*). For more information, contact our corporate/institutional sales department: (800) 998-9938 or *corporate@oreilly.com*.

Editor: Andy Oram
Production Editor: Sumita Mukherji
Copyeditor: Nancy Kotary
Proofreader: Kiel Van Horn

Indexer: Ellen Troutman Zaig
Cover Designer: Karen Montgomery
Interior Designer: David Futato
Illustrator: Robert Romano

Printing History:
   July 2009:   First Edition.

 This book uses RepKover™, a durable and flexible lay-flat binding.

ISBN: 978-0-596-15713-5

[M]   [5/10]

1271462549

Table of Contents

Preface

The combination of PHP and MySQL is the most convenient approach to dynamic, database-driven web design, holding its own in the face of challenges from integrated frameworks—such as Ruby on Rails—that are harder to learn. Due to its open source roots (unlike the competing Microsoft .NET framework), it is free to implement and is therefore an extremely popular option for web development.

Any would-be developer on a Unix/Linux or even a Windows/Apache platform will need to master these technologies. At the same time, the JavaScript is important, as it provides the hidden communication with the web server to create seamless interfaces.

Audience

This book is for people who wish to learn how to create effective and dynamic websites. This may include webmasters or graphic designers who are already creating static websites but wish to take their skills to the next level as well as high school and college students, recent graduates, and self-taught individuals.

In fact, anyone ready to learn the fundamentals behind the Web 2.0 technology known as Ajax will obtain a thorough grounding in all three of the core technologies: PHP, MySQL, and JavaScript.

Assumptions This Book Makes

This book assumes that you have a basic understanding of HTML and can at least put together a simple, static website, but does not assume that you have any prior knowledge of PHP, MySQL, or JavaScript—although if you do, your progress through the book will be even quicker.

Organization of This Book

The chapters in this book are written in a specific order, first introducing all three of the core technologies it covers and then walking you through their installation on a web development server, so that you will be ready to work through the examples.

In the following section, you will gain a grounding in the PHP programming language, covering the basics of syntax, arrays, functions, and object-oriented programming.

Then, with PHP under your belt, you will move on to an introduction to the MySQL database system, where you will learn everything from how MySQL databases are structured up to generating complex queries.

After that, you will learn how you can combine PHP and MySQL to start creating your own dynamic web pages by integrating forms and other HTML features. You will then spend some time looking at ways to speed up your web development using Smarty templates.

In the next three chapters, you will get down to the nitty-gritty practical aspects of PHP and MySQL development by learning a variety of useful functions and how to manage cookies and sessions, as well as how to maintain a high level of security.

In the following four chapters, you will gain a thorough grounding in JavaScript, from simple functions and event handling to accessing the Document Object Model and in-browser validation and error handling.

With an understanding of all three of these core technologies, you will then learn how to make behind-the-scenes Ajax calls and turn your websites into highly dynamic environments.

Finally, you'll put together everything you've learned in a complete set of PHP programs that together constitute a fully working social networking website.

Along the way, you'll also find plenty of pointers and advice on good programming practices and tips that could help you find and solve hard-to-detect programming errors. There are also plenty of links to websites containing further details on the topics covered.

Supporting Books

Once you have learned to develop using PHP, MySQL, and JavaScript you will be ready to take your skills to the next level using the following reference books:

- *Dynamic HTML: The Definitive Reference* by Danny Goodman (O'Reilly)
- *PHP in a Nutshell* by Paul Hudson (O'Reilly)
- *MySQL in a Nutshell* by Russell Dyer (O'Reilly)
- *JavaScript: The Definitive Guide* by David Flanagan (O'Reilly)

Conventions Used in This Book

The following typographical conventions are used in this book:

Plain text
> Indicates menu titles, options, and buttons.

Italic
> Indicates new terms, URLs, email addresses, filenames, file extensions, pathnames, directories, and Unix utilities.

`Constant width`
> Indicates command-line options, variables and other code elements, HTML tags, macros, the contents of files, and the output from commands.

`Constant width bold`
> Shows commands or other text that should be typed literally by the user; also occasionally used for emphasis.

`Constant width italic`
> Shows text that should be replaced with user-supplied values.

 This icon signifies a tip, suggestion, or general note.

 This icon indicates a warning or caution.

Using Code Examples

This book is here to help you get your job done. In general, you may use the code in this book in your programs and documentation. You do not need to contact us for permission unless you're reproducing a significant portion of the code. For example, writing a program that uses several chunks of code from this book does not require permission. Selling or distributing a CD-ROM of examples from O'Reilly books *does* require permission. Answering a question by citing this book and quoting example code does not require permission. Incorporating a significant amount of example code from this book into your product's documentation *does* require permission.

We appreciate, but do not require, attribution. An attribution usually includes the title, author, publisher, and ISBN. For example: "*Learning PHP, MySQL, and JavaScript*, by Robin Nixon. Copyright 2009 Robin Nixon, 978-0-596-15713-5."

If you feel your use of code examples falls outside fair use or the permission given here, feel free to contact us at *permissions@oreilly.com*.

We'd Like to Hear from You

Every example in this book has been tested on various platforms, but occasionally you may encounter problems; for example, if you have a nonstandard installation or a different version of PHP, and so on. The information in this book has also been verified at each step of the production process. However, mistakes and oversights can occur and we will gratefully receive details of any you find, as well as any suggestions you would like to make for future editions. You can contact the author and editors at:

> O'Reilly Media, Inc.
> 1005 Gravenstein Highway North
> Sebastopol, CA 95472
> (800) 998-9938 (in the United States or Canada)
> (707) 829-0515 (international or local)
> (707) 829-0104 (fax)

We have a web page for this book, where we list errata, examples, and any additional information. You can access this page at:

> *http://www.oreilly.com/catalog/9780596157135*

There is also a companion website to this book available online at:

> *http://lpmj.net*

where you can see all the examples with color-highlighted syntax. To comment or ask technical questions about this book, send email to the following address, mentioning its ISBN number (9780596157135):

> *bookquestions@oreilly.com*

For more information about our books, conferences, Resource Centers, and the O'Reilly Network, see our website at:

> *http://www.oreilly.com*

Safari® Books Online

When you see a Safari® Books Online icon on the cover of your favorite technology book, that means the book is available online through the O'Reilly Network Safari Bookshelf.

Safari offers a solution that's better than e-books. It's a virtual library that lets you easily search thousands of top tech books, cut and paste code samples, download chapters, and find quick answers when you need the most accurate, current information. Try it for free at *http://my.safaribooksonline.com*.

Acknowledgments

A huge thank you goes to my editor, Andy Oram, and all the folks at O'Reilly who worked so hard on this book, and without whom it could never have been written.

In particular I must thank my technical reviewers, Derek DeHart, Christoph Dorn, Tomislav Dugandzic, Becka Morgan, Harry Nixon, Alan Solis, and Demian Turner, for their help in ensuring the accuracy of this book.

I wish to also thank my wife, Julie, for her constant encouragement, and also Rachel, Hannah, Laura, Matthew, Harry, and Naomi, wonderful children who all helped with this project—each in their own way.

CHAPTER 1

Introduction to Dynamic Web Content

The World Wide Web is a constantly evolving network that has already traveled far beyond its conception in the early 1990s, when it was created to solve a specific problem. State-of-the-art experiments at CERN (the European Laboratory for Particle Physics—now best known as the operator of the Large Hadron Collider) were producing incredible amounts of data—so much that the data was proving unwieldy to distribute to the participating scientists who were spread out across the world.

At this time, the Internet was already in place, with several hundred thousand computers connected to it, so Tim Berners-Lee (a CERN fellow) devised a method of navigating between them using a hyperlinking framework, which came to be known as Hyper Text Transfer Protocol, or HTTP. He also created a markup language called HTML, or Hyper Text Markup Language. To bring these together, he wrote the first web browser and web server, tools that we now take for granted.

But back then, the concept was revolutionary. The most connectivity so far experienced by at-home modem users was dialing up and connecting to a bulletin board that was hosted by a single computer, where you could communicate and swap data only with other users of that service. Consequently, you needed to be a member of many bulletin board systems in order to effectively communicate electronically with your colleagues and friends.

But Berners-Lee changed all that with one fell swoop, and by the mid 1990s, there were three major graphical web browsers competing for the attention of five million users. It soon became obvious, though, that something was missing. Yes, pages of text and graphics with hyperlinks to take you to other pages was a brilliant concept, but the results didn't reflect the instantaneous potential of computers and the Internet to meet the particular needs of each user with dynamically changing content. Using the Web was a very dry and plain experience, even if we did now have scrolling text and animated GIFs!

Shopping carts, search engines, and social networks have clearly altered how we use the Web. In this chapter, we'll take a brief look at the various components that make up the Web, and the software that helps make it a rich and dynamic experience.

It is necessary to start using some acronyms more or less right away. I have tried to clearly explain them before proceeding. But don't worry too much about what they stand for or what these names mean, because the details will all become clear as you read on.

HTTP and HTML: Berners-Lee's Basics

HTTP is a communication standard governing the requests and responses that take place between the browser running on the end user's computer and the web server. The server's job is to accept a request from the client and attempt to reply to it in a meaningful way, usually by serving up a requested web page—that's why the term *server* is used. The natural counterpart to a server is a *client*, so that term is applied both to the web browser and the computer on which it's running.

Between the client and the server there can be several other devices, such as routers, proxies, gateways, and so on. They serve different roles in ensuring that the requests and responses are correctly transferred between the client and server. Typically, they use the Internet to send this information.

A web server can usually handle multiple simultaneous connections and—when not communicating with a client—spends its time listening for an incoming connection. When one arrives, the server sends back a response to confirm its receipt.

The Request/Response Procedure

At its most basic level, the request/response process consists of a web browser asking the web server to send it a web page and the server sending back the page. The browser then takes care of displaying the page (see Figure 1-1).

Each step in the request and response sequence is as follows:

1. You enter *http://server.com* into your browser's address bar.
2. Your browser looks up the IP address for *server.com*.
3. Your browser issues a request for the home page at *server.com*.
4. The request crosses the Internet and arrives at the *server.com* web server.
5. The web server, having received the request, looks for the web page on its hard disk.
6. The web page is retrieved by the server and returned to the browser.
7. Your browser displays the web page.

For an average web page, this process takes place once for each object within the page: a graphic, an embedded video or Flash file, and even a CSS template.

In step 2, notice that the browser looked up the IP address of *server.com*. Every machine attached to the Internet has an IP address—your computer included. But we generally access web servers by name, such as *google.com*. As you probably know, the browser

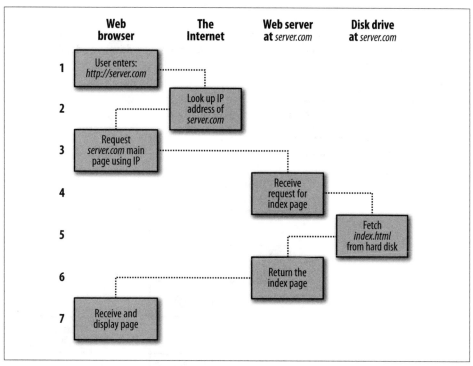

Figure 1-1. The basic client/server request/response sequence

consults an additional Internet service called the Domain Name Service (DNS) to find its associated IP address and then uses it to communicate with the computer.

For dynamic web pages, the procedure is a little more involved, because it may bring both PHP and MySQL into the mix (see Figure 1-2).

1. You enter *http://server.com* into your browser's address bar.

2. Your browser looks up the IP address for *server.com*.

3. Your browser issues a request to that address for the web server's home page.

4. The request crosses the Internet and arrives at the *server.com* web server.

5. The web server, having received the request, fetches the home page from its hard disk.

6. With the home page now in memory, the web server notices that it is a file incorporating PHP scripting and passes the page to the PHP interpreter.

7. The PHP interpreter executes the PHP code.

8. Some of the PHP contains MySQL statements, which the PHP interpreter now passes to the MySQL database engine.

9. The MySQL database returns the results of the statements back to the PHP interpreter.

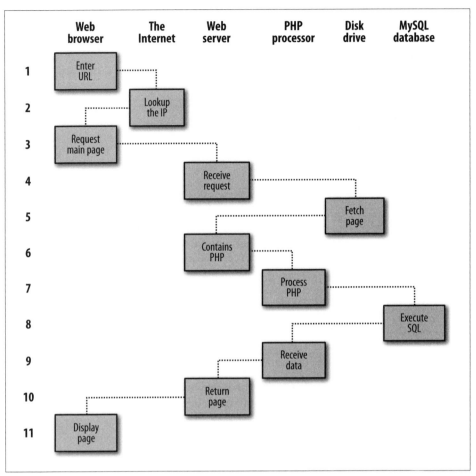

Figure 1-2. A dynamic client/server request/response sequence

10. The PHP interpreter returns the results of the executed PHP code, along with the results from the MySQL database, to the web server.

11. The web server returns the page to the requesting client, which displays it.

Although it's helpful to be aware of this process so that you know how the three elements work together, in practice you don't really need to concern yourself with these details, because they all happen automatically.

HTML pages returned to the browser in each example may well contain JavaScript, which will be interpreted locally by the client, and which could initiate another request—the same way embedded objects such as images would.

The Benefits of PHP, MySQL, and JavaScript

At the start of this chapter, I introduced the world of Web 1.0, but it wasn't long before the rush was on to create Web 1.1, with the development of such browser enhancements as Java, JavaScript, JScript (Microsoft's slight variant of JavaScript) and ActiveX. On the server side, progress was being made on the Common Gateway Interface (CGI) using scripting languages such as Perl (an alternative to the PHP language) and server-side scripting—inserting the contents of one file (or the output of a system call) into another one dynamically.

Once the dust had settled, three main technologies stood head and shoulders above the others. Although Perl was still a popular scripting language with a strong following, PHP's simplicity and built-in links to the MySQL database program had earned it more than double the number of users. And JavaScript, which had become an essential part of the equation for dynamically manipulating CSS (Cascading Style Sheets) now took on the even more muscular task of handling the client side of the Ajax process. Under Ajax, web pages perform data handling and send requests to web servers in the background—without the web user being aware that this is going on.

No doubt the symbiotic nature of PHP and MySQL helped propel them both forward, but what attracted developers to them in the first place? The simple answer has to be the ease with which you can use them to quickly create dynamic elements on websites. MySQL is a fast and powerful yet easy-to-use database system that offers just about anything a website would need in order to find and serve up data to browsers. When PHP allies with MySQL to store and retrieve this data, you have the fundamental parts required for the development of social networking sites and the beginnings of Web 2.0.

Using PHP

With PHP, it's a simple matter to embed dynamic activity in web pages. When you give pages the *.php* extension, they have instant access to the scripting language. From a developer's point of view, all you have to do is write code such as the following:

```php
<?php
echo "Hello World. Today is ".date("l").". ";
?>

How are you?
```

The opening `<?php` tells the web server to allow the PHP program to interpret all the following code up to the `?>` command. Outside of this construct, everything is sent to the client as direct HTML. So the text "How are you?" is simply output to the browser; within the PHP tags, the built-in **date** function displays the current day of the week according to the server's system time.

The final output of the two parts looks like this:

```
Hello World. Today is Wednesday. How are you?
```

PHP is a flexible language, and some people prefer to place the PHP construct directly next to PHP code, like this:

```
Hello World. Today is <?php echo date("l"); ?>. How are you?
```

There are also other ways of formatting and outputting information, which I'll explain in the chapters on PHP. The point is that with PHP, web developers have a scripting language that although not as fast as compiling your code in C or a similar language, is incredibly speedy and that also integrates seamlessly with HTML code.

 If you intend to type in the PHP examples in this book to work along with me, you must remember to add <?php in front and ?> after them to ensure that the PHP interpreter processes them. To facilitate this, you may wish to prepare a file called *example.php* with those tags in place.

Using PHP, you have unlimited control over your web server. Whether you need to modify HTML on the fly, process a credit card, add user details to a database, or fetch information from a third-party website, you can do it all from within the same PHP files in which the HTML itself resides.

Using MySQL

Of course, there's not a lot of point to being able to change HTML output dynamically unless you also have a means to track the changes that users make as they use your website. In the early days of the Web, many sites used "flat" text files to store data such as usernames and passwords. But this approach could cause problems if the file wasn't correctly locked against corruption from multiple simultaneous accesses. Also, a flat file can get only so big before it becomes unwieldy to manage—not to mention the difficulty of trying to merge files and perform complex searches in any kind of reasonable time.

That's where relational databases with structured querying become essential. And MySQL, being free to use and installed on vast numbers of Internet web servers, rises superbly to the occasion. It is a robust and exceptionally fast database management system that uses English-like commands.

The highest level of MySQL structure is a database, within which you can have one or more tables that contain your data. For example, let's suppose you are working on a table called users, within which you have created columns for surname, firstname, and email, and you now wish to add another user. One command that you might use to do this is:

```
INSERT INTO users VALUES('Smith', 'John', 'jsmith@mysite.com');
```

Of course, as mentioned earlier, you will have issued other commands to create the database and table and to set up all the correct fields, but the INSERT command here shows how simple it can be to add new data to a database. The INSERT command is an example of SQL (which stands for "Structured Query Language"), a language designed in the early 1970s and reminiscent of one of the oldest programming languages, COBOL. It is well suited, however, to database queries, which is why it is still in use after all this time.

It's equally easy to look up data. Let's assume that you have an email address for a user and need to look up that person's name. To do this, you could issue a MySQL query such as:

```
SELECT surname,firstname FROM users WHERE email='jsmith@mysite.com';
```

MySQL will then return Smith, John and any other pairs of names that may be associated with that email address in the database.

As you'd expect, there's quite a bit more that you can do with MySQL than just simple INSERT and SELECT commands. For example, you can join multiple tables according to various criteria, ask for results in a variety of different orders, make partial matches when you know only part of the string that you are searching for, return only the *n*th result, and a lot more.

Using PHP, you can make all these calls directly to MySQL without having to run the MySQL program yourself or use its command-line interface. This means you can save the results in arrays for processing and perform multiple lookups, each dependent on the results returned from earlier ones, to drill right down to the item of data you need.

For even more power, as you'll see later, there are additional functions built right in to MySQL that you can call up for common operations and extra speed.

Using JavaScript

The oldest of the three core technologies in this book, JavaScript, was created to enable scripting access to all the elements of an HTML document. In other words, it provides a means for dynamic user interaction such as checking email address validity in input forms, displaying prompts such as "Did you really mean that?", and so on (although it cannot be relied upon for security) which should always be performed on the web server.

Combined with CSS, JavaScript is the power behind dynamic web pages that change in front of your eyes rather than when a new page is returned by the server.

However, JavaScript can also be tricky to use, due to some major differences among the ways different browser designers have chosen to implement it. This mainly came about when some manufacturers tried to put additional functionality into their browsers at the expense of compatibility with their rivals.

Thankfully, the manufacturers have mostly now come to their senses and have realized the need for full compatibility between each other, so web developers don't have to write multiexception code. But there remain millions of legacy browsers that will be in use for a good many years to come. Luckily, there are solutions for the incompatibility problems, and later in this book we'll look at libraries and techniques that enable you to safely ignore these differences.

For now, let's take a quick look at how you can use basic JavaScript, accepted by all browsers:

```
<script type="text/javascript">
document.write("Hello World. Today is " + Date() );
</script>
```

This code snippet tells the web browser to interpret everything within the script tags as JavaScript, which the browser then does by writing the text "Hello World. Today is " to the current document, along with the date, by using the JavaScript function Date. The result will look something like this:

```
Hello World. Today is Sun Jan 01 2012 14:14:00
```

 It's worth knowing that unless you need to specify an exact version of JavaScript, you can normally omit the type="text/javascript" and just use <script> to start the interpretation of the JavaScript.

As previously mentioned, JavaScript was originally developed to offer dynamic control over the various elements within an HTML document, and that is still its main use. But more and more, JavaScript is being used for Ajax. This is a term for the process of accessing the web server in the background. (It originally meant "Asynchronous Java-Script and XML," but that phrase is already a bit outdated.)

Ajax is the main process behind what is now known as Web 2.0 (a term coined by Tim O'Reilly, the founder and CEO of this book's publishing company), in which web pages have started to resemble standalone programs, because they don't have to be reloaded in their entirety. Instead, a quick Ajax call can pull in and update a single element on a web page, such as changing your photograph on a social networking site or replacing a button that you click with the answer to a question. This subject is fully covered in Chapter 18.

The Apache Web Server

There's actually a fourth hero in the dynamic Web, in addition to our triumvirate of PHP, MySQL, and JavaScript: the web server. In the case of this book, that means the Apache web server. We've discussed a little of what a web server does during the HTTP server/client exchange, but it actually does much more behind the scenes.

For example, Apache doesn't serve up just HTML files—it handles a wide range of files, from images and Flash files to MP3 audio files, RSS (Really Simple Syndication) feeds, and so on. To do this, each element a web client encounters in an HTML page is also requested from the server, which then serves it up.

But these objects don't have to be static files such as GIF images. They can all be generated by programs such as PHP scripts. That's right: PHP can even create images and other files for you, either on the fly or in advance to serve up later.

To do this, you normally have modules either precompiled into Apache or PHP or called up at runtime. One such module is the GD library (short for Graphics Draw), which PHP uses to create and handle graphics.

Apache also supports a huge range of modules of its own. In addition to the PHP module, the most important for your purposes as a web programmer are the modules that handle security. Other examples are the Rewrite module, which enables the web server to handle a varying range of URL types and rewrite them to its own internal requirements, and the Proxy module, which you can use to serve up often-requested pages from a cache to ease the load on the server.

Later in the book, you'll see how to actually use some of these modules to enhance the features provided by the three core technologies.

About Open Source

Whether or not being open source is the reason these technologies are so popular has often been debated, but PHP, MySQL, and Apache *are* the three most commonly used tools in their categories (web scripting languages, databases, and web servers).

What can be said, though, is that being open source means that they have been developed in the community by teams of programmers writing the features they themselves want and need, with the original code available for all to see and change. Bugs can be found and security breaches can be prevented before they happen.

There's another benefit: all these programs are free to use. There's no worrying about having to purchase additional licenses if you have to scale up your website and add more servers. And you don't need to check the budget before deciding whether to upgrade to the latest versions of these products.

In fact, we'll cover a few other add-on products in this book that you'll find invaluable in getting the best out of your websites. They, too, are all open source. Of course, professional support is available to purchase for all these products, should you need it—but that shouldn't be the case for you once you've read this book.

Bringing It All Together

The real beauty of PHP, MySQL, and JavaScript is the wonderful way in which they all work together to produce dynamic web content: PHP handles all the main work on the web server, MySQL manages all the data, and JavaScript looks after web page presentation. JavaScript can also talk with your PHP code on the web server whenever it needs to update something (either on the server or on the web page).

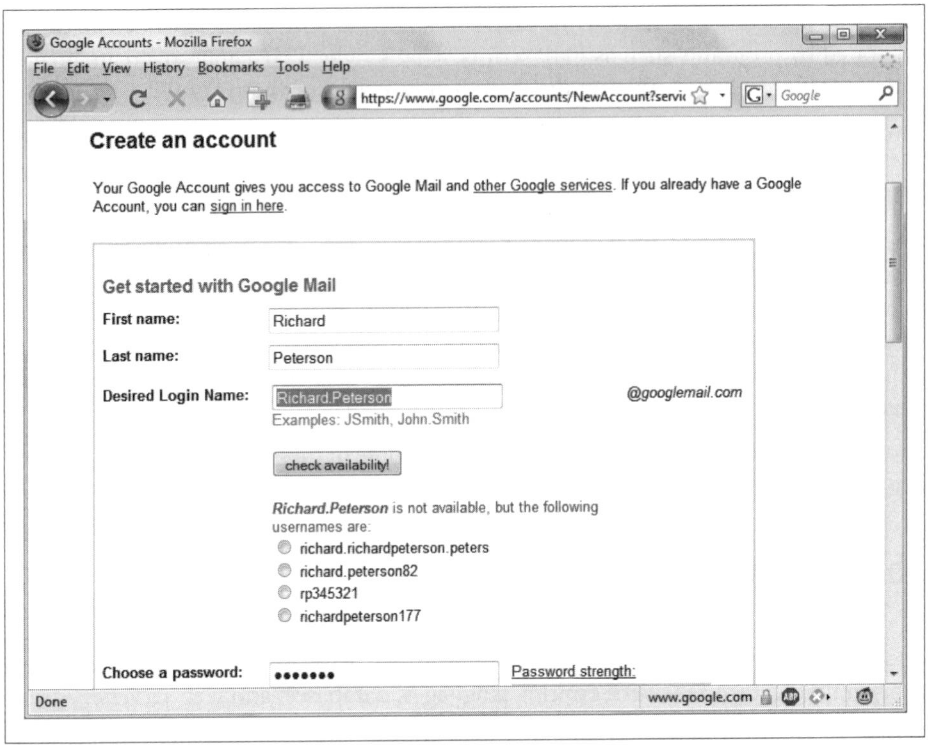

Figure 1-3. Gmail uses Ajax to check the availability of usernames

Without using program code, it's a good idea at this point to summarize the contents of this chapter by looking at the process of combining all three technologies into an everyday Ajax feature that many websites use: checking whether a desired username already exists on the site when a user is signing up for a new account. A good example of this can be seen with Google Mail (see Figure 1-3).

The steps involved in this Ajax process would be similar to the following:

1. The server outputs the HTML to create the web form, which asks for the necessary details, such as username, first name, last name, and email address.

2. At the same time, the server attaches some JavaScript to the HTML to monitor the username input box and check for two things: (a) whether some text has been typed into it, and (b) whether the input has been deselected because the user has clicked on another input box.

3. Once the text has been entered and the field deselected, in the background the JavaScript code passes the username that was typed in back to a PHP script on the web server and awaits a response.

4. The web server looks up the username and replies back to the JavaScript regarding whether that name has already been taken.

---

5. The JavaScript then places an indication next to the username input box to show whether the name is one available to the user—perhaps a green checkmark or a red cross graphic, along with some text.

6. If the username is not available and the user still submits the form, the JavaScript interrupts the submission and reemphasizes (perhaps with a larger graphic and/or an alert box) that the user needs to choose another username.

7. Optionally, an improved version of this process could even look at the username requested by the user and suggest an alternative that is currently available.

All of this takes place quietly in the background and makes for a comfortable and seamless user experience. Without using Ajax, the entire form would have to be submitted to the server, which would then send back HTML, highlighting any mistakes. It would be a workable solution, but nowhere near as tidy or pleasurable as on-the-fly form field processing.

Ajax can be used for a lot more than simple input verification and processing, though; we'll explore many additional things that you can do with it in the Ajax chapters later in this book.

In this chapter, you have read a good introduction to the core technologies of PHP, MySQL, and JavaScript (as well as Apache), and have learned how they work together with each other. In Chapter 2, we'll look at how you can install your own web development server on which to practice everything that you will be learning.

Test Your Knowledge: Questions

Question 1-1
   What four components are needed to create a fully dynamic web page?

Question 1-2
   What does HTML stand for?

Question 1-3
   Why does the name MySQL contain the letters SQL?

Question 1-4
   PHP and JavaScript are both programming languages that generate dynamic results for web pages. What is their main difference, and why would you use both of them?

Question 1-5
   If you encounter a bug (which is rare) in one of the open source tools, how do you think you could get it fixed?

See the section "Chapter 1 Answers" on page 435 in Appendix A for the answers to these questions.

CHAPTER 2

Setting Up a Development Server

If you wish to develop Internet applications but don't have your own development server, you will have to upload every modification you make to a server somewhere else on the Web before you can test it.

Even on a fast broadband connection, this can still represent a significant slowdown in development time. On a local computer, however, testing can be as easy as saving an update (usually just a matter of clicking once on an icon) and then hitting the Refresh button in your browser.

Another advantage of a development server is that you don't have to worry about embarrassing errors or security problems while you're writing and testing, whereas you need to be aware of what people may see or do with your application when it's on a public website. It's best to iron everything out while you're still on a home or small office system, presumably protected by firewalls and other safeguards.

Once you have your own development server, you'll wonder how you ever managed without one, and it's easy to set one up. Just follow the steps in the following sections, using the appropriate instructions for a PC, a Mac, or a Linux system.

In this chapter, we cover just the server side of the web experience, as described in Chapter 1. But to test the results of your work—particularly when we start using Java-Script later in this book—you should also have an instance of every major web browser running on some system convenient to you. Whenever possible, the list of browsers should include at least Internet Explorer, Mozilla Firefox, Opera, Safari, and Google Chrome.

What Is a WAMP, MAMP, or LAMP?

WAMP, MAMP, and LAMP are abbreviations for "Windows, Apache, MySQL, and PHP," "Mac, Apache, MySQL, and PHP," and "Linux, Apache, MySQL, and PHP." These abbreviations describe a fully functioning setup used for developing dynamic Internet web pages.

WAMPs, MAMPs, and LAMPs come in the form of a package that binds the bundled programs together so that you don't have to install and set them up separately. This means you can simply download and install a single program, and follow a few easy prompts, to get your web development server up and running in the quickest time with minimum hassle.

During installation, several default settings are created for you. The security configurations of such an installation will not be as tight as on a production web server, because it is optimized for local use. For these reasons, you should never install such a setup as a production server.

But for developing and testing websites and applications, one of these installations should be entirely sufficient.

 If you choose not to go the W/L/MAMP route for building your own development system, you should know that downloading and integrating the various parts yourself can be very time-consuming and may require a lot of research in order to configure everything fully. But if you already have all the components installed and integrated with each other, they should work with the examples in this book.

Installing a WAMP on Windows

There are several available WAMP servers, each offering slightly different configurations, but the easiest of these is the appropriately named EasyPHP. You can download it from a link toward the top of its website at *http://easyphp.org* (see Figure 2-1).

Follow the download link and you'll be taken to the SourceForge download area. The version used in this book is *EasyPHP-3.0-setup.exe*, which is about 15.6 MB in size.

Once you've downloaded the file, run the installer and follow the prompts, accepting the defaults you are given. Upon completion, EasyPHP will load and an icon will be added to your System Tray, at the bottom right of your screen (see Figure 2-2).

Double-click the System Tray icon and the control window will pop up. From here, you can start, stop, and restart both Apache and MySQL. Sometimes you may find that the initial installation will not correctly start one or the other program, so if you don't see a green traffic light next to one, select Restart to get it going (see Figure 2-3).

Overcoming Installation Problems

Should EasyPHP pop up any errors about either Apache or MySQL being unable to run because a port is blocked, this means that either a firewall you have running is preventing access, or another program is conflicting with EasyPHP.

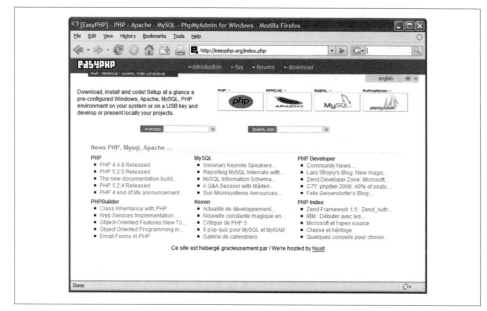

Figure 2-1. *You can download EasyPHP via the site's main page*

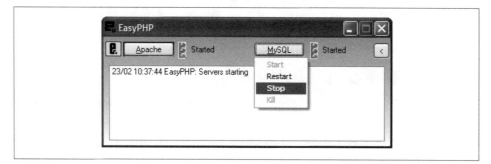

Figure 2-2. *Accessing EasyPHP's controls from the System Tray*

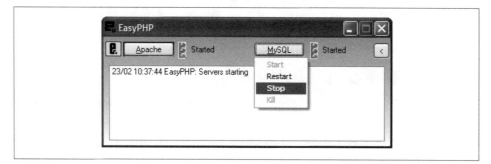

Figure 2-3. *The EasyPHP control window with both Apache and MySQL running*

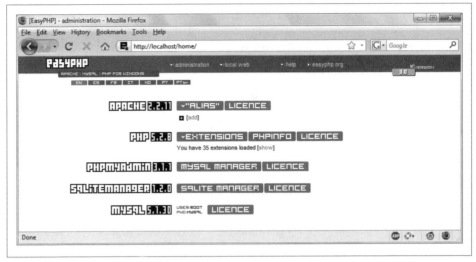

Figure 2-4. How the home page should look

Antivirus programs can sometimes block these ports, as can programs like Skype, which may try to grab port 80 for itself. The solution in such cases is to investigate the setup options for all such programs and ensure that port 80 for Apache and 3306 for MySQL are not blocked or otherwise taken up.

Also, if you are using Windows Vista and find that either Apache or MySQL stop soon after starting, odds are that the correct permissions have not been set for the EasyPHP folders. To correct this, navigate to your *Program Files* folder, right-click on the *EasyPHP 3.0* folder, and select Properties. Then from here click the Security tab followed by Edit to change the permissions for this folder and its subfolders, ensuring that all *users* have write access. This problem has been known to occur only after a Windows restart.

Testing the Installation

The first thing to do at this point is verify that everything is working correctly. To do this, you are going to try to display the default web page, which will have been saved in the server's root folder (see Figure 2-4). Enter either of the following two URLs into the address bar of your browser:

```
http://127.0.0.1/home
http://localhost/home
```

The first is the IP address that all computers use to refer to themselves. The second is an alias, which refers to exactly the same thing and is available for ease of use.

If all is well, you will see the default EasyPHP home screen. Assuming that you have been successful so far, you now need to perform one more task in order to have your development server fully operational. So create a folder on your hard disk called

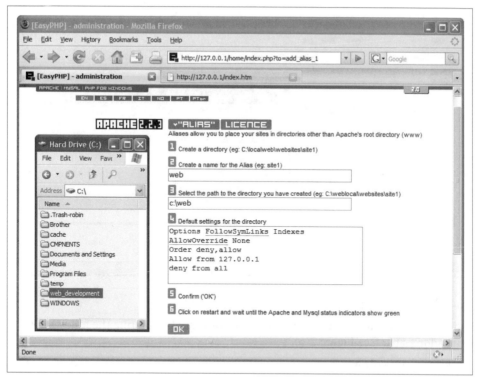

Figure 2-5. Creating a directory for your project files

c:\web and then click Add underneath the Apache section. Now type **web** as the alias requested in section 2, and enter **c:\web** for the directory in section 3. Then click OK, leaving the settings displayed in section 4 as they are (see Figure 2-5).

If you will be maintaining several projects, at some point you may wish to create all the directories you will need and the aliases Apache will recognize. An alias is a shortened, easily recognizable string used to refer to a longer path name, and it doesn't have to be the same as a directory name. So, if you wish to save on typing, you can have a directory several levels deep aliased to a single word. For example the alias "photos" could refer to a folder called *c:\myfiles\family\photos*.

To ensure that you have everything correctly configured, you should now run the obligatory "Hello World" program. So create a small HTML file along these lines using Windows Notepad—not a rich word processor such as Word (unless you save as Plain Text)—by selecting Start→Run, typing **notepad** and pressing Return:

```
<html><head><title>A quick test</title></head>
<body>A quick test</body></html>
```

Once you have done this, save it using the full filename *c:\web\index.html*, making sure that the "Save as type" box is changed from "Text Documents (*.txt)" to "All Files (*.*),"

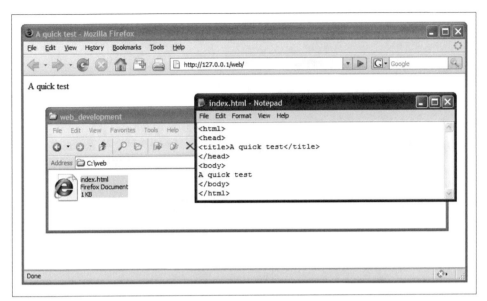

Figure 2-6. Our first web page

and you'll be able to call this page up in your browser by entering the following URL in its address bar (see Figure 2-6):

```
http://localhost/web
```

You should now have had a trouble-free installation, resulting in a fully working WAMP. But if you encountered any difficulties, check out the comprehensive EasyPHP FAQ at *http://easyphp.org/faq.php*, which should sort out your problem.

Alternative WAMPs

When software is updated, it sometimes works differently than you'd expect, and bugs can even be introduced. So if you encounter difficulties with EasyPHP that you cannot resolve, you may prefer to choose one of the various other solutions available on the Web instead.

You will still be able to make use of all the examples in this book, but you'll have to follow the instructions supplied with each WAMP, which may not be as easy to follow as the EasyPHP guide.

Here's a selection of the best in my opinion:

- XAMPP: *http://apachefriends.org/en/xampp.html*
- WAMPServer: *http://wampserver.com/en/*
- Glossword WAMP: *http://glossword.biz/glosswordwamp/*

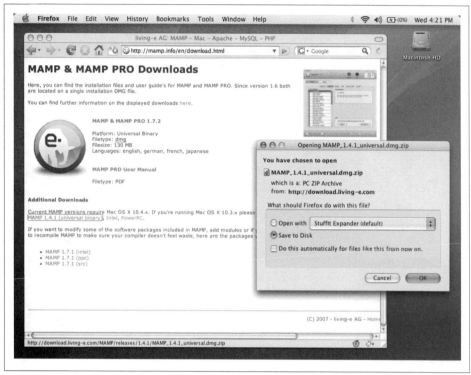

Figure 2-7. Select the correct MAMP version and download it

Installing a MAMP on Mac OS X

At the time of writing, probably the best MAMP solution is called simply *MAMP*. You can download it from *http://mamp.info/en/download.html*. The program comes in two flavors: regular and pro. The pro version is a commercial product that you might want to look at in the future, especially as it comes bundled with the regular version.

If you have trouble accessing the *http://mamp.info* website, you may wish to download the installer from *http://sourceforge.net/project/showfiles.php?group_id=121134*. The latest version (currently 1.7.2) will show by default, but for previous ones (such as 1.4.1), just click on the link entitled "mamp" under the "Package" Heading to see them all.

If you have OS X 10.4 or greater, you can download the latest version of MAMP, which will be 1.7.2 or higher. For Mac OS X 10.3, you'll need to download the correct version for that OS, which is likely to be 1.4.1 or similar (see Figure 2-7).

The downloaded file will have a filename such as *MAMP_1.7.2.dmg.zip* for version 1.7.2 or *MAMP_1.4.1_universal.dmg.zip* for the universal installer, and so on. You need to unzip the file using StuffIt Expander (or a similar product) to create a disk image

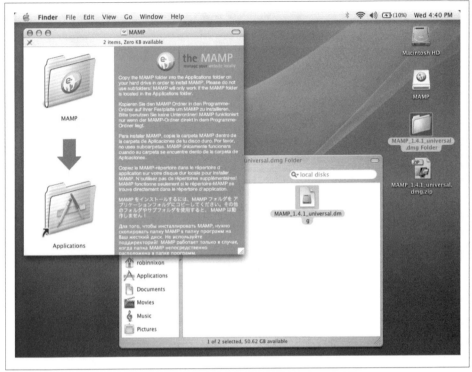

Figure 2-8. Installing MAMP takes a few simple mouse actions

with a name similar to *MAMP_1.7.2.dmg* or *MAMP_1.4.1_universal.dmg*, and double-click that image to mount it as a drive on your desktop.

You are now ready to double-click the new virtual drive, which will be called *MAMP 1.7.2* (or simply *MAMP* for version 1.4.1). When you do, the installer will appear, asking you to drag and drop the MAMP folder at the top left of the window down into the *Applications* folder alias at the bottom left. So go ahead and drop it in there (see Figure 2-8).

Open up your *Applications* folder, where you will find a new folder called *MAMP*. Open this up, and you'll be presented with several subfolders. The main three that should concern you for now are *htdocs*, which is where you will be saving your HTML and PHP files; *README.rtf*, which contains the latest release notes for the program; and *MAMP*, which is the program you will use to start and stop your web server and database.

To make things easier for yourself in the future, I recommend that you make an alias to the *MAMP* folder and place the alias on your desktop. That way, you'll find it a simple matter to click on that when you need to make any changes or run MAMP (see Figure 2-9).

Figure 2-9. The MAMP application in your Applications folder and after copying to your desktop

You are now ready to run the MAMP for the first time. Double-click the *MAMP* program and you'll see the main control window appear, along with the welcome page, which will display in your default web browser.

The Apache and MySQL servers should start automatically and display their status in the control window. If they don't, you can click on the Start Servers button to get them going. Then you'll see the welcome page in your browser (see Figure 2-10).

Now that you have your MAMP fully installed and running, it's time to test it with a quick HTML file. So, using an editor such as TextEdit, create a file called *index.html* as follows and save it in the *htdocs* folder of your MAMP installation (you may need to ensure that you have your TextEdit preferences set to "ignore rich text commands in HTML files" in order to use it as an HTML editor):

```
<html><head><title>A quick test</title></head>
<body>A quick test</body></html>
```

And now you can test your setup by entering the following into your browser's address bar:

```
http://localhost:8888
```

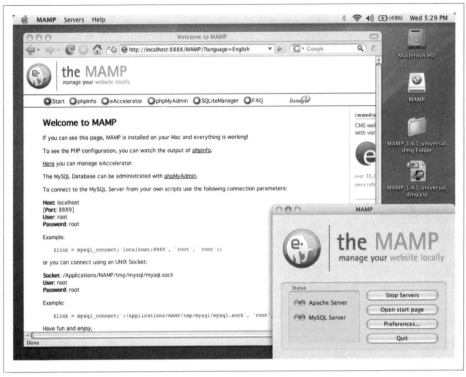

Figure 2-10. The MAMP—up and running and displaying a page

This tells your browser to serve up the default page stored locally in the MAMP *htdocs* folder, which, in this case, is your *index.html* file. All being well, you will see the simple test page displayed (see the browser window in the upper-left corner of Figure 2-11).

To get back to the main welcome page at any time, you can click on the "Open start page" button in the control window. Click it now and then click on the "phpinfo" button near the top of the web page, just to the right of the Start button.

If everything is working correctly, you will now be presented with a very long page of information all about your installation of PHP (see Figure 2-12). You should also ensure that MySQL is correctly installed: click on the "phpMyAdmin" button and you'll be presented with a control page.

At this point, there's no need to explain what this new page does. As long as you see similar screens to those in the figures, you can be confident that you now have a fully working MAMP installation.

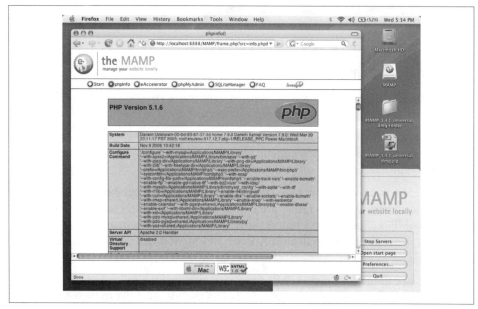

Figure 2-11. The MAMP—working and displaying the test page

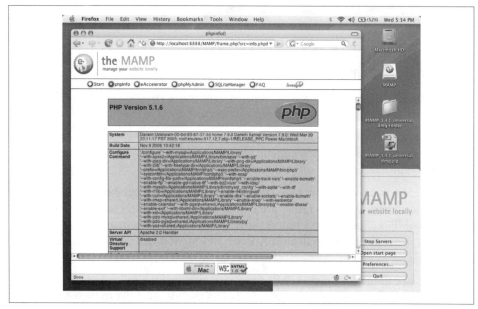

Figure 2-12. PHP, properly installed and running

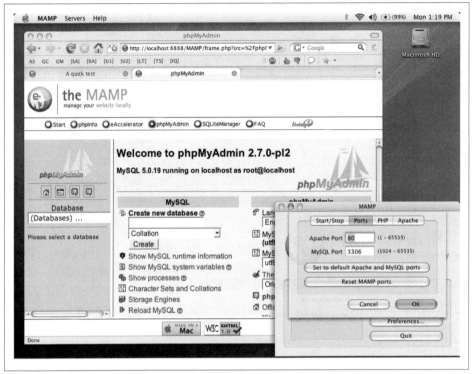

Figure 2-13. MAMP is easier to use with regular port settings

Some Final Tweaking

When you visit a site such as *google.com*, you are really visiting port 80 of the server hosting the website. Likewise, port 3306 is the one most commonly used for MySQL.

But by default, MAMP uses ports 8888 and 8889 for Apache and MySQL, respectively. This means that you will need to append the port number whenever you request a web page from your development server or access MySQL.

As you'll recall, instead of typing the URL *localhost* into your web browser, you had to type *localhost:8888*, which is rather annoying. So the last thing you need to do to set up your MAMP is click the Preferences button in the MAMP control window and then click Ports. Now click "Set to default Apache and MySQL ports," then click OK (see Figure 2-13).

You can now call up your test HTML page with either of the following shorter URLs (the latter being the IP address that all computers use for referring to themselves):

```
http://localhost
http://127.0.0.1
```

Other Alternatives

You may already be familiar with the XAMPP system, which you can download from *http://apachefriends.org/en/xampp.html*. If you have at least OS X 10.4, feel free to use it if you prefer, but make sure to carefully follow the instructions supplied with the package. You may also be interested in the new Zend Server CE (Community Edition) available at *http://zend.com/en/community/zend-server-ce*. This is another free W/M/LAMP and, as I write, it's available as a release candidate—but the final release should be ready by the time you read this.

If you are a beginner to PHP and MySQL web development, I wouldn't recommend that you try to set up Apache and MySQL on their own without following the MAMP route, as configuration can be tricky.

Users of versions of OS X prior to 10.3 (pre-2003) cannot use either of the current versions of MAMP described here (or the current releases of XAMPP or Zend Server CE). So I recommend that you upgrade your operating system, if you can, in order to make use of the simple installation processes available.

Installing a LAMP on Linux

If you know much about Linux, you may have already set up and installed PHP and MySQL. If not, your best bet is probably to look at XAMPP for Linux, which is available at *http://apachefriends.org/en/xampp-linux.html*.

The process is relatively simple. After downloading, go to a Linux shell and log in as the system administrator (*root*) by typing:

```
su
```

Enter your system administration password. Many desktop Linux systems allow you to use your personal account's password for the administration password. Some systems, including the popular Ubuntu, encourage you not to use *su* to log in as *root*, but to precede each system administration command with *sudo* instead. You'll know what to do if you've performed any administrative tasks on your system. Now extract the downloaded archive file to */opt* with the following command (inserting the appropriate filename if the version you downloaded is a later version):

```
tar xvfz xampp-linux-1.6.8a.tar.gz -C /opt
```

Any XAMPP version that was already installed will be overwritten by this command.

Once the command finishes, XAMPP will be installed below the */opt/lampp* directory. To start it, enter the following:

```
/opt/lampp/lampp start
```

You should now see something like this on your screen:

```
Starting XAMPP 1.6.8a...
LAMPP: Starting Apache...
```

```
LAMPP: Starting MySQL...
LAMPP started.

Ready. Apache and MySQL are running.
```

Now you are ready to test the setup. Type the following URL into your web browser's address bar:

```
http://localhost
```

You should now see the start page of XAMPP, containing some links to check the status of the installed software and some small programming examples (see Figure 2-14).

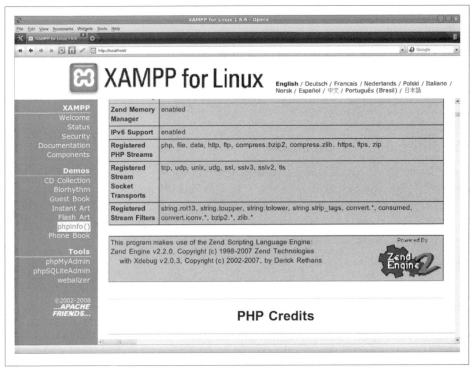

Figure 2-14. XAMPP for Linux, installed and running

Working Remotely

If you have access to a web server already configured with PHP and MySQL, you can always use that for your web development. But unless you have a high-speed connection, it is not always your best option. Developing locally allows you to test modifications with little or no upload delay.

Accessing MySQL remotely may not be easy either. You may have to Telnet or SSH into your server to manually create databases and set permissions from the command line. Your web hosting company will advise you on how best to do this and provide you with any password they have set for your MySQL access (as well as, of course, for getting into the server in the first place).

Logging In

I recommend that, at minimum, Windows users should install a program such as PuTTY, available at *http://putty.org*, for Telnet and SSH access (remember that SSH is much more secure than Telnet).

On a Mac, you already have SSH available. Just select the *Applications* folder, followed by *Utilities*, and then launch Terminal. In the terminal window, log in to a server using SSH as follows:

```
ssh mylogin @ server.com
```

where **server.com** is the name of the server you wish to log in to and **mylogin** is the username you will log in under. You will then be prompted for the correct password for that username and, if you enter it correctly, you will be logged in.

Using FTP

To transfer files to and from your web server, you will need an FTP program. If you go searching the Web for a good one, you'll find so many that it could take you quite a while to come across one with all the right features for you.

Nowadays I always recommend FireFTP, because of these advantages:

- It is an add-on for the Firefox 3 web browser, and will therefore work on any platform on which Firefox 3 runs.
- Calling it up can be as simple as selecting a bookmark.
- It is one of the fastest and easiest to use FTP programs that I have encountered.

 You may say "But I use only Microsoft Internet Explorer and FireFTP is not available for it," but I would counter that if you are going to develop web pages, you need a copy of each of the main browsers installed on your PC anyway, as suggested at the start of this chapter.

To install FireFTP, visit *http://fireftp.mozdev.org* using Firefox and click on the Download FireFTP link. It's about half a megabyte in size and installs very quickly. Once it's installed, restart Firefox; you can then access FireFTP from the Tools menu (see Figure 2-15).

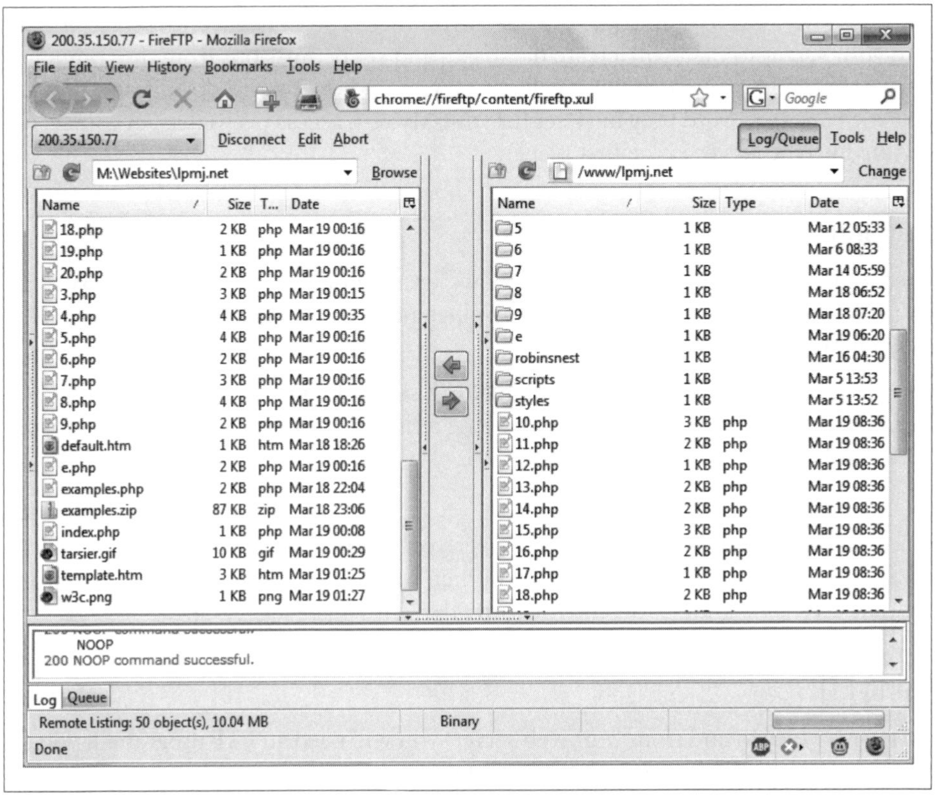

Figure 2-15. FireFTP offers full FTP access from within Firefox 3

Unfortunately, at the time of writing, Firefox 3 would not run on any versions of OS X prior to 10.4. If that is the case for you, I recommend that you install the excellent Classic FTP program available at *http://nchsoftware.com/ftp*. Unlike most other FTP programs for the Mac, it's free and it runs on OS X 10.2 and later (see Figure 2-16).

If you have an OS earlier than 10.2, you may wish to try a shareware program such as Hefty, available at *http://blackdiamond.co.za/bdhefty.html*. You can try it 50 times before having to register it for $20.

Another excellent FTP program is the open source FileZilla, available from *http://file zilla-project.org*, for Windows, Linux and Mac OS X 10.5 or newer.

Of course, if you already have an FTP program, all the better—stick with what you know.

Using a Program Editor

Although a plain-text editor works for editing HTML, PHP, and JavaScript, there have been some tremendous improvements in dedicated program editors, which now

Figure 2-16. Classic FTP for the Mac, which runs on OS X 10.2 and is free

incorporate very handy features such as colored syntax highlighting. Today's program editors are smart and can show you where you have syntax errors before you even run a program. Once you've used a modern editor, you'll wonder how you ever managed without one.

There are a number of good programs available, but I have settled on Editra, because it's free and available through a simple installer for both the Mac and the PC, and in source code form for Linux/Unix. You can download a copy by visiting *http://editra .org* and selecting the Download link toward the top left of the page, where you can also find the documentation for it.

As you can see from Figure 2-17, Editra understands HTML and highlights the syntax appropriately. It also notices when it encounters PHP code and correctly highlights that, too, using colors different from the HTML color tones to help clarify what's going on.

What's more, you can place the cursor next to brackets or braces and Editra will highlight the matching pair so that you can check whether you have too many or too few. In fact, Editra does a lot more in addition, which you will discover and enjoy as you use it.

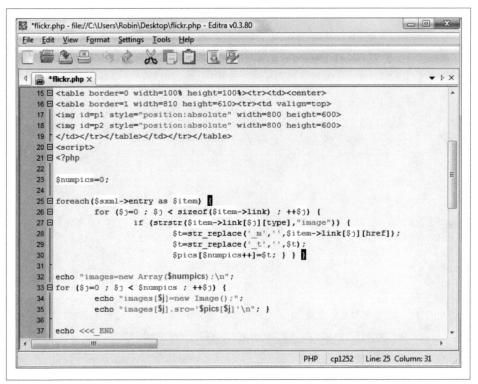

Figure 2-17. Program editors are superior to plain-text editors

Again, if you have a different preferred program editor, use that—it's always a good idea to use programs you're already familiar with.

Using an IDE

As good as dedicated program editors can be for your programming productivity, their utility pales into insignificance when compared to *Integrated Development Environments* (IDEs), which offer many additional features such as in-editor debugging and program testing, as well as function descriptions and much more.

Figure 2-18 shows the popular phpDesigner IDE with a PHP program loaded into the main frame, and the righthand Code Explorer listing the various classes, functions, and variables that it uses.

When developing with an IDE, you can set breakpoints and then run all (or portions) of your code, which will then stop at the breakpoints and provide you with information about the program's current state.

As an aid to learning programming, the examples in this book can be entered into an IDE and run there and then, without the need to call up your web browser.

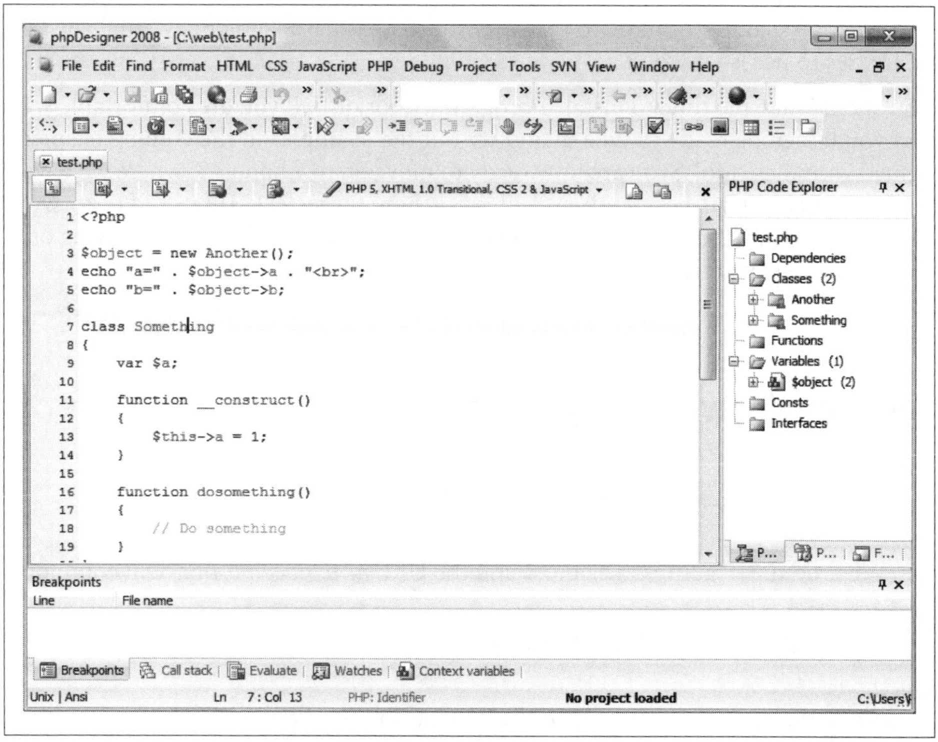

Figure 2-18. When using an IDE such as phpDesigner, PHP development becomes much quicker and easier

There are several IDEs available for different platforms, most of which are commercial, but there are some free ones, too. Table 2-1 lists some of the most popular PHP IDEs, along with their download URLs.

Table 2-1. A selection of PHP IDEs

IDE	Download URL	Price	Win	Mac	Linux
Eclipse PDT	*http://eclipse.org/pdt/downloads/*	Free	✓	✓	✓
Komodo IDE	*http://activestate.com/Products/komodo_ide*	$295	✓	✓	✓
NetBeans	*http://www.netbeans.org*	Free	✓	✓	✓
phpDesigner	*http://mpsoftware.dk*	$86	✓		
PHPEclipse	*http://phpeclipse.de*	Free	✓	✓	✓
PhpED	*http://nusphere.com*	$119	✓		✓
PHPEdit	*http://phpedit.com*	$130	✓		
Zend Studio	*http://zend.com/en/downloads*	$500	✓	✓	✓

Choosing an IDE can be a very personal thing, so if you intend to use one, I advise you to download a couple or more to try them out first—they all either have trial versions or are free to use, so it won't cost you anything.

You should take the time to install a program editor or IDE you are comfortable with and you'll then be ready to type in and try out the examples in the coming chapters. Armed with these tools, you are now ready to move on to Chapter 3, where we'll start exploring PHP in further depth and find out how to get HTML and PHP to work together, as well as how the PHP language itself is structured. But before moving on, I suggest you test your new knowledge with the following questions.

Test Your Knowledge: Questions

Question 2-1
>   What is the difference between a WAMP and a MAMP?

Question 2-2
>   What do the IP address 127.0.0.1 and the URL *http://localhost* have in common?

Question 2-3
>   What is the purpose of an FTP program?

Question 2-4
>   Name the main disadvantage of working on a remote web server.

Question 2-5
>   Why is it better to use a program editor instead of a plain-text editor?

See the section "Chapter 2 Answers" on page 436 in Appendix A for the answers to these questions.

CHAPTER 3

Introduction to PHP

In Chapter 1, I explained that PHP is the language that you use to make the server generate dynamic output—output that is potentially different each time a browser requests a page. In this chapter, you'll start learning this simple but powerful language; it will be the topic of the following chapters up through Chapter 6.

I encourage you to develop your PHP code in one of the IDEs listed in Chapter 2. It will help you catch typos and speed up learning tremendously in comparison to less feature-rich editors.

Many of these development environments let you run the PHP code and see the output discussed in this chapter. I'll also show you how to embed the PHP in an HTML file so that you can see what the output looks like in a web page (the way your users will ultimately see it). But that step, as thrilling as it may be at first, isn't really important at this stage.

In production, your web pages will be a combination of PHP, HTML, and JavaScript, and some MySQL statements. Furthermore, each page can lead to other pages to provide users with ways to click through links and fill out forms. We can avoid all that complexity while learning each language, though. Focus for now on just writing PHP code and making sure that you get the output you expect—or at least that you understand the output you actually get!

Incorporating PHP Within HTML

By default, PHP documents end with the extension *.php*. When a web server encounters this extension in a requested file, it automatically passes it to the PHP processor. Of course, web servers are highly configurable, and some web developers choose to force files ending with *.htm* or *.html* to also get parsed by the PHP processor, usually because developers want to hide the fact that they are using PHP.

Your PHP program is responsible for passing back a clean file suitable for display in a web browser. At its very simplest, a PHP document will output only HTML. To prove this, you can take any normal HTML document such as an *index.html* file, save it as *index.php*, and it will display identically to the original.

Calling the PHP Parser

To trigger the PHP commands, you need to learn a new tag. The first part is:

```
<?php
```

The first thing you may notice is that the tag has not been closed. This is because entire sections of PHP can be placed inside this tag and they finish only when the closing part is encountered, which looks like this:

```
?>
```

A small PHP "Hello World" program might look like Example 3-1.

Example 3-1. Invoking PHP

```
<?php
echo "Hello world";
?>
```

The way you use this tag is quite flexible. Some programmers open the tag at the start of a document and close it right at the end, outputting any HTML directly from PHP commands.

Others, however, choose to insert only the smallest possible fragments of PHP within these tags wherever dynamic scripting is required, leaving the rest of the document in standard HTML.

The latter type of programmer generally argues that their style of coding results in faster code, while the former say that the speed increase is so minimal that it doesn't justify the additional complexity of dropping in and out of PHP many times in a single document.

As you learn more, you will surely discover your preferred style of PHP development, but for the sake of making the examples in this book easier to follow, I have adopted the approach of keeping the number of transfers between PHP and HTML to a minimum—generally only once or twice in a document.

By the way, a slight variation to the PHP syntax exists. If you browse the Internet for PHP examples, you may also encounter code where the opening and closing syntax used is like this:

```
<?
echo "Hello world";
?>
```

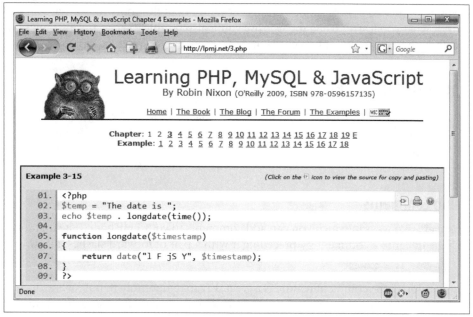

Figure 3-1. Viewing examples from this book at http://lpmj.net

Although it's not as obvious that the PHP parser is being called, this is a valid alternative syntax that also usually works (although not with the EasyPHP WAMP package), but should be discouraged, as it is incompatible with XML and its use is now deprecated (meaning that it is no longer recommended and could be removed in future versions).

 If you have only PHP code in a file, you may omit the closing ?>. This is actually good practice, as it will ensure you have no excess whitespace leaking from your PHP files (especially important when writing object-oriented code).

This Book's Examples

To save you the time it would take to type them in, all the examples from this book have been archived onto a specially created companion website at *http://lpmj.net*, where you can view each one individually—with color highlighting of syntax—and download them onto your computer (see Figure 3-1).

As well as having all the examples saved by chapter and example number (such as *example3-1.php*), the provided *examples.zip* archive also contains an extra folder called *named_examples*, in which you'll find all the examples, which I suggest saving using a specific filename, such as Example 3-4 (shown later; this file should be saved as *test1.php*).

If you read this book in front of a computer (and hopefully you will, so that you can try out what you learn), using the website you'll also be able to view any examples on-screen with a maximum of two clicks, making them easy to reference as you read.

The Structure of PHP

We're going to cover quite a lot of ground in this section. It's not too difficult, but I recommend that you work your way through it carefully, as it sets the foundation for everything else in this book. As always, there are some useful questions at the end of the chapter that you can use to test how much you've learned.

Using Comments

There are two ways in which you can add comments to your PHP code. The first turns a single line into a comment by preceding it with a pair of forward slashes, like this:

```
// This is a comment
```

This version of the comment feature is a great way to temporarily remove a line of code from a program that is giving you errors. For example, you could use such a comment to hide a debugging line of code until you need it, like this:

```
// echo "X equals $x";
```

You can also use this type of comment directly after a line of code to describe its action, like this:

```
$x += 10; // Increment $x by 10
```

When you need multiple-line comments, there's a second type of comment, which looks like Example 3-2.

Example 3-2. A multiline comment

```php
<?php
/* This is a section
   of multiline comments
   which will not be
   interpreted */
?>
```

You can use the /* and */ pairs of characters to open and close comments almost anywhere you like inside your code. Most, if not all, programmers use this construct to temporarily comment out entire sections of code that do not work or that, for one reason or another, they do not wish to be interpreted.

A common error is to use /* and */ to comment out a large section of code that already contains a commented-out section that uses those characters. You can't nest comments this way; the PHP interpreter won't know where a comment ends and will display an error message. However, if you use a program editor or IDE with syntax highlighting, this type of error is easier to spot.

Basic Syntax

PHP is quite a simple language with roots in C and Perl, yet looks more like Java. It is also very flexible, but there are a few rules that you need to learn about its syntax and structure.

Semicolons

You may have noticed in the previous examples that the PHP commands ended with a semicolon, like this:

```
$x += 10;
```

Probably the most common cause of errors you will encounter with PHP is to forget this semicolon, which causes PHP to treat multiple statements like one statement, find itself unable to understand it, and produce a "Parse error" message.

The $ symbol

The $ symbol has come to be used in many different ways by different programming languages. For example, if you have ever written in the BASIC language, you will have used the $ to terminate variable names to denote them as strings.

In PHP, however, you must place a $ in front of all variables. This is required to make the PHP parser faster, as it instantly knows whenever it comes across a variable. Whether your variables are numbers, strings, or arrays, they should all look something like those in Example 3-3.

Example 3-3. Three different types of variable assignment

```php
<?php
$mycounter = 1;
$mystring  = "Hello";
$myarray   = array("One", "Two", "Three");
?>
```

And really that's pretty much all the syntax that you have to remember. Unlike languages such as Python, which are very strict about how you indent and lay out code, PHP leaves you completely free to use (or not use) all the indenting and spacing you like. In fact, sensible use of what is called *whitespace* is generally encouraged (along with comprehensive commenting) to help you understand your code when you come back to it. It also helps other programmers when they have to maintain your code.

Figure 3-2. You can think of variables as matchboxes containing items

Understanding Variables

There's a simple metaphor that will help you understand what PHP variables are all about. Just think of them as little (or big) matchboxes! That's right, matchboxes that you've painted white and written names on.

String variables

Imagine you have a matchbox on which you have written the word *username*. You then write *Fred Smith* on a piece of paper and place it into the box (see Figure 3-2). Well, that's the same process as assigning a string value to a variable, like this:

```
$username = "Fred Smith";
```

The quotation marks indicate that "Fred Smith" is a *string* of characters. You must enclose each string in either quotation marks or apostrophes (single quotes), although there is a subtle difference between the two types of quote, which is explained later. When you want to see what's in the box, you open it, take the piece of paper out, and read it. In PHP, doing so looks like this:

```
echo $username;
```

Or you can assign it to another variable (photocopy the paper and place the copy in another matchbox), like this:

```
$current_user = $username;
```

If you are keen to start trying out PHP for yourself, you could try entering the examples in this chapter into an IDE (as recommended at the end of Chapter 2), to see instant results, or you could enter the code in Example 3-4 into a program editor and save it to your web development directory (also discussed in Chapter 2) as *test1.php*.

Example 3-4. Your first PHP program

```php
<?php // test1.php
$username = "Fred Smith";
echo $username;
echo "<br />";
$current_user = $username;
echo $current_user;
?>
```

Now you can call it up by entering the URL of your web development directory and the filename *test1.php* into the address bar of your browser. For example, if you are using a PC and the alias to your development directory is called *web*, you would enter the following into your browser:

```
http://localhost/web/test1.php
```

The result of running this code should be two occurrences of the name "Fred Smith", the first of which is the result of the echo $username command and the second is from the echo $current_user command.

Numeric variables

Variables don't contain just strings—they can contain numbers, too. Using the match-box analogy, to store the number 17 in the variable $count, the equivalent would be placing, say, 17 beads in a matchbox on which you have written the word *count*:

```
$count = 17;
```

You could also use a floating-point number (containing a decimal point); the syntax is the same:

```
$count = 17.5;
```

To read the contents of the matchbox, you would simply open it and count the beads. In PHP, you would assign the value of $count to another variable or perhaps just echo it to the web browser.

Arrays

So what are arrays? Well, you can think of them as several matchboxes glued together. For example, let's say we want to store the player names for a five-person soccer team in an array called $team. To do this, we could glue five matchboxes side by side and write down the names of all the players on separate pieces of paper, placing one in each matchbox.

Across the whole top of the matchbox assembly we would write the word *team* (see Figure 3-3). The equivalent of this in PHP would be:

```php
$team = array('Bill', 'Joe', 'Mike', 'Chris', 'Jim');
```

This syntax is more complicated than the ones I've explained so far. The array-building code consists of the following construct:

```
array();
```

with five strings inside. Each string is enclosed in apostrophes.

If we then wanted to know who player 4 is, we could use this command:

```
echo $team[3]; // Displays the name Chris
```

Figure 3-3. An array is like several matchboxes glued together

The reason the previous statement has the number 3 and not a 4 is because the first element of a PHP array is actually the zeroth element, so the player numbers will therefore be 0 through 4.

Two-dimensional arrays

There's a lot more you can do with arrays. For example, instead of being single-dimensional lines of matchboxes, they can be two-dimensional matrixes or can even have three or more dimensions.

As an example of a two-dimensional array, let's say we want to keep track of a game of tic-tac-toe, which requires a data structure of nine cells arranged in a 3×3 square. To represent this with matchboxes, imagine nine of them glued to each other in a matrix of three rows by three columns (see Figure 3-4).

You can now place a piece of paper with either an "x" or an "o" in the correct matchbox for each move played. To do this in PHP code, you have to set up an array containing

Figure 3-4. A multidimensional array simulated with matchboxes

three more arrays, as in Example 3-5, in which the array is set up with a game already in progress.

Example 3-5. Defining a two-dimensional array

```php
<?php
$oxo = array(array('x', '',  'o'),
             array('o', 'o', 'x'),
             array('x', 'o', '' ));
?>
```

Once again, we've moved up a step in complexity, but it's easy to understand if you grasp the basic array syntax. There are three `array()` constructs nested inside the outer `array()` construct.

To then return the third element in the second row of this array, you would use the following PHP command, which will display an "x":

```php
echo $oxo[1][2];
```

 Remember that array indexes (pointers at elements within an array) start from zero, not one, so the [1] in the previous command refers to the second of the three arrays, and the [2] references the third position within that array. It will return the contents of the matchbox three along and two down.

As mentioned, arrays with even more dimensions are supported by simply creating more arrays within arrays. However, we will not be covering arrays of more than two dimensions in this book.

And don't worry if you're still having difficulty getting to grips with using arrays, as the subject is explained in detail in Chapter 6.

Variable naming rules

When creating PHP variables, you must follow these four rules:

- Variable names must start with a letter of the alphabet or the _ (underscore) character.
- Variable names can contain only the characters: a-z, A-Z, 0-9, and _ (underscore).
- Variable names may not contain spaces. If a variable must comprise more than one word it should be separated with the _ (underscore) character. (e.g., $user_name).
- Variable names are case-sensitive. The variable $High_Score is not the same as the variable $high_score.

Operators

Operators are the mathematical, string, comparison, and logical commands such as plus, minus, times, and divide. PHP looks a lot like plain arithmetic; for instance, the following statement outputs 8:

```
echo 6 + 2;
```

Before moving on to learn what PHP can do for you, take a moment to learn about the various operators it provides.

Arithmetic operators

Arithmetic operators do what you would expect. They are used to perform mathematics. You can use them for the main four operations (plus, minus, times, and divide) as well as to find a modulus (the remainder after a division) and to increment or decrement a value (see Table 3-1).

Table 3-1. Arithmetic operators

Operator	Description	Example
+	Addition	$j + 1
-	Subtraction	$j - 6
*	Multiplication	$j * 11
/	Division	$j / 4
%	Modulus (division remainder)	$j % 9
++	Increment	++$j
--	Decrement	--$j

Assignment operators

These operators are used to assign values to variables. They start with the very simple = and move on to +=, -=, and so on (see Table 3-2). The operator += adds the value on the right side to the variable on the left, instead of totally replacing the value on the left. Thus, if $count starts with the value 5, the statement:

```
$count += 1;
```

sets $count to 6, just like the more familiar assignment statement:

```
$count = $count + 1;
```

Strings have their own operator, the period (.), detailed in the section "String concatenation" on page 46.

Table 3-2. Assignment operators

Operator	Example	Equivalent to
=	$j = 15	$j = 15
+=	$j += 5	$j = $j + 5
-=	$j -= 3	$j = $j - 3
*=	$j *= 8	$j = $j * 8
/=	$j /= 16	$j = $j / 16
.=	$j .= $k	$j = $j . $k
%=	$j %= 4	$j = $j % 4

Comparison operators

Comparison operators are generally used inside a construct such as an if statement in which you need to compare two items. For example, you may wish to know whether a variable you have been incrementing has reached a specific value, or whether another variable is less than a set value, and so on (see Table 3-3).

Note the difference between = and ==. The first is an assignment operator, and the second is a comparison operator. Even more advanced programmers can sometimes transpose the two when coding hurriedly, so be careful.

Table 3-3. Comparison operators

Operator	Description	Example
==	Is **equal** to	$j == 4
!=	Is **not equal** to	$j != 21
>	Is **greater than**	$j > 3
<	Is **less than**	$j < 100
>=	Is **greater than or equal** to	$j >= 15
<=	Is **less than or equal** to	$j <= 8

Logical operators

If you haven't used them before, logical operators may at first seem a little daunting. But just think of them the way you would use logic in English. For example, you might say to yourself "If the time is later than 12pm and earlier than 2pm, then have lunch." In PHP, the code for this might look something like the following (using military timing):

```
if ($hour > 12 && $hour < 14) dolunch();
```

Here we have moved the set of instructions for actually going to lunch into a function that we will have to create later called `dolunch`. The *then* of the statement is left out, because it is implied and therefore unnecessary.

As the previous example shows, you generally use a logical operator to combine the results of two of the comparison operators shown in the previous section. A logical operator can also be input to another logical operator ("If the time is later than 12pm and earlier than 2pm, or if the smell of a roast is permeating the hallway and there are plates on the table"). As a rule, if something has a `TRUE` or `FALSE` value, it can be input to a logical operator. A logical operator takes two true-or-false inputs and produces a true-or-false result.

Table 3-4 shows the logical operators.

Table 3-4. Logical operators

Operator	Description	Example
&&	**And**	$j == 3 **&&** $k == 2
and	Low-precedence **and**	$j == 3 **and** $k == 2
||	**Or**	$j < 5 **||** $j > 10
or	Low-precedence **or**	$j < 5 **or** $j > 10
!	**Not**	**!** ($j == $k)
xor	**Exclusive or**	$j **xor** $k

Note that && is usually interchangeable with and; the same is true for || and or. But and and or have a lower precedence, so in some cases, you may need extra parentheses to force the required precedence. On the other hand, there are times when *only* and or or are acceptable, as in the following statement, which uses an or operator (to be explained in Chapter 10):

```
mysql_select_db($database) or die("Unable to select database");
```

The most unusual of these operators is xor, which stands for *exclusive or* and returns a `true` value if either value is `true`, but a `false` value if both inputs are `true` or both inputs are `FALSE`. To understand this, imagine that you want to concoct your own cleaner for household items. Ammonia makes a good cleaner, and so does bleach, so you want your cleaner to have one of these. But the cleaner must not have both, because the combination is hazardous. In PHP, you could represent this as:

```
$ingredient = $ammonia xor $bleach;
```

In the example snippet, if either `$ammonia` or `$bleach` is `true`, `$ingredient` will also be set to `true`. But if both are `true` or both are `false`, `$ingredient` will be set to `false`.

Variable Assignment

The syntax to assign a value to a variable is always *variable = value*. Or, to reassign the value to another variable, it is *other variable = variable*.

There are also a couple of other assignment operators that you will find useful. For example, we've already seen:

```
$x += 10;
```

which tells the PHP parser to add the value on the right (in this instance, the value 10) to the variable `$x`. Likewise, we could subtract as follows:

```
$y -= 10;
```

Variable incrementing and decrementing

Adding or subtracting 1 is such a common operation that PHP provides special operators for it. You can use one of the following in place of the `+=` and `-=` operators:

```
++$x;
--$y;
```

In conjunction with a test (an `if` statement), you could use the following code:

```
if (++$x == 10) echo $x;
```

This tells PHP to *first* increment the value of `$x` and then test whether it has the value 10; if it does, output its value. But you can also require PHP to increment (or, in the following example, decrement) a variable *after* it has tested the value, like this:

```
if ($y-- == 0) echo $y;
```

which gives a subtly different result. Suppose `$y` starts out as 0 before the statement is executed. The comparison will return a `true` result, but `$y` will be set to –1 after the comparison is made. So what will the `echo` statement display: 0 or –1? Try to guess, and then try out the statement in a PHP processor to confirm. Because this combination of statements is confusing, it should be taken as just an educational example and not as a guide to good programming style.

In short, whether a variable is incremented or decremented before or after testing depends on whether the increment or decrement operator is placed before or after the variable.

By the way, the correct answer to the previous question is that the echo statement will display the result –1, because $y was decremented right after it was accessed in the if statement, and before the echo statement.

String concatenation

String concatenation uses the period (.) to append one string of characters to another. The simplest way to do this is as follows:

```
echo "You have " . $msgs . " messages.";
```

Assuming that the variable $msgs is set to the value 5, the output from this line of code will be:

```
You have 5 messages.
```

Just as you can add a value to a numeric variable with the += operator, you can append one string to another using .= like this:

```
$bulletin .= $newsflash;
```

In this case, if $bulletin contains a news bulletin and $newsflash has a news flash, the command appends the news flash to the news bulletin so that $bulletin now comprises both strings of text.

String types

PHP supports two types of strings that are denoted by the type of quotation mark that you use. If you wish to assign a literal string, preserving the exact contents, you should use the single quotation mark (apostrophe) like this:

```
$info = 'Preface variables with a $ like this: $variable';
```

In this case, every character within the single-quoted string is assigned to $info. If you had used double quotes, PHP would have attempted to evaluate $variable as a variable.

On the other hand, when you want to include the value of a variable inside a string, you do so by using double-quoted strings:

```
echo "There have been $count presidents of the US";
```

As you will realize, this syntax also offers a simpler form of concatenation in which you don't need to use a period, or close and reopen quotes, to append one string to another. This is called *variable substitution* and you will notice some applications using it extensively and others not using it at all.

Escaping characters

Sometimes a string needs to contain characters with special meanings that might be interpreted incorrectly. For example, the following line of code will not work, because the second quotation mark encountered in the word *sister's* will tell the PHP parser that the string end has been reached. Consequently, the rest of the line will be rejected as an error:

```
$text = 'My sister's car is a Ford'; // Erroneous syntax
```

To correct this, you can add a backslash directly before the offending quotation mark to tell PHP to treat the character literally and not to interpret it:

```
$text = 'My sister\'s car is a Ford';
```

And you can perform this trick in almost all situations in which PHP would otherwise return an error by trying to interpret a character. For example, the following double-quoted string will be correctly assigned:

```
$text = "My Mother always said \"Eat your greens\".";
```

Additionally you can use escape characters to insert various special characters into strings such as tabs, new lines, and carriage returns. These are represented, as you might guess, by \t, \n, and \r. Here is an example using tabs to lay out a heading; it is included here merely to illustrate escapes, because in web pages there are always better ways to do layout:

```
$heading = "Date\tName\tPayment";
```

These special backslash-preceded characters work only in double-quoted strings. In single-quoted strings, the preceding string would be displayed with the ugly \t sequences instead of tabs. Within single-quoted strings, only the escaped apostrophe (\') and escaped backslash itself (\\) are recognized as escaped characters.

Multiple-Line Commands

There are times when you need to output quite a lot of text from PHP and using several echo (or print) statements would be time-consuming and messy. To overcome this, PHP offers two conveniences. The first is just to put multiple lines between quotes, as in Example 3-6. Variables can also be assigned, as in Example 3-7.

Example 3-6. A multiline string echo statement

```
<?php
$author = "Alfred E Newman";

echo "This is a Headline

This is the first line.
This is the second.
Written by $author.";
?>
```

Example 3-7. A multiline string assignment

```
<?php
$author = "Alfred E Newman";
```

```
$text = "This is a Headline

This is the first line.
This is the second.
Written by $author.";
?>
```

PHP also offers a multiline sequence using the <<< operator, commonly referred to as *here-document* or *heredoc* for short, and is a way of specifying a string literal, preserving the line breaks and other whitespace (including indentation) in the text. Its use can be seen in Example 3-8.

Example 3-8. Alternative multiline echo statement

```
<?php
$author = "Alfred E Newman";

echo <<<_END
This is a Headline

This is the first line.
This is the second.
- Written by $author.
_END;
?>
```

What this code does is tell PHP to output everything between the two _END tags as if it were a double-quoted string. This means it's possible, for example, for a developer to write entire sections of HTML directly into PHP code and then just replace specific dynamic parts with PHP variables.

It is important to remember that the closing _END; tag *must* appear right at the start of a new line and it must be the *only* thing on that line—not even a comment is allowed to be added after it (nor even a single space). Once you have closed a multiline block, you are free to use the same tag name again.

 Remember: using the <<<_END..._END; heredoc construct, you don't have to add \n linefeed characters to send a linefeed—just press Return and start a new line. Also, unlike either a double-quote- or single-quote-delimited string, you are free to use all the single and double quotes you like within a heredoc, without escaping them by preceding them with a slash (\).

Example 3-9 shows how to use the same syntax to assign multiple lines to a variable.

Example 3-9. A multiline string variable assignment

```
<?php
$author = "Alfred E Newman";

$out = <<<_END
```

```
This is a Headline

This is the first line.
This is the second.
- Written by $author.
_END;
?>
```

The variable `$out` will then be populated with the contents between the two tags. If you were appending, rather than assigning, you could also have used `.=` in place of `=` to append the string to `$out`.

Be careful not to place a semicolon directly after the first occurrence of `_END` as that would terminate the multiline block before it had even started and cause a "Parse error" message. The only place for the semicolon is after the terminating `_END` tag, although it is safe to use semicolons within the block as normal text characters.

By the way, the `_END` tag is simply one I chose for these examples because it is unlikely to be used anywhere else in PHP code and is therefore unique. But you can use any tag you like such as `_SECTION1` or `_OUTPUT` and so on. Also, to help differentiate tags such as this from variables or functions, the general practice is to preface them with an underscore, but you don't have to use one if you choose not to.

Laying out text over multiple lines is usually just a convenience to make your PHP code easier to read, because once it is displayed in a web page, HTML formatting rules take over and whitespace is suppressed, but `$author` is still replaced with the variable's value.

Variable Typing

PHP is a very loosely typed language. This means that variables do not have to be declared before they are used, and that PHP always converts variables to the *type* required by their context when they are accessed.

For example, you can create a multiple-digit number and extract the nth digit from it simply by assuming it to be a string. In the following snippet of code, the numbers 12345 and 67890 are multiplied together, returning a result of 838102050, which is then placed in the variable `$number`, as shown in Example 3-10.

Example 3-10. Automatic conversion from a number to a string

```
<?php
$number = 12345 * 67890;
echo substr($number, 3, 1);
?>
```

At the point of the assignment, `$number` is a numeric variable. But on the second line, a call is placed to the PHP function `substr`, which asks for one character to be returned from `$number`, starting at the fourth position (remembering that PHP offsets start from zero). To do this, PHP turns `$number` into a nine-character string, so that `substr` can access it and return the character, which in this case is 1.

The same goes for turning a string into a number and so on. In Example 3-11, the variable $pi is set to a string value, which is then automatically turned into a floating-point number in the third line by the equation for calculating a circle's area, which outputs the value 78.5398175.

Example 3-11. Automatically converting a string to a number

```php
<?php
$pi = "3.1415927";
$radius = 5;
echo $pi * ($radius * $radius);
?>
```

In practice, what this all means is that you don't have to worry too much about your variable types. Just assign them values that make sense to you and PHP will convert them if necessary. Then, when you want to retrieve values, just ask for them—for example, with an echo statement.

Constants

Constants are similar to variables, holding information to be accessed later, except that they are what they sound like—constant. In other words, once you have defined one, its value is set for the remainder of the program and cannot be altered.

One example of a use for a constant might be to hold the location of your server *root* (the folder with the main files of your website). You would define such a constant like this:

```php
define("ROOT_LOCATION", "/usr/local/www/");
```

Then, to read the contents of the variable you just refer to it like a regular variable (but it isn't preceded by a dollar sign):

```php
$directory = ROOT_LOCATION;
```

Now, whenever you need to run your PHP code on a different server with a different folder configuration, you have only a single line of code to change.

 The main two things you have to remember about constants are that they must *not* be prefaced with a $ sign (as with regular variables), and that you can define them only using the define function.

It is generally agreed to be good practice to use only uppercase for constant variable names, especially if other people will also read your code.

Predefined constants

PHP comes ready-made with dozens of predefined constants that you generally will be unlikely to use as a beginner to PHP. However, there are a few—known as the *magic constants*—that you will find useful. The names of the magic constants always have two underscores at the beginning and two at the end, so that you won't accidentally try to name one of your own constants with a name that is already taken. They are detailed in Table 3-5. The concepts referred to in the table will be introduced in future chapters.

Table 3-5. PHP's magic constants

Magic constant	Description
__LINE__	The current line number of the file.
__FILE__	The full path and filename of the file. If used inside an include, the name of the included file is returned. In versions of PHP since 4.0.2, __FILE__ always contains an absolute path with symbolic links resolved, whereas in older versions it might contain a relative path under some circumstances.
__DIR__	The directory of the file. If used inside an include, the directory of the included file is returned. This is equivalent to *dirname*(__FILE__). This directory name does not have a trailing slash unless it is the root directory. (Added in PHP 5.3.0.)
__FUNCTION__	The function name. (Added in PHP 4.3.0.) As of PHP 5, returns the function name as it was declared (case-sensitive). In PHP 4, its value is always lowercase.
__CLASS__	The class name. (Added in PHP 4.3.0.) As of PHP 5, returns the class name as it was declared (case-sensitive). In PHP 4, its value is always lowercased.
__METHOD__	The class method name. (Added in PHP 5.0.0.) The method name is returned as it was declared (case-sensitive).
__NAMESPACE__	The name of the current namespace (case-sensitive). This constant is defined at compile time. (Added in PHP 5.3.0.)

One handy use of these variables is for debugging purposes, when you need to insert a line of code to see whether the program flow reaches it:

```
echo "This is line " . __LINE__ . " of file " . __FILE__;
```

This causes the current program line in the current file (including the path) being executed to be output to the web browser.

The Difference Between the echo and print Commands

So far, you have seen the echo command used in a number of different ways to output text from the server to your browser. In some cases, a string literal has been output. In others, strings have first been concatenated or variables have been evaluated. I've also shown output spread over multiple lines.

But there is also an alternative to echo that you can use: print. The two commands are quite similar to each other, but print is an actual function that takes a single parameter, whereas echo is a PHP language construct.

By and large, the echo command will be a tad faster than print in general text output, because, not being a function, it doesn't set a return value.

On the other hand, because it isn't a function, echo cannot be used as part of a more complex expression, whereas print can. Here's an example to output whether the value of a variable is TRUE or FALSE using print, something you could not perform in the same manner with echo, because it would display a "Parse error" message:

```
$b ? print "TRUE" : print "FALSE";
```

The question mark is simply a way of interrogating whether variable $b is true or false. Whichever command is on the left of the following colon is executed if $b is true, whereas the command to the right is executed if $b is false.

Generally, though, the examples in this book use echo and I recommend that you do so as well, until you reach such a point in your PHP development that you discover the need for using print.

Functions

Functions are used to separate out sections of code that perform a particular task. For example, maybe you often need to look up a date and return it in a certain format. That would be a good example to turn into a function. The code doing it might be only three lines long, but if you have to paste it into your program a dozen times, you're making your program unnecessarily large and complex, unless you use a function. And if you decide to change the data format later, putting it in a function means having to change it in only one place.

Placing it into a function not only shortens your source code and makes it more readable, it also adds extra functionality (pun intended), because functions can be passed parameters to make them perform differently. They can also return values to the calling code.

To create a function, declare it in the manner shown in Example 3-12.

Example 3-12. A simple function declaration

```php
<?php
function longdate($timestamp)
{
    return date("l F jS Y", $timestamp);
}
?>
```

This function takes a Unix timestamp (an integer number representing a date and time based on the number of seconds since 00:00 AM on January 1, 1970) as its input and then calls the PHP `date` function with the correct format string to return a date in the format *Wednesday August 1st 2012*. Any number of parameters can be passed between the initial parentheses; we have chosen to accept just one. The curly braces enclose all the code that is executed when you later call the function.

To output today's date using this function, place the following call in your code:

```
echo longdate(time());
```

This call uses the built-in PHP `time` function to fetch the current Unix timestamp and passes it to the new `longdate` function, which then returns the appropriate string to the `echo` command for display. If you need to print out the date 17 days ago, you now just have to issue the following call:

```
echo longdate(time() - 17 * 24 * 60 * 60);
```

which passes to `longdate` the current Unix timestamp less the number of seconds since 17 days ago (17 days × 24 hours × 60 minutes × 60 seconds).

Functions can also accept multiple parameters and return multiple results, using techniques that I'll develop over the following chapters.

Variable Scope

If you have a very long program, it's quite possible that you could start to run out of good variable names, but with PHP you can decide the scope of a variable. In other words, you can, for example, tell it that you want the variable `$temp` to be used only inside a particular function and to forget it was ever used when the function returns. In fact, this is the default scope for PHP variables.

Alternatively, you could inform PHP that a variable is global in scope and thus can be accessed by every other part of your program.

Local variables

Local variables are variables that are created within and can be accessed only by a function. They are generally temporary variables that are used to store partially processed results prior to the function's return.

One set of local variables is the list of arguments to a function. In the previous section, we defined a function that accepted a parameter named `$timestamp`. This is meaningful only in the body of the function; you can't get or set its value outside the function.

For another example of a local variable, take another look at the `longdate` function, which is modified slightly in Example 3-13.

Example 3-13. An expanded version of the longdate function

```php
<?php
function longdate($timestamp)
{
    $temp = date("l F jS Y", $timestamp);
    return "The date is $temp";
}
?>
```

Here we have assigned the value returned by the date function to the temporary variable $temp, which is then inserted into the string returned by the function. As soon as the function returns, the value of $temp is cleared, as if it had never been used at all.

Now, to see the effects of variable scope, let's look at some similar code in Example 3-14. Here $temp has been created *before* calling the longdate function.

Example 3-14. This attempt to access $temp in function longdate will fail

```php
<?php
$temp = "The date is ";
echo longdate(time());

function longdate($timestamp)
{
    return $temp . date("l F jS Y", $timestamp);
}
?>
```

However, because $temp was neither created within the longdate function nor passed to it as a parameter, longdate cannot access it. Therefore, this code snippet only outputs the date and not the preceding text. In fact it will first display the error message "Notice: Undefined variable: temp."

The reason for this is that, by default, variables created within a function are local to that function and variables created outside of any functions can be accessed only by nonfunction code.

Some ways to repair Example 3-14 appear in Examples 3-15 and 3-16.

Example 3-15. Rewriting to refer to $temp within its local scope fixes the problem

```php
<?php
$temp = "The date is ";
echo $temp . longdate(time());

function longdate($timestamp)
{
    return date("l F jS Y", $timestamp);
}
?>
```

Example 3-15 moves the reference to $temp out of the function. The reference appears in the same scope where the variable was defined.

Example 3-16. An alternative solution: passing $temp as an argument

```php
<?php
$temp = "The date is ";
echo longdate($temp, time());

function longdate($text, $timestamp)
{
    return $text . date("l F jS Y", $timestamp);
}
?>
```

The solution in Example 3-16 passes `$temp` to the `longdate` function as an extra argument. `longdate` reads it into a temporary variable that it creates called `$text` and outputs the desired result.

 Forgetting the scope of a variable is a common programming error, so remembering how variable scope works will help you debug some quite obscure problems. Unless you have declared a variable otherwise, its scope is limited to being local: either to the current function, or to the code outside of any functions, depending on whether it was first created or accessed inside or outside a function.

Global variables

There are cases when you need a variable to have *global* scope, because you want all your code to be able to access it. Also, some data may be large and complex, and you don't want to keep passing it as arguments to functions.

To declare a variable as having global scope, use the keyword `global`. Let's assume that you have a way of logging your users into your website and want all your code to know whether it is interacting with a logged-in user or a guest. One way to do this is to create a global variable such as `$is_logged_in`:

```php
global $is_logged_in;
```

Now your login function simply has to set that variable to 1 upon success of a login attempt, or 0 upon its failure. Because the scope of the variable is global, every line of code in your program can access it.

You should use global variables with caution, though. I recommend that you create them only when you absolutely cannot find another way of achieving the result you desire. In general, programs that are broken into small parts and segregated data are less buggy and easier to maintain. If you have a thousand-line program (and some day you will) in which you discover that a global variable has the wrong value at some point, how long will it take you to find the code that set it incorrectly?

Also, if you have too many global variables, you run the risk of using one of those names again locally, or at least thinking you have used it locally, when in fact it has already been declared as global. All manner of strange bugs can arise from such situations.

Static variables

In the section "Local variables" on page 53, I mentioned that the value of the variable is wiped out when the function ends. If a function runs many times, it starts with a fresh copy of the variable and the previous setting has no effect.

Here's an interesting case. What if you have a local variable inside a function that you don't want any other parts of your code to have access to, but that you would also like to keep its value for the next time the function is called? Why? Perhaps because you want a counter to track how many times a function is called. The solution is to declare a static variable, as shown in Example 3-17.

Example 3-17. A function using a static variable

```php
<?php
function test()
{
    static $count = 0;
    echo $count;
    $count++;
}
?>
```

Here the very first line of function test creates a static variable called $count and initializes it to a value of zero. The next line outputs the variable's value; the final one increments it.

The next time the function is called, because $count has already been declared, the first line of the function is skipped. Then the previously incremented value of $count is displayed before the variable is again incremented.

If you plan to use static variables, you should note that you cannot assign the result of an expression in their definitions. They can be initialized only with predetermined values (see Example 3-18).

Example 3-18. Allowed and disallowed static variable declarations

```php
<?php
static $int = 0;        // Allowed
static $int = 1+2;      // Disallowed (will produce a Parse error)
static $int = sqrt(144); // Disallowed
?>
```

Superglobal variables

Starting with PHP 4.1.0, several predefined variables are available. These are known as *superglobal variables*, which means that they are provided by the PHP environment but are global within the program, accessible absolutely everywhere.

These superglobals contain lots of useful information about the currently running program and its environment (see Table 3-6). They are structured as associative arrays, a topic discussed in Chapter 6.

Table 3-6. PHP's superglobal variables

Superglobal name	Contents
$GLOBALS	All variables that are currently defined in the global scope of the script. The variable names are the keys of the array.
$_SERVER	Information such as headers, paths, and script locations. The entries in this array are created by the web server and there is no guarantee that every web server will provide any or all of these.
$_GET	Variables passed to the current script via the HTTP GET method.
$_POST	Variables passed to the current script via the HTTP POST method.
$_FILES	Items uploaded to the current script via the HTTP POST method.
$_COOKIE	Variables passed to the current script via HTTP cookies.
$_SESSION	Session variables available to the current script.
$_REQUEST	Contents of information passed from the browser; by default, $_GET, $_POST and $_COOKIE.
$_ENV	Variables passed to the current script via the environment method.

All of the superglobals are named with a single initial underscore and only capital letters; therefore, you should avoid naming your own variables in this manner to avoid potential confusion.

To illustrate how you use them, let's look at a bit of information that many sites employ. Among the many nuggets of information supplied by superglobal variables is the URL of the page that referred the user to the current web page. This referring page information can be accessed like this:

```
$came_from = $_SERVER['HTTP_REFERRER'];
```

It's that simple. Oh, and if the user came straight to your web page, such as by typing its URL directly into a browser, $came_from will be set to an empty string.

Superglobals and security

A word of caution is in order before you start using superglobal variables, because they are often used by hackers trying to find exploits to break in to your website. What they do is load up $_POST, $_GET, or other superglobals with malicious code, such as Unix or MySQL commands that can damage or display sensitive data if you naïvely access them.

Therefore, you should always sanitize superglobals before using them. One way to do this is via the PHP htmlentities function. It converts all characters into HTML entities. For example, less-than and greater-than characters (< and >) are transformed into the strings < and > so that they are rendered harmless, as are all quotes and backslashes, and so on.

Therefore, a much better way to access $_SERVER (and other superglobals) is:

```
$came_from = htmlentities($_SERVER['HTTP_REFERRER']);
```

This chapter has provided you with a solid background in using PHP. In Chapter 4, we'll start using what's you've learned to build expressions and control program flow. In other words, some actual programming.

But before moving on, I recommend that you test yourself with some (if not all) of the following questions to ensure that you have fully digested the contents of this chapter.

Test Your Knowledge: Questions

Question 3-1
What tag is used to cause PHP to start interpreting program code? And what is the short form of the tag?

Question 3-2
What are the two types of comment tags?

Question 3-3
Which character must be placed at the end of every PHP statement?

Question 3-4
Which symbol is used to preface all PHP variables?

Question 3-5
What can a variable store?

Question 3-6
What is the difference between `$variable = 1` and `$variable == 1`?

Question 3-7
Why do you suppose that an underscore is allowed in variable names (`$current_user`) whereas hyphens are not (`$current-user`) ?

Question 3-8
Are variable names case-sensitive?

Question 3-9
Can you use spaces in variable names?

Question 3-10
How do you convert one variable type to another (say, a string to a number)?

Question 3-11
What is the difference between `++$j` and `$j++`?

Question 3-12
Are the operators `&&` and `and` interchangeable?

Question 3-13
How can you create a multiline `echo` or assignment?

Question 3-14
Can you redefine a constant?

Question 3-15

How do you escape a quotation mark?

Question 3-16

What is the difference between the `echo` and `print` commands?

Question 3-17

What is the purpose of functions?

Question 3-18

How can you make a variable accessible to all parts of a PHP program?

Question 3-19

If you generate data within a function, provide a couple of ways to convey the data to the rest of the program.

Question 3-20

What is the result of combining a string with a number?

See the section "Chapter 3 Answers" on page 436 in Appendix A for the answers to these questions.

CHAPTER 4

Expressions and Control Flow in PHP

The previous chapter introduced several topics in passing that this chapter covers more fully, such as making choices (branching) and creating complex expressions. In the previous chapter, I wanted to focus on the most basic syntax and operations in PHP, but I couldn't avoid touching on more advanced topics. Now I can fill in the background that you need to use these powerful PHP features properly.

In this chapter, you will get a thorough grounding in how PHP programming works in practice and how to control the flow of the program.

Expressions

Let's start with the most fundamental part of any programming language: *expressions*.

An expression is a combination of values, variables, operators, and functions that results in a value. It's familiar to anyone who has taken elementary-school algebra:

```
y = 3(abs(2x) + 4)
```

which in PHP would be:

```
$y = 3 * (abs(2*$x) + 4);
```

The value returned (y or $y in this case) can be a number, a string, or a *Boolean value* (named after George Boole, a nineteenth-century English mathematician and philosopher). By now, you should be familiar with the first two value types, but I'll explain the third.

A basic Boolean value can be either TRUE or FALSE. For example, the expression "20 > 9" (20 is greater than 9) is TRUE, and the expression "5 == 6" (5 is equal to 6) is FALSE. (Boolean operations can be combined using operators such as AND, OR, and XOR, which are covered later in this chapter.)

Note that I am using uppercase letters for the names TRUE and FALSE. This is because they are predefined constants in PHP. You can also use the lowercase versions, if you prefer, as they are also predefined. In fact, the lowercase versions are more stable, because PHP does not allow you to redefine them; the uppercase ones may be redefined—something you should bear in mind if you import third-party code.

Example 4-1 shows some simple expressions: the two I just mentioned, plus a couple more. For each line, it prints out a letter between a and d, followed by a colon and the result of the expressions (the <br /> tag is there to create a line break and thus separate the output into four lines in HTML).

Example 4-1. Four simple Boolean expressions

```
<?php
echo "a: [" . (20 > 9) . "]<br />";
echo "b: [" . (5 == 6) . "]<br />";
echo "c: [" . (1 == 0) . "]<br />";
echo "d: [" . (1 == 1) . "]<br />";
?>
```

The output from this code is as follows:

```
a: [1]
b: []
c: []
d: [1]
```

Notice that both expressions a: and d: evaluate to TRUE, which has a value of 1. But b: and c:, which evaluate to FALSE, do not show any value, because in PHP the constant FALSE is defined as NULL, or nothing. To verify this for yourself, you could enter the code in Example 4-2.

Example 4-2. Outputting the values of TRUE and FALSE

```
<?php // test2.php
echo "a: [" . TRUE  . "]<br />";
echo "b: [" . FALSE . "]<br />";
?>
```

which outputs the following:

```
a: [1]
b: []
```

By the way, in some languages FALSE may be defined as 0 or even –1, so it's worth checking on its definition in each language.

Literals and Variables

The simplest form of an expression is a *literal*, which simply means something that evaluates to itself, such as the number 73 or the string "Hello". An expression could also simply be a variable, which evaluates to the value that has been assigned to it. They are both types of expressions, because they return a value.

Example 4-3 shows five different literals, all of which return values, albeit of different types.

Example 4-3. Five types of literals

```php
<?php
$myname = "Brian";
$myage = 37;
echo "a: " . 73      . "<br />"; // Numeric literal
echo "b: " . "Hello" . "<br />"; // String literal
echo "c: " . FALSE   . "<br />"; // Constant literal
echo "d: " . $myname . "<br />"; // Variable string literal
echo "e: " . $myage  . "<br />"; // Variable numeric literal
?>
```

And, as you'd expect, you see a return value from all of these with the exception of
c:, which evaluates to FALSE, returning nothing in the following output:

```
a: 73
b: Hello
c:
d: Brian
e: 37
```

In conjunction with operators, it's possible to create more complex expressions that
evaluate to useful results.

When you combine assignment or control-flow constructs with expressions, the result
is a *statement*. Example 4-4 shows one of each. The first assigns the result of the expression 366 - $day_number to the variable $days_to_new_year, and the second outputs
a friendly message only if the expression $days_to_new_year < 30 evaluates to TRUE.

Example 4-4. An expression and a statement

```php
<?php
$days_to_new_year = 366 - $day_number;  // Expression
if ($days_to_new_year < 30)
{
    echo "Not long now till new year"; // Statement
}
?>
```

Operators

PHP offers a lot of powerful operators that range from arithmetic, string, and logical
operators to assignment, comparison, and more (see Table 4-1).

Table 4-1. PHP operator types

Operator	Description	Example
Arithmetic	Basic mathematics	$a + $b
Array	Array union	$a + $b
Assignment	Assign values	$a = $b + 23
Bitwise	Manipulate bits within bytes	12 ^ 9

Operator	Description	Example
Comparison	Compare two values	$a < $b
Execution	Executes contents of backticks	`ls -al`
Increment/Decrement	Add or subtract 1	$a++
Logical	Boolean	$a and $b
String	Concatenation	$a . $b

Each operator takes a different number of operands:

- *Unary* operators, such as incrementing (**$a++**) or negation (**-$a**), which take a single operand.
- *Binary* operators, which represent the bulk of PHP operators, including addition, subtraction, multiplication, and division.
- One *ternary* operator, which takes the form **? x : y**. It's a terse, single-line **if** statement that chooses between two expressions, depending on the result of a third one.

Operator Precedence

If all operators had the same precedence, they would be processed in the order in which they are encountered. In fact, many operators do have the same precedence, so let's look at a few in Example 4-5.

Example 4-5. Three equivalent expressions

```
1 + 2 + 3 - 4 + 5
2 - 4 + 5 + 3 + 1
5 + 2 - 4 + 1 + 3
```

Here you will see that although the numbers (and their preceding operators) have been moved, the result of each expression is the value 7, because the plus and minus operators have the same precedence. We can try the same thing with multiplication and division (see Example 4-6).

Example 4-6. Three expressions that are also equivalent

```
1 * 2 * 3 / 4 * 5
2 / 4 * 5 * 3 * 1
5 * 2 / 4 * 1 * 3
```

Here the resulting value is always 7.5. But things change when we mix operators with *different* precedences in an expression, as in Example 4-7.

Example 4-7. Three expressions using operators of mixed precedence

```
1 + 2 * 3 - 4 * 5
2 - 4 * 5 * 3 + 1
5 + 2 - 4 + 1 * 3
```

If there were no operator precedence, these three expressions would evaluate to 25, –29, and 12, respectively. But because multiplication and division take precedence over addition and subtraction, there are implied parentheses around these parts of the expressions, which would look like Example 4-8 if they were visible.

Example 4-8. Three expressions showing implied parentheses

```
1 + (2 * 3) - (4 * 5)
2 - (4 * 5 * 3) + 1
5 + 2 - 4 + (1 * 3)
```

Clearly, PHP must evaluate the subexpressions within parentheses first to derive the semicompleted expressions in Example 4-9.

Example 4-9. After evaluating the subexpressions in parentheses

```
1 + (6) - (20)
2 - (60) + 1
5 + 2 - 4 + (3)
```

The final results of these expressions are –13, –57, and 6, respectively (quite different from the results of 25, –29, and 12 that we would have seen had there been no operator precedence).

Of course, you can override the default operator precedence by inserting your own parentheses and force the original results that we would have seen, had there been no operator precedence (see Example 4-10).

Example 4-10. Forcing left-to-right evaluation

```
((1 + 2) * 3 - 4) * 5
(2 - 4) * 5 * 3 + 1
(5 + 2 - 4 + 1) * 3
```

With parentheses correctly inserted, we now see the values 25, –29, and 12, respectively.

Table 4-2 lists PHP's operators in order of precedence from high to low.

Table 4-2. The precedence of PHP operators (high to low)

Operator(s)	Type
()	Parentheses
++ --	Increment/Decrement
!	Logical
* / %	Arithmetic

Operator(s)	Type
+ - .	Arithmetic and String
<< >>	Bitwise
< <= > >= <>	Comparison
== != === !==	Comparison
&	Bitwise (and references)
^	Bitwise
|	Bitwise
&&	Logical
||	Logical
? :	Ternary
= += -= *= /= .= %= &= != ^= <<= >>=	Assignment
and	Logical
xor	Logical
or	Logical

Associativity

We've been looking at processing expressions from left to right, except where operator precedence is in effect. But some operators can also require processing from right to left. The direction of processing is called the operator's *associativity*.

This associativity becomes important in cases in which you do not explicitly force precedence. Table 4-3 lists all the operators that have right-to-left associativity.

Table 4-3. Operators with right-to-left associativity

Operator	Description
NEW	Create a new object
!	Logical NOT
~	Bitwise NOT
++ --	Increment and decrement
+ -	Unary plus and negation
(int)	Cast to an integer
(double)	Cast to a float
(string)	Cast to a string
(array)	Cast to an array
(object)	Cast to an object
@	Inhibit error reporting

Operator	Description
? :	Conditional
=	Assignment

For example, let's take a look at the assignment operator in Example 4-11, where three variables are all set to the value 0.

Example 4-11. A multiple-assignment statement

```php
<?php
$level = $score = $time = 0;
?>
```

This multiple assignment is possible only if the rightmost part of the expression is evaluated first and then processing continues in a right-to-left direction.

 As a beginner to PHP, you should learn to avoid the potential pitfalls of operator associativity by always nesting your subexpressions within parentheses to force the order of evaluation. This will also help other programmers who may have to maintain your code to understand what is happening.

Relational Operators

Relational operators test two operands and return a Boolean result of either TRUE or FALSE. There are three types of relational operators: *equality*, *comparison*, and *logical*.

Equality

As already encountered a few times in this chapter, the equality operator is == (two equals signs). It is important not to confuse it with the = (single equals sign) assignment operator. In Example 4-12, the first statement assigns a value and the second tests it for equality.

Example 4-12. Assigning a value and testing for equality

```php
<?php
$month = "March";
if ($month == "March") echo "It's springtime";
?>
```

As you see, returning either TRUE or FALSE, the equality operator enables you to test for conditions using, for example, an if statement. But that's not the whole story, because PHP is a loosely typed language. If the two operands of an equality expression are of different types, PHP will convert them to whatever type makes best sense to it.

For example, any strings composed entirely of numbers will be converted to numbers whenever compared with a number. In Example 4-13, $a and $b are two different strings and we would therefore expect neither of the if statements to output a result.

Example 4-13. The equality and identity operators

```
<?php
$a = "1000";
$b = "+1000";
if ($a == $b) echo "1";
if ($a === $b) echo "2";
?>
```

However, if you run the example, you will see that it outputs the number 1, which means that the first if statement evaluated to TRUE. This is because both strings were first converted to numbers, and 1000 is the same numerical value as +1000.

In contrast, the second if statement uses the *identity* operator—three equals signs in a row—which prevents PHP from automatically converting types. $a and $b are therefore compared as strings and are now found to be different, so nothing is output.

As with forcing operator precedence, whenever you feel there may be doubt about how PHP will convert operand types, you can use the identity operator to turn this behavior off.

In the same way that you can use the equality operator to test for operands being equal, you can test for them *not* being equal using !=, the inequality operator. Take a look at Example 4-14, which is a rewrite of Example 4-13 in which the equality and identity operators have been replaced with their inverses.

Example 4-14. The inequality and not identical operators

```
<?php
$a = "1000";
$b = "+1000";
if ($a != $b) echo "1";
if ($a !== $b) echo "2";
?>
```

And, as you might expect, the first if statement does not output the number 1, because the code is asking whether $a and $b are *not* equal to each other numerically.

Instead, it outputs the number 2, because the second if statement is asking whether $a and $b are *not* identical to each other in their present operand types, and the answer is TRUE; they are not the same.

Comparison operators

Using comparison operators, you can test for more than just equality and inequality. PHP also gives you > (is greater than), < (is less than), >= (is greater than or equal to), and <= (is less than or equal to) to play with. Example 4-15 shows these operators in use.

Example 4-15. The four comparison operators

```php
<?php
$a = 2; $b = 3;
if ($a > $b)  echo "$a is greater than $b<br />";
if ($a < $b)  echo "$a is less than $b<br />";
if ($a >= $b) echo "$a is greater than or equal to $b<br />";
if ($a <= $b) echo "$a is less than or equal to $b<br />";
?>
```

In this example, where $a is 2 and $b is 3, the following is output:

```
2 is less than 3
2 is less than or equal to 3
```

Try this example yourself, altering the values of $a and $b, to see the results. Try setting them to the same value and see what happens.

Logical operators

Logical operators produce true-or-false results, and therefore are also known as Boolean operators. There are four of them (see Table 4-4).

Table 4-4. The logical operators

Logical operator	Description
AND	TRUE if both operands are TRUE
OR	TRUE if either operand is TRUE
XOR	TRUE if one of the two operands is TRUE
NOT	TRUE if the operand is FALSE or FALSE if the operand is TRUE

You can see these operators used in Example 4-16. Note that the ! symbol is required by PHP in place of the word NOT. Furthermore, the operators can be lower- or uppercase.

Example 4-16. The logical operators in use

```php
<?php
$a = 1; $b = 0;
echo ($a AND $b) . "<br />";
echo ($a or $b)  . "<br />";
echo ($a XOR $b) . "<br />";
echo !$a          . "<br />";
?>
```

This example outputs NULL, 1, 1, NULL, meaning that only the second and third echo statements evaluate as TRUE. (Remember that NULL—or nothing—represents a value of FALSE.) This is because the AND statement requires both operands to be TRUE if it is going to return a value of TRUE, while the fourth statement performs a NOT on the value of $a, turning it from TRUE (a value of 1) to FALSE. If you wish to experiment with this, try out the code, giving $a and $b varying values of 1 and 0.

When coding, remember to bear in mind that AND and OR have lower precedence than the other versions of the operators, && and ||. In complex expressions, it may be safer to use && and || for this reason.

The OR operator can cause unintentional problems in if statements, because the second operand will not be evaluated if the first is evaluated as TRUE. In Example 4-17, the function getnext will never be called if $finished has a value of 1.

Example 4-17. A statement using the OR operator

```php
<?php
if ($finished == 1 OR getnext() == 1) exit;
?>
```

If you need getnext to be called at each if statement, you should rewrite the code as has been done in Example 4-18.

Example 4-18. The "if ... OR" statement modified to ensure calling of getnext

```php
<?php
$gn = getnext();
if ($finished == 1 OR $gn == 1) exit;
?>
```

In this case, the code in function getnext will be executed and the value returned stored in $gn before the if statement.

Table 4-5 shows all the possible variations of using the logical operators. You should also note that !TRUE equals FALSE and !FALSE equals TRUE.

Table 4-5. All possible PHP logical expressions

Inputs		Operators and results		
a	b	AND	OR	XOR
TRUE	TRUE	TRUE	TRUE	FALSE
TRUE	FALSE	FALSE	TRUE	TRUE
FALSE	TRUE	FALSE	TRUE	TRUE
FALSE	FALSE	FALSE	FALSE	FALSE

Conditionals

Conditionals alter program flow. They enable you to ask questions about certain things and respond to the answers you get in different ways. Conditionals are central to dynamic web pages—the goal of using PHP in the first place—because they make it easy to create different output each time a page is viewed.

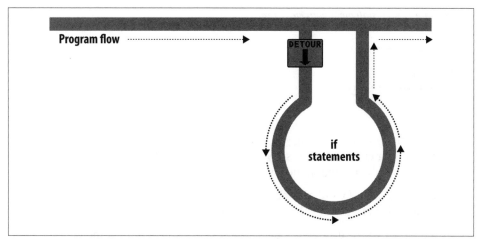

Figure 4-1. Program flow is like a single-lane highway

There are three types of nonlooping conditionals: the `if` statement, the `switch` statement, and the `?` operator. By nonlooping, I mean that the actions initiated by the statement take place and program flow then moves on, whereas looping conditionals (which we'll come to shortly) execute code over and over until a condition has been met.

The if Statement

One way of thinking about program flow is to imagine it as a single-lane highway that you are driving along. It's pretty much a straight line, but now and then you encounter various signs telling you where to go.

In the case of an `if` statement, you could imagine coming across a detour sign that you have to follow if a certain condition is TRUE. If so, you drive off and follow the detour until you return to where it started and then continue on your way in your original direction. Or, if the condition isn't TRUE, you ignore the detour and carry on driving (see Figure 4-1).

The contents of the `if` condition can be any valid PHP expression, including equality, comparison, tests for zero and NULL, and even the values returned by functions (either built-in functions or ones that you write).

The action to take when an `if` condition is TRUE are generally placed inside curly braces, `{ }`. However, you can ignore the braces if you have only a single statement to execute. But if you always use curly braces, you'll avoid having to hunt down difficult-to-trace bugs, such as when you add an extra line to a condition and it doesn't get evaluated due to lack of braces. (Note that for space and clarity, many of the examples in this book ignore this suggestion and omit the braces for single statements.)

In Example 4-19, imagine that it is the end of the month and all your bills have been paid, so you are performing some bank account maintenance.

Example 4-19. An if statement with curly braces

```php
<?php
if ($bank_balance < 100)
{
    $money += 1000;
    $bank_balance += $money;
}
?>
```

In this example, you are checking your balance to see whether it is less than 100 dollars (or whatever your currency is). If so, you pay yourself 1,000 dollars and then add it to the balance. (If only making money were that simple!)

If the bank balance is 100 dollars or greater, the conditional statements are ignored and program flow skips to the next line (not shown).

In this book, opening curly braces generally start on a new line. Some people like to place the first curly brace to the right of the conditional expression; others start a new line with it. Either of these is fine, because PHP allows you to set out your whitespace characters (spaces, newlines, and tabs) any way you choose. However, you will find your code easier to read and debug if you indent each level of conditionals with a tab.

The else Statement

Sometimes when a conditional is not TRUE, you may not want to continue on to the main program code immediately but might wish to do something else instead. This is where the else statement comes in. With it, you can set up a second detour on your highway, as in Figure 4-2.

What happens with an if...else statement is that the first conditional statement is executed if the condition is TRUE. But if it's FALSE, the second one is executed. One of the two choices *must* be executed. Under no circumstance can both (or neither) be executed. Example 4-20 shows the use of the if...else structure.

Example 4-20. An if...else statement with curly braces

```php
<?php
if ($bank_balance < 100)
{
    $money += 1000;
    $bank_balance += $money;
}
else
{
    $savings += 50;
    $bank_balance -= 50;
}
?>
```

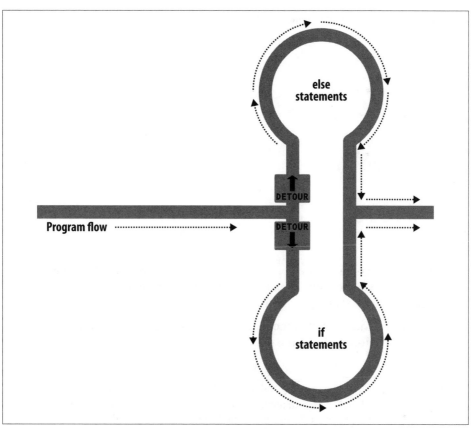

Figure 4-2. The highway now has an if detour and an else detour

In this example, having ascertained that you have over $100 in the bank, the else statement is executed, by which you place some of this money into your savings account.

As with if statements, if your else has only one conditional statement, you can opt to leave out the curly braces. (Curly braces are always recommended, though. First, they make the code easier to understand. Second, they let you easily add more statements to the branch later.)

The elseif Statement

There are also times when you want a number of different possibilities to occur, based upon a sequence of conditions. You can achieve this using the elseif statement. As you might imagine, it is like an else statement, except that you place a further conditional expression prior to the conditional code. In Example 4-21, you can see a complete if...elseif...else construct.

Example 4-21. An if...elseif...else statement with curly braces

```php
<?php
if ($bank_balance < 100)
{
    $money += 1000;
    $bank_balance += $money;
}
elseif ($bank_balance > 200)
{
    $savings += 100;
    $bank_balance -= 100;
}
else
{
    $savings += 50;
    $bank_balance -= 50;
}
?>
```

In the example, an `elseif` statement has been inserted between the `if` and `else` statements. It checks whether your bank balance exceeds $200 and, if so, decides that you can afford to save $100 of it this month.

Although I'm starting to stretch the metaphor a bit too far, you can imagine this as a multiway set of detours (see Figure 4-3).

> An `else` statement closes either an `if...else` or an `if...elseif...else` statement. You can leave out a final `else` if it is not required, but you cannot have one before an `elseif`; neither can you have an `elseif` before an `if` statement.

You may have as many `elseif` statements as you like. But as the number of `elseif` statements increase, you would probably be better advised to consider a `switch` statement if it fits your needs. We'll look at that next.

The switch Statement

The `switch` statement is useful in cases in which one variable or the result of an expression can have multiple values, which should each trigger a different function.

For example, consider a PHP-driven menu system that passes a single string to the main menu code according to what the user requests. Let's say the options are Home, About, News, Login, and Links, and we set the variable `$page` to one of these, according to the user's input.

The code for this written using `if...elseif...else` might look like Example 4-22.

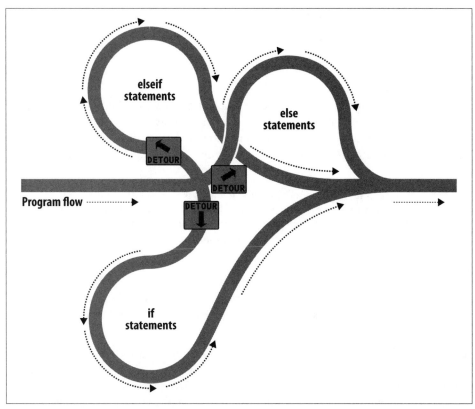

Figure 4-3. The highway with if, elseif, and else detours

Example 4-22. A multiple-line if...elseif... statement

```php
<?php
if      ($page == "Home")  echo "You selected Home";
elseif ($page == "About") echo "You selected About";
elseif ($page == "News")  echo "You selected News";
elseif ($page == "Login") echo "You selected Login";
elseif ($page == "Links") echo "You selected Links";
?>
```

Using a switch statement, the code might look like Example 4-23.

Example 4-23. A switch statement

```php
<?php
switch ($page)
{
    case "Home":  echo "You selected Home";
        break;
    case "About": echo "You selected About";
        break;
    case "News":  echo "You selected News";
        break;
```

```
    case "Login": echo "You selected Login";
        break;
    case "Links": echo "You selected Links";
        break;
}
?>
```

As you can see, `$page` is mentioned only once at the start of the `switch` statement. Thereafter, the `case` command checks for matches. When one occurs, the matching conditional statement is executed. Of course, in a real program you would have code here to display or jump to a page, rather than simply telling the user what was selected.

 One thing to note about `switch` statements is that you do not use curly braces inside `case` commands. Instead, they commence with a colon and end with the `break` statement. The entire list of cases in the `switch` statement is enclosed in a set of curly braces, though.

Breaking out

If you wish to break out of the `switch` statement because a condition has been fulfilled, use the `break` command. This command tells PHP to break out of the `switch` and jump to the following statement.

If you were to leave out the `break` commands in Example 4-23 and the `case` of "Home" evaluated to be TRUE, all five cases would then be executed. Or if `$page` had the value "News," then all the `case` commands from then on would execute. This is deliberate and allows for some advanced programming, but generally you should always remember to issue a `break` command every time a set of `case` conditionals has finished executing. In fact, leaving out the `break` statement is a common error.

Default action

A typical requirement in `switch` statements is to fall back on a default action if none of the `case` conditions are met. For example, in the case of the menu code in Example 4-23, you could add the code in Example 4-24 immediately before the final curly brace.

Example 4-24. A default statement to add to Example 4-23

```
default: echo "Unrecognized selection";
        break;
```

Although a `break` command is not required here because the default is the final substatement, and program flow will automatically continue to the closing curly brace, should you decide to place the `default` statement higher up it would definitely need a `break` command to prevent program flow from dropping into the following statements. Generally the safest practice is to always include the `break` command.

Alternative syntax

If you prefer, you may replace the first curly brace in a switch statement with a single colon, and the final curly brace with an `endswitch` command, as in Example 4-25. However this approach is not commonly used and is mentioned here only in case you encounter it in third-party code.

Example 4-25. Alternate switch statement syntax

```php
<?php
switch ($page):
    case "Home":
        echo "You selected Home";
        break;

    // etc...

    case "Links":
        echo "You selected Links";
        break;
endswitch;
?>
```

The ? Operator

One way of avoiding the verbosity of `if` and `else` statements is to use the more compact ternary operator, `?`, which is unusual in that it takes three operands rather than the more usual two.

We briefly came across this in Chapter 3 in the discussion about the difference between the `print` and `echo` statements as an example of an operator type that works well with `print` but not `echo`.

The `?` operator is passed an expression that it must evaluate, along with two statements to execute: one for when the expression evaluates to `TRUE`, the other for when it is `FALSE`. Example 4-26 shows code we might use for writing a warning about the fuel level of a car to its digital dashboard.

Example 4-26. Using the ? operator

```php
<?php
echo $fuel <= 1 ? "Fill tank now" : "There's enough fuel";
?>
```

In this statement, if there is one gallon or less of fuel (in other words `$fuel` is set to 1 or less), the string "Fill tank now" is returned to the preceding `echo` statement. Otherwise, the string "There's enough fuel" is returned. You can also assign the value returned in a `?` statement to a variable (see Example 4-27).

Example 4-27. Assigning a ? conditional result to a variable

```php
<?php
$enough = $fuel <= 1 ? FALSE : TRUE;
?>
```

Here $enough will be assigned the value TRUE only when there is more than a gallon of fuel; otherwise, it is assigned the value FALSE.

If you find the ? operator confusing, you are free to stick to if statements, but you should be familiar with it, because you'll see it in other people's code. It can be hard to read, because it often mixes multiple occurrences of the same variable. For instance, code such as the following is quite popular:

```php
$saved = $saved >= $new ? $saved : $new;
```

If you take it apart carefully, you can figure out what this code does:

```php
$saved =                    // Set the value of $saved
        $saved >= $new      // Check $saved against $new
    ?                       // Yes, comparison is true ...
        $saved                  // ... so assign the current value of $saved
    :                       // No, comparison is false ...
        $new;               // ... so assign the value of $new
```

It's a concise way to keep track of the largest value that you've seen as a program progresses. You save the largest value in $saved and compare it to $new each time you get a new value. Programmers familiar with the ? operator find it more convenient than if statements for such short comparisons. When not used for writing compact code, it is typically used to make some decision inline, such as when testing whether a variable is set before passing it to a function.

Looping

One of the great things about computers is that they can repeat calculating tasks quickly and tirelessly. Often you may want a program to repeat the same sequence of code again and again until something happens, such as a user inputting a value or the program reaching a natural end. PHP's various loop structures provide the perfect way to do this.

To picture how this works, take a look at Figure 4-4. It is much the same as the highway metaphor used to illustrate if statements, except that the detour also has a loop section that, once a vehicle has entered, can be exited only under the right program conditions.

while Loops

Let's turn the digital car dashboard in Example 4-26 into a loop that continuously checks the fuel level as you drive using a while loop (Example 4-28).

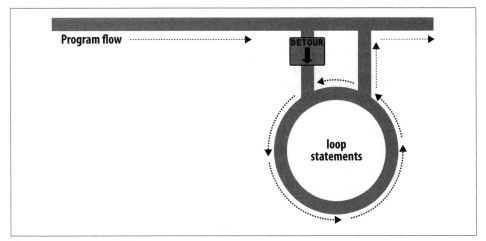

Program flow

DETOUR

loop
statements

Figure 4-4. Imagining a loop as part of a program highway layout

Example 4-28. A while loop

```php
<?php
$fuel = 10;

while ($fuel > 1)
{
    // Keep driving ...
    echo "There's enough fuel";
}
?>
```

Actually, you might prefer to keep a green light lit rather than output text, but the point is that whatever positive indication you wish to make about the level of fuel is placed inside the while loop. By the way, if you try this example for yourself, note that it will keep printing the string until you click the Stop button in your browser.

 As with if statements, you will notice that curly braces are required to hold the statements inside the while statements, unless there's only one.

For another example of a while loop that displays the 12 times table, see Example 4-29.

Example 4-29. A while loop to print the multiplication table for 12

```php
<?php
$count = 1;

while ($count <= 12)
{
    echo "$count times 12 is " . $count * 12 . "<br />";
    ++$count;
```

```
}
?>
```

Here the variable $count is initialized to a value of 1, then a while loop is started with the comparative expression $count <= 12. This loop will continue executing until the variable is greater than 12. The output from this code is as follows:

```
1 times 12 is 12
2 times 12 is 24
3 times 12 is 36
and so on...
```

Inside the loop, a string is printed along with the value of $count multiplied by 12. For neatness, this is also followed with a <br /> tag to force a new line. Then $count is incremented, ready for the final curly brace that tells PHP to return to the start of the loop.

At this point, $count is again tested to see whether it is greater than 12. It isn't, but it now has the value 2, and after another 11 times around the loop, it will have the value 13. When that happens, the code within the while loop is skipped and execution passes on to the code following the loop which, in this case, is the end of the program.

If the ++$count statement (which could equally have been $count++) had not been there, this loop would be like the first one in this section. It would never end and only the result of 1 * 12 would be printed over and over.

But there is a much neater way this loop can be written, which I think you will like. Take a look at Example 4-30.

Example 4-30. A shortened version of Example 4-29

```php
<?php
$count = 0;
while (++$count <= 12)
    echo "$count times 12 is " . $count * 12 . "<br />";
?>
```

In this example, it was possible to remove the ++$count statement from inside the while loop and place it directly into the conditional expression of the loop. What now happens is that PHP encounters the variable $count at the start of each iteration of the loop and, noticing that it is prefaced with the increment operator, first increments the variable and only then compares it to the value 12. You can therefore see that $count now has to be initialized to 0, and not 1, because it is incremented as soon as the loop is entered. If you keep the initialization at 1, only results between 2 and 12 will be output.

do...while Loops

A slight variation to the while loop is the do...while loop, used when you want a block of code to be executed at least once and made conditional only after that.

Example 4-31 shows a modified version of the multiplication table for 12 code using such a loop.

Example 4-31. A do...while loop for printing the times table for 12

```php
<?php
$count = 1;
do
    echo "$count times 12 is " . $count * 12 . "<br />";
while (++$count <= 12);
?>
```

Notice how we are back to initializing $count to 1 (rather than 0), because the code is being executed immediately, without an opportunity to increment the variable. Other than that, though, the code looks pretty similar.

Of course, if you have more than a single statement inside a do...while loop, remember to use curly braces, as in Example 4-32.

Example 4-32. Expanding Example 4-31 to use curly braces

```php
<?php
$count = 1;
do {
    echo "$count times 12 is " . $count * 12;
    echo "<br />";
} while (++$count <= 12);
?>
```

for Loops

The final kind of loop statement, the for loop, is also the most powerful, as it combines the abilities to set up variables as you enter the loop, test for conditions while iterating loops, and modify variables after each iteration.

Example 4-33 shows how you could write the multiplication table program with a for loop.

Example 4-33. Outputting the times table for 12 from a for loop

```php
<?php
for ($count = 1 ; $count <= 12 ; ++$count)
    echo "$count times 12 is " . $count * 12 . "<br />";
?>
```

See how the entire code has been reduced to a single for statement containing a single conditional statement? Here's what is going on. Each for statement takes three parameters:

- An initialization expression
- A condition expression

- A modification expression

These are separated by semicolons like this: for (*expr1* ; *expr2* ; *expr3*). At the start of the first iteration of the loop, the initialization expression is executed. In the case of the times table code, $count is initialized to the value 1. Then, each time round the loop, the condition expression (in this case, $count <= 12) is tested, and the loop is entered only if the condition is TRUE. Finally, at the end of each iteration, the modification expression is executed. In the case of the times table code, the variable $count is incremented.

All this structure neatly removes any requirement to place the controls for a loop within its body, freeing it up just for the statements you want the loop to perform.

Remember to use curly braces with a for loop if it will contain more than one statement, as in Example 4-34.

Example 4-34. The for loop from Example 4-33 with added curly braces

```
<?php
for ($count = 1 ; $count <= 12 ; ++$count)
{
    echo "$count times 12 is " . $count * 12;
    echo "<br />";
}
?>
```

Let's compare when to use for and while loops. The for loop is explicitly designed around a single value that changes on a regular basis. Usually you have a value that increments, as when you are passed a list of user choices and want to process each choice in turn. But you can transform the variable any way you like. A more complex form of the for statement even lets you perform multiple operations in each of the three parameters:

```
for ($i = 1, $j = 1 ; $i + $j < 10 ; $i++ , $j++)
{
    // ...
}
```

That's complicated and not recommended for first-time users. The key is to distinguish commas from semicolons. The three parameters must be separated by semicolons. Within each parameter, multiple statements can be separated by commas. Thus, in the previous example, the first and third parameters each contain two statements:

```
$i = 1, $j = 1  // Initialize $i and $j
$i + $j < 1     // Terminating condition
$i++ , $j++     // Modify $i and $j at the end of each iteration
```

The main thing to take from this example is that you must separate the three parameter sections with semicolons, not commas (which should be used only to separate statements within a parameter section).

So, when is a while statement more appropriate than a for statement? When your condition doesn't depend on a simple, regular change to a variable. For instance, if you want to check for some special input or error and end the loop when it occurs, use a while statement.

Breaking Out of a Loop

Just as you saw how to break out of a switch statement, you can also break out from a for loop using the same break command. This step can be necessary when, for example, one of your statements returns an error and the loop cannot continue executing safely.

One case in which this might occur might be when writing a file returns an error, possibly because the disk is full (see Example 4-35).

Example 4-35. Writing a file using a for loop with error trapping

```php
<?php
$fp = fopen("text.txt", 'wb');

for ($j = 0 ; $j < 100 ; ++$j)
{
    $written = fwrite($fp, "data");
    if ($written == FALSE) break;
}

fclose($fp);
?>
```

This is the most complicated piece of code that you have seen so far, but you're ready for it. We'll look into the file handling commands in a later chapter, but for now all you need to know is that the first line opens the file *text.txt* for writing in binary mode, and then returns a pointer to the file in the variable $fp, which is used later to refer to the open file.

The loop then iterates 100 times (from 0 to 99) writing the string data to the file. After each write, the variable $written is assigned a value by the fwrite function representing the number of characters correctly written. But if there is an error, the fwrite function assigns the value FALSE.

The behavior of fwrite makes it easy for the code to check the variable $written to see whether it is set to FALSE and, if so, to break out of the loop to the following statement closing the file.

If you are looking to improve the code, the line:

```php
    if ($written == FALSE) break;
```

can be simplified using the NOT operator, like this:

```php
    if (!$written) break;
```

In fact, the pair of inner loop statements can be shortened to the following single statement:

```
if (!fwrite($fp, "data")) break;
```

The break command is even more powerful than you might think, because if you have code nested more than one layer deep that you need to break out of, you can follow the break command with a number to indicate how many levels to break out of, like this:

```
break 2;
```

The continue Statement

The continue statement is a little like a break statement, except that it instructs PHP to stop processing the current loop and to move right to its next iteration. So, instead of breaking out of the whole loop, only the current iteration is exited.

This approach can be useful in cases where you know there is no point continuing execution within the current loop and you want to save processor cycles, or prevent an error from occurring, by moving right along to the next iteration of the loop. In Example 4-36, a continue statement is used to prevent a division-by-zero error from being issued when the variable $j has a value of 0.

Example 4-36. Trapping division-by-zero errors using continue

```
<?php
$j = 10;

while ($j > -10)
{
  $j--;
  if ($j == 0) continue;
  echo (10 / $j) . "<br />";
}
>
```

For all values of $j between 10 and –10, with the exception of 0, the result of calculating 10 divided by $j is displayed. But for the particular case of $j being 0, the continue statement is issued and execution skips immediately to the next iteration of the loop.

Implicit and Explicit Casting

PHP is a loosely typed language that allows you to declare a variable and its type simply by using it. It also automatically converts values from one type to another whenever required. This is called *implicit casting*.

However, there may be times when PHP's implicit casting is not what you want. In Example 4-37, note that the inputs to the division are integers. By default, PHP converts the output to floating-point so it can give the most precise value—4.66 recurring.

Example 4-37. This expression returns a floating-point number

```php
<?php
$a = 56;
$b = 12;
$c = $a / $b;
echo $c;
?>
```

But what if we had wanted $c to be an integer instead? There are various ways in which this could be achieved; one way is to force the result of $a/$b to be cast to an integer value using the integer cast type (int), like this:

```php
$c = (int) ($a / $b);
```

This is called *explicit* casting. Note that in order to ensure that the value of the entire expression is cast to an integer, the expression is placed within parentheses. Otherwise, only the variable $a would have been cast to an integer—a pointless exercise, as the division by $b would still have returned a floating-point number.

> You can explicitly cast to the types shown in Table 4-6, but you can usually avoid having to use a cast by calling one of PHP's built-in functions. For example, to obtain an integer value, you could use the intval function. As with some other sections in this book, this one is mainly here to help you understand third-party code that you may encounter.

Table 4-6. PHP's cast types

Cast type	Description
(int) (integer)	Cast to an integer by dropping the decimal portion
(bool) (boolean)	Cast to a Boolean
(float) (double) (real)	Cast to a floating-point number
(string)	Cast to a string
(array)	Cast to an array
(object)	Cast to an object

PHP Dynamic Linking

Because PHP is a programming language, and the output from it can be completely different for each user, it's possible for an entire website to run from a single PHP web page. Each time the user clicks on something, the details can be sent back to the same web page, which decides what to do next according to the various cookies and/or other session details it may have stored.

But although it is possible to build an entire website this way, it's not recommended, because your source code will grow and grow and start to become unwieldy, as it has to take account of every possible action a user could take.

Instead, it's much more sensible to split your website development into different parts. For example, one distinct process is signing up for a website, along with all the checking this entails to validate an email address, checking whether a username is already taken, and so on.

A second module might well be one for logging users in before handing them off to the main part of your website. Then you might have a messaging module with the facility for users to leave comments, a module containing links and useful information, another to allow uploading of images, and so on.

As long as you have created a means of tracking your user through your website by means of cookies or session variables (both of which we'll look at more closely in later chapters), you can split your website up into sensible sections of PHP code, each one self-contained, and therefore treat yourself to a much easier future developing each new feature and maintaining old ones.

Dynamic Linking in Action

One of the more popular PHP-driven applications on the web today is the blogging platform WordPress (see Figure 4-5). As a blogger or a blog reader, you might not realize it, but every major section has been given its own main PHP file, and a whole raft of generic, shared functions have been placed in separate files that are included by the main PHP pages as necessary.

Figure 4-5. The WordPress blogging platform is written in PHP

The whole platform is held together with behind-the-scenes session tracking, so that you hardly know when you are transitioning from one subsection to another. So, as a web developer, if you want to tweak WordPress, it's easy to find the particular file you need, make a modification, and test and debug it without messing around with unconnected parts of the program.

Next time you use WordPress, keep an eye on your browser's address bar, particularly if you are managing a blog, and you'll notice some of the different PHP files that it uses.

This chapter has covered quite a lot of ground, and by now you should be able to put together your own small PHP programs. But before you do, and before proceeding with the following chapter on functions and objects, you may wish to test your new knowledge on the following questions.

Test Your Knowledge: Questions

Question 4-1
What actual underlying values are represented by TRUE and FALSE?

Question 4-2
What are the simplest two forms of expressions?

Question 4-3
What is the difference between unary, binary, and ternary operators?

Question 4-4
What is the best way to force your own operator precedence?

Question 4-5
What is meant by "operator associativity"?

Question 4-6
When would you use the === (identity) operator?

Question 4-7
Name the three conditional statement types.

Question 4-8
What command can you use to skip the current iteration of a loop and move on to the next one?

Question 4-9
Why is a for loop more powerful than a while loop?

Question 4-10
How do if and while statements interpret conditional expressions of different data types?

See the section "Chapter 4 Answers" on page 438 in Appendix A for the answers to these questions.

CHAPTER 5

PHP Functions and Objects

The basic requirements of any programming language include somewhere to store data, a means of directing program flow, and a few bits and pieces such as expression evaluation, file management, and text output. PHP has all these, plus tools like `else` and `elseif` to make life easier. But even with all these in our toolkit, programming can be clumsy and tedious, especially if you have to rewrite portions of very similar code each time you need them.

That's where functions and objects come in. As you might guess, a *function* is a set of statements that performs a particular function and—optionally—returns a value. You can pull out a section of code that you have used more than once, place it into a function, and call the function by name when you want the code.

Functions have many advantages over contiguous, inline code:

- Less typing is involved.
- Functions reduce syntax and other programming errors.
- They decrease the loading time of program files.
- They also decrease execution time, because each function is compiled only once, no matter how often you call it.
- Functions accept arguments and can therefore be used for general as well as specific cases.

Objects take this concept a step further. An *object* incorporates one or more functions, and the data they use, into a single structure called a *class*.

In this chapter, you'll learn all about using functions, from defining and calling them to passing arguments back and forth. With that knowledge under your belt, you'll start creating functions and using them in your own objects (where they will be referred to as *methods*).

PHP Functions

PHP comes with hundreds of ready-made, built-in functions, making it a very rich language. To use a function, call it by name. For example, you can see the `print` function in action here:

```
print("print is a function");
```

The parentheses tell PHP that you're referring to a function. Otherwise, it thinks you're referring to a constant. You may see a warning such as this:

```
Notice: Use of undefined constant fname - assumed 'fname'
```

followed by the text string `fname`, under the assumption that you must have wanted to put a literal string in your code. (Things are even more confusing if there is actually a constant named `fname`, in which case PHP uses its value.)

 Strictly speaking, `print` is a pseudofunction, commonly called a *construct*. The difference is that you can omit the parentheses, as follows:

```
print "print doesn't require parentheses";
```

You do have to put parentheses after any other function you call, even if they're empty (that is, if you're not passing any argument to the function).

Functions can take any number of arguments, including zero. For example, `phpinfo`, as shown here, displays lots of information about the current installation of PHP and requires no argument. The result of calling this function can be seen in Figure 5-1.

```
phpinfo();
```

 The `phpinfo` function is extremely useful for obtaining information about your current PHP installation, but that information could also be very useful to potential hackers. Therefore, never leave a call to this function in any web-ready code.

Some of the built-in functions that use one or more arguments appear in Example 5-1.

Example 5-1. Three string functions

```
<?php
echo strrev(" .dlrow olleH"); // Reverse string
echo str_repeat("Hip ", 2);   // Repeat string
echo strtoupper("hooray!");   // String to uppercase
?>
```

This example uses three string functions to output the following text:

```
Hello world. Hip Hip HOORAY!
```

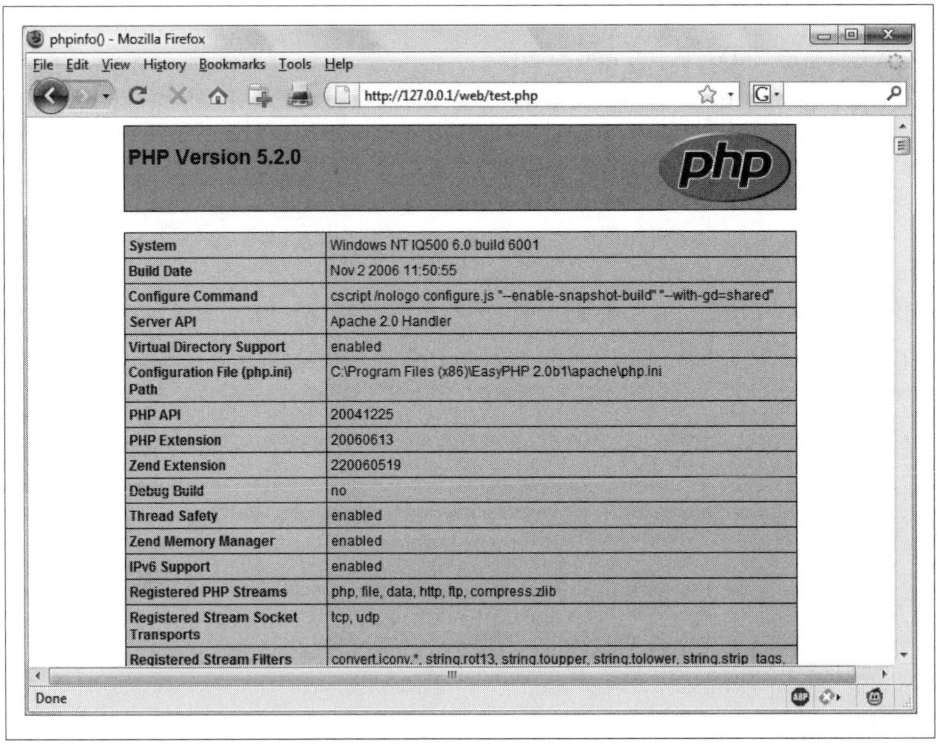

phpinfo() - Mozilla Firefox

File Edit View History Bookmarks Tools Help

http://127.0.0.1/web/test.php

PHP Version 5.2.0

System	Windows NT IQ500 6.0 build 6001
Build Date	Nov 2 2006 11:50:55
Configure Command	cscript /nologo configure.js "--enable-snapshot-build" "--with-gd=shared"
Server API	Apache 2.0 Handler
Virtual Directory Support	enabled
Configuration File (php.ini) Path	C:\Program Files (x86)\EasyPHP 2.0b1\apache\php.ini
PHP API	20041225
PHP Extension	20060613
Zend Extension	220060519
Debug Build	no
Thread Safety	enabled
Zend Memory Manager	enabled
IPv6 Support	enabled
Registered PHP Streams	php, file, data, http, ftp, compress.zlib
Registered Stream Socket Transports	tcp, udp
Registered Stream Filters	convert.iconv.*, string.rot13, string.toupper, string.tolower, string.strip_tags,

Done

Figure 5-1. The output of PHP's built-in phpinfo function

As you can see, the strrev function reversed the order of characters in the string,
str_repeat repeated the string "Hip " twice (as required by a second argument), and
strtoupper converted "hooray!" to uppercase.

Defining a Function

The general syntax for a function is:

```
function function_name([parameter [, ...]])
{
    // Statements
}
```

I'll explain all the square brackets, in case you find them confusing. The first line of the
syntax indicates that:

- A definition starts with the word function.
- A name follows, which must start with a letter or underscore, followed by any
  number of letters, numbers, or underscores.
- The parentheses are required.
- One or more parameters, separated by commas, are optional.

Function names are case-insensitive, so all of the following strings can refer to the print function: PRINT, Print, and PrInT.

The opening curly brace starts the statements that will execute when you call the function; a matching curly brace must close it. These statements may include one or more return statements, which force the function to cease execution and return to the calling code. If a value is attached to the return statement, the calling code can retrieve it, as we'll see next.

Returning a Value

Let's take a look at a simple function to convert a person's full name to lowercase and then capitalize the first letter of each name.

We've already seen an example of PHP's built-in strtoupper function in Example 5-1. For our current function, we'll use its counterpart: strtolower:

```
$lowered = strtolower("aNY # of Letters and Punctuation you WANT");

echo $lowered;
```

The output of this experiment is:

```
any # of letters and punctuation you want
```

We don't want names all lowercase, though; we want the first letter of each name capitalized. (We're not going to deal with subtle cases such as Mary-Ann or Jo-En-Lai, for this example.) Luckily, PHP also provides a ucfirst function that sets the first character of a string to uppercase:

```
$ucfixed = ucfirst("any # of letters and punctuation you want");

echo $ucfixed;
```

The output is:

```
Any # of letters and punctuation you want
```

Now we can do our first bit of program design: to get a word with its initial letter capitalized, we call strtolower on a string first, and then ucfirst. The way to do this is to nest a call to strtolower within ucfirst. Let's see why, because it's important to understand the order in which code is evaluated.

If you make a simple call to the print function:

```
print(5-8);
```

The expression 5-8 is evaluated first, and the output is –3. (As you saw in the previous chapter, PHP converts the result to a string in order to display it.) If the expression contains a function, that function is evaluated first as well:

```
print(abs(5-8));
```

PHP is doing several things in executing that short statement:

1. Evaluate **5-8** to produce –3.
2. Use the **abs** function to turn –3 into 3.
3. Convert the result to a string and output it using the **print** function.

It all works because PHP evaluates each element from the inside out. The same procedure is in operation when we call the following:

```
ucfirst(strtolower("aNY # of Letters and Punctuation you WANT"))
```

PHP passes our string to **strtolower** and then to **ucfirst**, producing (as we've already seen when we played with the functions separately):

```
Any # of letters and punctuation you want
```

Now let's define a function (shown in Example 5-2) that takes three names and makes each one lowercased with an initial capital letter.

Example 5-2. Cleaning up a full name

```php
<?php
echo fix_names("WILLIAM", "henry", "gatES");

function fix_names($n1, $n2, $n3)
{
    $n1 = ucfirst(strtolower($n1));
    $n2 = ucfirst(strtolower($n2));
    $n3 = ucfirst(strtolower($n3));
    return $n1 . " " . $n2 . " " . $n3;
}
?>
```

You may well find yourself writing this type of code, because users often leave their Caps Lock key on, accidentally insert capital letters in the wrong places, and even forget capitals altogether. The output from this example is:

```
William Henry Gates
```

Returning an Array

We just saw a function returning a single value. There are also ways of getting multiple values from a function.

The first method is to return them within an array. As you saw in Chapter 3, an array is like a bunch of variables stuck together in a row. Example 5-3 shows how you can use an array to return function values.

Example 5-3. Returning multiple values in an array

```php
<?php
$names = fix_names("WILLIAM", "henry", "gatES");
echo $names[0] . " " . $names[1] . " " . $names[2];
```

```
function fix_names($n1, $n2, $n3)
{
    $n1 = ucfirst(strtolower($n1));
    $n2 = ucfirst(strtolower($n2));
    $n3 = ucfirst(strtolower($n3));
    return array($n1, $n2, $n3);
}
?>
```

This method has the benefit of keeping all three names separate, rather than concatenating them into a single string, so you can refer to any user simply by their first or last
name, without having to extract either name from the returned string.

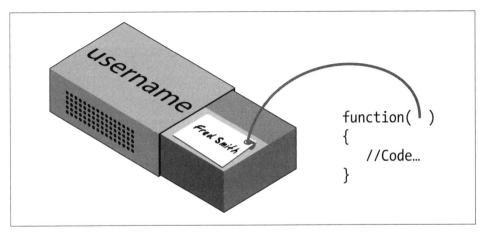

Figure 5-2. Imagining a reference as a thread attached to a variable

Passing by Reference

In PHP, the & symbol, when prefaced to a variable, tells the parser to pass a reference
to the variable's value, not the value itself. This concept can be hard to get your head
around, so let's go back to the matchbox metaphor from Chapter 3.

Imagine that, instead of taking a piece of paper out of a matchbox, reading it, copying
it to another piece of paper, putting the original back, and passing the copy to a function
(phew!), you simply attach a piece of thread to the original piece of paper and pass one
end of it to the function (see Figure 5-2).

Now the function can follow the thread to find the data to be accessed. This avoids all
the overhead of creating a copy of the variable just for the function's use. What's more,
the function can now modify the variable's value.

This means you can rewrite Example 5-3 to pass references to all the parameters, and
then the function can modify these directly (see Example 5-4).

Example 5-4. Returning values from a function by reference

```php
<?php
$a1 = "WILLIAM";
$a2 = "henry";
$a3 = "gatES";

echo $a1 . " " . $a2 . " " . $a3 . "<br />";
fix_names($a1, $a2, $a3);
echo $a1 . " " . $a2 . " " . $a3;

function fix_names(&$n1, &$n2, &$n3)
{
    $n1 = ucfirst(strtolower($n1));
    $n2 = ucfirst(strtolower($n2));
    $n3 = ucfirst(strtolower($n3));
}
?>
```

Rather than passing strings directly to the function, you first assign them to variables and print them out to see their "before" values. Then you call the function as before, but put a & symbol in front of each parameter, which tells PHP to pass the variables' references only.

Now the variables $n1, $n2, and $n3 are attached to "threads" that lead to the values of $a1, $a2, and $a3. In other words, there is one group of values, but two sets of variable names are allowed to access them.

Therefore, the function fix_names only has to assign new values to $n1, $n2, and $n3 to update the values of $a1, $a2, and $a3. The output from this code is:

```
WILLIAM henry gatES
William Henry Gates
```

As you see, both of the echo statements use only the values of $a1, $a2, and $a3.

> Be careful when passing values by reference. If you need to keep the original values, make copies of your variables and then pass the copies by reference.

Returning Global Variables

You can also give a function access to an externally created variable by declaring it a global variable from within the function. The **global** keyword followed by the variable name gives every part of your code full access to it (see Example 5-5).

Example 5-5. Returning values in global variables

```php
<?php
$a1 = "WILLIAM";
$a2 = "henry";
$a3 = "gatES";
```

```
echo $a1 . " " . $a2 . " " . $a3 . "<br />";
fix_names();
echo $a1 . " " . $a2 . " " . $a3;

function fix_names()
{
    global $a1; $a1 = ucfirst(strtolower($a1));
    global $a2; $a2 = ucfirst(strtolower($a2));
    global $a3; $a3 = ucfirst(strtolower($a3));
}
?>
```

Now you don't have to pass parameters to the function, and it doesn't have to accept them. Once declared, these variables remain global and available to the rest of your program, including its functions.

If at all possible, in order to retain as much local scope as possible, you should try returning arrays or using variables by association. Otherwise, you will begin to lose some of the benefits of functions.

Recap of Variable Scope

A quick reminder of what you know from Chapter 3:

- *Local variables* are accessible just from the part of code where you define them. If they're outside of a function, they can be accessed by all code outside of functions, classes, and so on. If a variable is inside a function, only that function can access the variable, and its value is lost when the function returns.
- *Global variables* are accessible from all parts of your code.
- *Static variables* are accessible only within the function that declared them but retain their value over multiple calls.

Including and Requiring Files

As you progress in your use of PHP programming, you are likely to start building a library of functions that you think you will need again. You'll also probably start using libraries created by other programmers.

There's no need to copy and paste these functions into your code. You can save them in separate files and use commands to pull them in. There are two types of commands to perform this action: `include` and `require`.

The include Statement

Using `include`, you can tell PHP to fetch a particular file and load all its contents. It's as if you pasted the included file into the current file at the insertion point. Example 5-6 shows how you would include a file called *library.php*.

Example 5-6. Including a PHP file

```php
<?php
include "library.php";

// Your code goes here
?>
```

Using include_once

Each time you issue the `include` directive, it includes the requested file again, even if you've already inserted it. For instance, suppose that *library.php* contains a lot of useful functions, so you include it in your file, but also include another library that includes *library.php*. Through nesting, you've inadvertently included *library.php* twice. This will produce error messages, because you're trying to define the same constant or function multiple times. So you should use `include_once` instead (see Example 5-7).

Example 5-7. Including a PHP file only once

```php
<?php
include_once "library.php";

// Your code goes here
?>
```

Then, whenever another `include` or `include_once` is encountered, if it has already been executed, it will be completely ignored. To determine whether the file has already been executed, the absolute file path is matched after all relative paths are resolved and the file is found in your *include* path.

> In general, it's probably best to stick with `include_once` and ignore the basic `include` statement. That way you will never have the problem of files being included multiple times.

Using require and require_once

A potential problem with `include` and `include_once` is that PHP will only *attempt* to include the requested file. Program execution continues even if the file is not found.

When it is absolutely essential to include a file, `require` it. For the same reasons I gave for using `include_once`, I recommend that you generally stick with `require_once` whenever you need to `require` a file (see Example 5-8).

Example 5-8. Requiring a PHP file only once

```php
<?php
require_once "library.php";
```

```
// Your code goes here
?>
```

PHP Version Compatibility

PHP is in an ongoing process of development, and there are multiple versions. If you need to check whether a particular function is available to your code, you can use the `function_exists` function, which checks all predefined and user-created functions.

Example 5-9 checks for the function `array_combine`, which is specific to PHP version 5.

Example 5-9. Checking for a function's existence

```
<?php
if (function_exists("array_combine"))
{
    echo "Function exists";
}
else
{
    echo "Function does not exist - better write our own";
}
?>
```

Using code such as this, you can take advantage of features in newer versions of PHP and yet still have your code run on earlier versions, as long as you replicate any features that are missing. Your functions may be slower than the built-in ones, but at least your code will be much more portable.

You can also use the `phpversion` function to determine which version of PHP your code is running on. The returned result will be similar to the following, depending on version:

```
5.2.8
```

PHP Objects

In much the same way that functions represent a huge increase in programming power over early days of computing, where sometimes the best program navigation available was a very basic `GOTO` or `GOSUB` statement, object-oriented programming (OOP) takes the use of functions to a whole new level.

Once you get the hang of condensing reusable bits of code into functions, it's not that great a leap to consider bundling the functions and their data into objects.

Let's take a social networking site that has many parts. One handles all user functions: code to enable new users to sign up and to enable existing users to modify their details. In standard PHP, you might create a few functions to handle this and embed some calls to the MySQL database to keep track of all the users.

Imagine how much easier it would be to create an object to represent the current user. To do this you could create a class, perhaps called User, which would contain all the code required for handling users and all the variables needed for manipulating the data within the class. Then, whenever you need to manipulate a user's data, you could simply create a new object with the User class.

You could treat this new object as if it were the actual user. For example, you could pass the object a name, password, and email address, ask it whether such a user already exists and, if not, have it create a new user with those attributes. You could even have an instant messaging object, or one for managing whether two users are friends.

Terminology

When creating a program to use objects, you need to design a composite of data and code called a *class*. Each new object based on this class is called an *instance* (or *occurrence*) of that class.

The data associated with an object are called its *properties*; the functions it uses are called *methods*. In defining a class, you supply the names of its properties and the code for its methods. See Figure 5-3 for a jukebox metaphor for an object. Think of the CDs that it holds in the carousel as its *properties*; the *method* of playing them is to press buttons on the front panel. There is also the slot for inserting coins (the method used to activate the object), and the laser disc reader (the method used to retrieve the music, or properties, from the CDs).

Figure 5-3. A jukebox: a great example of a self-contained object

When creating objects, it is best to use *encapsulation*, or writing a class in such a way that only its methods can be used to manipulate its properties. In other words, you deny outside code direct access to its data. The methods you supply are known as the object's *interface*.

This approach makes debugging easy: you have to fix faulty code only within a class. Additionally, when you want to upgrade a program, if you have used proper encapsulation and maintained the same interface, you can simply develop new replacement classes, debug them fully, and then swap them in for the old ones. If they don't work, you can swap the old ones back in to immediately fix the problem before further debugging the new classes.

Once you have created a class, you may find that you need another class that is similar to it but not quite the same. The quick and easy thing to do is to define a new class using *inheritance*. When you do this, your new class has all the properties of the one it has inherited from. The original class is now called the *superclass*, and the new one is the *subclass* (or *derived* class).

In our jukebox example, if you invent a new jukebox that can play a video along with the music, you can inherit all the properties and methods from the original jukebox superclass and add some new properties (videos) and new methods (a movie player).

An excellent benefit of this system is that if you improve the speed or any other aspect of the superclass, its subclasses will receive the same benefit.

Declaring a Class

Before you can use an object, you must define a class with the `class` keyword. Class definitions contain the class name (which is case-sensitive), its properties, and its methods. Example 5-10 defines the class `User` with two properties: `$name` and `$password` (indicated by the `public` keyword—see "Property and Method Scope in PHP 5" on page 107. It also creates a new instance (called `$object`) of this class.

Example 5-10. Declaring a class and examining an object

```
<?php
$object = new User;
print_r($object);

class User
{
    public $name, $password;

    function save_user()
    {
        echo "Save User code goes here";
    }
}
?>
```

Here I have also used an invaluable function called `print_r`. It asks PHP to display information about a variable in human readable form. The `_r` stands for "in human readable format." In the case of the new object `$object`, it prints the following:

```
User Object
(
    [name] =>
    [password] =>
)
```

However, a browser compresses all the whitespace, so the output in a browser is slightly harder to read:

```
User Object ( [name] => [password] => )
```

In any case, the output says that `$object` is a user-defined object that has the properties `name` and `password`.

Creating an Object

To create an object with a specified class, use the `new` keyword, like this: `object = new Class`. Here are a couple of ways in which we could do this:

```
$object = new User;
$temp = new User('name', 'password');
```

On the first line, we simply assign an object to the `User` class. In the second, we pass parameters to the call.

A class may require or prohibit arguments; it may also allow arguments, but not require them.

Accessing Objects

Let's add a few lines more to Example 5-10 and check the results. Example 5-11 extends the previous code by setting object properties and calling a method.

Example 5-11. Creating and interacting with an object

```php
<?php
$object = new User;
print_r($object); echo "<br />";

$object->name = "Joe";
$object->password = "mypass";
print_r($object); echo "<br />";

$object->save_user();

class User
{
    public $name, $password;
```

```
    function save_user()
    {
        echo "Save User code goes here";
    }
}
?>
```

As you can see, the syntax for accessing an object's property is `$object->property`. Likewise, you call a method like this: `$object->method()`.

You should note that the example `property` and `method` do not have $ signs in front of them. If you were to preface them with $ signs, the code would not work, as it would try to reference the value inside a variable. For example, the expression `$object->$property` would attempt to look up the value assigned to a variable named `$property` (let's say that value is the string "brown") and then attempt to reference the property `$object->brown`. If `$property` is undefined, an attempt to reference `$object->NULL` would occur and cause an error.

When looked at using a browser's View Source facility, the output from Example 5-11 is:

```
User Object
(
    [name] =>
    [password] =>
)
User Object
(
    [name] => Joe
    [password] => mypass
)
Save User code goes here
```

Again, `print_r` shows its utility by providing the contents of `$object` before and after property assignment. From now on I'll omit `print_r` statements, but if you are working along with this book on your development server, you can put some in to see exactly what is happening.

You can also see that the code in the method **save_user** was executed via the call to that method. It printed the string reminding us to create some code.

 You can place functions and class definitions anywhere in your code, before or after statements that use them. Generally, though, it is considered good practice to place them toward the end of a file.

Cloning objects

Once you have created an object, it is passed by reference when you pass it as a parameter. In the matchbox metaphor, this is like keeping several threads attached to an object stored in a matchbox, so that you can follow any attached thread to access it.

In other words, making object assignments does not copy objects in their entirety. You'll see how this works in Example 5-12, where we define a very simple User class with no methods and only the property name.

Example 5-12. Copying an object

```php
<?php
$object1 = new User();
$object1->name = "Alice";
$object2 = $object1;
$object2->name = "Amy";
echo "object1 name = " . $object1->name . "<br />";
echo "object2 name = " . $object2->name;

class User
{
    public $name;
}
?>
```

We've created the object $object1 and assigned the value "Alice" to the name property. Then we create $object2, assigning it the value of $object1, and assign the value "Amy" just to the name property of $object2—or so we might think. But this code outputs the following:

```
object1 name = Amy
object2 name = Amy
```

What has happened? Both $object1 and $object2 refer to the *same* object, so changing the name property of $object2 to "Amy" also sets that property for $object1.

To avoid this confusion, you can use the clone operator, which creates a new instance of the class and copies the property values from the original class to the new instance. Example 5-13 illustrates this usage.

Example 5-13. Cloning an object

```php
<?php
$object1 = new User();
$object1->name = "Alice";
$object2 = clone $object1;
$object2->name = "Amy";
echo "object1 name = " . $object1->name . "<br>";
echo "object2 name = " . $object2->name;

class User
{
    public $name;
}
?>
```

Voilà! The output from this code is what we initially wanted:

```
    object1 name = Alice
    object2 name = Amy
```

Constructors

When creating a new object, you can pass a list of arguments to the class being called. These are passed to a special method within the class, called the *constructor*, which initializes various properties.

In the past, you would normally give this method the same name as the class, as in Example 5-14.

Example 5-14. Creating a constructor method

```php
<?php
class User
{
    function User($param1, $param2)
    {
        // Constructor statements go here
    }
}
?>
```

However, PHP 5 provides a more logical approach to naming the constructor, which is to use the function name __construct (that is, construct preceded by two underscore characters), as in Example 5-15.

Example 5-15. Creating a constructor method in PHP 5

```php
<?php
class User
{
    function __construct($param1, $param2)
    {
        // Constructor statements go here
    }
}
?>
```

PHP 5 destructors

Also new in PHP 5 is the ability to create *destructor* methods. This ability is useful when code has made the last reference to an object or when a script reaches the end. Example 5-16 shows how to create a destructor method.

Example 5-16. Creating a destructor method in PHP 5

```php
<?php
class User
{
    function __destruct()
    {
```

```
            // Destructor code goes here
        }
}
?>
```

Writing Methods

As you have seen, declaring a method is similar to declaring a function, but there are a few differences. For example, method names beginning with a double underscore (__) are reserved and you should not create any of this form.

You also have access to a special variable called $this, which can be used to access the current object's properties. To see how this works, take a look at Example 5-17, which contains a different method from the User class definition called get_password.

Example 5-17. Using the variable $this in a method

```php
<?php
class User
{
    public $name, $password;

    function get_password()
    {
        return $this->password;
    }
}
?>
```

What get_password does is use the $this variable to access the current object and then return the value of that object's password property. Note how the preceding $ of the property $password is omitted when using the -> operator. Leaving the $ in place is a typical error you may run into, particularly when you first use this feature.

Here's how you would use the class defined in Example 5-17:

```php
$object = new User;
$object->password = "secret";
echo $object->get_password();
```

This code prints the password "secret".

Static methods in PHP 5

If you are using PHP 5, you can also define a method as *static*, which means that it is called on a class and not on an object. A static method has no access to any object properties and is created and accessed as in Example 5-18.

Example 5-18. Creating and accessing a static method

```php
<?php
User::pwd_string();
```

```
class User
{
    static function pwd_string()
    {
        echo "Please enter your password";
    }
}
?>
```

Note how the class itself is called, along with the static method, using a double colon (also known as the *scope resolution* operator) and not ->. Static functions are useful for performing actions relating to the class itself, but not to specific instances of the class. You can see another example of a static method in Example 5-21.

 If you try to access $this->property, or other object properties from within a static class, you will receive an error message.

Declaring Properties

It is not necessary to explicitly declare properties within classes, as they can be implicitly defined when first used. To illustrate this, in Example 5-19 the class User has no properties and no methods but is legal code.

Example 5-19. Defining a property implicitly

```
<?php
$object1 = new User();
$object1->name = "Alice";
echo $object1->name;

class User {}
?>
```

This code correctly outputs the string "Alice" without a problem, because PHP implicitly declares the variable $object1->name for you. But this kind of programming can lead to bugs that are infuriatingly difficult to discover, because name was declared from outside the class.

To help yourself and anyone else who will maintain your code, I advise that you get into the habit of always declaring your properties explicitly within classes. You'll be glad you did.

Also, when you declare a property within a class, you may assign a default value to it. The value you use must be a constant and not the result of a function or expression. Example 5-20 shows a few valid and invalid assignments.

Example 5-20. Valid and invalid property declarations

```php
<?php
class Test
{
    public $name    = "Paul Smith"; // Valid
    public $age     = 42;           // Valid
    public $time    = time();       // Invalid - calls a function
    public $score   = $level * 2;   // Invalid - uses an expression
}
?>
```

Declaring Constants

In the same way that you can create a global constant with the `define` function, you can define constants inside classes. The generally accepted practice is to use uppercase letters to make them stand out, as in Example 5-21.

Example 5-21. Defining constants within a class

```php
<?php
Translate::lookup();

class Translate
{
    const ENGLISH = 0;
    const SPANISH = 1;
    const FRENCH  = 2;
    const GERMAN  = 3;
    // ...

    function lookup()
    {
        echo self::SPANISH;
    }
}
?>
```

Constants can be referenced directly, using the `self` keyword and double colon operator. Note that this code calls the class directly, using the double colon operator at line one, without creating an instance of it first. As you would expect, the value printed when you run this code is `1`.

Remember that once you define a constant, you can't change it.

Property and Method Scope in PHP 5

PHP 5 provides three keywords for controlling the scope of properties and methods:

`public`

> These properties are the default when declaring a variable using the `var` or `public` keywords, or when a variable is implicitly declared the first time it is used.

The keywords var and public are interchangeable, because, although deprecated, var is retained for compatibility with previous versions of PHP. Methods are assumed to be public by default.

protected

These properties and methods (*members*) can be referenced only by the object's class methods and those of any subclasses.

private

These members can be referenced only by methods within the same class—not by subclasses.

Here's how to decide which you need to use:

- Use public when outside code *should* access this member and extending classes *should* also inherit it.

- Use protected when outside code *should not* access this member but extending classes *should* inherit it.

- Use private when outside code *should not* access this member and extending classes also *should not* inherit it.

Example 5-22 illustrates the use of these keywords.

Example 5-22. Changing property and method scope

```php
<?php
class Example
{
    var $name = "Michael";   // Same as public but deprecated
    public $age = 23;        // Public property
    protected $usercount;    // Protected property

    private function admin() // Private method
    {
        // Admin code goes here
    }
}
?>
```

Static properties and methods

Most data and methods apply to instances of a class. For example, in a User class, you want to do such things as set a particular user's password or check when the user has been registered. These facts and operations apply separately to each user and therefore use instance-specific properties and methods.

But occasionally you'll want to maintain data about a whole class. For instance, to report how many users are registered, you will store a variable that applies to the whole User class. PHP provides static properties and methods for such data.

As shown briefly in Example 5-18, declaring members of a class **static** makes them accessible without an instantiation of the class. A property declared **static** cannot be directly accessed within an instance of a class, but a static method can.

Example 5-23 defines a class called **Test** with a static property and a public method.

Example 5-23. Defining a class with a static property

```php
<?php
$temp = new Test();
echo "Test A: " . Test::$static_property . "<br />";
echo "Test B: " . $temp->get_sp()          . "<br />";
echo "Test C: " . $temp->static_property . "<br />";

class Test
{
    static $static_property = "I'm static";

    function get_sp()
    {
        return self::$static_property;
    }
}
?>
```

When you run this code, it returns the following output:

```
Test A: I'm static
Test B: I'm static

Notice: Undefined property: Test::$static_property
Test C:
```

This example shows that the property **$static_property** could be directly referenced from the class itself using the double colon operator in *Test A*. Also, *Test B* could obtain its value by calling the **get_sp** method of the object **$temp**, created from class **Test**. But *Test C* failed, because the static property **$static_property** was not accessible to the object **$temp**.

Note how the method **get_sp** accesses **$static_property** using the keyword **self**. This is the way in which a static property or constant can be directly accessed within a class.

Inheritance

Once you have written a class, you can derive subclasses from it. This can save lots of painstaking code rewriting: you can take a class similar to the one you need to write, extend it to a subclass, and just modify the parts that are different. This is achieved using the **extends** operator.

In Example 5-24, the class **Subscriber** is declared a subclass of **User** by means of the **extends** operator.

Example 5-24. Inheriting and extending a class

```php
<?php
$object            = new Subscriber;
$object->name      = "Fred";
$object->password  = "pword";
$object->phone     = "012 345 6789";
$object->email     = "fred@bloggs.com";
$object->display();

class User
{
    public $name, $password;

    function save_user()
    {
        echo "Save User code goes here";
    }
}

class Subscriber extends User
{
    public $phone, $email;

    function display()
    {
        echo "Name:  " . $this->name     . "<br />";
        echo "Pass:  " . $this->password . "<br />";
        echo "Phone: " . $this->phone    . "<br />";
        echo "Email: " . $this->email;
    }
}
?>
```

The original `User` class has two properties, `$name` and `$password`, and a method to save the current user to the database. `Subscriber` extends this class by adding an additional two properties, `$phone` and `$email`, and includes a method of displaying the properties of the current object using the variable `$this`, which refers to the current values of the object being accessed. The output from this code is:

```
Name:  Fred
Pass:  pword
Phone: 012 345 6789
Email: fred@bloggs.com
```

The parent operator

If you write a method in a subclass with the same name of one in its parent class, its statements will override those of the parent class. Sometimes this is not the behavior you want and you need to access the parent's method. To do this, you can use the **parent** operator, as in Example 5-25.

Example 5-25. Overriding a method and using the parent operator

```php
<?php
$object = new Son;
$object->test();
$object->test2();

class Dad
{
    function test()
    {
        echo "[Class Dad] I am your Father<br />";
    }
}

class Son extends Dad
{
    function test()
    {
        echo "[Class Son] I am Luke<br />";
    }

    function test2()
    {
        parent::test();
    }
}
?>
```

This code creates a class called Dad and then a subclass called Son that inherits its properties and methods, then overrides the method test. Therefore, when line 2 calls the method test, the new method is executed. The only way to execute the overridden test method in the Dad class is to use the parent operator, as shown in function test2 of class Son. The code outputs the following:

```
[Class Son] I am Luke
[Class Dad] I am your Father
```

If you wish to ensure that your code calls a method from the current class, you can use the self keyword, like this:

```
self::method();
```

Subclass constructors

When you extend a class and declare your own constructor, you should be aware that PHP will not automatically call the constructor method of the parent class. To be certain that all initialization code is executed, subclasses should always call the parent constructors, as in Example 5-26.

Example 5-26. Calling the parent class constructor

```php
<?php
$object = new Tiger();
echo "Tigers have...<br>";
echo "Fur: " . $object->fur . "<br />";
echo "Stripes: " . $object->stripes;

class Wildcat
{
    public $fur; // Wildcats have fur

    function __construct()
    {
        $this->fur = "TRUE";
    }
}

class Tiger extends Wildcat
{
    public $stripes; // Tigers have stripes

    function __construct()
    {
        parent::__construct(); // Call parent constructor first
        $this->stripes = "TRUE";
    }
}
?>
```

This example takes advantage of inheritance in the typical manner. The `Wildcat` class has created the property `$fur`, which we'd like to reuse, so we create the `Tiger` class to inherit `$fur` and additionally create another property, `$stripes`. To verify that both constructors have been called, the program outputs the following:

```
Tigers have...
Fur: TRUE
Stripes: TRUE
```

Final methods

In cases in which you wish to prevent a subclass from overriding a superclass method, you can use the `final` keyword. Example 5-27 shows how.

Example 5-27. Creating a final method

```php
<?php
class User
{
    final function copyright()
    {
        echo "This class was written by Joe Smith";
    }
}
?>
```

Once you have digested the contents of this chapter, you should have a strong feel for what PHP can do for you. You should be able to use functions with ease and, if you wish, write object-oriented code. In Chapter 6, we'll finish off our initial exploration of PHP by looking at the workings of PHP arrays.

Test Your Knowledge: Questions

Question 5-1
   What is the main benefit of using a function?

Question 5-2
   How many values can a function return?

Question 5-3
   What is the difference between accessing a variable by name and by reference?

Question 5-4
   What is the meaning of "scope" in PHP?

Question 5-5
   How can you incorporate one PHP file within another?

Question 5-6
   How is an object different from a function?

Question 5-7
   How do you create a new object in PHP?

Question 5-8
   What syntax would you use to create a subclass from an existing one?

Question 5-9
   How can you call an initializing piece of code when an object is created?

Question 5-10
   Why is it a good idea to explicitly declare properties within a class?

See the section "Chapter 5 Answers" on page 439 in Appendix A for the answers to these questions.

CHAPTER 6

PHP Arrays

In Chapter 3, I gave a very brief introduction to PHP's arrays—just enough for a little taste of their power. In this chapter, I'll show you many more things that you can do with arrays, some of which—if you are have ever used a strongly typed language such as C—may surprise you with their elegance and simplicity.

Arrays are an example of what has made PHP so popular. Not only do they remove the tedium of writing code to deal with complicated data structures, but they also provide numerous ways to access data while remaining amazingly fast.

Basic Access

We've already looked at arrays as if they were clusters of matchboxes glued together. Another way to think of an array is like a string of beads, with the beads representing variables that can be numeric, string, or even other arrays. They are like bead strings, because each element has its own location and (with the exception of the first and last ones) each has other elements on either side.

Some arrays are referenced by numeric indexes; others allow alphanumeric identifiers. Built-in functions let you sort them, add or remove sections, and walk through them to handle each item through a special kind of loop. And by placing one or more arrays inside another, you can create arrays of two, three, or any number of dimensions.

Numerically Indexed Arrays

Let's assume that you've been tasked with creating a simple website for a local office supplies company and you're currently working on the section devoted to paper. One way to manage the various items of stock in this category would be to place them in a numeric array. You can see the simplest way of doing so in Example 6-1.

Example 6-1. Adding items to an array

```php
<?php
$paper[] = "Copier";
$paper[] = "Inkjet";
$paper[] = "Laser";
$paper[] = "Photo";

print_r($paper);
?>
```

In this example, each time you assign a value to the array $paper, the first empty location within that array is used to store the value and a pointer internal to PHP is incremented to point to the next free location, ready for future insertions. The familiar print_r function (which prints out the contents of a variable, array, or object) is used to verify that the array has been correctly populated. It prints out the following:

```
Array
(
        [0] => Copier
        [1] => Inkjet
        [2] => Laser
        [3] => Photo
)
```

The previous code could equally have been written as in Example 6-2, where the exact location of each item within the array is specified. But, as you can see, that approach requires extra typing and makes your code harder to maintain if you want to insert or remove supplies from the array. So unless you wish to specify a different order, it's usually better to simply let PHP handle the actual location numbers.

Example 6-2. Adding items to an array using explicit locations

```php
<?php
$paper[0] = "Copier";
$paper[1] = "Inkjet";
$paper[2] = "Laser";
$paper[3] = "Photo";

print_r($paper);
?>
```

The output from these examples is identical, but you are not likely to use print_r in a developed website, so Example 6-3 shows how you might print out the various types of paper the website offers using a for loop.

Example 6-3. Adding items to an array and retrieving them

```php
<?php
$paper[] = "Copier";
$paper[] = "Inkjet";
$paper[] = "Laser";
$paper[] = "Photo";
```

```
for ($j = 0 ; $j < 4 ; ++$j)
    echo "$j: $paper[$j]<br>";
?>
```

This example prints out the following:

```
0: Copier
1: Inkjet
2: Laser
3: Photo
```

So far, you've seen a couple of ways in which you can add items to an array and one way of referencing them, but PHP offers many more—which I'll get to shortly. But first, we'll look at another type of array.

Associative Arrays

Keeping track of array elements by index works just fine, but can require extra work in terms of remembering which number refers to which product. It can also make code hard for other programmers to follow.

This is where associative arrays come into their own. Using them, you can reference the items in an array by name rather than by number. Example 6-4 expands on the previous code by giving each element in the array an identifying name and a longer, more explanatory string value.

Example 6-4. Adding items to an associative array and retrieving them

```
<?php
$paper['copier'] = "Copier & Multipurpose";
$paper['inkjet'] = "Inkjet Printer";
$paper['laser']  = "Laser Printer";
$paper['photo']  = "Photographic Paper";

echo $paper['laser'];
?>
```

In place of a number (which doesn't convey any useful information, aside from the position of the item in the array), each item now has a unique name that you can use to reference it elsewhere, as with the echo statement—which simply prints out Laser Printer. The names (copier, inkjet, and so on) are called *indexes* or *keys* and the items assigned to them (such as "Laser Printer") are called *values*.

This very powerful feature of PHP is often used when extracting information from XML and HTML. For example, an HTML parser such as those used by a search engine could place all the elements of a web page into an associative array whose names reflect the page's structure:

```
$html['title'] = "My web page";
$html['body']  = "... body of web page ...";
```

The program would also probably break down all the links found within a page into another array, and all the headings and subheadings into another. When you use associative rather than numeric arrays, the code to refer to all of these items is easy to write and debug.

Assignment Using the array Keyword

So far, you've seen how to assign values to arrays by just adding new items one at a time. Whether you specify keys, specify numeric identifiers, or let PHP assign numeric identifiers implicitly, this is a long-winded approach. A more compact and faster assignment method uses the **array** keyword. Example 6-5 shows both a numeric and an associative array assigned using this method.

Example 6-5. Adding items to an array using the array keyword

```php
<?php
$p1 = array("Copier", "Inkjet", "Laser", "Photo");

echo "p1 element: " . $p1[2] . "<br>";

$p2 = array('copier' => "Copier & Multipurpose",
            'inkjet' => "Inkjet Printer",
            'laser'  => "Laser Printer",
            'photo'  => "Photographic Paper");

echo "p2 element: " . $p2['inkjet'] . "<br>";
?>
```

The first half of this snippet assigns the old, shortened product descriptions to the array **$p1**. There are four items, so they will occupy slots 0 through 3. Therefore the **echo** statement prints out the following:

```
p1 element: Laser
```

The second half assigns associative identifiers and accompanying longer product descriptions to the array **$p2** using the format **index => value**. The use of **=>** is similar to the regular = assignment operator, except that you are assigning a value to an *index* and not to a *variable*. The index is then inextricably linked with that value, unless it is reassigned a new value. The **echo** command therefore prints out:

```
p2 element: Inkjet Printer
```

You can verify that **$p1** and **$p2** are different types of array, because both of the following commands, when appended to the code, will cause an "undefined index" or "undefined offset" error, as the array identifier for each is incorrect:

```
echo $p1['inkjet']; // Undefined index
echo $p2['3'];      // Undefined offset
```

The foreach...as Loop

The creators of PHP have gone to great lengths to make the language easy to use. So, not content with the loop structures already provided, they added another one especially for arrays: the `foreach...as` loop. Using it, you can step through all the items in an array, one at a time, and do something with them.

The process starts with the first item and ends with the last one, so you don't even have to know how many items there are in an array. Example 6-6 shows how `foreach` can be used to rewrite Example 6-3.

Example 6-6. Walking through a numeric array using foreach...as

```php
<?php
$paper = array("Copier", "Inkjet", "Laser", "Photo");
$j = 0;

foreach ($paper as $item)
{
    echo "$j: $item<br>";
    ++$j;
}
?>
```

When PHP encounters a `foreach` statement, it takes the first item of the array and places it in the variable following the `as` keyword, and each time control flow returns to the `foreach`, the next array element is placed in the `as` keyword. In this case, the variable `$item` is set to each of the four values in turn in the array `$paper`. Once all values have been used, execution of the loop ends. The output from this code is exactly the same as Example 6-3.

Now let's see how `foreach` works with an associative array by taking a look at Example 6-7, which is a rewrite of the second half of Example 6-5.

Example 6-7. Walking through an associative array using foreach...as

```php
<?php
$paper = array('copier' => "Copier & Multipurpose",
               'inkjet' => "Inkjet Printer",
               'laser'  => "Laser Printer",
               'photo'  => "Photographic Paper");

foreach ($paper as $item => $description)
    echo "$item: $description<br>";
?>
```

Remember that associative arrays do not require numeric indexes, so the variable `$j` is not used in this example. Instead, each item of the array `$paper` is fed into the key and value pair of variables `$item` and `$description`, from where they are printed out. The result of this code is as follows:

```
copier: Copier & Multipurpose
inkjet: Inkjet Printer
laser: Laser Printer
photo: Photographic Paper
```

As an alternative syntax to `foreach...as`, you can use the `list` function in conjunction with the `each` function, as in Example 6-8.

Example 6-8. Walking through an associative array using each and list

```php
<?php
$paper = array('copier' => "Copier & Multipurpose",
               'inkjet' => "Inkjet Printer",
               'laser'  => "Laser Printer",
               'photo'  => "Photographic Paper");

while (list($item, $description) = each($paper))
    echo "$item: $description<br>";
?>
```

In this example, a `while` loop is set up and will continue looping until the `each` function returns a value of `FALSE`. The `each` function acts like `foreach`: it returns an array containing a key and value pair from the array `$paper` and then moves its built-in pointer to the next pair in that array. When there are no more pairs to return, `each` returns `FALSE`.

The `list` function takes an array as its argument (in this case the key and value pair returned by function `each`) and then assigns the values of the array to the variables listed within parentheses.

You can see how `list` works a little more clearly in Example 6-9, where an array is created out of the two strings "Alice" and "Bob" and then passed to the `list` function, which assigns those strings as values to the variables `$a` and `$b`.

Example 6-9. Using the list function

```php
<?php
list($a, $b) = array('Alice', 'Bob');
echo "a=$a b=$b";
?>
```

The output from this code is:

```
a=Alice b=Bob
```

So you can take your pick when walking through arrays. Use `foreach...as` to create a loop that extracts values to the variable following the `as`, or use the `each` function and create your own looping system.

Multidimensional Arrays

A simple design feature in PHP's array syntax makes it possible to create arrays of more than one dimension. In fact, they can be as many dimensions as you like (although it's a rare application that goes further than three).

And that feature is the ability to include an entire array as a part of another one, and to be able to keep on doing so, just like the old rhyme: "Big fleas have little fleas upon their backs to bite 'em. Little fleas have lesser fleas, add flea, ad infinitum."

Let's look at how this works by taking the associative array in the previous example and extending it—see Example 6-10.

Example 6-10. Creating a multidimensional associative array

```php
<?php
$products = array(
    'paper' =>      array(
        'copier' => "Copier & Multipurpose",
        'inkjet' => "Inkjet Printer",
        'laser'  => "Laser Printer",
        'photo'  => "Photographic Paper"),

    'pens' => array(
        'ball'   => "Ball Point",
        'hilite' => "Highlighters",
        'marker' => "Markers"),

    'misc' => array(
        'tape'  => "Sticky Tape",
        'glue'  => "Adhesives",
        'clips' => "Paperclips") );

echo "<pre>";
foreach ($products as $section => $items)
    foreach ($items as $key => $value)
        echo "$section:\t$key\t($value)<br>";
echo "</pre>";
?>
```

To make things clearer now that the code is starting to grow, I've renamed some of the elements. For example, seeing as the previous array $paper is now just a subsection of a larger array, the main array is now called $products. Within this array there are three items: paper, pens, and misc, and each of these contains another array with key/value pairs.

If necessary, these subarrays could have contained even further arrays. For example, under ball there might be many different types and colors of ballpoint pens available in the online store. But for now I've restricted the code to just a depth of two.

Once the array data has been assigned, I use a pair of nested `foreach...as` loops to print out the various values. The outer loop extracts the main sections from the top level of the array, and the inner loop extracts the key/value pairs for the categories within each section.

As long as you remember that each level of the array works the same way (it's a key/value pair), you can easily write code to access any element at any level.

The `echo` statement makes use of the PHP escape character `\t`, which outputs a tab. Although tabs are not normally significant to the web browser, I let them be used for layout by using the `<pre>...</pre>` tags, which tell the web browser to format the text as preformatted and monospaced, and *not* to ignore whitespace characters such as tabs and line feeds. The output from this code looks like the following:

```
paper:    copier    (Copier & Multipurpose)
paper:    inkjet    (Inkjet Printer)
paper:    laser     (Laser Printer)
paper:    photo     (Photographic Paper)
pens:     ball      (Ball Point)
pens:     hilite    (Highlighters)
pens:     marker    (Markers)
misc:     tape      (Sticky Tape)
misc:     glue      (Adhesives)
misc:     clips     (Paperclips)
```

You can directly access a particular element of the array using square brackets, like this:

```
echo $products['misc']['glue'];
```

which outputs the value "Adhesives".

You can also create numeric multidimensional arrays that are accessed directly by indexes rather than by alphanumeric identifiers. Example 6-11 creates the board for a chess game with the pieces in their starting positions.

Example 6-11. Creating a multidimensional numeric array

```php
<?php
$chessboard = array(
    array('r', 'n', 'b', 'k', 'q', 'b', 'n', 'r'),
    array('p', 'p', 'p', 'p', 'p', 'p', 'p', 'p'),
    array(' ', ' ', ' ', ' ', ' ', ' ', ' ', ' '),
    array(' ', ' ', ' ', ' ', ' ', ' ', ' ', ' '),
    array(' ', ' ', ' ', ' ', ' ', ' ', ' ', ' '),
    array(' ', ' ', ' ', ' ', ' ', ' ', ' ', ' '),
    array(' ', ' ', ' ', ' ', ' ', ' ', ' ', ' '),
    array(' ', ' ', ' ', ' ', ' ', ' ', ' ', ' '),
    array('P', 'P', 'P', 'P', 'P', 'P', 'P', 'P'),
    array('R', 'N', 'B', 'K', 'Q', 'B', 'N', 'R'));

echo "<pre>";
foreach ($chessboard as $row)
{
    foreach ($row as $piece)
```

```
        echo "$piece ";
    echo "<br />";
}
echo "</pre>";
?>
```

In this example, the lowercase letters represent black pieces and the uppercase white. The key is *r=rook*, *n=knight*, *b=bishop*, *k=king*, *q=queen*, and *p=pawn*. Again, a pair of nested `foreach...as` loops walk through the array and display its contents. The outer loop processes each row into the variable `$row`, which itself is an array, because the `$chessboard` array uses a subarray for each row. This loop has two statements within it, so curly braces enclose them.

The inner loop then processes each square in a row, outputting the character (`$piece`) stored in it, followed by a space (to square up the printout). This loop has a single statement, so curly braces are not required to enclose it. The `<pre>` and `</pre>` tags ensure that the output displays correctly, like this:

```
r n b k q b n r
p p p p p p p p



p p p p p p p p
R N B K Q B N R
```

You can also directly access any element within this array using square brackets, like this:

```
echo $chessboard[7][4];
```

This statement outputs the uppercase letter Q, the eighth element down and the fifth along (remembering that array indexes start at 0, not 1).

Using Array Functions

You've already seen the `list` and `each` functions, but PHP comes with numerous other functions for handling arrays. The full list is at *http://php.net/manual/en/ref.array.php*. However, some of these functions are so fundamental that it's worth taking the time to look at them here.

is_array()

Arrays and variables share the same namespace. This means that you cannot have a string variable called `$fred` and an array also called `$fred`. If you're in doubt and your code needs to check whether a variable is an array, you can use the `is_array` function like this:

```
echo (is_array($fred)) ? "Is an array" : "Is not an array";
```

Note that if $fred has not yet been assigned a value, an "Undefined variable" message will be generated.

count()

Although the each function and foreach...as loop structure are excellent ways to walk through an array's contents, sometimes you need to know exactly how many elements there are in your array, particularly if you will be referencing them directly. To count all the elements in the top level of an array, use a command such as the following:

```
echo count($fred);
```

Should you wish to know how many elements there are altogether in a multidimensional array, you can use a statement such as:

```
echo count($fred, 1);
```

The second parameter is optional and sets the mode to use. It should be either a 0 to limit counting to only the top level, or 1 to force recursive counting of all subarray elements, too.

sort()

Sorting is so common that PHP provides a built-in function. In its simplest form, you would use it like this:

```
sort($fred);
```

Unlike some other functions, sort will act directly on the supplied array rather than returning a new array of sorted elements. Instead it returns TRUE on success and FALSE on error and also supports a few flags, but the main two that you might wish to use force sorting to be made either numerically or as strings, like this:

```
sort($fred, SORT_NUMERIC);
sort($fred, SORT_STRING);
```

You can also sort an array in reverse order using the rsort function, like this:

```
rsort($fred, SORT_NUMERIC);
rsort($fred, SORT_STRING);
```

shuffle()

There may be times when you need the elements of an array to be put in random order, such as when creating a game of playing cards:

```
shuffle($cards);
```

Like sort, shuffle acts directly on the supplied array and returns TRUE on success or FALSE on error.

---

explode()

This is a very useful function with which you can take a string containing several items separated by a single character (or string of characters) and then place each of these items into an array. One handy example is to split a sentence up into an array containing all its words, as in Example 6-12.

Example 6-12. Exploding a string into an array using spaces

```php
<?php
$temp = explode(' ', "This is a sentence with seven words");
print_r($temp);
?>
```

This example prints out the following (on a single line when viewed in a browser):

```
Array
(
    [0] => This
    [1] => is
    [2] => a
    [3] => sentence
    [4] => with
    [5] => seven
    [6] => words
)
```

The first parameter, the delimiter, need not be a space or even a single character. Example 6-13 shows a slight variation.

Example 6-13. Exploding a string delimited with *** into an array

```php
<?php
$temp = explode('***', "A***sentence***with***asterisks");
print_r($temp);
?>
```

The code in Example 6-13 prints out the following:

```
Array
(
    [0] => A
    [1] => sentence
    [2] => with
    [3] => asterisks
)
```

extract()

Sometimes it can be convenient to turn the key/value pairs from an array into PHP variables. One such time might be when processing the $_GET or $_POST variables as sent to a PHP script by a form.

When a form is submitted over the Web, the web server unpacks the variables into a global array for the PHP script. If the variables were sent using the GET method, they will be placed in an associative array called $_GET, and if they were sent using POST, they will be placed in an associative array called $_POST.

You could, of course, walk through such associative arrays in the manner shown in the examples so far. However, sometimes you just want to store the values sent into variables for later use. In this case, you can have PHP do the job automatically for you:

```
extract($_GET);
```

So, for example, if the query string parameter q is sent to a PHP script along with the associated value "Hi there", a new variable called $q will be created and assigned that value.

Be careful with this approach, though, because if any extracted variables conflict with ones that you have already defined, your existing values will be overwritten. To avoid this possibility, you can use one of the many additional parameters available to this function, like this:

```
extract($_GET, EXTR_PREFIX_ALL, 'fromget');
```

In this case, all the new variables will begin with the given prefix string followed by an underscore, so $q will become $fromget_q. I strongly recommend that you use this version of the function when handling the $_GET and $_POST arrays, or any other array whose keys could be controlled by the user, because malicious users could submit keys chosen deliberately to overwrite commonly used variable names and compromise your website.

compact()

There are also times when you want to use compact, the inverse of extract, to create an array from variables and their values. Example 6-14 shows how you might use this function.

Example 6-14. Using the compact function

```
<?php
$fname   = "Elizabeth";
$sname   = "Windsor";
$address = "Buckingham Palace";
$city    = "London";
$country = "United Kingdom";

$contact = compact('fname', 'sname', 'address', 'city', 'country');
print_r($contact);
?>
```

The result of running Example 6-14 is:

```
Array
(
```

```
        [fname] => Elizabeth
        [sname] => Windsor
        [address] => Buckingham Palace
        [city] => London
        [country] => United Kingdom
    )
```

Note how `compact` requires the variable names to be supplied in quotes and not as variables preceded with a $ symbol. This is because `compact` is looking for an array of variable names.

Another use of this function is for debugging, when you wish to quickly view several variables and their values, as in Example 6-15.

Example 6-15. Using compact to help with debugging

```php
<?php
$j       = 23;
$temp    = "Hello";
$address = "1 Old Street";
$age     = 61;

print_r (compact (explode (' ','j temp address age')));
?>
```

This works by using the `explode` function to extract all the words from the string into an array, which is then passed to the `compact` function, which returns an array to `print_r`, which shows its contents.

If you copy and paste the `print_r` line of code, you only need to alter the variables named there for a quick print out of a group of variables' values. In this example, the output is:

```
Array
(
    [j] => 23
    [temp] => Hello
    [address] => 1 Old Street
    [age] => 61
)
```

reset()

When the `foreach...as` construct or the `each` function walk through an array, they keep an internal PHP pointer that makes a note of which element of the array they should return next. If your code ever needs to return to the start of an array, you can issue `reset`, which also returns the value of that element. Examples of how to use this function are:

```php
reset($fred);        // Throw away return value
$item = reset($fred); // Keep first element of the array in $item
```

end()

As with **reset**, you can move PHP's internal array pointer to the final element in an array using the **end** function, which also returns the value of the element, and can be used as in these examples:

```
end($fred);
$item = end($fred);
```

This chapter concludes your basic introduction to PHP, and you should now be able to write quite complex programs using the skills you have learned. In the next chapter, we'll look at using PHP for common, practical tasks.

Test Your Knowledge: Questions

Question 6-1
  What is the difference between a numeric and an associative array?

Question 6-2
  What is the main benefit of the **array** keyword?

Question 6-3
  What is the difference between **foreach** and **each**?

Question 6-4
  How can you create a multidimensional array?

Question 6-5
  How can you determine the number of elements there are in an array?

Question 6-6
  What is the purpose of the **explode** function?

Question 6-7
  How can you set PHP's internal pointer into an array back to the first element of the array?

See the section "Chapter 6 Answers" on page 440 in Appendix A for the answers to these questions.

CHAPTER 7

Practical PHP

Previous chapters went over the elements of the PHP language. This chapter builds on your new programming skills to teach you some common but important practical tasks. You will learn the best ways to manage string handling to achieve clear and concise code that displays in web browsers exactly how you want it to, including advanced date and time management. You'll also find out how to create and otherwise modify files, including those uploaded by users.

There's also a comprehensive introduction to XHTML, a markup language similar to HTML (and which conforms to the XML syntax used to store data such as RSS feeds), and intended to supersede HTML. Together these topics will extend your understanding of both practical PHP programming and developing international web standards.

Using printf

You've already seen the `print` and `echo` functions, which simply output text to the browser. But a much more powerful function, `printf`, controls the format of the output by letting you put special formatting characters in a string.

For each formatting character, `printf` expects you to pass an argument that it will display using that format. For instance, the following example uses the `%d` conversion specifier to display the value 3 in decimal:

```
printf("There are %d items in your basket", 3);
```

If you replace the `%d` with `%b`, the value 3 would be displayed in binary (11). Table 7-1 shows the conversion specifiers supported.

Table 7-1. The printf conversion specifiers

Specifier	Conversion action on argument arg	Example (for an arg of 123)
%	Display a % character (no arg is required)	%
b	Display arg as a binary integer	1111011
c	Display ASCII character for the arg	{
d	Display arg as a signed decimal integer	123
e	Display arg using scientific notation	1.23000e+2
f	Display arg as floating point	123.000000
o	Display arg as an octal integer	173
s	Display arg as a string	123
u	Display arg as an unsigned decimal	123
x	Display arg in lowercase hexadecimal	7b
X	Display arg in uppercase hexadecimal	7B

You can have as many specifiers as you like in a `printf` function, as long as you pass a matching number of arguments, and as long as each specifier is prefaced by a `%` symbol. Therefore the following code is valid, and will output "My name is Simon. I'm 33 years old, which is 21 in hexadecimal":

```
printf("My name is %s. I'm %d years old, which is %X in hexadecimal",
    'Simon', 33, 33);
```

If you leave out any arguments, you will receive a parse error informing you that a right bracket,), was unexpectedly encountered.

A more practical example of `printf` sets colors in HTML using decimal. For example, suppose you know you want a color that has a triplet value of 65 red, 127 green, and 245 blue, but don't want to convert this to hexadecimal yourself. An easy solution is:

```
printf("<font color='#%X%X%X'>Hello</font>", 65, 127, 245);
```

Check the format of the color specification between the apostrophes (' ') carefully. First comes the pound sign (#) expected by the color specification. Then come three `%X` format specifiers, one for each of your numbers. The resulting output from this command is:

```
<font color='#417FF5'>Hello</font>
```

Usually, you'll find it convenient to use variables or expressions as arguments to `printf`. For instance, if you stored values for your colors in the three variables `$r`, `$g`, and `$b`, you could create a darker color with:

```
printf("<font color='#%X%X%X'>Hello</font>", $r-20, $g-20, $b-20);
```

Precision Setting

Not only can you specify a conversion type, you can also set the precision of the displayed result. For example, amounts of currency are usually displayed with only two digits of precision. However, after a calculation, a value may have a greater precision than this, such as 123.42/12, which results in 10.285. To ensure that such values are correctly stored internally, but displayed with only two digits of precision, you can insert the string ".2" between the % symbol and the conversion specifier:

```php
printf("The result is: $%.2f", 123.42 / 12);
```

The output from this command is:

```
The result is $10.29
```

But you actually have even more control than that, because you can also specify whether to pad output with either zeros or spaces by prefacing the specifier with certain values. Example 7-1 shows five possible combinations.

Example 7-1. Precision setting

```php
<?php
echo "<pre>"; // Enables viewing of the spaces

// Pad to 15 spaces
    printf("The result is $%15f\n", 123.42 / 12);

// Pad to 15 spaces, fill with zeros
    printf("The result is $%015f\n", 123.42 / 12);

// Pad to 15 spaces, 2 decimal places precision
    printf("The result is $%15.2f\n", 123.42 / 12);

// Pad to 15 spaces, 2 decimal places precision, fill with zeros
    printf("The result is $%015.2f\n", 123.42 / 12);

// Pad to 15 spaces, 2 decimal places precision, fill with # symbol
    printf("The result is $%'#15.2f\n", 123.42 / 12);
?>
```

The output from this example looks like this:

```
The result is $       10.285000
The result is $00000010.285000
The result is $          10.29
The result is $000000000010.29
The result is $##########10.29
```

The way it works is simple if you go from right to left (see Table 7-2). Notice that:

- The rightmost character is the conversion specifier. In this case, it is f for floating point.
- Just before the conversion specifier, if there is a period and a number together, then the precision of the output is specified as the value of the number.

- Regardless of whether there's a precision specifier, if there is a number, then that represents the amount of characters to which the output should be padded. In the previous example, this is 15 characters. If the output is already equal to or greater than the padding length, then this argument is ignored.
- The leftmost parameter allowed before the % symbol is a 0, which is ignored unless a padding value has been set, in which case the output is padded with zeros instead of spaces. If a pad character other than zero or a space is required, you can use any one of your choice as long as you preface it with a single quotation mark, like this: '#.
- On the left is the % symbol, which starts the conversion.

Table 7-2. Conversion specifier components

Start conversion	Pad character	Number of pad characters	Display precision	Conversion specifier	Examples
%		15		f	10.285000
%	0	15	.2	f	000000000010.29
%	'#	15	.4	f	########10.2850

String Padding

You can also pad strings to required lengths as you can with numbers, select different padding characters, and even choose between left and right justification. Example 7-2 shows various examples.

Example 7-2. String padding

```php
<?php
echo "<pre>"; // Enables viewing of the spaces

$h = 'House';

printf("[%s]\n",       $h); // Standard string output
printf("[%10s]\n",     $h); // Right justify with spaces
printf("[%-10s]\n",    $h); // Left justify with spaces
printf("[%010s]\n",    $h); // Zero padding
printf("[%'#10s]\n\n", $h); // Use the custom padding character '#'

$d = 'Doctor House';

printf("[%10.8s]\n",    $d); // Right justify, cutoff of 8 characters
printf("[%-10.6s]\n",   $d); // Left justify, cutoff of 6 characters
printf("[%-'@10.6s]\n", $d); // Left justify, pad '@', cutoff 6 chars
?>
```

Note how for purposes of layout in a web page, I've used the `<pre>` HTML tag to preserve all the spaces and the \n newline character after each of the lines to be displayed. The output from this example is as follows:

```
[House]
[    House]
[House    ]
[00000House]
[#####House]

[  Doctor H]
[Doctor    ]
[Doctor@@@@]
```

When specifying a padding value, if a string is already of equal or greater length than that value it will be ignored, *unless* a cutoff value is given that shortens the string back to less than the padding value.

Table 7-3 shows a breakdown of the components available to string conversion specifiers.

Table 7-3. String conversion specifier components

Start conversion	Left or right justify	Padding character	Number of pad characters	Cutoff	Conversion specifier	Examples
%					s	[House]
%	-		10		s	[House]
%		'#	8	.4	s	[####Hous]

Using sprintf

Often you don't want to output the result of a conversion but need to use it elsewhere in your code. This is where the `sprintf` function comes in. With it, you can send the output to another variable rather than to the browser.

You might use it simply to make a conversion, as in the following example, which returns the hexadecimal string value for the RGB color group 65, 127, 245 in `$hexstring`:

```
$hexstring = sprintf("%X%X%X", 65, 127, 245);
```

Or you may wish to store output ready to display later on:

```
$out = sprintf("The result is: $%.2f", 123.42 / 12);
echo $out;
```

Date and Time Functions

To keep track of the date and time, PHP uses standard Unix timestamps, which are simply the number of seconds since the start of January 1, 1970. To determine the current timestamp, you can use the `time` function:

```
echo time();
```

Because the value is stored as seconds, to obtain the timestamp for this time next week, you would use the following, which adds 7 days × 24 hours × 60 minutes × 60 seconds to the returned value:

```
echo time() + 7 * 24 * 60 * 60;
```

If you wish to create a timestamp for a given date, you can use the `mktime` function. Its output is the timestamp 946684800 for the first second of the first minute of the first hour of the first day of the year 2000:

```
echo mktime(0, 0, 0, 1, 1, 2000);
```

The parameters to pass are, in order from left to right:

- The number of the hour (0–23)
- The number of the minute (0–59)
- The number of seconds (0–59)
- The number of the month (1–12)
- The number of the day (1–31)
- The year (1970–2038, or 1901–2038 with PHP 5.1.0+ on 32-bit signed systems)

> You may ask why you are limited to the years 1970 through 2038. Well, it's because the original developers of Unix chose the start of the year 1970 as the base date that no programmer should need to go before! Luckily, because as of version 5.1.0, PHP supports systems using a signed 32-bit integer for the timestamp, dates 1901 to 2038 are allowed on them. However, a problem even worse than the first comes about because the Unix designers also decided that nobody would be using Unix after about 70 years or so, and therefore believed they could get away with storing the timestamp as a 32-bit value—which will run out on January 19, 2038! This will create what has come to be known as the Y2K38 bug (much like the millennium bug, which was caused by storing years as two-digit values, and which also had to be fixed). We have to hope it will all be solved well before we get too close to that date.

To display the date, use the `date` function, which supports a plethora of formatting options, enabling you to display the date any way you could wish. The format is as follows:

```
date($format, $timestamp);
```

The parameter `$format` should be a string containing formatting specifiers as detailed in Table 7-4 and `$timestamp` should be a Unix timestamp. For the complete list of specifiers, please see *http://php.net/manual/en/function.date.php*. The following command will output the current date and time in the format "Thursday April 15th, 2010 - 1:38pm":

```
echo date("l F jS, Y - g:ia", time());
```

Table 7-4. The major date function format specifiers

Format	Description	Returned value
Day specifiers		
d	Day of month, 2 digits, with leading zeros	*01* to *31*
D	Day of the week, three letters	*Mon* to *Sun*
j	Day of the month, no leading zeros	*1* to *31*
l	Day of week, full names	*Sunday* to *Saturday*
N	Day of week, numeric, Monday to Sunday	*1* to *7*
S	Suffix for day of month (useful with specifier j)	*st, nd, rd,* or *th*
w	Day of week, numeric, Sunday to Saturday	*0* to *6*
z	Day of year	*0* to *365*
Week specifier		
W	Week number of year	*1* to *52*
Month specifiers		
F	Month name	*January* to *December*
m	Month number with leading zeros	*01* to *12*
M	Month name, three letters	*Jan* to *Dec*
n	Month number, no leading zeros	*1* to *12*
t	Number of days in given month	*28, 29, 30* or *31*
Year specifiers		
L	Leap year	*1* = Yes, *0* = No
Y	Year, 4 digits	*0000* to *9999*
y	Year, 2 digits	*00* to *99*
Time specifiers		
a	Before or after midday, lowercase	*am* or *pm*
A	Before or after midday, uppercase	*AM* or *PM*
g	Hour of day, 12-hour format, no leading zeros	*1* to *12*
G	Hour of day, 24-hour format, no leading zeros	*1* to *24*
h	Hour of day, 12-hour format, with leading zeros	*01* to *12*
H	Hour of day, 24-hour format, with leading zeros	*01* to *24*
i	Minutes, with leading zeros	*00* to *59*
s	Seconds, with leading zeros	*00* to *59*

Date Constants

There are a number of useful constants that you can use with the `date` command to return the date in specific formats. For example, `date(DATE_RSS)` returns the current date and time in the valid format for an RSS feed. Some of the more commonly used constants are:

DATE_ATOM
> This is the format for Atom feeds. The PHP format is "Y-m-d\TH:i:sP" and example output is "2012-08-16T12:00:00+0000".

DATE_COOKIE
> This is the format for cookies set from a web server or JavaScript. The PHP format is "l, d-M-y H:i:s T" and example output is "Thu, 16 Aug 2012 12:00:00 UTC".

DATE_RSS
> This is the format for RSS feeds. The PHP format is "D, d M Y H:i:s T" and example output is "Thu, 16 Aug 2012 12:00:00 UTC".

DATE_W3C
> This is the format for "World Wide Web Consortium." The PHP format is "Y-m-d\TH:i:sP" and example output is "2012-08-16T12:00:00+0000".

The complete list can be found at *http://php.net/manual/en/class.datetime.php*.

Using checkdate

You've seen how to display a valid date in a variety of formats. But how can you check whether a user has submitted a valid date to your program? The answer is to pass the month, day and year to the `checkdate` function, which returns a value of `TRUE` if the date is valid, or `FALSE` if it is not.

For example, if February 30 of any year is input, it will always be an invalid date. Example 7-3 shows code that you could use for this. As it stands, it will find the given date invalid.

Example 7-3. Checking for the validity of a date

```php
<?php
$month = 9;      // September (only has 30 days)
$day   = 31;     // 31st
$year  = 2012;   // 2012

if (checkdate($month, $day, $year)) echo "Date is valid";
else echo "Date is invalid";
?>
```

File Handling

Powerful as it is, MySQL is not the only (or necessarily the best) way to store all data on a web server. Sometimes it can be quicker and more convenient to directly access files on the hard disk. Cases in which you might need to do this are modifying images such as uploaded user avatars, or log files that you wish to process.

First, though, a note about file naming. If you are writing code that may be used on various PHP installations, there is no way of knowing whether these systems are case-sensitive. For example, Windows and Mac OS X filenames are not case-sensitive, but Linux and Unix ones are. Therefore you should always assume that the system is case-sensitive and stick to a convention such as all lowercase filenames.

Checking Whether a File Exists

To determine whether a file already exists, you can use the `file_exists` function, which returns either `TRUE` or `FALSE`, and is used like this:

```
if (file_exists("testfile.txt")) echo "File exists";
```

Creating a File

At this point *testfile.txt* doesn't exist, so let's create it and write a few lines to it. Type in Example 7-4 and save it as *testfile.php*.

Example 7-4. Creating a simple text file

```
<?php // testfile.php
$fh = fopen("testfile.txt", 'w') or die("Failed to create file");
$text = <<<_END
Line 1
Line 2
Line 3

_END;
fwrite($fh, $text) or die("Could not write to file");
fclose($fh);
echo "File 'testfile.txt' written successfully";
?>
```

When you run this in a browser, all being well, you will receive the message "File 'testfile.txt' written successfully". If you receive an error message, your hard disk may be full or, more likely, you may not have permission to create or write to the file, in which case you should modify the attributes of the destination folder according to your operating system. Otherwise, the file *testfile.txt* should now be residing in the same folder in which you saved the *testfile.php* program. Try opening the file in a text or program editor—the contents will look like this:

```
Line 1
Line 2
Line 3
```

This simple example shows the sequence that all file handling takes:

1. Always start by opening the file. This is done through a call to fopen.

2. Then you can call other functions; here we write to the file (fwrite), but you can also read from an existing file (fread or fgets) and do other things.

3. Finish by closing the file (fclose). Although the program does this for you when it ends, you should clean up yourself by closing the file when you're finished.

Every open file requires a file resource so that PHP can access and manage it. The preceding example sets the variable $fh (which I chose to stand for *file handle*) to the value returned by the fopen function. Thereafter, each file handling function that accesses the opened file, such as fwrite or fclose, must be passed $fh as a parameter to identify the file being accessed. Don't worry about the content of the $fh variable; it's a number PHP uses to refer to internal information about the file—you just pass the variable to other functions.

Upon failure, FALSE will be returned by fopen. The previous example shows a simple way to capture and respond to the failure: it calls the **die** function to end the program and gives the user an error message. A web application would never abort in this crude way (you would create a web page with an error message instead), but this is fine for our testing purposes.

Notice the second parameter to the fopen call. It is simply the character w, which tells the function to open the file for writing. The function creates the file if it doesn't already exist. Be careful when playing around with these functions: if the file already exists, the w mode parameter causes the fopen call to delete the old contents (even if you don't write anything new!).

There are several different mode parameters that can be used here, as detailed in Table 7-5.

Table 7-5. The supported fopen modes

Mode	Action	Description
'r'	Read from file start	Open for reading only; place the file pointer at the beginning of the file. Return FALSE if the file doesn't already exist.
'r+'	Read from file start and allow writing	Open for reading and writing; place the file pointer at the beginning of the file. Return FALSE if the file doesn't already exist.
'w'	Write from file start and truncate file	Open for writing only; place the file pointer at the beginning of the file and truncate the file to zero length. If the file doesn't exist, attempt to create it.
'w+'	Write from file start, truncate file and allow reading	Open for reading and writing; place the file pointer at the beginning of the file and truncate the file to zero length. If the file doesn't exist, attempt to create it.

Mode	Action	Description
'a'	Append to file end	Open for writing only; place the file pointer at the end of the file. If the file doesn't exist, attempt to create it.
'a+'	Append to file end and allow reading	Open for reading and writing; place the file pointer at the end of the file. If the file doesn't exist, attempt to create it.

Reading from Files

The easiest way to read from a text file is to grab a whole line through `fgets` (think of the final `s` as standing for "string"), as in Example 7-5.

Example 7-5. Reading a file with fgets

```php
<?php
$fh = fopen("testfile.txt", 'r') or
    die("File does not exist or you lack permission to open it");
$line = fgets($fh);
fclose($fh);
echo $line;
?>
```

If you created the file as shown in Example 7-4, you'll get the first line:

```
Line 1
```

Or you can retrieve multiple lines or portions of lines through the `fread` function, as in Example 7-6.

Example 7-6. Reading a file with fread

```php
<?php
$fh = fopen("testfile.txt", 'r') or
    die("File does not exist or you lack permission to open it");
$text = fread($fh, 3);
fclose($fh);
echo $text;
?>
```

I've requested three characters in the `fread` call, so the program displays the following:

```
Lin
```

The `fread` function is commonly used with binary data. But if you use it on text data that spans more than one line, remember to count newline characters.

Copying Files

Let's try out the PHP `copy` function to create a clone of *testfile.txt*. Type in Example 7-7 and save it as *copyfile.php*, then call the program up in your browser.

Example 7-7. Copying a file

```
<?php // copyfile.php
copy('testfile.txt', 'testfile2.txt') or die("Could not copy file");
echo "File successfully copied to 'testfile2.txt'";
?>
```

If you check your folder again, you'll see that you now have the new file *testfile2.txt* in it. By the way, if you don't want your programs to exit on a failed copy attempt, you could try the alternate syntax in Example 7-8.

Example 7-8. Alternate syntax for copying a file

```
<?php // copyfile2.php
if (!copy('testfile.txt', 'testfile2.txt')) echo "Could not copy file";
else echo "File successfully copied to 'testfile2.txt'";
?>
```

Moving a File

To move a file, rename it with the `rename` function, as in Example 7-9.

Example 7-9. Moving a file

```
<?php // movefile.php
if (!rename('testfile2.txt', 'testfile2.new'))
    echo "Could not rename file";
else echo "File successfully renamed to 'testfile2.new'";
?>
```

You can use the `rename` function on directories, too. To avoid any warning messages, if the original file doesn't exist, you can call the `file_exists` function first to check.

Deleting a File

Deleting a file is just a matter of using the `unlink` function to remove it from the file system, as in Example 7-10.

Example 7-10. Deleting a file

```
<?php // deletefile.php
if (!unlink('testfile2.new')) echo "Could not delete file";
else echo "File 'testfile2.new' successfully deleted";
?>
```

 Whenever you access files on your hard disk directly, you must also always ensure that it is impossible for your filesystem to be compromised. For example, if you are deleting a file based on user input, you must make absolutely certain it is a file that can be safely deleted and that the user is allowed to delete it.

As with moving a file, a warning message will be displayed if the file doesn't exist, which you can avoid by using `file_exists` to first check for its existence before calling `unlink`.

Updating Files

Often you will want to add more data to a saved file, which you can do in many ways. You can use one of the append write modes (see Table 7-5), or you can simply open a file for reading and writing with one of the other modes that supports writing, and move the file pointer to the correct place within the file that you wish to write to or read from.

The *file pointer* is the position within a file at which the next file access will take place, whether it's a read or a write. It is not the same as the file handle (as stored in the variable `$fh` in Example 7-4), which contains details about the file being accessed.

You can see this in action by typing in Example 7-11 and saving it as *update.php*. Then call it up in your browser.

Example 7-11. Updating a file

```
<?php // update.php
$fh = fopen("testfile.txt", 'r+') or die("Failed to open file");
$text = fgets($fh);
fseek($fh, 0, SEEK_END);
fwrite($fh, "$text") or die("Could not write to file");
fclose($fh);
echo "File 'testfile.txt' successfully updated";
?>
```

What this program does is open *testfile.txt* for both reading and writing by setting the mode with '+r', which puts the file pointer right at the start. It then uses the `fgets` function to read in a single line from the file (up to the first line feed). After that, the `fseek` function is called to move the file pointer right to the file end, at which point the line of text that was extracted from the start of the file (stored in `$text`) is then appended to file's end and the file is closed. The resulting file now looks like this:

```
Line 1
Line 2
Line 3
Line 1
```

The first line has successfully been copied and then appended to the file's end.

As used here, in addition to the `$fh` file handle, the `fseek` function was passed two other parameters, 0 and `SEEK_END`. The `SEEK_END` tells the function to move the file pointer to the end of the file and the 0 parameter tells it how many positions it should then be moved backward from that point. In the case of Example 7-11, a value of 0 is used, because the pointer is required to remain at the file's end.

There are two other seek options available to the **fseek** function: **SEEK_SET** and **SEEK_CUR**. The **SEEK_SET** option tells the function to set the file pointer to the exact position given by the preceding parameter. Thus, the following example moves the file pointer to position 18:

```
fseek($fh, 18, SEEK_SET);
```

SEEK_CUR sets the file pointer to the current position *plus* the value of the given offset. Therefore, if the file pointer is currently at position 18, the following call will move it to position 23:

```
fseek($fh, 5, SEEK_CUR);
```

Although this is not recommended unless you have very specific reasons for it, it is even possible to use text files such as this (but with fixed line lengths) as simple flat-file databases. Your program can then use **fseek** to move back and forth within such a file to retrieve, update, and add new records. Records can also be deleted by overwriting them with zero characters, and so on.

Locking Files for Multiple Accesses

Web programs are often called by many users at the same time. If more than one person tries to write to a file simultaneously, it can become corrupted. And if one person writes to it while another is reading from it, the file is all right but the person reading it can get odd results. To handle simultaneous users, it's necessary to use the file locking **flock** function. This function queues up all other requests to access a file until your program releases the lock. So, whenever your programs use write access on files that may be accessed concurrently by multiple users, you should also add file locking to them, as in Example 7-12, which is an updated version of Example 7-11.

Example 7-12. Updating a file with file locking

```php
<?php
$fh = fopen("testfile.txt", 'r+') or die("Failed to open file");
$text = fgets($fh);

if (flock($fh, LOCK_EX))
{
    fseek($fh, 0, SEEK_END);
    fwrite($fh, "$text") or die("Could not write to file");
    flock($fh, LOCK_UN);
}
fclose($fh);
echo "File 'testfile.txt' successfully updated";
?>
```

There is a trick to file locking to preserve the best possible response time for your website visitors: perform it directly before you make a change to a file, and then unlock it immediately afterward. Having a file locked for any longer than this will slow your application down unnecessarily. This is why the calls to `flock` in Example 7-12 are directly before and after the `fwrite` call.

The first call to `flock` sets an exclusive file lock on the file referred to by `$fh` using the `LOCK_EX` parameter:

```
flock($fh, LOCK_EX);
```

From this point onward, no other processes can write to (or even read from) the file until the lock is released by using the `LOCK_UN` parameter, like this:

```
flock($fh, LOCK_UN);
```

As soon as the lock is released, other processes are allowed access again to the file. This is one reason why you should reseek to the point you wish to access in a file each time you need to read or write data, because another process could have changed the file since the last access.

However, did you notice that the call to request an exclusive lock is nested as part of an `if` statement? This is because `flock` is not supported on all systems and therefore it is wise to check whether you successfully secured a lock, just in case one could not be obtained.

Something else you must consider is that `flock` is what is known as an *advisory* lock. This means that it locks out only other processes that call the function. If you have any code that goes right in and modifies files without implementing `flock` file locking, it will always override the locking and could wreak havoc on your files.

By the way, implementing file locking and then accidentally leaving it out in one section of code can lead to an extremely hard-to-locate bug.

 `flock` will not work on NFS (Network File System) and many other networked filesystems. Also, when using a multithreaded server like ISAPI, you may not be able to rely on `flock` to protect files against other PHP scripts running in parallel threads of the same server instance. Additionally, `flock` is not supported on the FAT filesystem and its derivates, and will therefore always return `FALSE` under this environment (this is especially true for Windows 98 users).

Reading an Entire File

A handy function for reading in an entire file without having to use file handles is `file_get_contents`. It's very easy to use, as you can see in Example 7-13.

Example 7-13. Using file_get_contents

```php
<?php
echo "<pre>";  // Enables display of line feeds
echo file_get_contents("testfile.txt");
echo "</pre>"; // Terminates pre tag
?>
```

Figure 7-1. The O'Reilly home page grabbed with file_get_contents

But the function is actually a lot more useful than that, because you can also use it to fetch a file from a server across the Internet, as in Example 7-14, which requests the HTML from the O'Reilly home page, and then displays it as if the page itself had been surfed to. The result will be similar to the screenshot in Figure 7-1.

Example 7-14. Grabbing the O'Reilly home page

```php
<?php
echo file_get_contents("http://oreilly.com");
?>
```

Uploading Files

Uploading files to a web server is a subject area that seems daunting to many people, but it actually couldn't be much easier. All you need to do to upload a file from a form is choose a special type of encoding called *multipart/form-data* and your browser will handle the rest. To see how this works, type in the program in Example 7-15 and save it as *upload.php*. When you run it, you'll see a form in your browser that lets you upload a file of your choice.

Example 7-15. Image uploader upload.php

```php
<?php // upload.php
echo <<<_END
<html><head><title>PHP Form Upload</title></head><body>
<form method='post' action='upload.php' enctype='multipart/form-data'>
Select File: <input type='file' name='filename' size='10' />
<input type='submit' value='Upload' />
</form>
_END;

if ($_FILES)
{
    $name = $_FILES['filename']['name'];
    move_uploaded_file($_FILES['filename']['tmp_name'], $name);
    echo "Uploaded image '$name'<br /><img src='$name' />";
}

echo "</body></html>";
?>
```

Let's examine this program a section at a time. The first line of the multiline `echo` statement starts an HTML document, displays the title, and then starts the document's body.

Next we come to the form that selects the POST method of form submission, sets the target for posted data to the program *upload.php* (the program itself), and tells the web browser that the data posted should be encoded using the content type of *multipart/ form-data*.

With the form set up, the next lines display the prompt "Select File:" and then request two inputs. The first input being asked for is a file, which is done by using an input type of *file* and a name of *filename*, and the input field has a width of 10 characters.

The second requested input is just a Submit button that is given the label "Upload" (replacing the default button text of "Submit Query"). And then the form is closed.

This short program shows a common technique in web programming in which a single program is called twice: once when the user first visits a page, and again when the user presses the Submit button.

The PHP code to receive the uploaded data is fairly simple, because all uploaded files are placed into the associative system array $_FILES. Therefore a quick check to see whether $_FILES has anything in it is sufficient to determine whether the user has up-loaded a file. This is done with the statement `if ($_FILES)`.

The first time the user visits the page, before uploading a file, $_FILES is empty, so the program skips this block of code. When the user uploads a file, the program runs again and discovers an element in the $_FILES array.

Figure 7-2. *Uploading an image as form data*

Once the program realizes that a file was uploaded, the actual name, as read from the uploading computer, is retrieved and placed into the variable $name. Now all that's necessary is to move the file from the temporary location in which PHP stored the uploaded file to a more permanent one. This is done using the move_uploaded_file function, passing it the original name of the file, with which it is saved to the current directory.

Finally, the uploaded image is displayed within an IMG tag, and the result should look like the screenshot in Figure 7-2.

> If you run this program and receive warning messages such as "Permission denied" for the move_uploaded_file function call, then you may not have the correct permissions set for the folder in which the program is running.

Using $_FILES

Five things are stored in the $_FILES array when a file is uploaded, as shown by Table 7-6 (where *file* is the file upload field name supplied by the submitting form).

Table 7-6. *The contents of the $_FILES array*

Array Element	Contents
$_FILES['*file*']['*name*']	The name of the uploaded file (e.g., *smiley.jpg*)
$_FILES['*file*']['*type*']	The content type of the file (e.g., *image/jpeg*)

Array Element	Contents
$_FILES['*file*']['*size*']	The file's size in bytes
$_FILES['*file*']['*tmp_name*']	The name of the temporary file stored on the server
$_FILES['*file*']['*error*']	The error code resulting from the file upload

Content types used to be known as MIME (Multipurpose Internet Mail Extension) types, but because their use later expanded to the whole Internet, they are nowadays often called *Internet media types*. Table 7-7 shows some of the more frequently used types that turn up in $_FILES['*file*']['*type*'].

Table 7-7. Some common Internet media content types

application/pdf	image/gif	multipart/form-data	text/xml
application/zip	image/jpeg	text/css	video/mpeg
audio/mpeg	image/png	text/html	video/mp4
audio/x-wav	image/tiff	text/plain	video/quicktime

Validation

Hopefully it now goes without saying (although I'll do so anyway) that form-data validation is of the utmost importance, due to the possibility of users attempting to hack into your server.

In addition to maliciously formed input data, some of the things you also have to check are whether a file was actually received and, if so, whether the right type of data was sent.

Taking all these things into account, Example 7-16, *upload2.php*, is a rewrite of *upload.php*.

Example 7-16. A more secure version of upload.php

```
<?php // upload2.php
echo <<<_END
<html><head><title>PHP Form Upload</title></head><body>
<form method='post' action='upload2.php' enctype='multipart/form-data'>
Select a JPG, GIF, PNG or TIF File:
<input type='file' name='filename' size='10' />
<input type='submit' value='Upload' /></form>
_END;

if ($_FILES)
{
    $name = $_FILES['filename']['name'];

    switch($_FILES['filename']['type'])
    {
        case 'image/jpeg': $ext = 'jpg'; break;
        case 'image/gif':  $ext = 'gif'; break;
        case 'image/png':  $ext = 'png'; break;
```

```
            case 'image/tiff': $ext = 'tif'; break;
            default:           $ext = '';    break;
    }
    if ($ext)
    {
        $n = "image.$ext";
        move_uploaded_file($_FILES['filename']['tmp_name'], $n);
        echo "Uploaded image '$name' as '$n':<br />";
        echo "<img src='$n' />";
    }
    else echo "'$name' is not an accepted image file";
}
else echo "No image has been uploaded";

echo "</body></html>";
?>
```

The non-HTML section of code has been expanded from the half-dozen lines of Example 7-15 to more than 20 lines, starting at: if ($_FILES).

As with the previous version, this if line checks whether any data was actually posted, but there is now a matching else near the bottom of the program that echoes a message to screen when nothing has been uploaded.

Within the if statement, the variable $name is assigned the value of the filename as retrieved from the uploading computer (just as before), but this time we won't rely on the user having sent us valid data. Instead a switch statement is used to check the uploaded content type against the four types of image this program supports. If a match is made, the variable $ext is set to the three-letter file extension for that type. Should no match be found, the file uploaded was not of an accepted type and the variable $ext is set to the empty string "".

The next section of code then checks the variable $ext to see whether it contains a string and, if so, creates a new filename called $n with the base name *image* and the extension stored in $ext. This means that the program is in full control over the name of the file to be created, as it can be only one of *image.jpg*, *image.gif*, *image.png*, or *image.tif*.

Safe in the knowledge that the program has not been compromised, the rest of the PHP code is much the same as in the previous version. It moves the uploaded temporary image to its new location and then displays it, while also displaying the old and new image names.

 Don't worry about having to delete the temporary file that PHP creates during the upload process, because if the file has not been moved or renamed, it will be automatically removed when the program exits.

After the if statement there is a matching else, which is executed only if an unsupported image type was uploaded, in which case it displays an appropriate error message.

When you write your own file uploading routines, I strongly advise you to use a similar approach and have prechosen names and locations for uploaded files. That way no attempts to add path names and other malicious data to the variables you use can get through. If this means that more than one user could end up having a file uploaded with the same name, you could prefix such files with their usernames, or save them to individually created folders for each user.

But if you must use a supplied filename, you should sanitize it by allowing only alphanumeric characters and the period, which you can do with the following command, using a regular expression (see Chapter 17) to perform a search and replace on $name:

```
$name = ereg_replace("[^A-Za-z0-9.]", "", $name);
```

This leaves only the characters A–Z, a–z, 0–9 and periods in the string $name, and strips out everything else.

Even better, to ensure that your program will work on all systems, regardless of whether they are case-sensitive or case-insensitive, you should probably use the following command instead, which changes all uppercase characters to lowercase at the same time:

```
$name = strtolower(ereg_replace("[^A-Za-z0-9.]", "", $name));
```

Sometimes you may encounter the media type of *image/pjpeg*, which indicates a progressive jpeg, but you can safely add this to your code as an alias of *image/jpeg*, like this:

```
case 'image/pjpeg':
case 'image/jpeg': $ext = 'jpg'; break;
```

System Calls

Sometimes PHP will not have the function you need to perform a certain action, but the operating system it is running on may. In such cases, you can use the **exec** system call to do the job.

For example, to quickly view the contents of the current directory, you can use a program such as Example 7-17. If you are on a Windows system, it will run as-is using the Windows **dir** command. On Linux, Unix, or Mac OS X, comment out or remove the first line and uncomment the second to use the **ls** system command. You may wish to type this program in, save it as *exec.php* and call it up in your browser.

Example 7-17. Executing a system command

```
<?php // exec.php
$cmd = "dir";    // Windows
// $cmd = "ls"; // Linux, Unix & Mac

exec(escapeshellcmd($cmd), $output, $status);

if ($status) echo "Exec command failed";
else
```

```
{
    echo "<pre>";
    foreach($output as $line) echo "$line\n";
}
?>
```

Depending on the system you are using, the result of running this program will look something like this (from a Windows `dir` command):

```
Volume in drive C is HP
Volume Serial Number is E67F-EE11

Directory of C:\web

20/01/2011  10:34
            .
    20/01/2011  10:34
                ..
        19/01/2011  16:26              236 maketest.php
        20/01/2011  10:47              198 exec.php
        20/01/2011  08:04           13,741 smiley.jpg
        19/01/2011  18:01               54 test.php
        19/01/2011  16:59               35 testfile.txt
        20/01/2011  09:35              886 upload.php
                    6 File(s)       15,150 bytes
                    2 Dir(s)   382,907,748,352 bytes free
```

exec takes three arguments:

1. The command itself (in the previous case, $cmd)

2. An array in which the system will put the output from the command (in the previous case, $output)

3. A variable to contain the returned status of the call (in the previous case, $status)

If you wish, you can omit the $output and $status parameters, but you will not know the output created by the call or even whether it completed successfully.

You should also note the use of the escapeshellcmd function. It is a good habit to always use this when issuing an exec call, because it sanitizes the command string, preventing the execution of arbitrary commands, should you supply user input to the call.

 The system calling functions are typically disabled on shared web hosts as they pose a security risk. You should always try to solve your problems within PHP if you can, and go to the system directly only if it is really necessary. Also, going to the system is relatively slow and you need to code two implementations if your application is expected to run on both Windows and Linux/Unix systems.

XHTML

I've used some elements of XHTML (eXtensible Hypertext Markup Language) already in this book, although you may not have realized it. For example, instead of the simple HTML tag `<br>`, I've been using the XHTML `<br />` version. But what's the difference between the two markup languages?

Well, not a lot at first glance, but XHTML improves on HTML by clearing up a lot of little inconsistencies that make it hard to process. HTML requires quite a complex and very lenient parser, whereas XHTML, which uses standard syntax more like XML (eXtensible Markup Language), is very easily processed with quite a simple parser—a parser being a piece of code that processes tags and commands and works out what they mean.

The Benefits of XHTML

XHTML documents can be quickly processed by any program that can handle XML files. As more and more devices such as iPhones and BlackBerries become web-enabled, it is increasingly important to ensure that web content looks good on them as well as on a computer's web browser. The tighter syntax required by XHTML is a big factor in helping this cross-platform compatibility.

So what is happening right now is that browser developers, in order to be able to provide faster and more powerful programs, are trying to push web developers over to using XHTML, and the time may eventually come when HTML is superseded by XHTML— so it's a good idea to start using it now.

XHTML Versions

The XHTML standard is constantly evolving, and there are a few versions in use:

XHTML 1.0
> This incorporates the contents from the HTML 4.01 standard but requires the use of XML syntax.

XHTML 1.1
> This version has not been widely adopted, although it is largely compatible with XHTML 1.0 and HTML 4. A major feature of this version is that CSS is used to control browser presentation.

XHTML 1.2
> This version is only in the proposal stage and is not currently implemented.

XHTML 2.0
> This version of XHTML makes a totally clean break from previous versions and also from HTML 4. Unsurprisingly, there are a tremendous number of changes.

Luckily for us, for now XHTML 1.0 is the main version that you need to understand. And that holds true even if you will be writing to XHTML 2.0 specifications, because XHTML 1.0 introduces the XML aspects used by all versions.

What's Different?

The following XHTML rules differentiate it from HTML:

- All tags must be closed by another tag. In cases in which there is no matching closing tag, the tag must close itself using a space followed by the symbols / and >. So, for example, a tag such as `<input type='submit'>` needs to be changed into `<input type='submit' />`. In addition, all opening `<p>` tags now require a closing `</p>` tag, too. And no, you can't replace them with `<p />`.

- All tags must be correctly nested. Therefore the string `<b>My first name is <i>Robin</b></i>` is not allowed, because the opening `<b>` has been closed before the `<i>`. The corrected version is `<b>My first name is <i>Robin</i></b>`.

- All tag attributes must be enclosed in quotation marks. Instead of using tags such as `<form method=post action=post.php>` you should instead use `<form method='post' action='post.php'>`. You can also use double quotes: `<form method="post" action="post.php">`.

- The ampersand (&) character cannot be used on its own. For example, the string "Batman & Robin" must be replaced with "Batman & Robin". This means that URLs require modification, too. So the HTML syntax `<a href="index.php?page=12&item=15">` should be replaced with `<a href="index.php?page=12&amp;item=15">`.

- XHTML tags are case-sensitive and must be all in lowercase. Therefore HTML such as `<BODY><DIV ID="heading">` must be changed to the following syntax: `<body><div id="heading">`.

- Attributes cannot be minimized any more, so tags such as `<option name="bill" selected>` now must be replaced with an assigned value: `<option name="bill" selected="selected">`. All other attributes such as `checked` and `disabled` also need to be changed to `checked="checked"`, `disabled="disabled"`, and so on.

- XHTML documents must start with a new XML declaration on the very first line, like this: `<?xml version="1.0" encoding="UTF-8"?>`.

- The `DOCTYPE` declaration has been changed.

- The `<html>` tag now requires an `xmlns` attribute.

So let's take a look at the XHTML 1.0 conforming document in Example 7-18.

Example 7-18. An example XML document

```
<?xml version="1.0" encoding="UTF-8"?>
<!DOCTYPE html PUBLIC "-//W3C//DTD XHTML 1.0 Strict//EN"
    "http://www.w3.org/TR/xhtml1/DTD/xhtml1-strict.dtd">
```

```
<html xmlns="http://www.w3.org/1999/xhtml" xml:lang="en" lang="en">
    <head>
        <meta http-equiv="Content-Type"
            content="text/html; charset=utf-8" />
        <title>XHTML 1.0 Document</title>
    </head>
    <body>
        <p>This is an example XHTML 1.0 document</p>
        <h1>This is a heading</h1>
        <p>This is some text</p>
    </body>
</html>
```

As previously discussed, the document begins with an XML declaration, followed by the DOCTYPE declaration, and the <html> tag with an xmlns attribute. From there on, it all looks like straightforward HTML, except that the meta tag is closed properly with />.

HTML 4.01 Document Types

To tell the browser precisely how to handle a document, use the DOCTYPE declaration, which defines the syntax that is allowed. HTML 4.01 supports three DTDs (Document Type Declarations), as can be seen in the following examples.

The strict DTD in Example 7-19 requires complete adherence to HTML 4.01 syntax.

Example 7-19. The HTML 4.01 Strict DTD

```
<!DOCTYPE HTML PUBLIC "-//W3C//DTD HTML 4.01//EN"
    "http://www.w3.org/TR/html4/strict.dtd">
```

The loose DTD in Example 7-20 allows some older elements and deprecated attributes. (The standards at *http://w3.org/TR/xhtml1* explain which items are deprecated.)

Example 7-20. The HTML 4.01 Transitional DTD

```
<!DOCTYPE HTML PUBLIC "-//W3C//DTD HTML 4.01 Transitional//EN"
    "http://www.w3.org/TR/html4/loose.dtd">
```

Finally, Example 7-21 signifies an HTML 4.01 document containing a frameset.

Example 7-21. The HTML 4.01 Frameset DTD

```
<!DOCTYPE HTML PUBLIC "-//W3C//DTD HTML 4.01 Frameset//EN"
    "http://www.w3.org/TR/html4/frameset.dtd">
```

XHTML 1.0 Document Types

You may well have come across one or more of the HTML document types before. However, the syntax is slightly changed when it comes to XHTML 1.0, as shown in the following examples.

The strict DTD in Example 7-22 rules out the use of deprecated attributes and requires code that is completely correct.

Example 7-22. The XHTML 1.0 Strict DTD

```
<!DOCTYPE html PUBLIC "-//W3C//DTD XHTML 1.0 Strict//EN"
    "http://www.w3.org/TR/xhtml1/DTD/xhtml1-strict.dtd">
```

The transitional XHTML 1.0 DTD in Example 7-23 allows deprecated attributes and is the most commonly used DTD.

Example 7-23. The XHTML 1.0 Transitional DTD

```
<!DOCTYPE html PUBLIC "-//W3C//DTD XHTML 1.0 Transitional//EN"
    "http://www.w3.org/TR/xhtml1/DTD/xhtml1-transitional.dtd">
```

Example 7-24 shows the only XHTML 1.0 DTD that supports framesets.

Example 7-24. The XHTML 1.0 Frameset DTD

```
<!DOCTYPE html PUBLIC "-//W3C//DTD XHTML 1.0 Frameset//EN"
    "http://www.w3.org/TR/xhtml1/DTD/xhtml1-frameset.dtd">
```

XHTML Validation

To validate your XHTML, visit the W3C validation site at *http://validator.w3.org*, where you can validate a document by URL, form upload, or by typing it in or copying and pasting it into a web form. Before you code some PHP to create a web page, submit a sample of the output that you want to create to the validation site. No matter how carefully you code your XHTML, you will be surprised how many errors you left in.

Whenever a document is not fully compatible with XHTML, you will be given helpful messages explaining how you can correct it. Figure 7-3 shows that the document in Example 7-18 successfully passes the XHTML 1.0 Strict validation test.

 You will find that your XHTML 1.0 documents are so close to HTML that even if they are called up on a browser that is unaware of XHTML, they should display correctly. The only potential problem is with the `<script>` tag. To ensure compatibility, avoid using the `<script src="script.src" />` syntax and replace it with `<script src="script.src"></script>`.

This chapter represented another long journey in your task to master PHP. Now that you have formatting, file handling, XHTML, and a lot of other important concepts under your belt, the next chapter will introduce you to another major topic, MySQL.

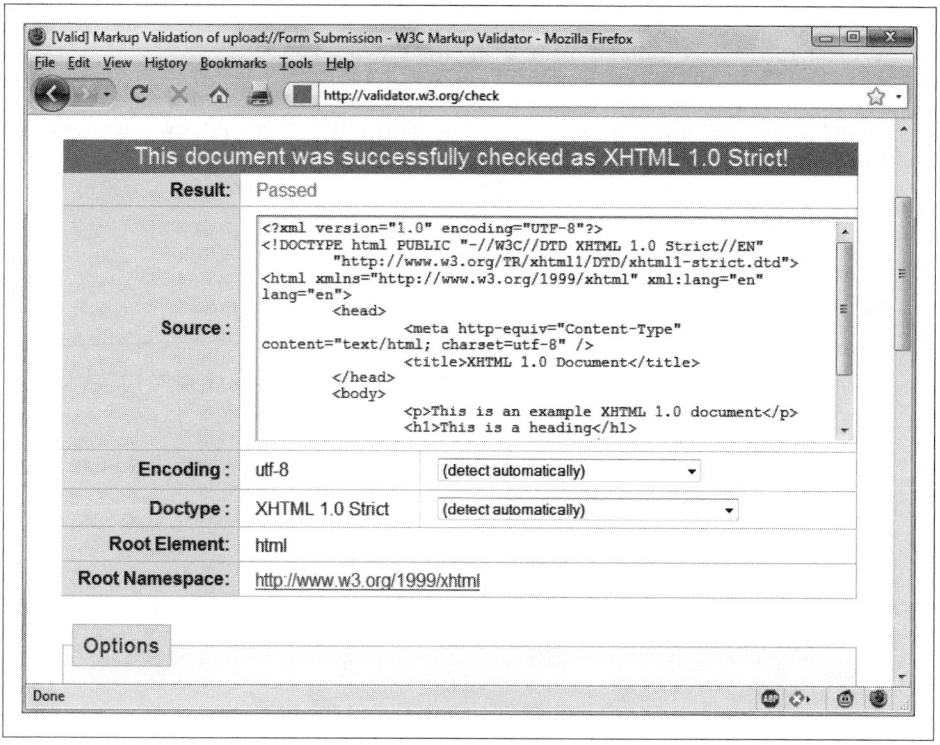

Figure 7-3. The document in Example 7-18, having passed validation

Test Your Knowledge: Questions

Question 7-1

Which `printf` conversion specifier would you use to display a floating-point number?

Question 7-2

What `printf` statement could be used to take the input string "Happy Birthday" and output the string "**Happy"?

Question 7-3

To send the output from `printf` to a variable instead of to a browser, what alternative function would you use?

Question 7-4

How would you create a Unix timestamp for 7:11am on May 2nd, 2016?

Question 7-5

Which file access mode would you use with `fopen` to open a file in write and read mode, with the file truncated and the file pointer at the start?

Question 7-6
What is the PHP command for deleting the file *file.txt*?

Question 7-7
Which PHP function is used to read in an entire file in one go, even from across the Web?

Question 7-8
Which PHP system variable holds the details on uploaded files?

Question 7-9
Which PHP function enables the running of system commands?

Question 7-10
What is wrong with the following XHTML 1.0 tag: `<input type=file name=file size=10>`?

See the section "Chapter 7 Answers" on page 440 in Appendix A for the answers to these questions.

CHAPTER 8

Introduction to MySQL

With well over ten million installations, MySQL is probably the most popular database management system for web servers. Developed in the mid 1990s, it's now a mature technology that powers many of today's most-visited Internet destinations.

One reason for its success must be the fact that, like PHP, it's free to use. But it's also extremely powerful and exceptionally fast—it can run on even the most basic of hardware, and it hardly puts a dent in system resources.

MySQL is also highly scalable, which means that it can grow with your website. In fact, in a comparison of several databases by *eWEEK*, MySQL and Oracle tied for both best performance and for greatest scalability (*http://mysql.com/why-mysql/benchmarks*).

MySQL Basics

A database is a structured collection of records or data stored in a computer system and organized in such a way that it can be quickly searched and information can be rapidly retrieved.

The SQL in MySQL stands for Structured Query Language. This language is loosely based on English and is also used on other databases such as Oracle and Microsoft SQL Server. It is designed to allow simple requests from a database via commands such as:

```
SELECT title FROM publications WHERE author = 'Charles Dickens';
```

A MySQL database contains one or more *tables*, each of which contain *records* or *rows*. Within these rows are various *columns* or *fields* that contain the data itself. Table 8-1 shows the contents of an example database of five publications detailing the author, title, type, and year of publication.

Table 8-1. Example of a simple database

Author	Title	Type	Year
Mark Twain	*The Adventures of Tom Sawyer*	Fiction	1876
Jane Austen	*Pride and Prejudice*	Fiction	1811
Charles Darwin	*The Origin of Species*	Non-fiction	1856
Charles Dickens	*The Old Curiosity Shop*	Fiction	1841
William Shakespeare	*Romeo and Juliet*	Play	1594

Each row in the table is the same as a row in a MySQL table, and each element within a row is the same as a MySQL field.

To uniquely identify this database, I'll refer to it as the *publications* database in the examples that follow. And, as you will have observed, all these publications are considered to be classics of literature, so I'll call the table within the database that holds the details *classics*.

Summary of Database Terms

The main terms you need to acquaint yourself with for now are:

Database
    The overall container for a collection of MySQL data.

Table
    A subcontainer within a database that stores the actual data.

Row
    A single record within a table, which may contain several fields.

Column
    The name of a field within a row.

I should note that I'm not trying to reproduce the precise terminology used in academic literature about relational databases, but just to provide simple, everyday terms to help you quickly grasp basic concepts and get started with a database.

Accessing MySQL via the Command Line

There are three main ways in which you can interact with MySQL: using a command line, via a web interface such as phpMyAdmin, and through a programming language like PHP. We'll start doing the third of these in Chapter 10, but for now, let's look at the first two.

Starting the Command-Line Interface

The following sections describe relevant instructions for Windows, Mac OS X, and Linux.

Windows users

If you installed the EasyPHP WAMP as explained in Chapter 2, you will be able to access the MySQL executable from the following directory:

```
\Program Files\EasyPHP 3.0\mysql\bin
```

> If you installed EasyPHP in a place other than *\Program Files*, you will need to use that directory instead. Also, if the version of EasyPHP is not 3.0, you will need to change that, too.

By default, the initial MySQL user will be *root* and will not have had a password set. Seeing as this is a development server that only you should be able to access, we won't worry about creating one yet.

So, to enter MySQL's command-line interface, select Start→Run and enter CMD into the Run box, then press Return. This will call up a Windows Command prompt. From there, enter the following (making any appropriate changes as discussed previously):

```
"\Program Files\EasyPHP 3.0\mysql\bin\mysql" -u root
```

> Note the quotation marks surrounding the main path and filename. These are present because the name contains spaces, which the Command prompt doesn't correctly interpret, and the quotation marks group the parts of the filename into a single string for the Command program to understand.

This command tells MySQL to log you in as user *root*, without a password. You will now be logged into MySQL and can start entering commands. So, to be sure everything is working as it should be, enter the following—the results should be similar to Figure 8-1:

```
SHOW databases;
```

If this has not worked and you get an error such as "Can't connect to MySQL server on 'localhost,'" make sure that you have EasyPHP running in your System Tray and that MySQL is enabled. Otherwise, you are ready to move on to the next section, "Using the Command-Line Interface" on page 163.

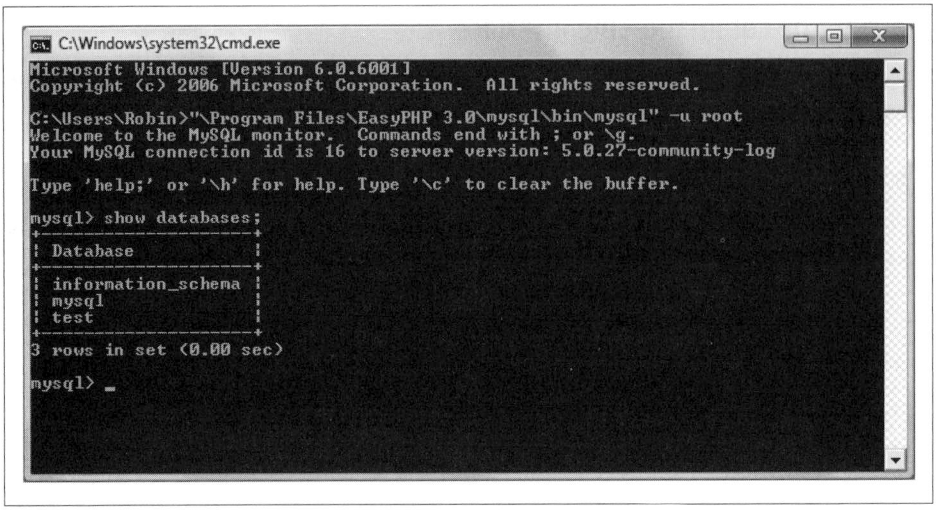

Figure 8-1. Accessing MySQL from a Windows Command prompt

Mac OS X users

To proceed with this chapter, you should have installed MAMP as detailed in Chapter 2. You should also have MAMP already running with the MySQL server started, as shown previously in Figure 2-10.

To enter the MySQL command-line interface, start the Terminal program (which should be available in Finder→Utilities). Then call up the MySQL program, which will have been installed in the directory */Applications/MAMP/Library/bin*.

By default, the initial MySQL user is *root* and it will have a password of *root*, too. So, to start the program, type the following:

```
/Applications/MAMP/Library/bin/mysql -u root -p
```

This command tells MySQL to log you in as user *root* and to request your password. When prompted, type **root**, press Return, and you should be set to go. To verify that all is well, type in the following—Figure 8-2 should be the result:

```
SHOW databases;
```

If you receive an error such as "Can't connect to local MySQL server through socket," you haven't started up MAMP, so locate it in your *Applications* folder, run it, redo the commands in Terminal, and everything should be fine.

You should now be ready to move on to the next section, "Using the Command-Line Interface" on page 163.

Linux users

On a system running a Unix-like operating system such as Linux, you will almost certainly already have PHP and MySQL installed and running, and you will be able to

```
 ⊖ ⊖ ⊖              Terminal — mysql — 80x24
Last login: Wed Nov 26 11:35:14 on ttyp1
Welcome to Darwin!
Unknown-00-0d-93-87-37-3d:~ robinnixon$ /Applications/MAMP/Library/bin/mysql -u
root -p
Enter password:
Welcome to the MySQL monitor.  Commands end with ; or \g.
Your MySQL connection id is 18 to server version: 5.0.19

Type 'help;' or '\h' for help. Type '\c' to clear the buffer.

mysql> show databases;
+--------------------+
| Database           |
+--------------------+
| information_schema |
| mysql              |
| test               |
+--------------------+
3 rows in set (0.00 sec)

mysql> █
```

Figure 8-2. Accessing MySQL from the Mac OS X Terminal program

enter the examples in the next section. But first you should type the following to log in to your MySQL system:

```
mysql -u root -p
```

This tells MySQL to log you in as the user *root* and to request your password. If you have a password, enter it; otherwise, just press Return.

Once you are logged in, type the following to test the program—you should see something like Figure 8-3 in response:

```
SHOW databases;
```

If this procedure fails at any point, please refer to the section "Installing a LAMP on Linux" on page 25 in Chapter 2 to ensure that you have MySQL properly installed. Otherwise, you should now be ready to move on to the next section, "Using the Command-Line Interface" on page 163.

MySQL on a remote server

If you are accessing MySQL on a remote server, you should Telnet (or preferably, for security, use SSH) into the remote machine, which will probably be a Linux/FreeBSD/Unix type of box. Once in there, things may be a little different for you, depending on how the system administrator has set the server up, especially if it's a shared hosting server. Therefore, you need to ensure that you have been given access to MySQL and

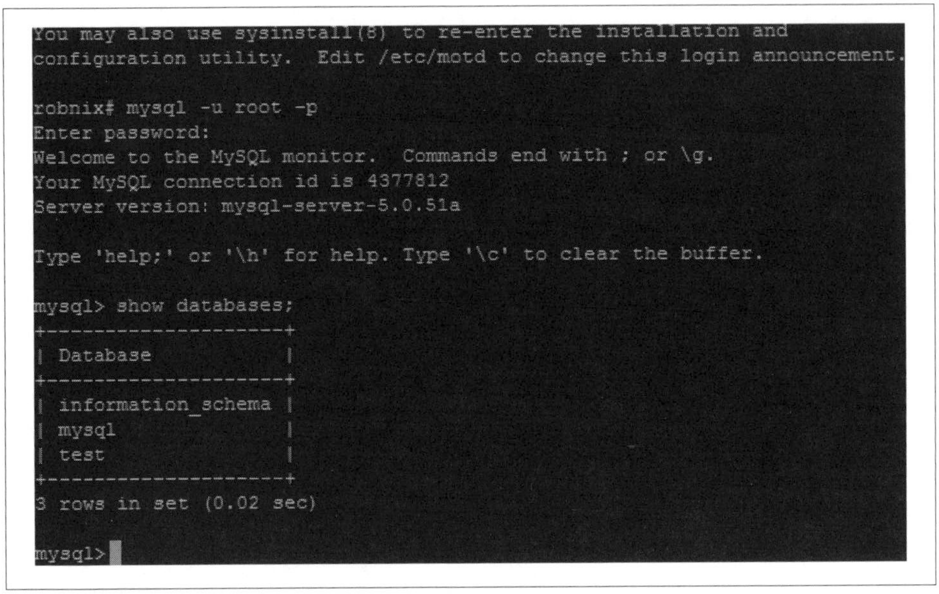

```
You may also use sysinstall(8) to re-enter the installation and
configuration utility.  Edit /etc/motd to change this login announcement.

robnix# mysql -u root -p
Enter password:
Welcome to the MySQL monitor.  Commands end with ; or \g.
Your MySQL connection id is 4377812
Server version: mysql-server-5.0.51a

Type 'help;' or '\h' for help. Type '\c' to clear the buffer.

mysql> show databases;
+--------------------+
| Database           |
+--------------------+
| information_schema |
| mysql              |
| test               |
+--------------------+
3 rows in set (0.02 sec)

mysql>
```

Figure 8-3. Accessing MySQL using Linux

that you have your username and password. Armed with these you can then type the following, where *username* is the name supplied:

```
mysql -u username -p
```

Enter your password when prompted. You can then try the following command, which should result in something like the screenshot in Figure 8-3:

```
SHOW databases;
```

There may be other databases already created and the *test* database may not be there.

Bear in mind also that system administrators have ultimate control over everything and that you can encounter some unexpected setups. For example, you may find that you are required to preface all database names that you create with a unique identifying string to ensure that you do not conflict with databases created by other users.

Therefore, if you have any problems, have a word with your sysadmin and he or she will get you sorted out. Just let the sysadmin know that you need a username and password. You should also ask for the ability to create new databases or, at a minimum, to have at least one database created for you ready to use. You can then create all the tables you require within that database.

Using the Command-Line Interface

From here on out, it makes no difference whether you are using Windows, Mac OS X, or Linux to access MySQL directly, as all the commands used (and errors you may receive) are identical.

The semicolon

Let's start with the basics. Did you notice the semicolon (;) at the end of the SHOW databases; command that you typed? The semicolon is used by MySQL to separate or end commands. If you forget to enter it, MySQL will issue a prompt and wait for you to do so. The required semicolon was made part of the syntax to let you enter multiple-line commands, which can be convenient, because some commands get quite long. It also allows you to issue more than one command at a time by placing a semicolon after each one. The interpreter gets them all in a batch when you press the Return key and executes them in order.

> It's very common to receive a MySQL prompt instead of the results of your command; it means that you forgot the final semicolon. Just enter the semicolon, press the Return key, and you'll get what you want.

There are six different prompts that MySQL may present you with (see Table 8-2), so you will always know where you are during a multiline input.

Table 8-2. MySQL's six command prompts

MySQL prompt	Meaning
mysql>	MySQL is ready and waiting for a command
->	Waiting for the next line of a command
'>	Waiting for the next line of a string started with a single quote
">	Waiting for the next line of a string started with a double quote
`>	Waiting for the next line of a string started with a back tick
/*>	Waiting for the next line of a comment started with /*

Canceling a command

If you are partway through entering a command and decide you don't wish to execute it after all, whatever you do don't press Ctrl-C! That will close the program. Instead, you can enter \c and press Return. Example 8-1 shows how to use it.

Example 8-1. Canceling a line of input

```
meaningless gibberish to mysql \c
```

When you type that line in, MySQL will ignore everything you typed and issue a new prompt. Without the \c, it would have displayed an error message. Be careful, though: if you have opened a string or comment, close it first before using the \c or MySQL will think the \c is just part of the string. Example 8-2 shows the right way to do this.

Example 8-2. Canceling input from inside a string

```
this is "meaningless gibberish to mysql" \c
```

Also note that using \c after a semicolon will not work, as it is then a new statement.

MySQL Commands

You've already seen the SHOW command, which lists tables, databases, and many other items. The commands you'll use most often are listed in Table 8-3.

Table 8-3. A selection of common MySQL commands (and/or shorthand forms where available)

Command	Parameter(s)	Meaning
ALTER	DATABASE, TABLE	Alter DATABASE or TABLE
BACKUP	TABLE	Back up TABLE
\c		Cancel input
CREATE	DATABASE, TABLE,	Create DATABASE or TABLE
DELETE	(expression with TABLE & ROW)	Delete ROW from TABLE
DESCRIBE	TABLE	Describe the TABLE'S columns
DROP	DATABASE, TABLE	Delete DATABASE or TABLE
EXIT (CTRL-C)		Exit
GRANT	(*user* details)	Change *user* privileges
HELP (\h, \?)	*item*	Display help on *item*
INSERT	(expression with *data*)	Insert *data*
LOCK	TABLE(s)	Lock TABLE(s)
QUIT (\q)		Same as EXIT
RENAME	TABLE	Rename TABLE
SHOW	(too many *items* to list)	List *item*'s details
SOURCE	*filename*	Execute commands from *filename*
STATUS (\s)		Display current status
TRUNCATE	TABLE	Empty TABLE
UNLOCK	table(s)	Unlock TABLE(s)
UPDATE	(expression with *data*)	Update an existing record
USE	*database*	Use *database*

I'll cover most of these as we proceed, but first, you need to remember a couple of points about MySQL commands:

- SQL commands and keywords are case-insensitive. `CREATE`, `create`, and `CrEaTe` all mean the same thing. However, for the sake of clarity, the recommended style is to use uppercase.

- Table names are case-sensitive on Linux and Mac OS X, but case-insensitive on Windows. So for portability purposes, you should always choose a case and stick to it. The recommended style is to use lowercase for tables.

Creating a database

If you are working on a remote server and have only a single user account and access to a single database that was created for you, move on to the section "Creating a table" on page 166. Otherwise, get the ball rolling by issuing the following command to create a new database called *publications*:

```
CREATE DATABASE publications;
```

A successful command will return a message that doesn't mean much yet—"Query OK, 1 row affected (0.00 sec)"—but will make sense soon. Now that you've created the database, you want to work with it, so issue:

```
USE publications;
```

You should now see the message `Database changed` and will then be set to proceed with the following examples.

Creating users

Now that you've seen how easy it is to use MySQL, and created your first database, it's time to look at how you create users, as you probably won't want to grant your PHP scripts root access to MySQL—it could cause a real headache should you get hacked.

To create a user, issue the `GRANT` command, which takes the following form (don't type this in—it's not an actual working command):

```
GRANT PRIVILEGES ON database.object TO 'username@hostname'
    IDENTIFIED BY 'password';
```

This should be pretty straightforward, with the possible exception of the `database.object` part. What this refers to is the database itself and the objects it contains, such as tables (see Table 8-4).

Table 8-4. Example parameters for the GRANT command

Arguments	Meaning
.	All databases and all their objects
database.*	Only the database called *database* and all its objects
database.object	Only the database called *database* and its object called *object*

So let's create a user who can access just the new `publications` database and all its objects, by entering the following (replacing the username `jim` and the password `mypasswd` with ones of your choosing):

```
GRANT ALL ON publications.* TO 'jim' IDENTIFIED BY 'mypasswd';
```

What this does is allow the user `jim@localhost` full access to the publications database using the password `mypasswd`. You can test whether this step has worked by entering `quit` to exit and then rerunning MySQL the way you did before, but instead of entering `-u root -p`, type `-u jim -p`, or whatever the username is that you created. See Table 8-5 for the correct command for your operating system. Modify it as necessary if the `mysql` client is installed in a different directory on your system.

Table 8-5. Starting MySQL and logging in as jim@localhost

OS	Example command
Windows	`"\Program Files\EasyPHP 3.0\mysql\bin\mysql" -u jim -p`
Mac OS X	`/Applications/MAMP/Library/bin/mysql -u jim -p`
Linux	`mysql -u jim -p`

All you now have to do is enter your password when prompted and you will be logged in. By the way, if you prefer, you can place your password immediately following the `-p` (without any spaces) to avoid having to enter it when prompted. But this is considered a poor practice, because if other people are logged in to your system, there may be ways for them to look at the command you entered and find out your password.

 You can grant only privileges that you already have, and you must also have the privilege to issue `GRANT` commands. There are a whole range of privileges you can choose to grant if you are not granting all privileges. For further details, please visit the following site, which also covers the `REVOKE` command, which can remove privileges once granted: *http://dev .mysql.com/doc/refman/5.0/en/grant.html*.

You also need to be aware that if you create a new user but do not specify an `IDENTIFIED BY` clause, the user will have no password, a situation that is very insecure and should be avoided.

Creating a table

At this point, you should now be logged into MySQL with `ALL` privileges granted for the database *publications* (or a database that was created for you)—you're ready to create your first table. So make sure that database is in use by typing the following (replacing *publications* with the name of your database if it is different):

```
USE publications;
```

Now enter the commands in Example 8-3 one line at a time:

Example 8-3. Creating a table called classics

```
CREATE TABLE classics (
 author VARCHAR(128),
 title VARCHAR(128),
 type VARCHAR(16),
 year CHAR(4)) ENGINE MyISAM;
```

 You could also issue this command on a single line like this:

```
CREATE TABLE classics (author VARCHAR(128), title
    VARCHAR(128), type VARCHAR(16), year CHAR(4)) ENGINE MyISAM;
```

but MySQL commands can be long and complicated, so I recommend a single line at a time until you are comfortable with longer ones.

MySQL should then issue the response "Query OK, 0 rows affected," along with how long it took to execute the command. If you see an error message instead, check your syntax carefully. Every parenthesis and comma counts, and typing errors are easy to make. In case you are wondering, the `ENGINE MyISAM` tells MySQL the type of database engine to use for this table.

To check whether your new table has been created, type:

```
DESCRIBE classics;
```

All being well, you will see the sequence of commands and responses shown in Example 8-4, where you should particularly note the table format displayed.

Example 8-4. A MySQL session: Creating and checking a new table

```
mysql> USE publications;
Database changed
mysql> CREATE TABLE classics (
    ->    author VARCHAR(128),
    ->    title VARCHAR(128),
    ->    type VARCHAR(16),
    ->    year CHAR(4)) ENGINE MyISAM;
Query OK, 0 rows affected (0.03 sec)

mysql> DESCRIBE classics;
+--------+--------------+------+-----+---------+-------+
| Field  | Type         | Null | Key | Default | Extra |
+--------+--------------+------+-----+---------+-------+
| author | varchar(128) | YES  |     | NULL    |       |
| title  | varchar(128) | YES  |     | NULL    |       |
| type   | varchar(16)  | YES  |     | NULL    |       |
| year   | char(4)      | YES  |     | NULL    |       |
+--------+--------------+------+-----+---------+-------+
4 rows in set (0.00 sec)
```

The DESCRIBE command is an invaluable debugging aid when you need to ensure that you have correctly created a MySQL table. You can also use it to remind yourself about a table's field or column names and the types of data in each one. Let's look at each of the headings in detail:

Field
> The name of each field or column within a table.

Type
> The type of data being stored in the field.

Null
> Whether a field is allowed to contain a value of NULL.

Key
> MySQL supports *keys* or *indexes*, which are quick ways to look up and search for data. The Key heading shows what type of key (if any) has been applied.

Default
> The default value that will be assigned to the field if no value is specified when a new row is created.

Extra
> Additional information, such as whether a field is set to auto-increment.

Data Types

In Example 8-3, you may have noticed that three of the table's fields were given the data type of VARCHAR, and one was given the type CHAR. The term VARCHAR stands for *VARiable length CHARacter string* and the command takes a numeric value that tells MySQL the maximum length allowed to a string stored in this field.

This data type is very useful, as MySQL can then plan the size of databases and perform lookups and searches more easily. The downside is that if you ever attempt to assign a string value longer than the length allowed, it will be truncated to the maximum length declared in the table definition.

The year field, however, has more predictable values, so instead of VARCHAR we use the more efficient CHAR(4) data type. The parameter of 4 allows for four bytes of data, supporting all years from –999 to 9999. You could, of course, just store two-digit values for the year, but if your data is going to still be needed in the following century, or may otherwise wrap around, it will have to be sanitized first—much like the "millennium bug" that would have caused dates beginning on January 1, 2000, to be treated as 1900 on many of the world's biggest computer installations.

The reason I didn't use the YEAR data type in the *classics* table is because it supports only the years 0000 and 1901 through 2155. This is because MySQL stores the year in a single byte for reasons of efficiency, but it also means that only 256 years are available, and the publication years of the titles in the *classics* table are well before this.

Both CHAR and VARCHAR accept text strings and impose a limit on the size of the field. The difference is that every string in a CHAR field has the specified size. If you put in a smaller string, it is padded with spaces. A VARCHAR field does not pad the text; it lets the size of the field vary to fit the text that is inserted. But VARCHAR requires a small amount of overhead to keep track of the size of each value. So CHAR is slightly more efficient if the sizes are similar in all records, whereas VARCHAR is more efficient if sizes can vary a lot and get large. In addition, the overhead causes access to VARCHAR data to be slightly slower than to CHAR data.

The CHAR data type

Table 8-6 lists the CHAR data types. All these types offer a parameter that sets the maximum (or exact) length of the string allowed in the field. As the table shows, each type also has a built-in maximum.

Table 8-6. MySQL's CHAR data types

Data type	Bytes used	Examples
CHAR(n)	Exactly n (<= 255)	CHAR(5) "Hello" uses 5 bytes
		CHAR(57) "New York" uses 57 bytes
VARCHAR(n)	Up to n (<= 65535)	VARCHAR(100) "Greetings" uses 9 bytes
		VARCHAR(7) "Morning" uses 7 bytes

The BINARY data type

The BINARY data type is used for storing strings of full bytes that do not have an associated character set. For example, you might use the BINARY data type to store a GIF image (see Table 8-7).

Table 8-7. MySQL's BINARY data types

Data type	Bytes used	Examples
BINARY(n) or BYTE(n)	Exactly n (<= 255)	As CHAR but contains binary data
VARBINARY(n)	Up to n (<= 65535)	As VARCHAR but contains binary data

The TEXT and VARCHAR data types

The differences between TEXT and VARCHAR are small:

- Prior to version 5.0.3, MySQL would remove leading and trailing spaces from VARCHAR fields.
- TEXT fields cannot have default values.
- MySQL indexes only the first n characters of a TEXT column (you specify n when you create the index).

What this means is that VARCHAR is the better and faster data type to use if you need to search the entire contents of a field. If you will never search more than a certain number of leading characters in a field, you should probably use a TEXT data type (see Table 8-8).

Table 8-8. MySQL's TEXT data types

Data type	Bytes used	Attributes
TINYTEXT(n)	Up to n (<= 255)	Treated as a string with a character set
TEXT(n)	Up to n (<= 65535)	Treated as a string with a character set
MEDIUMTEXT(n)	Up to n (<= 16777215)	Treated as a string with a character set
LONGTEXT(n)	Up to n (<= 4294967295)	Treated as a string with a character set

The BLOB data type

The term BLOB stands for *Binary Large OBject* and therefore, as you would think, the BLOB data type is most useful for binary data in excess of 65,536 bytes in size. The main other difference between the BLOB and BINARY data types is that BLOBs cannot have default values (see Table 8-9).

Table 8-9. MySQL's BLOB data types

Data type	Bytes used	Attributes
TINYBLOB(n)	Up to n (<= 255)	Treated as binary data—no character set
BLOB(n)	Up to n (<= 65535)	Treated as binary data—no character set
MEDIUMBLOB(n)	Up to n (<= 16777215)	Treated as binary data—no character set
LONGBLOB(n)	Up to n (<= 4294967295)	Treated as binary data—no character set

Numeric data types

MySQL supports various numeric data types from a single byte up to double-precision floating-point numbers. Although the most memory that a numeric field can use up is eight bytes, you are well advised to choose the smallest data type that will adequately handle the largest value you expect. Your databases will be small and quickly accessible.

Table 8-10 lists the numeric data types supported by MySQL and the ranges of values they can contain. In case you are not acquainted with the terms, a signed number is one with a possible range from a negative value, through zero, to a positive one, and an unsigned one has a value ranging from zero to a positive one. They can both hold the same number of values—just picture a signed number as being shifted halfway to the left so that half its values are negative and half are positive. Note that floating-point values (of any precision) may only be signed.

Table 8-10. MySQL's numeric data types

Data type	Bytes used	Minimum value (Signed/Unsigned)	Maximum value (Signed/Unsigned)
TINYINT	1	−128	127
		0	255
SMALLINT	2	−32768	32767
		0	65535
MEDIUMINT	3	−8388608	8388607
		0	16777215
INT or INTEGER	4	−2147483648	2147483647
		0	4294967295
BIGINT	8	−9223372036854775808	9223372036854775807
		0	18446744073709551615
FLOAT	4	−3.402823466E+38	3.402823466E+38
		(no unsigned)	(no unsigned)
DOUBLE or REAL	8	−1.7976931348623157E+308	1.7976931348623157E+308
		(no unsigned)	(no unsigned)

To specify whether a data type is signed or unsigned, use the UNSIGNED qualifier. The following example creates a table called *tablename* with a field in it called *fieldname* of the data type UNSIGNED INTEGER:

```
CREATE TABLE tablename (fieldname INT UNSIGNED);
```

When creating a numeric field, you can also pass an optional number as a parameter, like this:

```
CREATE TABLE tablename (fieldname INT(4));
```

But you must remember that, unlike BINARY and CHAR data types, this parameter does not indicate the number of bytes of storage to use. It may seem counterintuitive, but what the number actually represents is the display width of the data in the field when it is retrieved. It is commonly used with the ZEROFILL qualifier like this:

```
CREATE TABLE tablename (fieldname INT(4) ZEROFILL);
```

What this does is cause any numbers with a width of less than four characters to be padded with one or more zeros, sufficient to make the display width of the field four characters long. When a field is already of the specified width or greater no padding takes place.

DATE and TIME

The main remaining data types supported by MySQL relate to the date and time and can be seen in Table 8-11.

Table 8-11. MySQL's DATE and TIME data types

Data type	Time/date format
DATETIME	'0000-00-00 00:00:00'
DATE	'0000-00-00'
TIMESTAMP	'0000-00-00 00:00:00'
TIME	'00:00:00'
YEAR	0000 (Only years 0000 and 1901–2155)

The DATETIME and TIMESTAMP data types display the same way. The main difference is that TIMESTAMP has a very narrow range (from the years 1970 through 2037), whereas DATETIME will hold just about any date you're likely to specify, unless you're interested in ancient history or science fiction.

TIMESTAMP is useful, however, because you can let MySQL set the value for you. If you don't specify the value when adding a row, the current time is automatically inserted. You can also have MySQL update a TIMESTAMP column each time you change a row.

The AUTO_INCREMENT data type

Sometimes you need to ensure that every row in your database is guaranteed to be unique. You could do this in your program by carefully checking the data you enter and making sure that there is at least one value that differs in any two rows, but this approach is error-prone and works only in certain circumstances. In the *classics* table, for instance, an author may appear multiple times. Likewise, the year of publication will also be frequently duplicated, and so on. It would be hard to guarantee that you have no duplicate rows.

The general solution is to use an extra column just for this purpose. In a while, we'll look at using a publication's ISBN (International Standard Book Number), but first I'd like to introduce the AUTO_INCREMENT data type.

As its name implies, a column given this data type will set the value of its contents to that of the column entry in the previously inserted row, plus 1. Example 8-5 shows how to add a new column called *id* to the table *classics* with auto-incrementing:

Example 8-5. Adding the auto-incrementing column id

```
ALTER TABLE classics ADD id INT UNSIGNED NOT NULL AUTO_INCREMENT KEY;
```

This is your introduction to the `ALTER` command, which is very similar to `CREATE`. `ALTER` operates on an existing table, and can add, change, or delete columns. Our example adds a column named *id* with the following characteristics:

`INT UNSIGNED`
Makes the column take an integer large enough for you to store more than 4 billion records in the table.

`NOT NULL`
Ensures that every column has a value. Many programmers use `NULL` in a field to indicate that the field doesn't have any value. But that would allow duplicates, which would violate the whole reason for this column's existence. So we disallow `NULL` values.

`AUTO_INCREMENT`
Causes MySQL to set a unique value for this column in every row, as described earlier. We don't really have control over the value that this column will take in each row, but we don't care: all we care about is that we are guaranteed a unique value.

`KEY`
An auto-increment column is useful as a key, because you will tend to search for rows based on this column. This will be explained in the section "Indexes" on page 177.

Each entry in the column *id* will now have a unique number, with the first starting at 1 and the others counting upward from there. And whenever a new row is inserted, its *id* column will automatically be given the next number in sequence.

Rather than applying the column retroactively, you could have included it by issuing the `CREATE` command in slightly different format. In that case, the command in Example 8-3 would be replaced with Example 8-6. Check the final line in particular.

Example 8-6. Adding the auto-incrementing id column at table creation

```
CREATE TABLE classics (
 author VARCHAR(128),
 title VARCHAR(128),
 type VARCHAR(16),
 year CHAR(4),
 id INT UNSIGNED NOT NULL AUTO_INCREMENT KEY) ENGINE MyISAM;
```

If you wish to check whether the column has been added, use the following command to view the table's columns and data types:

```
DESCRIBE classics;
```

Now that we've finished with it, the *id* column is no longer needed, so if you created it using Example 8-5, you should now remove the column using the command in Example 8-7.

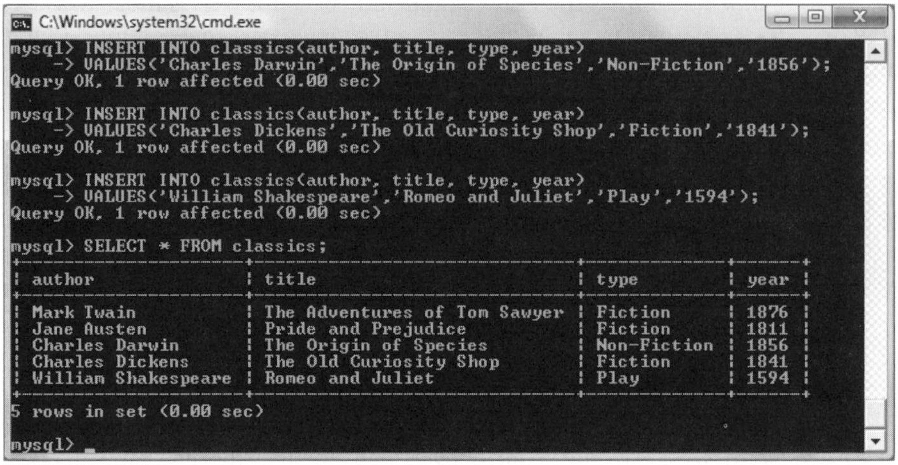

Figure 8-4. Populating the classics table and viewing its contents

Example 8-7. Removing id column

```
ALTER TABLE classics DROP id;
```

Adding data to a table

To add data to a table, use the `INSERT` command. Let's see this in action by populating the table *classics* with the data from Table 8-1, using one form of the `INSERT` command repeatedly (Example 8-8).

Example 8-8. Populating the classics table

```
INSERT INTO classics(author, title, type, year)
 VALUES('Mark Twain','The Adventures of Tom Sawyer','Fiction','1876');
INSERT INTO classics(author, title, type, year)
 VALUES('Jane Austen','Pride and Prejudice','Fiction','1811');
INSERT INTO classics(author, title, type, year)
 VALUES('Charles Darwin','The Origin of Species','Non-Fiction','1856');
INSERT INTO classics(author, title, type, year)
 VALUES('Charles Dickens','The Old Curiosity Shop','Fiction','1841');
INSERT INTO classics(author, title, type, year)
 VALUES('William Shakespeare','Romeo and Juliet','Play','1594');
```

After every second line, you should see a "Query OK" message. Once all lines have been entered, type the following command, which will display the table's contents. The result should look like Figure 8-4:

```
SELECT * FROM classics;
```

Don't worry about the `SELECT` command for now—we'll come to it in the upcoming section "Querying a MySQL Database" on page 183. Suffice it to say that as typed, it will display all the data you just entered.

Let's go back and look at how we used the INSERT command. The first part, INSERT INTO classics, tells MySQL where to insert the following data. Then, within parentheses, the four column names are listed—*author*, *title*, *type*, and *year*—all separated by commas. This tells MySQL that these are the fields into which the data is to be inserted.

The second line of each INSERT command contains the keyword VALUES followed by four strings within parentheses, and separated by commas. This supplies MySQL with the four values to be inserted into the four columns previously specified. (As always, my choice of where to break the lines was arbitrary.)

Each item of data will be inserted into the corresponding column, in a one-to-one correspondence. If you accidentally listed the columns in a different order from the data, the data would go into the wrong columns. And the number of columns must match the number of data items.

Renaming a table

Renaming a table, like any other change to the structure or meta-information about a table, is achieved via the ALTER command. So, for example, to change the name of table *classics* to *pre1900*, use the following command:

```
ALTER TABLE classics RENAME pre1900;
```

If you tried that command, you should rename the table back again by entering the following, so that later examples in this chapter will work as printed:

```
ALTER TABLE pre1900 RENAME classics;
```

Changing the data type of a column

Changing a column's data type also makes use of the ALTER command, this time in conjunction with the MODIFY keyword. So to change the data type of column *year* from CHAR(4) to SMALLINT (which requires only two bytes of storage and so will save disk space), enter the following:

```
ALTER TABLE classics MODIFY year SMALLINT;
```

When you do this, if the conversion of data type makes sense to MySQL, it will automatically change the data while keeping the meaning. In this case, it will change each string to a comparable integer, and so on, as the string is recognizable as referring to an integer.

Adding a new column

Let's suppose that you have created a table and populated it with plenty of data, only to discover you need an additional column. Not to worry. Here's how to add the new column *pages*, which will be used to store the number of pages in a publication:

```
ALTER TABLE classics ADD pages SMALLINT UNSIGNED;
```

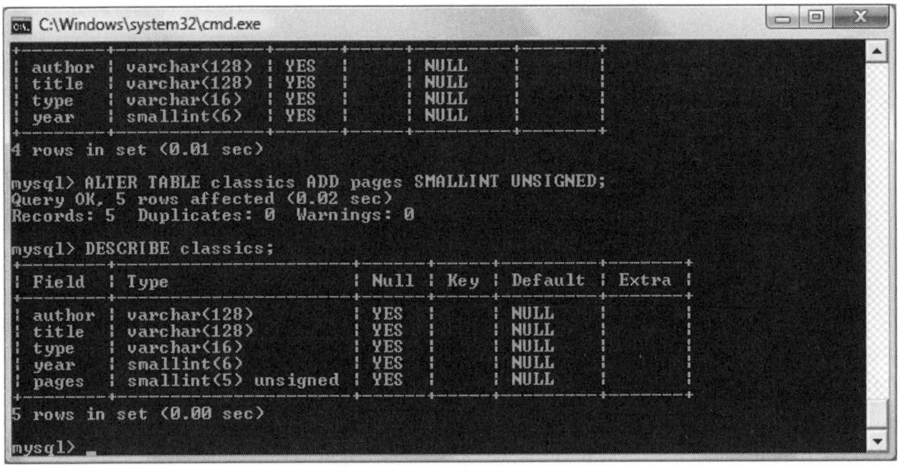

Figure 8-5. Adding the new pages column and viewing the table

This adds the new column with the name *pages* using the `UNSIGNED SMALLINT` data type, sufficient to hold a value of up to 65,535—hopefully that's more than enough for any book ever published!

And, if you ask MySQL to describe the updated table using the `DESCRIBE` command, as follows, you will see the change has been made (see Figure 8-5):

```
DESCRIBE classics;
```

Renaming a column

Looking again at Figure 8-5, you may decide that having a column named *type* can be confusing, because that is the name used by MySQL to identify data types. Again, no problem—let's change its name to *category*, like this:

```
ALTER TABLE classics CHANGE type category VARCHAR(16);
```

Note the addition of `VARCHAR(16)` on the end of this command. That's because the `CHANGE` keyword requires the data type to be specified, even if you don't intend to change it, and `VARCHAR(16)` was the data type specified when that column was initially created as *type*.

Removing a column

Actually, upon reflection, maybe the page count column *pages* isn't actually all that useful for this particular database, so here's how to remove that column using the `DROP` keyword:

```
ALTER TABLE classics DROP pages;
```

```
C:\Windows\system32\cmd.exe

1 row in set (0.00 sec)

mysql> CREATE TABLE disposable(trash INT);
Query OK, 0 rows affected (0.01 sec)

mysql> DESCRIBE disposable;
+-------+---------+------+-----+---------+-------+
| Field | Type    | Null | Key | Default | Extra |
+-------+---------+------+-----+---------+-------+
| trash | int(11) | YES  |     | NULL    |       |
+-------+---------+------+-----+---------+-------+
1 row in set (0.01 sec)

mysql> DROP TABLE disposable;
Query OK, 0 rows affected (0.00 sec)

mysql> SHOW tables;
+----------------------+
| Tables_in_publications |
+----------------------+
| classics             |
+----------------------+
1 row in set (0.00 sec)

mysql>
```

Figure 8-6. Creating, viewing, and deleting a table

 Remember that DROP is irreversible and you should always use it with caution, because you could delete entire tables (and even databases) with it if you are not careful!

Deleting a table

Deleting a table is very easy indeed. But, because I don't want you to have to reenter all the data for the *classics* table, let's quickly create a new table, verify its existence, and then delete it by typing in the commands in Example 8-9. The result of these four commands should look like Figure 8-6.

Example 8-9. Creating, viewing, and deleting a table

```
CREATE TABLE disposable(trash INT);
DESCRIBE disposable;
DROP TABLE disposable;
SHOW tables;
```

Indexes

As things stand, the table *classics* works and can be searched without problem by MySQL—until it grows to more than a couple hundred rows, that is. At that point, database accesses will get slower and slower with every new row added, because MySQL has to search through every row whenever a query is issued. This is like searching through every book in a library whenever you need to look something up.

Of course, you don't have to search libraries that way, because they have either a card index system or, most likely, a database of their own. And the same goes for MySQL, because at the expense of a slight overhead in memory and disk space, you can create a "card index" for a table that MySQL will use to conduct lightning-fast searches.

Creating an Index

The way to achieve fast searches is to add an *index*, either when creating a table or at any time afterward. But the decision is not so simple. For example, there are different index types, such as `INDEX`, `PRIMARY KEY`, and `FULLTEXT`. Also you must decide which columns require an index, a judgment that requires you to predict whether you will be searching any of the data in that column. Indexes can also get complicated, because you can combine multiple columns in one index. And even when you've decided that, you still have the option of reducing index size by limiting the amount of each column to be indexed.

If we imagine the searches that may be made on the *classics* table, it becomes apparent that all of the columns may need to be searched. However, if the *pages* column created in the earlier section ("Adding a new column" on page 175) had not been deleted, it would probably not have needed an index, as most people would be unlikely to search for books by the number of pages they have. Anyway, go ahead and add an index to each of the columns, using the commands in Example 8-10.

Example 8-10. Adding indexes to the classics table

```
ALTER TABLE classics ADD INDEX(author(20));
ALTER TABLE classics ADD INDEX(title(20));
ALTER TABLE classics ADD INDEX(category(4));
ALTER TABLE classics ADD INDEX(year);
DESCRIBE classics;
```

The first two commands create indexes on both the *author* and *title* columns, limiting each index to only the first 20 characters. For instance, when MySQL indexes the following title:

```
The Adventures of Tom Sawyer
```

It will actually store in the index only the first 20 characters:

```
The Adventures of To
```

This is done to minimize the size of the index, and to optimize database access speed. I chose 20 because it's likely to be sufficient to ensure uniqueness for most strings in these columns. If MySQL finds two indexes with the same contents, it will have to waste time going to the table itself and checking the column that was indexed to find out which rows really matched.

With the *category* column, currently only the first character is required to identify a string as unique (F for Fiction, N for Non-Fiction, and P for Play), but I chose an index of four characters to allow for future category types that may be unique only after four characters. You can also reindex this column later, when you have a more complete set

---

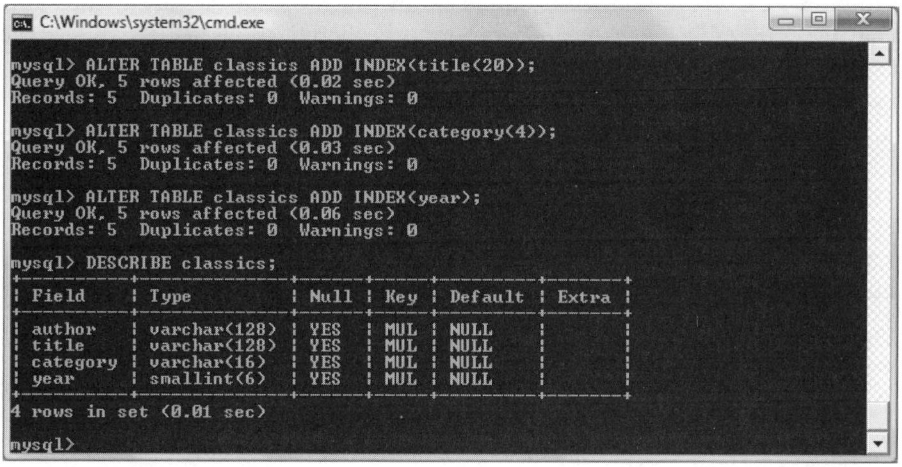

Figure 8-7. Adding indexes to the classics table

of categories. And finally, I set no limit to the *year* column's index, because it's an integer, not a string.

The results of issuing these commands (and a DESCRIBE command to confirm that they worked) can be seen in Figure 8-7, which shows the key *MUL* for each column. This key means that multiple occurrences of a value may occur within that column, which is exactly what we want, as authors may appear many times, the same book title could be used by multiple authors, and so on.

Using CREATE INDEX

An alternative to using ALTER TABLE to add an index is to use the CREATE INDEX command. They are equivalent, except that CREATE INDEX cannot be used to create a PRIMARY KEY (see the section "Primary keys" on page 180). The format of this command can be seen in the second line of Example 8-11.

Example 8-11. These two commands are equivalent

```
ALTER TABLE classics ADD INDEX(author(20));
CREATE INDEX author ON classics (author(20));
```

Adding indexes when creating tables

You don't have to wait until after creating a table to add indexes. In fact, doing so can be time-consuming, as adding an index to a large table can take a very long time. Therefore, let's look at a command that creates the table *classics* with indexes already in place.

Example 8-12 is a reworking of Example 8-3 in which the indexes are created at the same time as the table. Note that to incorporate the modifications made in this chapter, this version uses the new column name *category* instead of *type* and sets the data type of *year* to SMALLINT instead of CHAR(4). If you want to try it out without first deleting your current *classics* table, change the word *classics* in line one to something else like *classics1*, then drop *classics1* after you have finished with it.

Example 8-12. Creating the table classics with indexes

```
CREATE TABLE classics (
  author VARCHAR(128),
  title VARCHAR(128),
  category VARCHAR(16),
  year SMALLINT,
  INDEX(author(20)),
  INDEX(title(20)),
  INDEX(category(4)),
  INDEX(year)) ENGINE MyISAM;
```

Primary keys

So far you've created the table *classics* and ensured that MySQL can search it quickly by adding indexes, but there's still something missing. All the publications in the table can be searched, but there is no single unique key for each publication to enable instant accessing of a row. The importance of having a key with a unique value for each row will come up when we start to combine data from different tables.

The earlier section "The AUTO_INCREMENT data type" on page 172 briefly introduced the idea of a primary key when creating the auto incrementing column *id*, which could have been used as a primary key for this table. However, I wanted to reserve that task for a more appropriate column: the internationally recognized ISBN number.

So let's go ahead and create a new column for this key. Now, bearing in mind that ISBN numbers are 13 characters long, you might think that the following command would do the job:

```
    ALTER TABLE classics ADD isbn CHAR(13) PRIMARY KEY;
```

But it doesn't. If you try it, you'll get the error "Duplicate entry" for key 1. The reason is that the table is already populated with some data and this command is trying to add a column with the value NULL to each row, which is not allowed, as all columns using a primary key index must be unique. However, if there were no data already in the table, this command would work just fine, as would adding the primary key index upon table creation.

In our current situation, we have to be a bit sneaky and create the new column without an index, populate it with data, and then add the index retrospectively using the commands in Example 8-13. Luckily, each of the years is unique in the current set of data, so we can use the *year* column to identify each row for updating. Note that this example

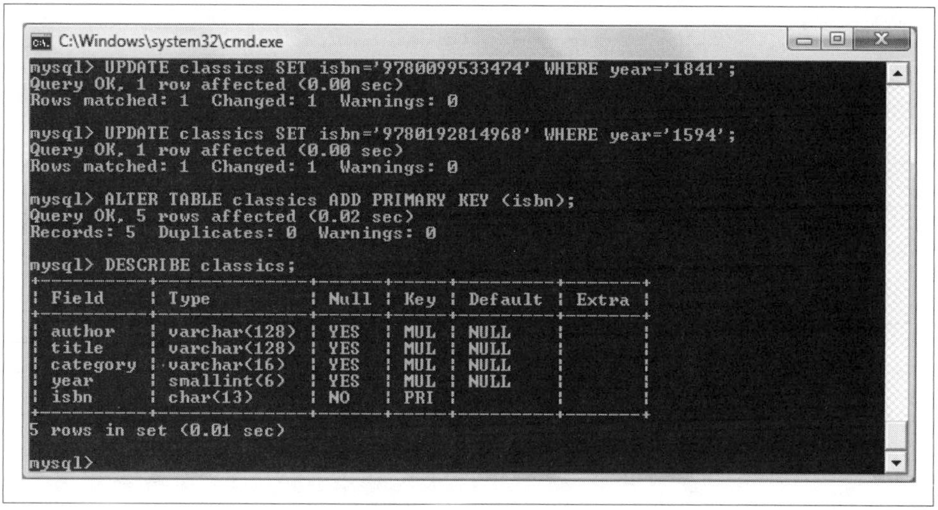

Figure 8-8. Retrospectively adding a primary key to the classics table

uses the UPDATE and WHERE keywords, which are explained in more detail in the upcoming section "Querying a MySQL Database" on page 183.

Example 8-13. Populating the isbn column with data and using a primary key

```
ALTER TABLE classics ADD isbn CHAR(13);
UPDATE classics SET isbn='9781598184891' WHERE year='1876';
UPDATE classics SET isbn='9780582506206' WHERE year='1811';
UPDATE classics SET isbn='9780517123201' WHERE year='1856';
UPDATE classics SET isbn='9780099533474' WHERE year='1841';
UPDATE classics SET isbn='9780192814968' WHERE year='1594';
ALTER TABLE classics ADD PRIMARY KEY(isbn);
DESCRIBE classics;
```

Once you have typed in these commands, the results should look like the screenshot in Figure 8-8. Note that the keywords PRIMARY KEY replace the keyword INDEX in the ALTER TABLE syntax (compare Examples 8-10 and 8-13).

To have created a primary key when the table *classics* was created, you could have used the commands in Example 8-14. Again, rename *classics* in line 1 to something else if you wish to try this example for yourself, and then delete the test table afterward.

Example 8-14. Creating the classics table with indexes

```
CREATE TABLE classics (
 author VARCHAR(128),
 title VARCHAR(128),
 category VARCHAR(16),
 year SMALLINT,
 isbn CHAR(13),
 INDEX(author(20)),
 INDEX(title(20)),
 INDEX(category(4)),
```

```
INDEX(year),
PRIMARY KEY (isbn)) ENGINE MyISAM;
```

Creating a FULLTEXT index

Unlike a regular index, MySQL's `FULLTEXT` allows super-fast searches of entire columns of text. What it does is it stores every word in every data string in a special index that you can search using "natural language," in a similar manner to using a search engine.

 Actually, it's not strictly true that MySQL stores *all* the words in a `FULLTEXT` index, because it has a built-in list of more than 500 words that it chooses to ignore because they are so common that they aren't very helpful when searching anyway. This list, called *stopwords*, includes *the*, *as*, *is*, *of*, and so on. The list helps MySQL run much more quickly when performing a `FULLTEXT` search and keeps database sizes down. Appendix C contains the full list of stopwords.

Here are some things that you should know about `FULLTEXT` indexes:

- `FULLTEXT` indexes can be used only with MyISAM tables, the type used by MySQL's default storage engine (MySQL supports at least 10 different storage engines). If you need to convert a table to MyISAM, you can usually use the MySQL command: `ALTER TABLE tablename ENGINE = MyISAM;`.
- `FULLTEXT` indexes can be created for `CHAR`, `VARCHAR`, and `TEXT` columns only.
- A `FULLTEXT` index definition can be given in the `CREATE TABLE` statement when a table is created, or added later using `ALTER TABLE` (or `CREATE INDEX`).
- For large data sets, it is *much* faster to load your data into a table that has no `FULLTEXT` index and then create the index than to load data into a table that has an existing `FULLTEXT` index.

To create a `FULLTEXT` index, apply it to one or more records as in Example 8-15, which adds a `FULLTEXT` index to the pair of columns *author* and *title* in the table *classics* (this index is in addition to the ones already created and does not affect them).

Example 8-15. Adding a FULLTEXT index to the classics table

```
ALTER TABLE classics ADD FULLTEXT(author,title);
```

You can now perform `FULLTEXT` searches across this pair of columns. This feature could really come into its own if you could now add the entire text of these publications to the database (particularly as they're out of copyright protection) and they would be fully searchable. See the section "MATCH...AGAINST" on page 188 for a description of searches using `FULLTEXT`.

If you find that MySQL is running slower than you think it should be when accessing your database, the problem is usually related to your indexes. Either you don't have an index where you need one, or the indexes are not optimally designed. Tweaking a table's indexes will often solve such a problem. Performance is beyond the scope of this book, but in Chapter 9 I'll give you a few tips so you know what to look for.

Querying a MySQL Database

So far we've created a MySQL database and tables, populated them with data, and added indexes to make them fast to search. Now it's time to look at how these searches are performed, and the various commands and qualifiers available.

SELECT

As you saw in Figure 8-4, the SELECT command is used to extract data from a table. In that section, I used its simplest form to select all data and display it—something you will never want to do on anything but the smallest tables, because all the data will scroll by at an unreadable pace. Let's now examine SELECT in more detail.

The basic syntax is:

```
SELECT something FROM tablename;
```

The *something* can be an * (asterisk) as you saw before, which means "every column," or you can choose to select only certain columns. For instance, Example 8-16 shows how to select just the *author* and *title* and just the *title* and *isbn*. The result of typing these commands can be seen in Figure 8-9.

Example 8-16. Two different SELECT statements

```
SELECT author,title FROM classics;
SELECT title,isbn FROM classics;
```

SELECT COUNT

Another replacement for the *something* parameter is COUNT, which can be used in many ways. In Example 8-17, it displays the number of rows in the table by passing * as a parameter, which means "all rows." As you'd expect, the result returned is 5, as there are five publications in the table.

Example 8-17. Counting rows

```
SELECT COUNT(*) FROM classics;
```

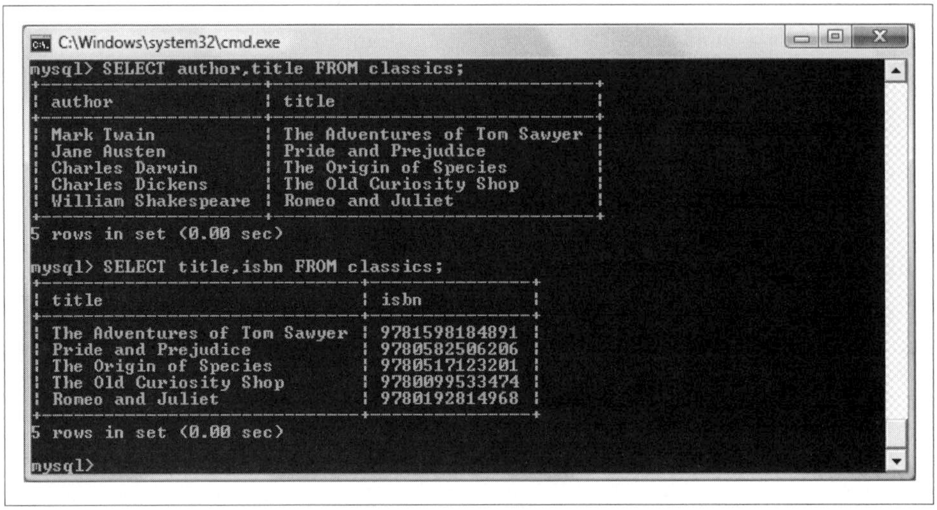

Figure 8-9. The output from two different SELECT statements

SELECT DISTINCT

This qualifier (and its synonym `DISTINCTROW`) allows you to weed out multiple entries when they contain the same data. For instance, suppose that you want a list of all authors in the table. If you select just the *author* column from a table containing multiple books by the same author, you'll normally see a long list with the same author names over and over. But by adding the `DISTINCT` keyword, you can show each author just once. So let's test that out by adding another row that repeats one of our existing authors (Example 8-18).

Example 8-18. Duplicating data

```
INSERT INTO classics(author, title, category, year, isbn)
VALUES('Charles Dickens','Little Dorrit','Fiction','1857','9780141439969');
```

Now that Charles Dickens appears twice in the table, we can compare the results of using `SELECT` with and without the `DISTINCT` qualifier. Example 8-19 and Figure 8-10 show that the simple `SELECT` lists Dickens twice, and the command with the `DISTINCT` qualifier shows him only once.

Example 8-19. With and without the DISTINCT qualifier

```
SELECT author FROM classics;
SELECT DISTINCT author FROM classics;
```

DELETE

When you need to remove a row from a table, use the `DELETE` command. Its syntax is similar to the `SELECT` command and allows you to narrow down the exact row or rows to delete using qualifiers such as `WHERE` and `LIMIT`.

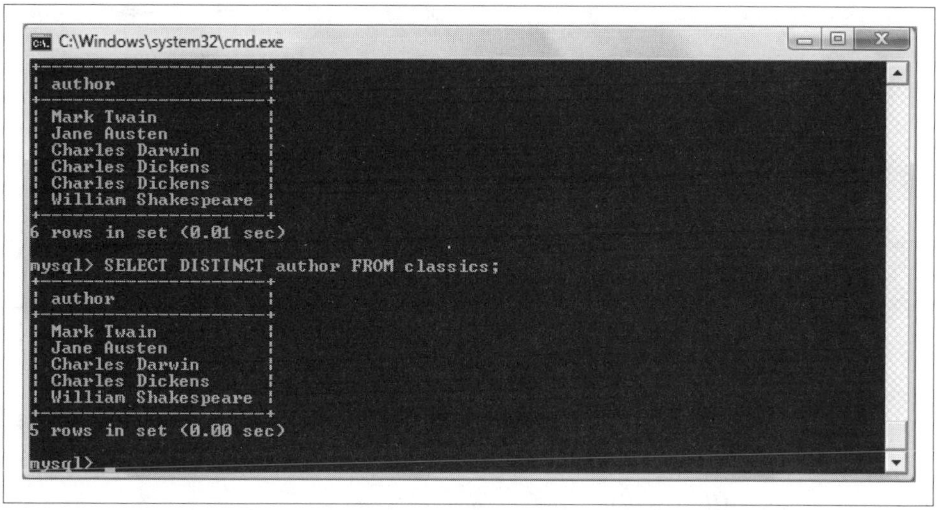

Figure 8-10. Selecting data with and without DISTINCT

Now that you've seen the effects of the DISTINCT qualifier, if you typed in Example 8-18, you should remove *Little Dorrit* by entering the commands in Example 8-20.

Example 8-20. Removing the new entry

```
DELETE FROM classics WHERE title='Little Dorrit';
```

This example issues a DELETE command for all rows whose *title* column contains the string 'Little Dorrit'.

The WHERE keyword is very powerful, and important to enter correctly; an error could lead a command to the wrong rows (or have no effect in cases where nothing matches the WHERE clause). So now we'll spend some time on that clause, which is the heart and soul of SQL.

WHERE

The WHERE keyword enables you to narrow down queries by returning only those *where* a certain expression is true. Example 8-20 returns only the rows where the column exactly matches the string 'Little Dorrit', using the equality operator =. Example 8-21 shows a couple more examples of using WHERE with =.

Example 8-21. Using the WHERE keyword

```
SELECT author,title FROM classics WHERE author="Mark Twain";
SELECT author,title FROM classics WHERE isbn="9781598184891 ";
```

Given our current table, the two commands in Example 8-21 display the same results. But we could easily add more books by Mark Twain, in which case the first line would display all titles he wrote and the second line would continue (because we know the

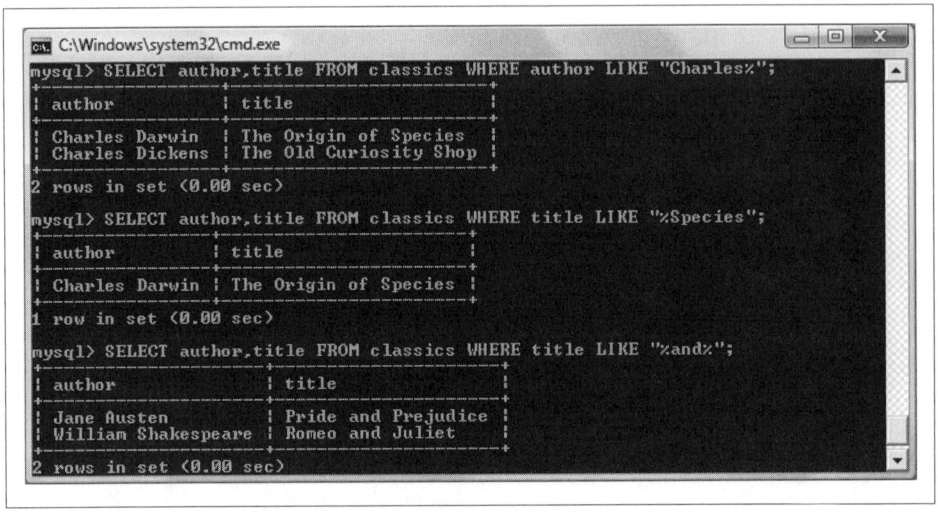

Figure 8-11. Using WHERE with the LIKE qualifier

ISBN is unique) to display *The Adventures of Tom Sawyer*. In other words, searches using a unique key are more predictable, and you'll see further evidence later of the value of unique and primary keys.

You can also do pattern matching for your searches using the `LIKE` qualifier, which allows searches on parts of strings. This qualifier should be used with a % character before or after some text. When placed before a keyword, % means "anything before" and after a keyword it means "anything after." Example 8-22 performs three different queries, one for the start of a string, one for the end, and one for anywhere in a string. You can see the results of these commands in Figure 8-11.

Example 8-22. Using the LIKE qualifier

```
SELECT author,title FROM classics WHERE author LIKE "Charles%";
SELECT author,title FROM classics WHERE title LIKE "%Species";
SELECT author,title FROM classics WHERE title LIKE "%and%";
```

The first command outputs the publications by both *Charles Darwin* and *Charles Dickens* because the `LIKE` qualifier was set to return anything matching the string *Charles* followed by any other text. Then just *The Origin of Species* is returned, because it's the only row whose column ends with the string *Species*. Lastly both *Pride and Prejudice* and *Romeo and Juliet* are returned, because they both matched the string *and* anywhere in the column.

The % will also match if there is nothing in the position it occupies; in other words, it can match an empty string.

```
C:\Windows\system32\cmd.exe

mysql> SELECT author,title FROM classics LIMIT 3;
+---------------+--------------------------------+
| author        | title                          |
+---------------+--------------------------------+
| Mark Twain    | The Adventures of Tom Sawyer   |
| Jane Austen   | Pride and Prejudice            |
| Charles Darwin| The Origin of Species          |
+---------------+--------------------------------+
3 rows in set (0.00 sec)

mysql> SELECT author,title FROM classics LIMIT 1,2;
+---------------+--------------------------------+
| author        | title                          |
+---------------+--------------------------------+
| Jane Austen   | Pride and Prejudice            |
| Charles Darwin| The Origin of Species          |
+---------------+--------------------------------+
2 rows in set (0.00 sec)

mysql> SELECT author,title FROM classics LIMIT 3,1;
+----------------+---------------------------+
| author         | title                     |
+----------------+---------------------------+
| Charles Dickens| The Old Curiosity Shop    |
+----------------+---------------------------+
```

Figure 8-12. Restricting the rows returned with LIMIT

LIMIT

The LIMIT qualifier enables you to choose how many rows to return in a query, and where in the table to start returning them. When passed a single parameter, it tells MySQL to start at the beginning of the results and just return the number of rows given in that parameter. If you pass it two parameters, the first indicates the offset from the start of the results where MySQL should start the display, and the second indicates how many to return. You can think of the first parameter as saying, "Skip this number of results at the start."

Example 8-23 includes three commands. The first returns the first three rows from the table. The second returns two rows starting at position 1 (skipping the first row). The last command returns a single row starting at position 3 (skipping the first three rows). Figure 8-12 shows the results of issuing these three commands.

Example 8-23. Limiting the number of results returned

```
SELECT author,title FROM classics LIMIT 3;
SELECT author,title FROM classics LIMIT 1,2;
SELECT author,title FROM classics LIMIT 3,1;
```

 Be careful with the LIMIT keyword, because offsets start at zero, but the number of rows to return starts at 1. So LIMIT 1,3 means return *three* rows starting from the *second* row.

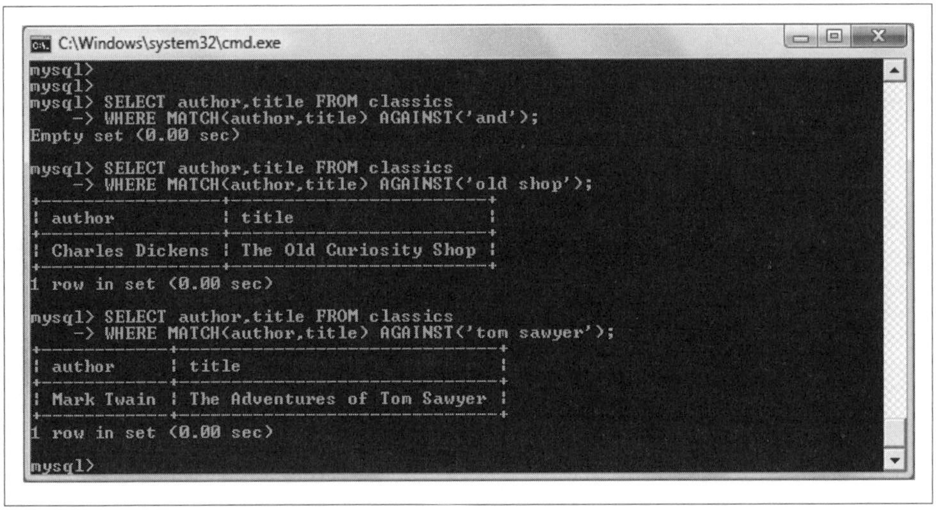

Figure 8-13. Using MATCH...AGAINST on a FULLTEXT index

MATCH...AGAINST

The `MATCH...AGAINST` construct can be used on columns that have been given a `FULLTEXT` index (see the earlier section "Creating a FULLTEXT index" on page 182). With it, you can make natural language searches as you would in an Internet search engine. Unlike the use of `WHERE...=` or `WHERE...LIKE`, `MATCH...AGAINST` lets you enter multiple words in a search query and checks them against all words in the `FULLTEXT` columns. `FULLTEXT` indexes are case-insensitive, so it makes no difference what case is used in your queries.

Assuming that you have added a `FULLTEXT` index to the *author* and *title* columns, enter the three queries shown in Example 8-24. The first asks for any of these columns that contain the word *and* to be returned. Because *and* is a stopword, MySQL will ignore it and the query will always produce an empty set—no matter what is stored in the columns. The second query asks for any rows that contain both of the words *old* and *shop* anywhere in them, in any order, to be returned. And the last query applies the same kind of search for the words *tom* and *sawyer*. The screenshot in Figure 8-13 shows the results of these queries.

Example 8-24. Using MATCH... AGAINST on FULLTEXT indexes

```
SELECT author,title FROM classics
 WHERE MATCH(author,title) AGAINST('and');
SELECT author,title FROM classics
 WHERE MATCH(author,title) AGAINST('old shop');
SELECT author,title FROM classics
 WHERE MATCH(author,title) AGAINST('tom sawyer');
```

```
C:\Windows\system32\cmd.exe                                    _ □ X

mysql>
mysql>
mysql>
mysql>
mysql> SELECT author,title FROM classics
    ->   WHERE MATCH(author,title)
    ->   AGAINST('+charles -species' IN BOOLEAN MODE);
+-----------------+-----------------------------+
| author          | title                       |
+-----------------+-----------------------------+
| Charles Dickens | The Old Curiosity Shop      |
+-----------------+-----------------------------+
1 row in set (0.00 sec)

mysql> SELECT author,title FROM classics
    ->   WHERE MATCH(author,title)
    ->   AGAINST('"origin of"' IN BOOLEAN MODE);
+----------------+-----------------------------+
| author         | title                       |
+----------------+-----------------------------+
| Charles Darwin | The Origin of Species       |
+----------------+-----------------------------+
1 row in set (0.00 sec)

mysql>
```

Figure 8-14. Using MATCH…AGAINST…IN BOOLEAN MODE

MATCH…AGAINST…IN BOOLEAN MODE

If you wish to give your MATCH...AGAINST queries even more power, use Boolean mode. This changes the effect of the standard FULLTEXT query so that it searches for any combination of search words, instead of requiring all search words to be in the text. The presence of a single word in a column causes the search to return the row.

Boolean mode also allows you to preface search words with a + or - sign to indicate whether they must be included or excluded. If normal Boolean mode says, "Any of these words will do," a plus sign means, "This word must be present; otherwise, don't return the row." A minus sign means, "This word must not be present; its presence disqualifies the row from being returned."

Example 8-25 illustrates Boolean mode through two queries. The first asks for all rows containing the word *charles* and not the word *species* to be returned. The second uses double quotes to request that all rows containing the exact phrase "origin of" be returned. Figure 8-14 shows the results of these queries.

As you would expect, the first request only returns *The Old Curiosity Shop* by *Charles Dickens*, because any rows containing the word *species* have been excluded, so *Charles Darwin*'s publication is ignored.

> There is something of interest to note in the second query: the stopword *of* is part of the search string, but is still used by the search because the double quotation marks override stopwords.

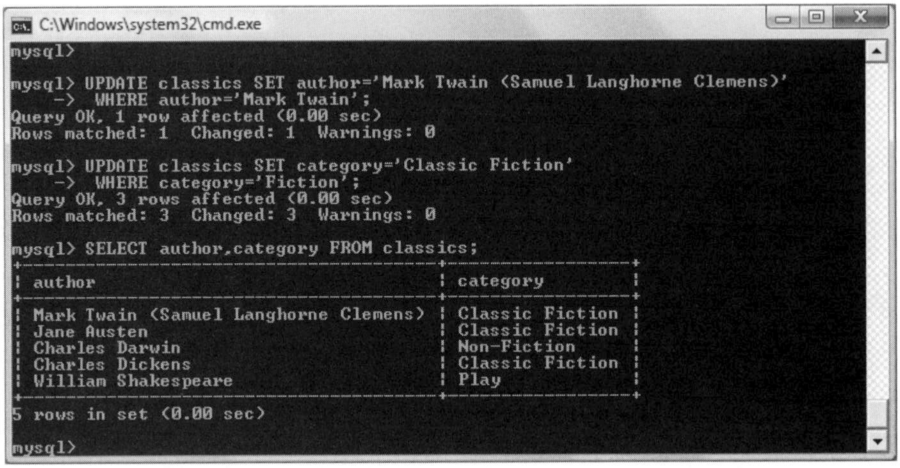

Figure 8-15. Updating columns in the classics table

Example 8-25. Using MATCH...AGAINST...IN BOOLEAN MODE

```
SELECT author,title FROM classics
 WHERE MATCH(author,title)
 AGAINST('+charles -species' IN BOOLEAN MODE);
SELECT author,title FROM classics
 WHERE MATCH(author,title)
 AGAINST('"origin of"' IN BOOLEAN MODE);
```

UPDATE...SET

This construct allows you to update the contents of a field. If you wish to change the contents of one or more fields, you need to first narrow in on just the field or fields to be changed, in much the same way you use the SELECT command. Example 8-26 shows the use of UPDATE...SET in two different ways. You can see a screenshot of the results in Figure 8-15.

Example 8-26. Using UPDATE...SET

```
UPDATE classics SET author='Mark Twain (Samuel Langhorne Clemens)'
 WHERE author='Mark Twain';
UPDATE classics SET category='Classic Fiction'
 WHERE category='Fiction';
```

In the first query *Mark Twain*'s real name of *Samuel Langhorne Clemens* was appended to his pen name in brackets, which affected only one row. The second query, however, affected three rows, because it changed all occurrences of the word *Fiction* in the *category* column to the term *Classic Fiction*.

When performing an update you can also make use of the qualifiers you have already seen, such as LIMIT, and the following ORDER BY and GROUP BY keywords.

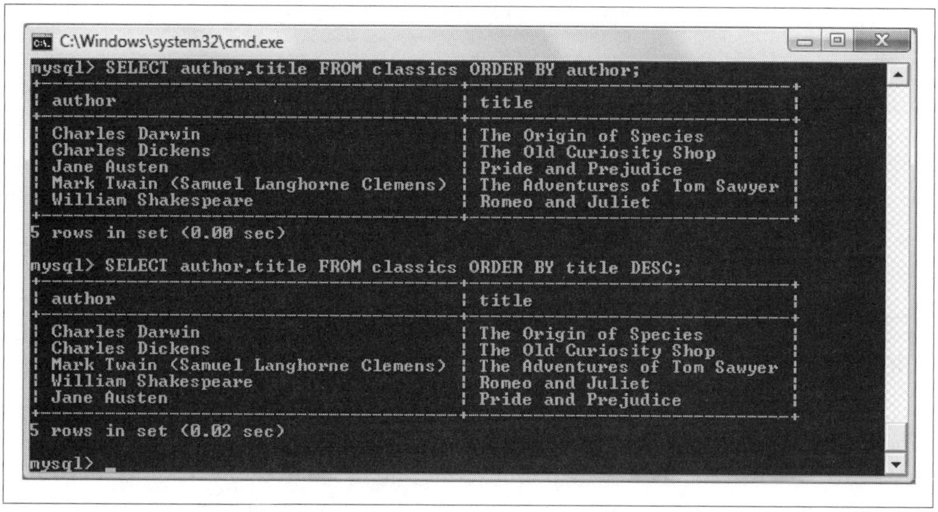

Figure 8-16. Sorting the results of requests

ORDER BY

ORDER BY sorts returned results by one or more columns in ascending or descending order. Example 8-27 shows two such queries, the results of which can be seen in Figure 8-16.

Example 8-27. Using ORDER BY

```
SELECT author,title FROM classics ORDER BY author;
SELECT author,title FROM classics ORDER BY title DESC;
```

As you can see, the first query returns the publications by *author* in ascending alphabetical order (the default), and the second returns them by *title* in descending order.

If you wanted to sort all the rows by *author* and then by descending *year* of publication (to view the most recent first), you would issue the following query:

```
SELECT author,title,year FROM classics ORDER BY author,year DESC;
```

This shows that each ascending and descending qualifier applies to a single column. The DESC keyword applies only to the preceding column, *year*. Because you allow *author* to use the default sort order, it is sorted in ascending order. You could also have explicitly specified ascending order for that column, with the same results:

```
SELECT author,title,year FROM classics ORDER BY author ASC,year DESC;
```

GROUP BY

In a similar fashion to ORDER BY, you can group results returned from queries using GROUP BY, which is good for retrieving information about a group of data. For example, if you want to know how many publications there are of each category in the *classics* table, you can issue the following query:

```
SELECT category,COUNT(author) FROM classics GROUP BY category;
```

which returns the following output:

```
+-----------------+---------------+
| category        | COUNT(author) |
+-----------------+---------------+
| Classic Fiction |             3 |
| Non-Fiction     |             1 |
| Play            |             1 |
+-----------------+---------------+
3 rows in set (0.00 sec)
```

Joining Tables Together

It is quite normal to maintain multiple tables within a database, each holding a different type of information. For example, consider the case of a *customers* table that needs to be able to be cross-referenced with publications purchased from the *classics* table. Enter the commands in Example 8-28 to create this new table and populate it with three customers and their purchases. Figure 8-17 shows the result.

Example 8-28. Creating and populating the customers table

```
CREATE TABLE customers (
 name VARCHAR(128),
 isbn VARCHAR(128),
 PRIMARY KEY (isbn)) ENGINE MyISAM;
INSERT INTO customers(name,isbn)
 VALUES('Joe Bloggs','9780099533474');
INSERT INTO customers(name,isbn)
 VALUES('Mary Smith','9780582506206');
INSERT INTO customers(name,isbn)
 VALUES('Jack Wilson','9780517123201');
SELECT * FROM customers;
```

 There's also a shortcut for inserting multiple rows of data, as in Example 8-28, in which you can replace the three separate INSERT INTO queries with a single one listing the data to be inserted, separated by commas, like this:

```
INSERT INTO customers(name,isbn) VALUES
('Joe Bloggs','9780099533474'),
('Mary Smith','9780582506206'),
('Jack Wilson','9780517123201');
```

Of course, in a proper table containing customers' details there would also be addresses, phone numbers, email addresses, and so on, but they aren't necessary for this explanation. While creating the new table, you should have noticed that it has something in common with the *classics* table: a column called *isbn*. Because it has the same meaning

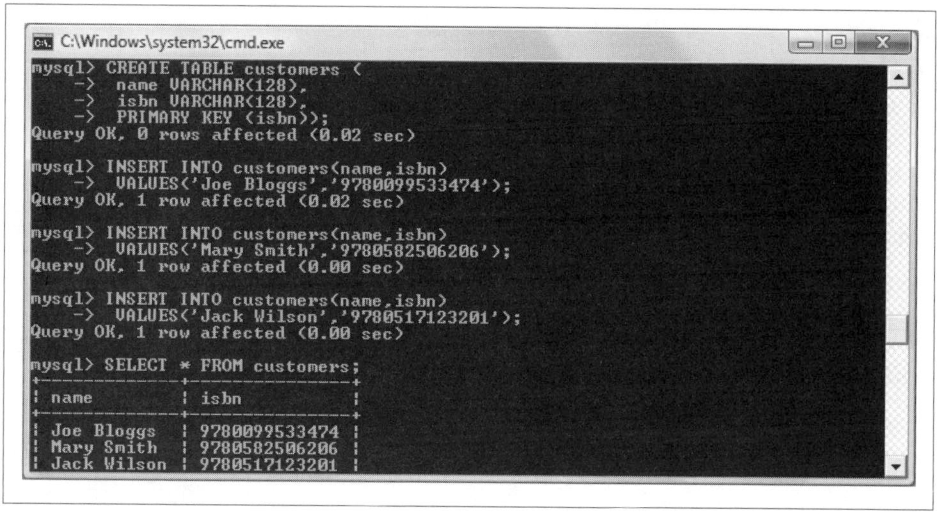

Figure 8-17. Creating the table customers

in both tables (an ISBN refers to a book, and always the same book), we can use this column to tie the two tables together into a single query, as in Example 8-29.

Example 8-29. Joining two tables into a single SELECT

```
SELECT name,author,title from customers,classics
 WHERE customers.isbn=classics.isbn;
```

The result of this operation is the following:

```
+-------------+----------------+------------------------+
| name        | author         | title                  |
+-------------+----------------+------------------------+
| Joe Bloggs  | Charles Dickens | The Old Curiosity Shop |
| Mary Smith  | Jane Austen    | Pride and Prejudice    |
| Jack Wilson | Charles Darwin  | The Origin of Species  |
+-------------+----------------+------------------------+
3 rows in set (0.00 sec)
```

See how this query has neatly tied both tables together to show the publications purchased from the *classics* table by the people in the *customers* table?

NATURAL JOIN

Using NATURAL JOIN, you can save yourself some typing and make queries a little clearer. This kind of join takes two tables and automatically joins columns that have the same name. So, to achieve the same results as from Example 8-29, you would enter:

```
SELECT name,author,title FROM customers NATURAL JOIN classics;
```

JOIN...ON

If you wish to specify the column on which to join two tables, use the `JOIN...ON` construct, as follows, to achieve results identical to those of Example 8-29:

```
SELECT name,author,title FROM customers
 JOIN classics ON customers.isbn=classics.isbn;
```

Using AS

You can also save yourself some typing and improve query readability by creating aliases using the `AS` keyword. Follow a table name with `AS` and the alias to use. The following code, therefore, is also identical in action to Example 8-29. Aliases can be particularly useful when you have long queries that reference the same table names many times.

```
SELECT name,author,title from
  customers AS cust, classics AS class WHERE cust.isbn=class.isbn;
```

Using Logical Operators

You can also use the logical operators `AND`, `OR`, and `NOT` in your MySQL `WHERE` queries to further narrow down your selections. Example 8-30 shows one instance of each, but you can mix and match them in any way you need.

Example 8-30. Using logical operators

```
SELECT author,title FROM classics WHERE
 author LIKE "Charles%" AND author LIKE "%Darwin";
SELECT author,title FROM classics WHERE
 author LIKE "%Mark Twain%" OR author LIKE "%Samuel Langhorne Clemens%";
SELECT author,title FROM classics WHERE
 author LIKE "Charles%" AND author NOT LIKE "%Darwin";
```

I've chosen the first query, because Charles Darwin might be listed in some rows by his full name, *Charles Robert Darwin*. Thus, the query returns publications as long as the *author* column starts with *Charles* and ends with *Darwin*. The second query searches for publications written using either *Mark Twain*'s pen name or his real name, *Samuel Langhorne Clemens*. The third query returns publications written by authors with the first name *Charles* but not the surname *Darwin*.

MySQL Functions

You might wonder why anyone would want to use MySQL functions when PHP comes with a whole bunch of powerful functions of its own. The answer is very simple: the MySQL functions work on the data right there in the database. If you were to use PHP, you would first have to extract raw data from MySQL, manipulate it, and then perform the database query you first wanted.

By having functions built into MySQL, the time needed for performing complex queries is substantially reduced, as is their complexity. If you wish to learn more about the available functions, you can visit the following URLs:

- String functions: *http://dev.mysql.com/doc/refman/5.0/en/string-functions.html*
- Date and time: *http://dev.mysql.com/doc/refman/5.0/en/date-and-time-functions.html*

However, to get you started, Appendix D describes a subset containing the most useful of these functions.

Accessing MySQL via phpMyAdmin

Although to use MySQL it is essential to learn these main commands and how they work, once you have learned them, it can be much quicker and simpler to use a program such as phpMyAdmin to manage your databases and tables.

The following explanation assumes you have worked through the previous examples in this chapter and have created the tables *classics* and *customers* in the database *publications*. Please choose the section relevant to your operating system.

Windows Users

Ensure that you have EasyPHP up and running so that the MySQL database is ready, then type the following into the address bar of your browser:

```
http://localhost/home/mysql/
```

Your browser should now look like Figure 8-18, and you are now ready to proceed to the section "Using phpMyAdmin" on page 197.

Mac OS X Users

Ensure that MAMP is running and that the Apache and MySQL servers are started, then type the following into your browser:

```
http://localhost/MAMP/
```

Now click on the link titled *phpMyAdmin*—your browser should look like Figure 8-19. You will now be ready to proceed to the section "Using phpMyAdmin" on page 197.

Linux Users

Ensure that you have installed XAMPP, then type the following into your browser:

```
http://localhost
```

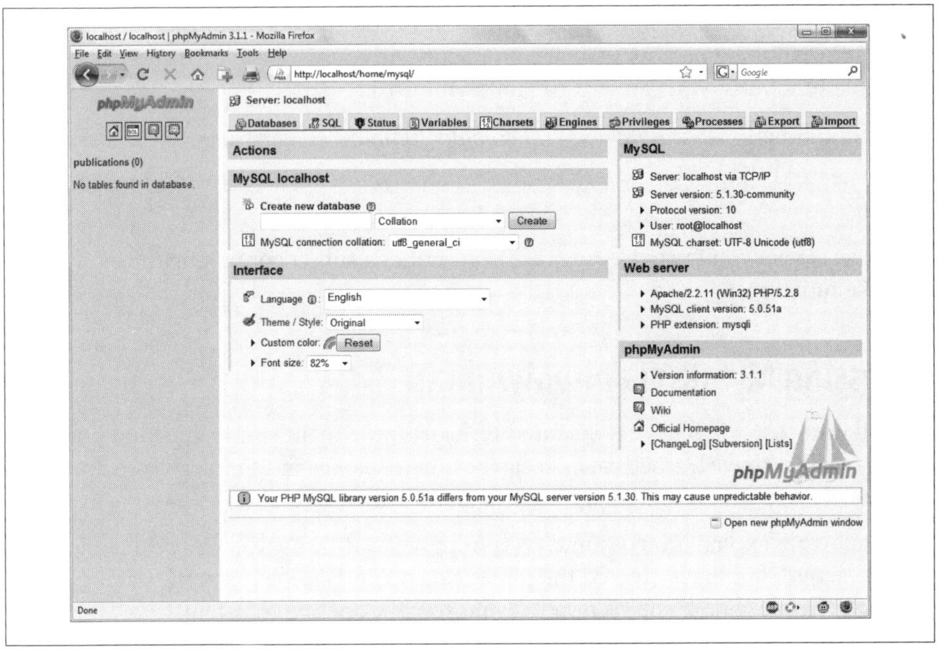

Figure 8-18. The Windows phpMyAdmin main screen

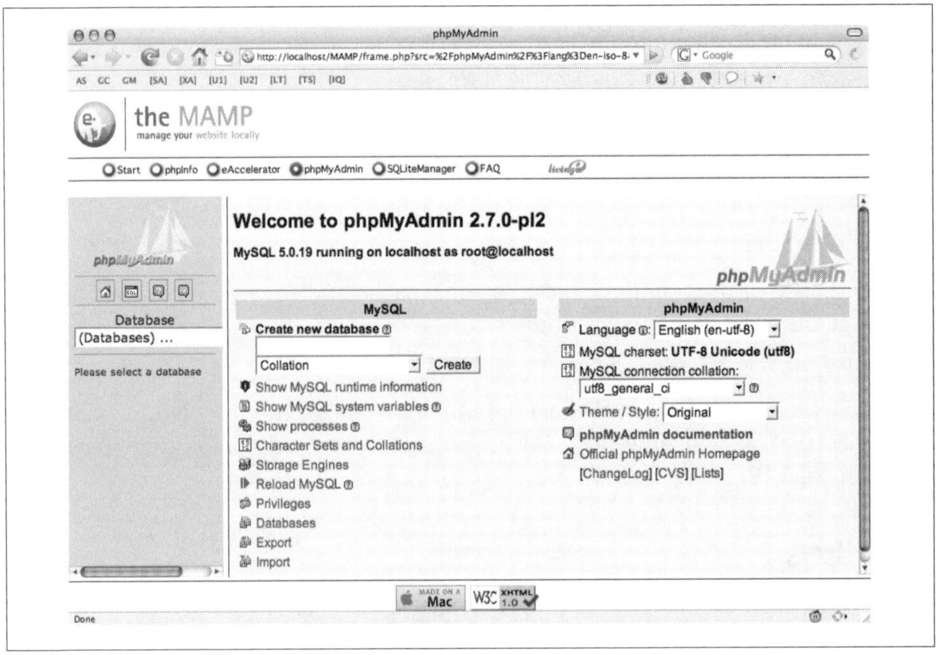

Figure 8-19. The Mac OS X phpMyAdmin main screen

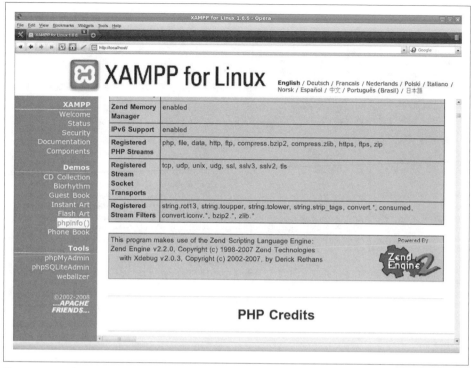

Figure 8-20. The Linux XAMPP main screen

Your browser should now look like Figure 8-20. Click on the *phpMyAdmin* link in the Tools section of the lefthand pane and you will be ready to proceed with the next section.

Using phpMyAdmin

In the lefthand pane of the main phpMyAdmin screen, which should now be in your browser, click on the drop-down menu that says "Databases" and select the database *publications*, which will open the database and display its two tables just below. Then click on the *classics* table, and you'll see a host of information about it appear in the righthand frame (see Figure 8-21).

From here you can perform all the main operations for your databases, such as creating databases, adding tables, creating indexes, and much more. To read the supporting documentation for phpMyAdmin, visit *http://www.phpmyadmin.net/documentation/*.

If you worked with me through the examples in this chapter, congratulations—it's been quite a long journey. You've come all the way from learning how to create a MySQL database through issuing complex queries that combine multiple tables, use Boolean operators, and leverage MySQL's various qualifiers.

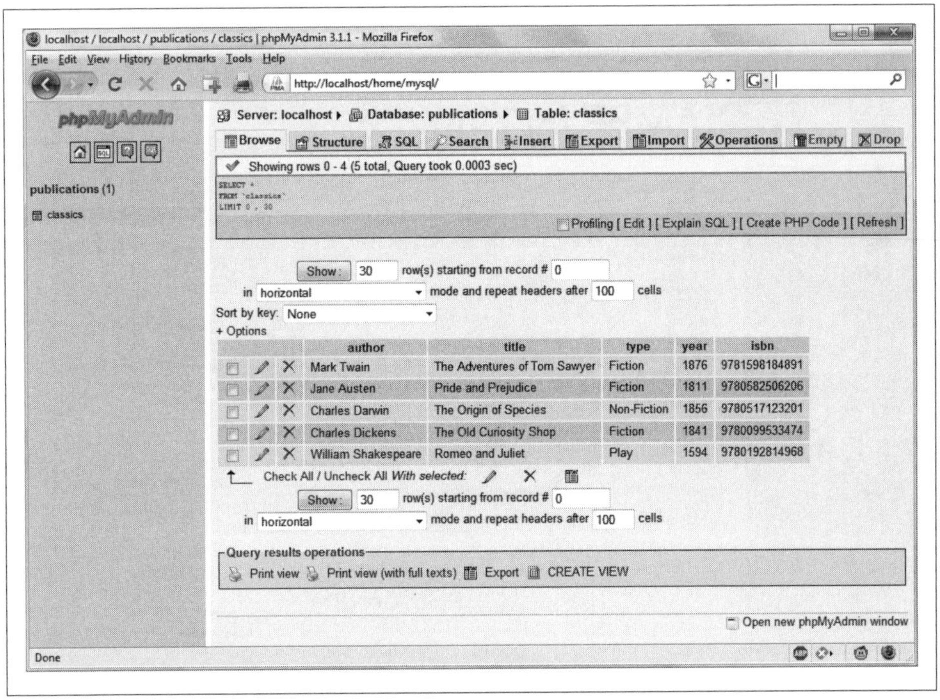

Figure 8-21. The classics table as viewed in phpMyAdmin

In the next chapter, we'll start looking at how to approach efficient database design, advanced SQL techniques, and MySQL functions and transactions.

Test Your Knowledge: Questions

Question 8-1
> What is the purpose of the semicolon in MySQL queries?

Question 8-2
> Which command would you use to view the available databases or tables?

Question 8-3
> How would you create a new MySQL user on the local host called *newuser* with a password of *newpass* and access to everything in the database *newdatabase*?

Question 8-4
> How can you view the structure of a table?

Question 8-5
> What is the purpose of a MySQL index?

Question 8-6

What benefit does a FULLTEXT index provide?

Question 8-7

What is a stopword?

Question 8-8

Both SELECT DISTINCT and GROUP BY cause the display to show only one output row for each value in a column, even if multiple rows contain that value. What are the main differences between SELECT DISTINCT and GROUP BY?

Question 8-9

Using the SELECT...WHERE construct, how would you return only rows containing the word *Langhorne* somewhere in the *author* column of the *classics* table used in this chapter?

Question 8-10

What needs to be defined in two tables to make it possible for you to join them together?

Question 8-11

Observant readers may have noticed that three book publication dates are incorrect in this chapter. *Pride and Prejudice* was actually published in 1813, *The Origin of Species* in 1859 and *Romeo and Juliet* in 1597. How could you correct these entries?

See the section "Chapter 8 Answers" on page 441 in Appendix A for the answers to these questions.

CHAPTER 9

Mastering MySQL

Chapter 8 provided you with a good grounding in the practice of using relational databases with structured query language. You've learned about creating databases and the tables that comprise them, as well as inserting, looking up, changing, and deleting data.

With that knowledge under your belt, we now need to look at how to design databases for maximum speed and efficiency. For example, how do you decide what data to place in which table? Well, over the years, a number of guidelines have been developed that—if you follow them—ensure that your databases will be efficient and capable of growing as you feed them more and more data.

Database Design

It's very important that you design a database correctly before you start to create it; otherwise, you are almost certainly going to have to go back and change it by splitting up some tables, merging others, and moving various columns about in order to achieve sensible relationships that MySQL can easily use.

Sitting down with a sheet of paper and a pencil and writing down a selection of the queries that you think you and your users are likely to ask is an excellent starting point. In the case of an online bookstore's database, some of the questions you write down could be:

- How many authors, books, and customers are in the database?
- Which author wrote a certain book?
- Which books were written by a certain author?
- What is the most expensive book?

- What is the best-selling book?
- Which books have not sold this year?
- Which books did a certain customer buy?
- Which books have been purchased along with the same other books?

Of course, there are many more queries that could be made on such a database, but even this small sample will begin to give you insights into how to lay out your tables. For example, books and ISBNs can probably be combined into one table, because they are closely linked (we'll examine some of the subtleties later). In contrast, books and customers should be in separate tables, because their connection is very loose. A customer can buy any book, and even multiple copies of a book, yet a book can be bought by many customers and be ignored by still more potential customers.

When you plan to do a lot of searches on something, it can often benefit by having its own table. And when couplings between things are loose, it's best to put them in separate tables.

Taking into account those simple rules of thumb, we can guess we'll need at least three tables to accommodate all these queries:

Authors
> There will be lots of searches for authors, many of whom have collaborated on titles, and many of whom will be featured in collections. Listing all the information about each author together, linked to that author, will produce optimal results for searches—hence an authors table.

Books
> Many books appear in different editions. Sometimes they change publisher and sometimes they have the same titles as other, unrelated books. So the links between books and authors are complicated enough to call for a separate table.

Customers
> It's even more clear why customers should get their own table, as they are free to purchase any book by any author.

Primary Keys: The Keys to Relational Databases

Using the power of relational databases, we can define information for each author, book, and customer in just one place. Obviously, what interests us are the links between them, such as who wrote each book and who purchased it—but we can store that information just by making links between the three tables. I'll show you the basic principles, and then it just takes practice for it to feel natural.

The magic involves giving every author a unique identifier. Do the same for every book and for every customer. We saw the means of doing that in the previous chapter: the *primary key*. For a book, it makes sense to use the ISBN, although you then have to deal with multiple editions that have different ISBNs. For authors and customers, you can just assign arbitrary keys, which the `AUTO_INCREMENT` feature that you saw in the last chapter makes easy.

In short, every table will be designed around some object that you're likely to search for a lot—an author, book, or customer, in this case—and that object will have a primary key. Don't choose a key that could possibly have the same value for different objects. The ISBN is a rare case for which an industry has provided a primary key that you can rely on to be unique for each product. Most of the time, you'll create an arbitrary key for this purpose, using `AUTO_INCREMENT`.

Normalization

The process of separating your data into tables and creating primary keys is called *normalization*. Its main goal is to make sure each piece of information appears in the database only once. Duplicating data is very inefficient, because it makes databases larger than they need to be and therefore slows down access.

But, more importantly, the presence of duplicates creates a strong risk that you'll update only one row of duplicated data, creating inconsistencies in a database and potentially causing serious errors.

Thus, if you list the titles of books in the *authors* table as well as the *books* table, and you have to correct a typographic error in a title, you'll have to search through both tables and make sure you make the same change every place the title is listed. It's better to keep the title in one place and use the ISBN in other places.

But in the process of splitting a database into multiple tables, it's important not to go too far and create more tables than is necessary, which would also lead to inefficient design and slower access.

Luckily, E. F. Codd, the inventor of the relational model, analyzed the concept of normalization and split it into three separate schemas called *First*, *Second*, and *Third Normal Form*. If you modify a database to satisfy each of these forms in order, you will ensure that your database is optimally balanced for fast access, and minimum memory and disk space usage.

To see how the normalization process works, let's start with the rather monstrous database in Table 9-1, which shows a single table containing all of the author names, book titles, and (fictional) customer details. You could consider it a first attempt at a table intended to keep track of which customers have ordered books.

Obviously, this is inefficient design, because data is duplicated all over the place (duplications are highlighted), but it represents a starting point.

Table 9-1. A highly inefficient design for a database table

Author 1	Author 2	Title	ISBN	Price U.S.	Cust. name	Cust. address	Purch. date
David Sklar	Adam Trachtenberg	*PHP Cookbook*	0596101015	44.99	Emma Brown	1565 Rainbow Road, Los Angeles, CA 90014	Mar 03 2009
Danny Goodman		*Dynamic HTML*	0596 527403	59.99	**Darren Ryder**	**4758 Emily Drive, Richmond, VA 23219**	**Dec 19 2008**
Hugh E. Williams	David Lane	*PHP and MySQL*	0596005436	44.95	Earl B. Thurston	862 Gregory Lane, Frankfort, KY 40601	Jun 22 2009
David Sklar	Adam Trachtenberg	*PHP Cookbook*	0596101015	44.99	**Darren Ryder**	**4758 Emily Drive, Richmond, VA 23219**	**Dec 19 2008**
Rasmus Lerdorf	Kevin Tatroe & Peter MacIntyre	*Programming PHP*	0596006815	39.99	David Miller	3647 Cedar Lane, Waltham, MA 02154	Jan 16 2009

In the following three sections, we will examine this database design and you'll see how it can be improved by removing the various duplicate entries and splitting the single table into sensible tables, each containing one type of data.

First Normal Form

For a database to satisfy the *First Normal Form*, it must fulfill three requirements:

1. There should be no repeating columns containing the same kind of data.
2. All columns should contain a single value.
3. There should be a primary key to uniquely identify each row.

Looking at these requirements in order, you should notice straight away that the *Author 1* and *Author 2* columns constitute repeating data types. So we already have a target column for pulling into a separate table, as the repeated *Author* columns violate Rule 1.

Second, there are three authors listed for the final book, *Programming PHP*. I've handled that by making Kevin Tatroe and Peter MacIntyre share the *Author 2* column, which violates Rule 2. Yet another reason to transfer the *Author* details to a separate table.

However, Rule 3 is satisfied, because the primary key of ISBN has already been created.

Table 9-2 shows the result of removing the *Authors* columns from Table 9-1. Already it looks a lot less cluttered, although there remain duplications that are highlighted.

Table 9-2. The result of stripping the Authors column from Table 9-1

Title	ISBN	Price	Cust. name	Cust. address	Purch. date
PHP Cookbook	0596101015	44.99	Emma Brown	1565 Rainbow Road, Los Angeles, CA 90014	Mar 03 2009
Dynamic HTML	0596527403	59.99	**Darren Ryder**	**4758 Emily Drive, Richmond, VA 23219**	**Dec 19 2008**
PHP and MySQL	0596005436	44.95	Earl B. Thurston	862 Gregory Lane, Frankfort, KY 40601	Jun 22 2009
PHP Cookbook	0596101015	44.99	**Darren Ryder**	**4758 Emily Drive, Richmond, VA 23219**	**Dec 19 2008**
Programming PHP	0596006815	39.99	David Miller	3647 Cedar Lane, Waltham, MA 02154	Jan 16 2009

The new *Authors* table shown in Table 9-3 is small and simple. It just lists the ISBN of a title along with an author. If a title has more than one author, additional authors get their own rows. At first you may feel ill at ease with this table, because you can't tell which author wrote which book. But don't worry: MySQL can quickly tell you. All you have to do is tell it which book you want information for, and MySQL will use its ISBN to search the *Authors* table in a matter of milliseconds.

Table 9-3. The new Authors table

ISBN	Author
0596101015	David Sklar
0596101015	Adam Trachtenberg
0596527403	Danny Goodman
0596005436	Hugh E Williams
0596005436	David Lane
0596006815	Rasmus Lerdorf
0596006815	Kevin Tatroe
0596006815	Peter MacIntyre

As I mentioned earlier, the ISBN will be the primary key for the *Books* table, when we get around to creating that table. I mention that here in order to emphasize that the ISBN is not, however, the primary key for the *Authors* table. In the real world, the *Authors* table would deserve a primary key, too, so that each author would have a key to uniquely identify him or her.

So, in the *Authors* table, the ISBN is just a column for which—for the purposes of speeding up searches—we'll probably make a key, but not the primary key. In fact, it *cannot* be the primary key in this table, because it's not unique: the same ISBN appears multiple times whenever two or more authors have collaborated on a book.

Because we'll use it to link authors to books in another table, this column is called a *foreign* key.

 Keys (also called *indexes*) have several purposes in MySQL. The fundamental reason for defining a key is to make searches faster. You've seen examples in Chapter 8 in which keys are used in WHERE clauses for searching. But a key can also be useful to uniquely identify an item. Thus, a unique key is often used as a primary key in one table, and as a foreign key to link rows in that table to rows in another table.

Second Normal Form

The First Normal Form deals with duplicate data (or redundancy) across multiple columns. The *Second Normal Form* is all about redundancy across multiple rows. In order to achieve Second Normal Form, your tables must already be in First Normal Form. Once this has been done, Second Normal Form is achieved by identifying columns whose data repeats in different places and then removing them to their own tables.

So let's look again at Table 9-2. Notice how Darren Ryder bought two books and therefore his details are duplicated. This tells us that the *Customer* columns need to be pulled into their own tables. Table 9-4 shows the result of removing the *Customer* columns from Table 9-2.

Table 9-4. The new Titles table

ISBN	Title	Price
0596101015	PHP Cookbook	44.99
0596527403	Dynamic HTML	59.99
0596005436	PHP and MySQL	44.95
0596006815	Programming PHP	39.99

As you can see, all that's left in Table 9-4 are the *ISBN*, *Title*, and *Price* columns for four unique books, so this now constitutes an efficient and self-contained table that satisfies the requirements of both the First and Second Normal Forms. Along the way, we've managed to reduce the information to data closely related to book titles. This table could also include years of publication, page counts, numbers of reprints, and so on, as these details are also closely related. The only rule is that we can't put in any column that could have multiple values for a single book, because then we'd have to list the same book in multiple rows and would thus violate Second Normal Form. Restoring an *Author* column, for instance, would violate this normalization.

However, looking at the extracted *Customer* columns, now in Table 9-5, we can see that there's still more normalization work to do, because Darren Ryder's details are still duplicated. And it could also be argued that First Normal Form Rule 2 (all columns should contain a single value) has not been properly complied with, because the addresses really need to be broken into separate columns for *Address*, *City*, *State*, and *Zip code*.

Table 9-5. The Customer details from Table 9-2

ISBN	Cust. name	Cust. address	Purch. date
0596101015	Emma Brown	1565 Rainbow Road, Los Angeles, CA 90014	Mar 03 2009
0596527403	Darren Ryder	4758 Emily Drive, Richmond, VA 23219	Dec 19 2008
0596005436	Earl B. Thurston	862 Gregory Lane, Frankfort, KY 40601	Jun 22 2009
0596101015	Darren Ryder	4758 Emily Drive, Richmond, VA 23219	Dec 19 2008
0596006815	David Miller	3647 Cedar Lane, Waltham, MA 02154	Jan 16 2009

What we have to do is split this table further to ensure that each customer's details are entered only once. Because the ISBN is not and cannot be used as a primary key to identify customers (or authors), a new key must be created.

Table 9-6 is the result of normalizing the *Customers* table into both First and Second Normal Forms. Each customer now has a unique customer number called *CustNo* that is the table's primary key, and that will most likely have been created using AUTO_INCREMENT. All the parts of their addresses have also been separated into distinct columns to make them easily searchable and updateable.

Table 9-6. The new Customers table

CustNo	Name	Address	City	State	Zip
1	Emma Brown	1565 Rainbow Road	Los Angeles	CA	90014
2	Darren Ryder	4758 Emily Drive	Richmond	VA	23219
3	Earl B. Thurston	862 Gregory Lane	Frankfort	KY	40601
4	David Miller	3647 Cedar Lane	Waltham	MA	02154

At the same time, in order to normalize Table 9-6, it was necessary to remove the information on customer purchases, because otherwise there would be multiple instances of customer details for each book purchased. Instead, the purchase data is now placed in a new table called *Purchases* (see Table 9-7).

Table 9-7. The new Purchases table

CustNo	ISBN	Date
1	0596101015	Mar 03 2009
2	0596527403	Dec 19 2008

CustNo	ISBN	Date
2	0596101015	Dec 19 2008
3	0596005436	Jun 22 2009
4	0596006815	Jan 16 2009

Here the *CustNo* column from Table 9-6 is reused as a key to tie both the *Customers* and the *Purchases* tables together. Because the ISBN column is also repeated here, this table can be linked with either of the *Authors* or the *Titles* tables, too.

The *CustNo* column can be a useful key in the *Purchases* table, but it's not a primary key. A single customer can buy multiple books (and even multiple copies of one book), so the *CustNo* column is not a primary key. In fact, the *Purchases* table has no primary key. That's all right, because we don't expect to need to keep track of unique purchases. If one customer buys two copies of the same book on the same day, we'll just allow two rows with the same information. For easy searching, we can define both *CustNo* and *ISBN* as keys—just not as primary keys.

 There are now four tables, one more than the three we had initially assumed would be needed. We arrived at this decision through the normalization processes, by methodically following the First and Second Normal Form rules, which made it plain that a fourth table called *Purchases* would also be required.

The tables we now have are: *Authors* (Table 9-3), *Titles* (Table 9-4), *Customers* (Table 9-6), and *Purchases* (Table 9-7), and each table can be linked to any other using either the *CustNo* or the *ISBN* keys.

For example, to see which books Darren Ryder has purchased, you can look him up in Table 9-6, the *Customers* table, where you will see his *CustNo* is 2. Armed with this number, you can now go to Table 9-7, the *Purchases* table; looking at the ISBN column here, you will see that he purchased titles 0596527403 and 0596101015 on December 19, 2008. This looks like a lot of trouble for a human, but it's not so hard for MySQL.

To determine what these titles were, you can then refer to Table 9-4, the *Titles* table, and see that the books he bought were *Dynamic HTML* and *PHP Cookbook*. Should you wish to know the authors of these books, you could also use the ISBN numbers you just looked up on Table 9-3, the *Authors* table, and you would see that ISBN 0596527403, *Dynamic HTML*, was written by Danny Goodman, and that ISBN 0596101015, *PHP Cookbook*, was written by David Sklar and Adam Trachtenberg.

Third Normal Form

Once you have a database that complies to both the First and Second Normal Forms, it is in pretty good shape and you might not have to modify it any further. However, if you wish to be very strict with your database, you can ensure that it adheres to the *Third Normal Form*, which requires data that is *not* directly dependent on the primary key but that *is* dependent on another value in the table should also be moved into separate tables, according to the dependence.

For example, in Table 9-6, the *Customers* table, it could be argued that the State, City, and Zip code keys are not directly related to each customer, because many other people will have the same details in their addresses, too. However, they are directly related to each other, in that the street *Address* relies on the *City*, and the *City* relies on the *State*.

Therefore, to satisfy Third Normal Form for Table 9-6, you would need to split it into Tables 9-8, 9-9, 9-10, and 9-11.

Table 9-8. Third Normal Form Customers table

CustNo	Name	Address	Zip
1	Emma Brown	1565 Rainbow Road	90014
2	Darren Ryder	4758 Emily Drive	23219
3	Earl B. Thurston	862 Gregory Lane	40601
4	David Miller	3647 Cedar Lane	02154

Table 9-9. Third Normal Form Zip codes table

Zip	CityID
90014	1234
23219	5678
40601	4321
02154	8765

Table 9-10. Third Normal Form Cities table

CityID	Name	StateID
1234	Los Angeles	5
5678	Richmond	46
4321	Frankfort	17
8765	Waltham	21

Table 9-11. Third Normal Form States table

StateID	Name	Abbreviation
5	California	CA
46	Virginia	VA
17	Kentucky	KY
21	Massachusetts	MA

So, how would you use this set of four tables instead of the single Table 9-6? Well, you would look up the *Zip code* in Table 9-8, then find the matching *CityID* in Table 9-9. Given this information, you could then look up the city *Name* in Table 9-10 and then also find the *StateID*, which you could use in Table 9-11 to look up the State's *Name*.

Although using the Third Normal Form in this way may seem like overkill, it can have advantages. For example, take a look at Table 9-11, where it has been possible to include both a state's name and its two-letter abbreviation. It could also contain population details and other demographics, if you desired.

Table 9-10 could also contain even more localized demographics that could be useful to you and/or your customers. By splitting these pieces of data up, you can make it easier to maintain your database in the future, should it be necessary to add additional columns.

Deciding whether to use the Third Normal Form can be tricky. Your evaluation should rest on what additional data you may need to add at a later date. If you are absolutely certain that the name and address of a customer is all that you will ever require, you probably will want to leave out this final normalization stage.

On the other hand, suppose you are writing a database for a large organization such as the U.S. Postal Service. What would you do if a city were to be renamed? With a table such as Table 9-6, you would need to perform a global search and replace on every instance of that city. But if you have your database set up according to the Third Normal Form, you would have to change only a single entry in Table 9-10 for the change to be reflected throughout the entire database.

Therefore, I suggest that you ask yourself two questions to help you decide whether to perform a Third Normal Form normalization on any table:

1. Is it likely that many new columns will need to be added to this table?
2. Could any of this table's fields require a global update at any point?

If either of the answers is yes, you should probably consider performing this final stage of normalization.

When Not to Use Normalization

Now that you know all about normalization, I'm going to tell you why you should throw these rules out of the window on high-traffic sites. That's right—you should never fully normalize your tables on sites that will cause MySQL to thrash.

Normalization requires spreading data across multiple tables, and this means making multiple calls to MySQL for each query. On a very popular site, if you have normalized tables, your database access will slow down considerably once you get above a few dozen concurrent users, because they will be creating hundreds of database accesses between them. In fact I would go so far as to say you should denormalize any commonly looked-up data as much as you can.

You see, if you have data duplicated across your tables, you can substantially reduce the number of additional requests that need to be made, because most of the data you want is available in each table. This means that you can simply add an extra column to a query and that field will be available for all matching results.

Of course, you have to deal with the downsides previously mentioned, such as using up large amounts of disk space, and ensuring that you update every single duplicate copy of data when one of them needs modifying.

Multiple updates can be computerized, though. MySQL provides a feature called *triggers* that make automatic changes to the database in response to changes you make. (Triggers are, however, beyond the scope of this book.) Another way to propagate redundant data is to set up a PHP program to run regularly and keep all copies in sync. The program reads changes from a "master" table and updates all the others. (You'll see how to access MySQL from PHP in the next chapter.)

However, until you are very experienced with MySQL, I recommend you fully normalize all your tables, as this will instill the habit and put you in good stead. Only when you actually start to see MySQL logjams should you consider looking at denormalization.

Relationships

MySQL is called a *relational* database management system because its tables store not only data but the *relationships* among the data. There are three categories of relationships.

One-to-One

A one-to-one relationship is like a (traditional) marriage: each item has a relationship to only one item of the other type. This is surprisingly rare. For instance, an author can write multiple books, a book can have multiple authors, and even an address can be associated with multiple customers. Perhaps the best example in this chapter so far of a one-to-one relationship is the relationship between the name of a state and its two-character abbreviation.

However, for the sake of argument, let's assume that there can ever be only one customer at any address. In such a case, the Customers-Addresses relationship in Figure 9-1 is a one-to-one relationship: only one customer lives at each address and each address can have only one customer.

Usually, when two items have a one-to-one relationship, you just include them as columns in the same table. There are two reasons for splitting them into separate tables:

- You want to be prepared in case the relationship changes later.
- The table has a lot of columns and you think that performance or maintenance would be improved by splitting it.

	Table 9-8a (Customers)	Table 9-8b (Addresses)	
CustNo	Name	Address	Zip
1	Emma Brown	1565 Rainbow Road	90014
2	Darren Ryder	4758 Emily Drive	23219
3	Earl B. Thurston	862 Gregory Lane	40601
4	David Miller	3647 Cedar Lane	02154

Figure 9-1. The Customers table, Table 9-8, split into two tables

Of course, when you come to build your own databases in the real world, you will have to create one-to-many Customer-Address relationships (*one* address, *many* customers).

One-to-Many

One-to-many (or many-to-one) relationships occur when one row in one table is linked to many rows in another table. You have already seen how Table 9-8 would take on a one-to-many relationship if multiple customers were allowed at the same address, which is why it would have to be split up if that were the case.

So, looking at Table 9-8a within Figure 9-1, you can see that it shares a one-to-many relationship with Table 9-7 because there is only one of each customer in Table 9-8a. However Table 9-7, the *Purchases* table, can (and does) contain more than one purchase from customers. Therefore *one* customer has a relationship with *many* purchases.

You can see these two tables alongside each other in Figure 9-2, where the dashed lines joining rows in each table start from a single row in the lefthand table but can connect to more than one row on the right-hand table. This one-to-many relationship is also the preferred scheme to use when describing a many-to-one relationship, in which case you would normally swap the left and right tables to view them as a one-to-many relationship.

Many-to-Many

In a many-to-many relationship, many rows in one table are linked to many rows in another table. To create this relationship, add a third table containing the same key

Table 9-8a (Customers)   Table 9-7. (Purchases)

CustNo	Name		CustNo	ISBN	Date
1	Emma Brown	....	1	0596101015	Mar 03 2009
2	Darren Ryder	....	2	0596527403	Dec 19 2008
	(etc...)		2	0596101015	Dec 19 2008
3	Earl B. Thurston	....	3	0596005436	Jun 22 2009
4	David Miller	....	4	0596006815	Jan 16 2009

Figure 9-2. Illustrating the relationship between two tables

column from each of the other tables. This third table contains nothing else, as its sole purpose is to link up the other tables.

Table 9-12 is just such a table. It was extracted from Table 9-7, the *Purchases* table, but omitting the purchase date information. What it now contains is a copy of the ISBN number of every title sold, along with the customer number of the purchaser.

Table 9-12. An intermediary table

Customer	ISBN
1	0596101015
2	0596527403
2	0596101015
3	0596005436
4	0596006815

With this intermediary table in place, you can traverse all the information in the database through a series of relations. You can take an address as a starting point and find out the authors of any books purchased by the customer living at that address.

For example, let's suppose that you want to find out about purchases in the 23219 zip code. Look that zip code up in Table 9-8b within Figure 9-2 and you'll find that customer number 2 has bought at least one item from the database. At this point, you can use Table 9-8a within Figure 9-1 to find out his or her name, or use the new intermediary Table 9-12 to see the book(s) purchased.

From here, you will find that two titles were purchased and can follow them back to Table 9-4 to find the titles and prices of these books, or to Table 9-3 to see who the authors were.

If it seems to you that this is really combining multiple one-to-many relationships, then you are absolutely correct. To illustrate, Figure 9-3 brings three tables together.

Columns from Table 9-8b (Customers)		Intermediary Table 9-12 (Customer/ISBN)		Columns from Table 9-4 (Titles)	
Zip	**Cust.**	**CustNo**	**ISBN**	**ISBN**	**Title**
90014	1·············· 1		0596101015 ···········	0596101015	PHP Cookbook
23219	2·········· 2		0596527403 ·······	(etc...)	
(etc...)	······ 2		0596101015 ···········	0596527403	Dynamic HTML
40601	3·············· 3		0596005436 ···········	0596005436	PHP and MySQL
02154	4············· 4		0596006815 ···········	0596006815	Programming PHP

Figure 9-3. Creating a many-to-many relationship via a third table

Follow any zip code in the left table to associated customer IDs. From there, you can link to the middle table, which joins the left and right tables by linking customer IDs and ISBN numbers. Now all you have to do is follow an ISBN over to the right table to see which book it relates to.

You can also use the intermediary table to work your way backward from book titles to zip codes. The *Titles* table can tell you the ISBN, which you can use in the middle table to find ID numbers of customers who bought the books, and finally, the *Customers* table matches the customer ID numbers to the customers' zip codes.

Databases and Anonymity

An interesting aspect of using relations is that you can accumulate a lot of information about some item—such as a customer—without actually knowing who that customer is. Note that we went from customers' zip codes to customers' purchases, and back again, in the previous example, without finding out the name of a customer. Databases can be used to track people, but they can also be used to help preserve people's privacy while still finding useful information.

Transactions

In some applications, it is vitally important that a sequence of queries runs in the correct order and that every single query successfully completes. For example, suppose that you are creating a sequence of queries to transfer funds from one bank account to another. You would not want either of the following events to occur:

- You add the funds to the second account, but when you try to subtract them from the first account the update fails, and now both accounts have the funds.
- You subtract the funds from the first bank account, but the update request to add them to the second account fails, and the funds have now disappeared into thin air.

As you can see, not only is the order of queries important in this type of transaction, but it is also vital that all parts of the transaction complete successfully. But how can you ensure this happens, because surely after a query has occurred, it cannot be undone? Do you have to keep track of all parts of a transaction and then undo them all one at a time if any one fails? The answer is absolutely not, because MySQL comes with powerful transaction handling features to cover just these types of eventualities.

In addition, transactions allow concurrent access to a database by many users or programs at the same time, by ensuring all transactions are queued up and each user or program takes their turn, and doesn't tread on each others' toes—all handled seamlessly by MySQL.

Transaction Storage Engines

In order to be able to use MySQL's transaction facility, you have to be using MySQL's *InnoDB* storage engine. This is easy to do, as it's simply another parameter that you use when creating a table. So go ahead and create a table of bank accounts by typing in the commands in Example 9-1. (Remember that to do this you will need access to the MySQL command line, and must also have already selected a suitable database in which to create this table.)

Example 9-1. Creating a transaction-ready table

```
CREATE TABLE accounts (
number INT, balance FLOAT, PRIMARY KEY(number)
) ENGINE InnoDB;
DESCRIBE accounts;
```

The final line of this example displays the contents of the new table so you can ensure that it was correctly created. The output from it should look like this:

```
+---------+---------+------+-----+---------+-------+
| Field   | Type    | Null | Key | Default | Extra |
+---------+---------+------+-----+---------+-------+
| number  | int(11) | NO   | PRI | 0       |       |
| balance | float   | YES  |     | NULL    |       |
+---------+---------+------+-----+---------+-------+
2 rows in set (0.00 sec)
```

Now let's create two rows within the table so that you can practice using transactions. Type in the commands in Example 9-2.

Example 9-2. Populating the accounts table

```
INSERT INTO accounts(number, balance) VALUES(12345, 1025.50);
INSERT INTO accounts(number, balance) VALUES(67890, 140.00);
SELECT * FROM accounts;
```

The third line displays the contents of the table to confirm that the rows were correctly inserted. The output should look like this:

```
+--------+---------+
| number | balance |
+--------+---------+
|  12345 |  1025.5 |
|  67890 |     140 |
+--------+---------+
2 rows in set (0.00 sec)
```

With this table created and prepopulated, you are now ready to start using transactions.

Using BEGIN

Transactions in MySQL start with either a BEGIN or a START TRANSACTION statement. Type in the commands in Example 9-3 to send a transaction to MySQL.

Example 9-3. A MySQL transaction

```
BEGIN;
UPDATE accounts SET balance=balance+25.11 WHERE number=12345;
COMMIT;
SELECT * FROM accounts;
```

The result of this transaction is displayed by the final line, and should look like this:

```
+--------+---------+
| number | balance |
+--------+---------+
|  12345 | 1050.61 |
|  67890 |     140 |
+--------+---------+
2 rows in set (0.00 sec)
```

As you can see, the balance of account number 12345 was increased by 25.11 and is now 1050.61. You may also have noticed the COMMIT command in Example 9-3, which is explained next.

Using COMMIT

When you are satisfied that a series of queries in a transaction has successfully completed, issue a COMMIT command to commit all the changes to the database. Until a COMMIT is received, all the changes you make are considered to be merely temporary by MySQL. This feature gives you the opportunity to cancel a transaction by not sending a COMMIT but by issuing a ROLLBACK command instead.

Using ROLLBACK

Using the ROLLBACK command, you can tell MySQL to forget all the queries made since the start of a transaction and to end the transaction. Check this out in action by entering the funds transfer transaction in Example 9-4.

Example 9-4. A funds transfer transaction

```
BEGIN;
UPDATE accounts SET balance=balance-250 WHERE number=12345;
UPDATE accounts SET balance=balance+250 WHERE number=67890;
SELECT * FROM accounts;
```

Once you have entered these lines, you should see the following result:

```
+--------+---------+
| number | balance |
+--------+---------+
|  12345 |  800.61 |
|  67890 |     390 |
+--------+---------+
2 rows in set (0.00 sec)
```

The first bank account now has a value that is 250 less than before, and the second has been incremented by 250—you have transferred a value of 250 between them. But let's assume that something went wrong and you wish to undo this transaction. All you have to do is issue the commands in Example 9-5.

Example 9-5. Cancelling a transaction using ROLLBACK

```
ROLLBACK;
SELECT * FROM accounts;
```

You should now see the following output, showing that the two accounts have had their previous balances restored, due to the entire transaction being cancelled using the ROLLBACK command:

```
+--------+---------+
| number | balance |
+--------+---------+
|  12345 | 1050.61 |
|  67890 |     140 |
+--------+---------+
2 rows in set (0.00 sec)
```

Using EXPLAIN

MySQL comes with a powerful tool for investigating how the queries you issue to it are interpreted. Using EXPLAIN, you can get a snapshot of any query to find out whether you could issue it in a better or more efficient way. Example 9-6 shows how to use it with the accounts table you created earlier.

Example 9-6. Using the EXPLAIN command

```
EXPLAIN SELECT * FROM accounts WHERE number='12345';
```

The results of this EXPLAIN command should look like the following:

```
+--+-----------+--------+-----+-------------+-------+-------+-----+----+-----+
|id|select_type|table   |type |possible_keys|key    |key_len|ref  |rows|Extra|
+--+-----------+--------+-----+-------------+-------+-------+-----+----+-----+
| 1|SIMPLE     |accounts|const|PRIMARY      |PRIMARY|4      |const|  1 |     |
+--+-----------+--------+-----+-------------+-------+-------+-----+----+-----+
1 row in set (0.00 sec)
```

The information that MySQL is giving you here is as follows:

select_type
>   The selection type is SIMPLE. If you were joining tables together, this would show the join type.

table
>   The current table being queried is accounts.

type
>   The query type is const. From worst to best, the possible values can be: ALL, index, range, ref, eq_ref, const, system, and NULL.

possible_keys
>   There is a possible PRIMARY key, which means that accessing should be fast.

key
>   The key actually used is PRIMARY. This is good.

key_len
>   The key length is 4. This is the number of bytes of the index that MySQL will use.

ref
>   The ref column displays which columns or constants are used with the key. In this case, a constant key is being used.

rows
>   The number of rows that need to be searched by this query is 1. This is good.

Whenever you have a query that seems to be taking longer than you think it should to execute, try using EXPLAIN to see where you can optimize it. You will discover which keys, if any, are being used, their lengths, and so on, and will be able to adjust your query or the design of your table(s) accordingly.

> When you have finished experimenting with the temporary *accounts* table, you may wish to remove it by entering the following command:
>
> ```
> DROP TABLE accounts;
> ```

Backing Up and Restoring

Whatever kind of data you are storing in your database it must have some value to you, even if it's only the cost of the time required for reentering it should the hard disk fail. Therefore it's important that you keep backups to protect your investment. Also there will be times when you have to migrate your database over to a new server; the best way to do this is usually to back it up first. It is also important that you test your backups from time to time to ensure that they are valid and will work if they need to be used.

Thankfully, backing up and restoring MySQL data is easy using the `mysqldump` command.

Using mysqldump

With `mysqldump`, you can dump a database or collection of databases into one or more files containing all the instructions necessary to recreate all your tables and repopulate them with your data. It can also generate files in CSV (Comma-Separated Values) and other delimited text formats, or even in XML format. Its main drawback is that you must make sure that no one writes to a table while you're backing it up. There are various ways to do this, but the easiest is to shut down the MySQL server before `mysqldump` and start up the server again after `mysqldump` finishes.

Or you can lock the tables you are backing up before running `mysqldump`. To lock tables for reading (as we want to read the data), from the MySQL command line issue the command:

```
LOCK TABLES tablename1 READ, tablename2 READ, ...;
```

Then, to release the lock(s), enter:

```
UNLOCK TABLES;
```

By default, the output from `mysqldump` is simply printed out, but you can capture it in a file through the > redirect symbol.

The basic format of the `mysqldump` command is:

```
mysqldump -u user -ppassword database
```

However, before you can dump the contents of a database, you must make sure that `mysqldump` is in your path, or that you specify its location as part of your command. Table 9-13 shows the likely locations of the program for the different installations and operating systems covered in Chapter 2. If you have a different installation, it may be in a slightly different location.

Table 9-13. Likely locations of mysqldump for different installations

Operating system & program	Likely folder location
Windows EasyPHP WAMP	\Program Files\EasyPHP 3.0\mysql\bin\
Mac MAMP	/Applications/MAMP/Library/bin/
Linux LAMP	/usr/local/bin/

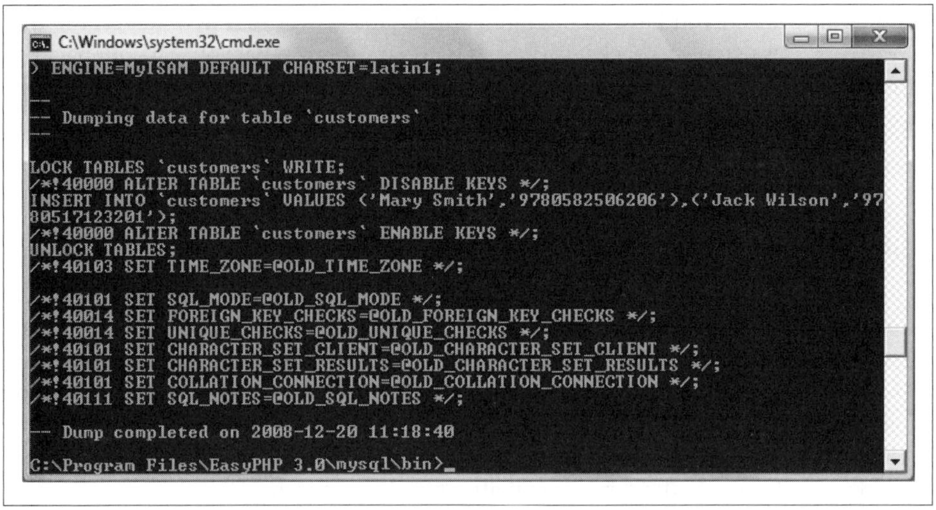

Figure 9-4. Dumping the publications database to screen

So, to dump the contents of the *publications* database that you created in Chapter 8 to the screen, enter `mysqldump` (or the full path if necessary) and the command in Example 9-7.

Example 9-7. Dumping the publications database to screen

```
mysqldump -u user -ppassword publications
```

Make sure that you replace *user* and *password* with the correct details for your installation of MySQL. If there is no password set for the user, you can omit that part of the command, but the `-u` *user* part is mandatory—unless you have root access without a password and are executing as root (not recommended). The result of issuing this command will look something like the screenshot in Figure 9-4.

Creating a Backup File

Now that you have `mysqldump` working, and have verified it outputs correctly to the screen, you can send the backup data directly to a file using the `>` redirect symbol. Assuming that you wish to call the backup file *publications.sql*, type in the command in Example 9-8 (remembering to replace *user* and *password* with the correct details).

Example 9-8. Dumping the publications database to screen

```
mysqldump -u user -ppassword publications > publications.sql
```

The command in Example 9-8 stores the backup file into the current directory. If you need it to be saved elsewhere, you should insert a file path before the filename. You must also ensure that the directory you are backing up to has the right permissions set to allow the file to be written.

If you echo the backup file to screen or load it into a text editor, you will see that it comprises sequences of SQL commands such as the following:

```
DROP TABLE IF EXISTS `classics`;
CREATE TABLE `classics` (
  `author` varchar(128) default NULL,
  `title` varchar(128) default NULL,
  `category` varchar(16) default NULL,
  `year` smallint(6) default NULL,
  `isbn` char(13) NOT NULL default '',
  PRIMARY KEY (`isbn`),
  KEY `author` (`author`(20)),
  KEY `title` (`title`(20)),
  KEY `category` (`category`(4)),
  KEY `year` (`year`),
  FULLTEXT KEY `author_2` (`author`,`title`)
) ENGINE=MyISAM DEFAULT CHARSET=latin1;
```

This is smart code that can be used to restore a database from a backup, even if it currently exists, because it will first drop any tables that need to be recreated, thus avoiding potential MySQL errors.

To back up only a single table from a database (such as the *classics* table from the *publications* database), you should first lock the table from within the MySQL command line, by issuing a command such as the following:

```
LOCK TABLES publications.classics READ
```

This ensures that MySQL remains running for read purposes, but writes cannot be made. Then, while keeping the MySQL command line open, use another terminal window to issue the following command from the operating system command line:

```
mysqldump -u user -ppassword publications classics > classics.sql
```

You must now release the table lock by entering the following command from the MySQL command line, which unlocks all tables that have been locked during the current session:

```
UNLOCK TABLES
```

Example 9-9. Dumping just the classics table from publications

```
$ mysql -u user -ppassword
mysql> LOCK TABLES classics READ
mysql> QUIT
$ mysqldump -u user -ppassword publications classics > classics.sql
$ mysql -u user -ppassword
```

```
mysql> UNLOCK TABLES
mysql> QUIT
```

Or, if you want to back up all your MySQL databases at once (including the system databases such as *mysql*), you can use a command such as the one in Example 9-10, which would make it possible to restore an entire MySQL database installation—remembering to use locking where required.

Example 9-10. Dumping all the MySQL databases to file

```
mysqldump -u user -ppassword --all-databases > all_databases.sql
```

 Of course, there's a lot more than just a few lines of SQL code in backed-up database files. I recommend that you take a few minutes to examine a couple in order to familiarize yourself with the types of commands that appear in backup files and how they work.

Restoring from a Backup File

To perform a restore from a file, call the *mysql* executable, passing it the file to restore from using the < symbol. So, to recover an entire database that you dumped using the *--all-databases* option, use a command such as that in Example 9-11.

Example 9-11. Restoring an entire set of databases

```
mysql -u user -ppassword < all_databases.sql
```

To restore a single database, use the -D option followed by the name of the database, as in Example 9-12, where the *publications* database is being restored from the backup made in Example 9-8.

Example 9-12. Restoring the publications database

```
mysql -u user -ppassword -D publications < publications.sql
```

To restore a single table to a database, use a command such as that in Example 9-13, where just the *classics* table, backed up in Example 9-9, is being restored to the *publications* database.

Example 9-13. Restoring the classics table to the publications database

```
mysql -u user -ppassword -D publications < classics.sql
```

Dumping Data in CSV Format

As previously mentioned, the `mysqldump` program is very flexible and supports various types of output, such as the CSV format. Example 9-14 shows how you can dump the data from the *classics* and *customers* tables in the *publications* database to the files *classics.txt* and *customers.txt* in the folder *c:/web*. By default, on an EasyPHP 3.0 installation, the user should be *root* and no password is used. On OS X or Linux systems, you should modify the destination path to an existing folder.

Example 9-14. Dumping data to CSV format files

```
mysqldump -u user -ppassword --no-create-info --tab=c:/web
  --fields-terminated-by=',' publications
```

This command is quite long and is shown here wrapped over two lines, but you must type it all in as a single line, ensuring there is a space between *web* and *--fields*. The result is the following:

```
Mark Twain (Samuel Langhorne Clemens)','The Adventures
 of Tom Sawyer','Classic Fiction','1876','9781598184891
Jane Austen','Pride and Prejudice','Classic Fiction','1811','9780582506206
Charles Darwin','The Origin of Species','Non-Fiction','1856','9780517123201
Charles Dickens','The Old Curiosity Shop','Classic Fiction','1841','9780099533474
William Shakespeare','Romeo and Juliet','Play','1594','9780192814968

Mary Smith','9780582506206
Jack Wilson','9780517123201
```

Planning Your Backups

The golden rule to backing up is to do so as often as you find practical. The more valuable the data, the more often you should back it up, and the more copies you should make. If your database gets updated at least once a day, you should really back it up on a daily basis. If, on the other hand, it is not updated very often, you could probably get by with backups less often.

> You should also consider making multiple backups and storing them in different locations. If you have several servers, it is a simple matter to copy your backups between them. You would also be well advised to make physical backups of removable hard disks, thumb drives, CDs or DVDs, and so on, and to keep these in separate locations—preferably somewhere like a fireproof safe.

Once you've digested the contents of this chapter, you will be proficient in using both PHP and MySQL; the next chapter will show you to bring these two technologies together.

Test Your Knowledge: Questions

Question 9-1

What does the word *relationship* mean in reference to a relational database?

Question 9-2

What is the term for the process of removing duplicate data and optimizing tables?

Question 9-3

What are the three rules of First Normal Form?

Question 9-4

How can you make a table satisfy Second Normal Form?

Question 9-5

What do you put in a column to tie together two tables that contain items having a one-to-many relationship?

Question 9-6

How can you create a database with a many-to-many relationship?

Question 9-7

What commands initiate and end a MySQL transaction?

Question 9-8

What feature does MySQL provide to enable you to examine how a query will work in detail?

Question 9-9

What command would you use to back up the database *publications* to a file called *publications.sql*?

See the section "Chapter 9 Answers" on page 442 in Appendix A for the answers to these questions.

CHAPTER 10

Accessing MySQL Using PHP

If you worked through the previous chapters, you're proficient in using both MySQL and PHP. In this chapter, you will learn how to integrate the two by using PHP's built-in functions to access MySQL.

Querying a MySQL Database with PHP

The reason for using PHP as an interface to MySQL is to format the results of SQL queries in a form visible in a web page. As long as you can log into your MySQL installation using your username and password, you can also do so from PHP. However, instead of using MySQL's command line to enter instructions and view output, you will create query strings that are passed to MySQL. When MySQL returns its response, it will come as a data structure that PHP can recognize instead of the formatted output you see when you work on the command line. Further PHP commands can retrieve the data and format it for the web page.

The Process

The process of using MySQL with PHP is:

1. Connect to MySQL.
2. Select the database to use.
3. Build a query string.
4. Perform the query.
5. Retrieve the results and output it to a web page.
6. Repeat Steps 3 to 5 until all desired data have been retrieved.
7. Disconnect from MySQL.

We'll work through these sections in turn, but first it's important to set up your login details in a secure manner so people snooping around on your system have trouble getting access to your database.

Creating a Login File

Most websites developed with PHP contain multiple program files that will require access to MySQL and will therefore need the login and password details. Therefore, it's sensible to create a single file to store these and then include that file wherever it's needed. Example 10-1 shows such a file, which I've called *login.php*. Type it in, replacing values (such as *username*) with the actual values you use for your MySQL database, and save it to the web development directory you set up in Chapter 2. We'll be making use of the file shortly. The hostname `localhost` should work as long as you're using a MySQL database on your local system, and the database *publications* should work if you're typing in the examples I've used so far.

Example 10-1. The login.php file

```
<?php // login.php
$db_hostname = 'localhost';
$db_database = 'publications';
$db_username = 'username';
$db_password = 'password';
?>
```

The enclosing `<?php` and `?>` tags are especially important for the *login.php* file in Example 10-1, because they mean that the lines between can be interpreted *only* as PHP code. If you were to leave them out and someone were to call up the file directly from your website, it would display as text and reveal your secrets. But, with the tags in place, all they will see is a blank page. The file will correctly include in your other PHP files.

The `$db_hostname` variable will tell PHP which computer to use when connecting to a database. This is required, because you can access MySQL databases on any computer connected to your PHP installation, and that potentially includes any host anywhere on the Web. However, the examples in this chapter will be working on the local server. So in place of specifying a domain such as *mysql.myserver.com*, the word `localhost` (or the IP address 127.0.0.1) will correctly refer to it.

The database we'll be using, `$db_database`, is the one called *publications*, which you probably created in Chapter 8, or the one you were provided with by your server administrator (in which case you have to modify *login.php* accordingly).

The variables `$db_username` and `$db_password` should be set to the username and password that you have been using with MySQL.

Another benefit of keeping these login details in a single place is that you can change your password as frequently as you like and there will be only one file to update when you do, no matter how many PHP files access MySQL.

Connecting to MySQL

Now that you have the *login.php* file saved, you can include it in any PHP files that will need to access the database by using the `require_once` statement. This has been chosen in preference to an `include` statement, as it will generate a fatal error if the file is not found. And believe me, not finding the file containing the login details to your database *is* a fatal error.

Also, using `require_once` instead of `require` means that the file will be read in only when it has not previously been included, which prevents wasteful duplicate disk accesses. Example 10-2 shows the code to use.

Example 10-2. Connecting to a MySQL database

```
<?php
require_once 'login.php';
$db_server = mysql_connect($db_hostname, $db_username, $db_password);

if (!$db_server) die("Unable to connect to MySQL: " . mysql_error());
?>
```

This example runs PHP's `mysql_connect` function, which requires three parameters, the *hostname*, *username*, and *password* of a MySQL server. Upon success it returns an *identifier* to the server; otherwise, `FALSE` is returned. Notice that the second line uses an `if` statement with the `die` function, which does what it sounds like and quits from PHP with an error message if `$db_server` is not `TRUE`.

The `die` message explains that it was not possible to connect to the MySQL database, and—to help identify why this happened—includes a call to the `mysql_error` function. This function outputs the error text from the last called MySQL function.

The database server pointer `$db_server` will be used in some of the following examples to identify the MySQL server to be queried. Using identifiers this way, it is possible to connect to and access multiple MySQL servers from a single PHP program.

> The `die` function is great for when you are developing PHP code, but of course you will want more user-friendly error messages on a production server. In this case you won't abort your PHP program, but format a message that will be displayed when the program exits normally, such as:
>
> ```
> function mysql_fatal_error($msg)
>     {
>         $msg2 - mysql_error();
>         echo <<< _END
> We are sorry, but it was not possible to complete
> the requested task. The error message we got was:
>
>     <p>$msg: $msg2</p>
>
> Please click the back button on your browser
> and try again. If you are still having problems,
> ```

```
                     please <a href="mailto:admin@server.com">email
                     our administrator</a>. Thank you.
                     _END;
                     }
```

Selecting a database

Having successfully connected to MySQL, you are now ready to select the database that you will be using. Example 10-3 shows how to do this.

Example 10-3. Selecting a database

```
<?php
mysql_select_db($db_database)
    or die("Unable to select database: " . mysql_error());
?>
```

The command to select the database is `mysql_select_db`. Pass it the name of the database you want and the server to which you connected. As with the previous example, a `die` statement has been included to provide an error message and explanation, should the selection fail—the only difference being that there has been no need to retain the return value from the `mysql_select_db` function, as it simply returns either `TRUE` or `FALSE`. Therefore the PHP `or` statement was used, which means "if the previous command failed, do the following." Note that for the `or` to work, there must be no semicolon at the end of the first line of code.

Building and executing a query

Sending a query to MySQL from PHP is as simple as issuing it using the `mysql_query` function. Example 10-4 shows you how to use it.

Example 10-4. Querying a database

```
<?php
$query = "SELECT * FROM classics";
$result = mysql_query($query);

if (!$result) die ("Database access failed: " . mysql_error());
?>
```

First, the variable `$query` is set to the query to be made. In this case it is asking to see all rows in the table *classics*. Note that, unlike using MySQL's command line, no semicolon is required at the tail of the query, because the `mysql_query` function is used to issue a complete query, and cannot be used to query by sending multiple parts, one at a time. Therefore, MySQL knows the query is complete and doesn't look for a semicolon.

This function returns a result that we place in the variable `$result`. Having used MySQL at the command line, you might think that the contents of `$result` will be the same as the result returned from a command-line query, with horizontal and vertical lines, and so on. However, this is not the case with the result returned to PHP. Instead, upon success, $result will contain a *resource* that can be used to extract the results of the query. You'll see how to extract the data in the next section. Upon failure, $result contains FALSE. So the example finishes by checking $result. If it's FALSE, it means that there was an error and the die command is executed.

Fetching a result

Once you have a resource returned from a mysql_query function, you can use it to retrieve the data you want. The simplest way to do this is to fetch the cells you want, one at a time, using the mysql_result function. Example 10-5 combines and extends the previous examples into a program that you can type in and run yourself to retrieve the returned results. I suggest that you save it in the same folder as *login.php* and give it the name *query.php*.

Example 10-5. Fetching results one cell at a time

```php
<?php // query.php
require_once 'login.php';
$db_server = mysql_connect($db_hostname, $db_username, $db_password);

if (!$db_server) die("Unable to connect to MySQL: " . mysql_error());

mysql_select_db($db_database)
    or die("Unable to select database: " . mysql_error());

$query = "SELECT * FROM classics";
$result = mysql_query($query);

if (!$result) die ("Database access failed: " . mysql_error());

$rows = mysql_num_rows($result);

for ($j = 0 ; $j < $rows ; ++$j)
{
    echo 'Author: '    . mysql_result($result,$j,'author')   . '<br />';
    echo 'Title: '     . mysql_result($result,$j,'title')    . '<br />';
    echo 'Category: '  . mysql_result($result,$j,'category') . '<br />';
    echo 'Year: '      . mysql_result($result,$j,'year')     . '<br />';
    echo 'ISBN: '      . mysql_result($result,$j,'isbn')     . '<br /><br />';
}
?>
```

The final 10 lines of code are the new ones, so let's look at them. They start by setting the variable $rows to the value returned by a call to mysql_num_rows. This function reports the number of rows returned by a query.

Armed with the row count, we enter a for loop that extracts each cell of data from each row using the mysql_result function. The parameters supplied to this function are the resource $result, which was returned by mysql_query, the row number $j, and the name of the column from which to extract the data.

Author: Mark Twain (Samuel Langhorne Clemens)
Title: The Adventures of Tom Sawyer
Category: Classic Fiction
Year: 1876
ISBN: 9781598184891

Author: Jane Austen
Title: Pride and Prejudice
Category: Classic Fiction
Year: 1811
ISBN: 9780582506206

Author: Charles Darwin
Title: The Origin of Species
Category: Non-Fiction
Year: 1856
ISBN: 9780517123201

Author: Charles Dickens
Title: The Old Curiosity Shop
Category: Classic Fiction
Year: 1841
ISBN: 9780099533474

Author: William Shakespeare

Figure 10-1. The output from the query.php program in Example 10-5

The results from each call to `mysql_result` are then incorporated within `echo` statements to display one field per line, with an additional line feed between rows. Figure 10-1 shows the result of running this program.

As you may recall, we populated the *classics* table with five rows in Chapter 8, and indeed, five rows of data are returned by *query.php*. But, as it stands, this code is actually extremely inefficient and slow, because a total of 25 calls are made to the function `mysql_result` in order to retrieve all the data, a single cell at a time. Luckily, there is a much better way of retrieving the data, which is getting a single row at a time using the `mysql_fetch_row` function.

 In Chapter 9, I talked about First, Second, and Third Normal Form, so you may have now noticed that the *classics* table doesn't satisfy these, because both author and book details are included within the same table. That's because we created this table before encountering normalization. However, for the purposes of illustrating access to MySQL from PHP, reusing this table avoids the hassle of typing in a new set of test data, so we'll stick with it for the time being.

Fetching a row

It was important to show how you can fetch a single cell of data from MySQL, but now let's look at a much more efficient method. So, replace the `for` loop of *query.php* (in Example 10-5) with the new loop in Example 10-6, and you will find that you get exactly the same result that was displayed in Figure 10-1.

Example 10-6. Replacement for loop for fetching results one row at a time

```php
<?php
for ($j = 0 ; $j < $rows ; ++$j)
{
    $row = mysql_fetch_row($result);
    echo 'Author: ' .        $row[0] . '<br />';
    echo 'Title: ' .         $row[1] . '<br />';
    echo 'Category: ' .      $row[2] . '<br />';
    echo 'Year: ' .          $row[3] . '<br />';
    echo 'ISBN: ' .          $row[4] . '<br /><br />';
}
?>
```

In this modified code, only one-fifth of the calls are made to a MySQL-calling function (a full 80 percent less), because each row is fetched in its entirety using the `mysql_fetch_row` function. This returns a single row of data in an array, which is then assigned to the variable `$row`.

All that's necessary then is to reference each element of the array `$row` in turn (starting at an offset of zero). Therefore `$row[0]` contains the *Author* data, `$row[1]` the *Title*, and so on, because each column is placed in the array in the order in which it appears in the MySQL table. Also, by using `mysql_fetch_row` instead of `mysql_result`, you use substantially less PHP code and achieve much faster execution time, due to simply referencing each item of data by offset rather than by name.

Closing a connection

When you have finished using a database, you should close the connection. This is done by issuing the command in Example 10-7.

Example 10-7. Closing a MySQL database connection

```php
<?php
mysql_close($db_server);
?>
```

We have to pass the identifier returned by `mysql_connect` back in Example 10-2, which we stored in the variable `$db_server`.

All database connections are automatically closed when PHP exits, so it doesn't matter that the connection wasn't closed in Example 10-5. But in longer programs, where you may continually open and close database connections, you are strongly advised to close each one as soon as accessing it is complete.

A Practical Example

It's time to write our first example of inserting data in and deleting it from a MySQL table using PHP. I recommend that you type in Example 10-8 and save it to your web development directory using the filename *sqltest.php*. You can see an example of the program's output in Figure 10-2.

Figure 10-2. The output from Example 10-8, sqltest.php

Example 10-8 creates a standard HTML form. The following chapter explains forms in detail, but in this chapter I take form handling for granted and just deal with database interaction.

Example 10-8. Inserting and deleting using sqltest.php

```php
<?php // sqltest.php
require_once 'login.php';
$db_server = mysql_connect($db_hostname, $db_username, $db_password);

if (!$db_server) die("Unable to connect to MySQL: " . mysql_error());

mysql_select_db($db_database, $db_server)
    or die("Unable to select database: " . mysql_error());

if (isset($_POST['author']) &&
    isset($_POST['title']) &&
    isset($_POST['category']) &&
    isset($_POST['year']) &&
    isset($_POST['isbn']))
{
    $author   = get_post('author');
    $title    = get_post('title');
    $category = get_post('category');
    $year     = get_post('year');
    $isbn     = get_post('isbn');

    if (isset($_POST['delete']) && $isbn != "")
    {
        $query = "DELETE FROM classics WHERE isbn='$isbn'";

        if (!mysql_query($query, $db_server))
            echo "DELETE failed: $query<br />" .
            mysql_error() . "<br /><br />";
    }
    else
    {
        $query = "INSERT INTO classics VALUES" .
        "('$author', '$title', '$category', '$year', '$isbn')";

        if (!mysql_query($query, $db_server))
            echo "INSERT failed: $query<br />" .
            mysql_error() . "<br /><br />";
    }
}

echo <<<_END
<form action="sqltest.php" method="post"><pre>
  Author <input type="text" name="author" />
   Title <input type="text" name="title" />
Category <input type="text" name="category" />
    Year <input type="text" name="year" />
    ISBN <input type="text" name="isbn" />
         <input type="submit" value="ADD RECORD" />
</pre></form>
_END;

$query = "SELECT * FROM classics";
$result = mysql_query($query);
```

```php
if (!$result) die ("Database access failed: " . mysql_error());
$rows = mysql_num_rows($result);

for ($j = 0 ; $j < $rows ; ++$j)
{
    $row = mysql_fetch_row($result);
    echo <<<_END
<pre>
  Author $row[0]
   Title $row[1]
Category $row[2]
    Year $row[3]
    ISBN $row[4]
</pre>
<form action="sqltest.php" method="post">
<input type="hidden" name="delete" value="yes" />
<input type="hidden" name="isbn" value="$row[4]" />
<input type="submit" value="DELETE RECORD" /></form>
_END;
}

mysql_close($db_server);

function get_post($var)
{
    return mysql_real_escape_string($_POST[$var]);
}
?>
```

At over 80 lines of code, this program may appear daunting, but don't worry—you've already covered many of them in Example 10-5, and what the code does is actually quite simple.

It first checks for any inputs that may have been made and then either inserts new data into the *classics* table of the *publications* database or deletes a row from it, according to the input supplied. Regardless of whether there was input, the program then outputs all rows in the table to the browser. So let's see how it works.

The first section of new code starts by using the `isset` function to check whether values for all the fields have been posted to the program. Upon such confirmation, each of the first six lines within the `if` statement call the function `get_post`, which appears at the end of the program. This function has one small but critical job: fetching the input from the browser.

The $_POST Array

I mentioned in an earlier chapter that a browser sends user input through either a GET request or a POST request. The POST request is usually preferred, and we use it here. The web server bundles up all the user input (even if the form was filled out with a hundred fields) and puts it into an array named $_POST.

$_POST is an associative array, which you encountered in Chapter 6. Depending on whether a form has been set to use the POST or the GET method, either the $_POST or the $_GET associative array will be populated with the form data. They can both be read in exactly the same way.

Each field has an element in the array named after that field. So if a form contained a field named isbn, the $_POST array contains an element keyed by the word isbn. The PHP program can read that field by referring to either $_POST['isbn'] or $_POST["isbn"] (single and double quotes have the same effect in this case).

If the $_POST syntax still seems complex to you, rest assured that you can just use the convention I've shown in Example 10-8, copy the user's input to other variables, and forget about $_POST after that. This is normal in PHP programs: they retrieve all the fields from $_POST at the beginning of the program and then ignore it.

> There is no reason to write to an element in the $_POST array. Its only purpose is to communicate information from the browser to the program, and you're better off copying data to your own variables before altering it.

So, back to the get_post function, which passes each item it retrieves through the mysql_real_escape_string function to strip out any characters that a hacker may have inserted in order to break into or alter your database.

Deleting a Record

Having loaded up the various possible variables that could have been posted with any values that were passed, the program then checks whether the variable $_POST['delete'] has a value. If so, the user has clicked on a DELETE RECORD button to erase a record. In this case, the value of $isbn will also have been posted.

As you'll recall, the ISBN uniquely identifies each record. The HTML form appends the ISBN to the DELETE FROM query string created in the variable $query, which is then passed to the mysql_query function to issue it to MySQL. mysql_query returns either TRUE or FALSE, and FALSE causes an error message to be displayed explaining what went wrong.

If $delete didn't contain the word "yes," then the following else statement is executed. $query is set to an INSERT INTO command, followed by the five values to be inserted. The variable is then passed to mysql_query, which upon completion returns either TRUE or FALSE. If FALSE is returned, an error message is displayed.

Displaying the Form

Next we get to the part of code that displays the little form at the top of Figure 10-2. You should recall the `echo <<<_END` structure from previous chapters, which outputs everything between the `_END` tags.

 Instead of the `echo` command, the program could also drop out of PHP using `?>`, issue the HTML, and then reenter PHP processing with `<?php`. Whichever style used is a matter of programmer preference, but I always recommend staying within PHP code for these reasons:

- It makes it very clear when debugging (and also for other users) that everything within a *.php* file is PHP code. Therefore, there is no need to go hunting for dropouts to HTML.
- When you wish to include a PHP variable directly within HTML, you can just type it in. If you had dropped back to HTML, you would have had to temporarily reenter PHP processing, output the variable, and then drop back out again.

The HTML form section simply sets the form's action to *sqltest.php*. This means that when the form is submitted, the contents of the form fields will be sent to the file *sqltest.php*, which is the program itself. The form is also set up to send the fields as a `POST` rather than a `GET` request. This is because `GET` requests are appended to the URL being submitted and can look messy in your browser. They also allow users to easily modify submissions and try to hack your server. Therefore, whenever possible, you should use `POST` submissions, which also have the benefit of hiding the posted data from view.

Having output the form fields, the HTML displays a Submit button with the name ADD RECORD and closes the form. Note the use of the `<pre>` and `</pre>` tags here, which have been used to force a monospaced font and allow all the inputs to line up neatly. The carriage returns at the end of each line are also output when inside `<pre>` tags.

Querying the Database

Next, the code returns to the familiar territory of Example 10-5 where, in the following four lines of code, a query is sent to MySQL asking to see all the records in the *classics* table. After that, `$rows` is set to a value representing the number of rows in the table and a `for` loop is entered to display the contents of each row.

I have altered the next bit of code to simplify things. Instead of using the `<br />` tags for line feeds in Example 10-5, I have chosen to use a `<pre>` tag to line up the display of each record in a pleasing manner.

After the display of each record there is a second form that also posts to *sqltest.php* (the program itself) but this time contains two hidden fields: *delete* and *isbn*. The *delete* field is set to "yes" and *isbn* to the value held in $row[4], which contains the ISBN for the record. Then a Submit button with the name DELETE RECORD is displayed and the form is closed. A curly brace then completes the for loop, which will continue until all records have been displayed.

Finally, you see the definition for the function get_post, which we've already looked at. And that's it—our first PHP program to manipulate a MySQL database. So, let's check out what it can do.

Once you have typed the program in (and corrected any typing errors), try entering the following data into the various input fields to add a new record for the book *Moby Dick* to the database:

```
Herman Melville
Moby Dick
Fiction
1851
9780199535729
```

Running the Program

When you have submitted this data using the ADD RECORD button, scroll down to the bottom of the web page to see the new addition. It should look like Figure 10-3.

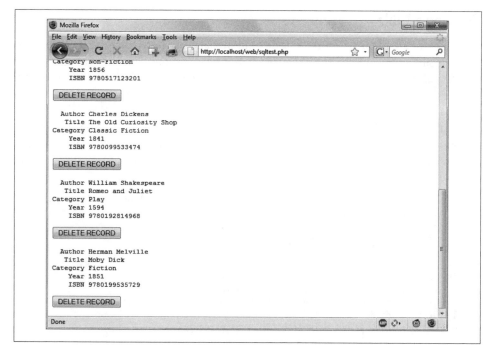

Figure 10-3. The result of adding Moby Dick to the database

Now let's look at how deleting a record works by creating a dummy record. So try entering just the number 1 in each of the five fields and click on the ADD RECORD button. If you now scroll down, you'll see a new record consisting just of 1s. Obviously this record isn't useful in this table, so now click on the DELETE RECORD button and scroll down again to confirm that the record has been deleted.

 Assuming that everything worked, you are now able to add and delete records at will. Try doing this a few times, but leave the main records in place (including the new one for *Moby Dick*), as we'll be using them later. You could also try adding the record with all 1s again a couple of times and note the error message that you receive the second time, indicating that there is already an ISBN with the number 1.

Practical MySQL

You are now ready to look at some practical techniques that you can use in PHP to access the MySQL database, including tasks such as creating and dropping tables, inserting, updating, and deleting data, and protecting your database and website from malicious users. Note that the following examples assume that you've created the *login.php* program discussed earlier in this chapter.

Creating a Table

Let's assume that you are working for a wildlife park and need to create a database to hold details about all the types of cats it houses. You are told that there are nine *families* of cats: Lion, Tiger, Jaguar, Leopard, Cougar, Cheetah, Lynx, Caracal, and Domestic, so you'll need a column for that. Then each cat has been given a *name*, so that's another column, and you also want to keep track of their *ages*, which is another. Of course, you will probably need more columns later, perhaps to hold dietary requirements, inoculations, and other details, but for now that's enough to get going. A unique identifier is also needed for each animal, so you also decide to create a column for that called *id*.

Example 10-9 shows the code you might use to create a MySQL table to hold this data, with the main query assignment in bold text.

Example 10-9. Creating a table called cats

```
<?php
require_once 'login.php';
$db_server = mysql_connect($db_hostname, $db_username, $db_password);
if (!$db_server) die("Unable to connect to MySQL: " . mysql_error());
mysql_select_db($db_database)
    or die("Unable to select database: " . mysql_error());

$query = "CREATE TABLE cats (
          id SMALLINT NOT NULL AUTO_INCREMENT,
```

```
        family VARCHAR(32) NOT NULL,
        name VARCHAR(32) NOT NULL,
        age TINYINT NOT NULL,
        PRIMARY KEY (id)
    )";

$result = mysql_query($query);
if (!$result) die ("Database access failed: " . mysql_error());
?>
```

As you can see, the MySQL query looks pretty similar to how you would type it in directly to the command line, except that there is no trailing semicolon, as none is needed when accessing MySQL from PHP.

Describing a Table

When you aren't logged into the MySQL command line, here's a handy piece of code that you can use to verify that a table has been correctly created from inside a browser. It simply issues the query DESCRIBE cats and then outputs an HTML table with four headings: *Column*, *Type*, *Null*, and *Key*, underneath which all columns within the table are shown. To use it with other tables, simply replace the name "cats" in the query with that of the new table (see Example 10-10).

Example 10-10. Describing the cats table

```
<?php
require_once 'login.php';
$db_server = mysql_connect($db_hostname, $db_username, $db_password);
if (!$db_server) die("Unable to connect to MySQL: " . mysql_error());
mysql_select_db($db_database)
    or die("Unable to select database: " . mysql_error());

$query = "DESCRIBE cats";

$result = mysql_query($query);
if (!$result) die ("Database access failed: " . mysql_error());
$rows = mysql_num_rows($result);

echo "<table><tr> <th>Column</th> <th>Type</th>
    <th>Null</th> <th>Key</th> </tr>";

for ($j = 0 ; $j < $rows ; ++$j)
{
    $row = mysql_fetch_row($result);
    echo "<tr>";
    for ($k = 0 ; $k < 4 ; ++$k) echo "<td>$row[$k]</td>";
    echo "</tr>";
}

echo "</table>";
?>
```

The output from the program should look like this:

```
Column Type        Null Key
id     smallint(6) NO   PRI
family varchar(32) NO
name   varchar(32) NO
age    tinyint(4)  NO
```

Dropping a Table

Dropping a table is very easy to do and is therefore very dangerous, so be careful. Example 10-11 shows the code that you need. However, I don't recommend that you try it until you have been through the other examples, as it will drop the table *cats* and you'll have to recreate it using Example 10-9.

Example 10-11. Dropping the table cats

```php
<?php
require_once 'login.php';
$db_server = mysql_connect($db_hostname, $db_username, $db_password);
if (!$db_server) die("Unable to connect to MySQL: " . mysql_error());
mysql_select_db($db_database)
    or die("Unable to select database: " . mysql_error());

$query = "DROP TABLE cats";

$result = mysql_query($query);
if (!$result) die ("Database access failed: " . mysql_error());
?>
```

Adding Data

Let's add some data to the table using the code in Example 10-12.

Example 10-12. Adding data to table cats

```php
<?php
require_once 'login.php';
$db_server = mysql_connect($db_hostname, $db_username, $db_password);
if (!$db_server) die("Unable to connect to MySQL: " . mysql_error());
mysql_select_db($db_database)
    or die("Unable to select database: " . mysql_error());

$query = "INSERT INTO cats VALUES(NULL, 'Lion', 'Leo', 4)";

$result = mysql_query($query);
if (!$result) die ("Database access failed: " . mysql_error());
?>
```

You may wish to add a couple more items of data by modifying $query as follows and calling the program up in your browser again:

```
$query = "INSERT INTO cats VALUES(NULL, 'Cougar', 'Growler', 2)";
$query = "INSERT INTO cats VALUES(NULL, 'Cheetah', 'Charly', 3)";
```

By the way, notice the NULL value passed as the first parameter? This is done because the *id* column is of the AUTO_INCREMENT type and MySQL will decide what value to assign according to the next available number in sequence, so we simply pass a NULL value, which will be ignored.

Of course, the most efficient way to populate MySQL with data is to create an array and insert the data with a single query.

Retrieving Data

Now that some data has been entered into the *cats* table, Example 10-13 shows how you can check that it was correctly inserted.

Example 10-13. Retrieving rows from the cats table

```
<?php
require_once 'login.php';
$db_server = mysql_connect($db_hostname, $db_username, $db_password);
if (!$db_server) die("Unable to connect to MySQL: " . mysql_error());
mysql_select_db($db_database)
    or die("Unable to select database: " . mysql_error());

$query = "SELECT * FROM cats";

$result = mysql_query($query);
if (!$result) die ("Database access failed: " . mysql_error());
$rows = mysql_num_rows($result);

echo "<table><tr> <th>Id</th> <th>Family</th>
    <th>Name</th><th>Age</th></tr>";

for ($j = 0 ; $j < $rows ; ++$j)
{
    $row = mysql_fetch_row($result);
    echo "<tr>";
    for ($k = 0 ; $k < 4 ; ++$k) echo "<td>$row[$k]</td>";
    echo "</tr>";
}

echo "</table>";
?>
```

This code simply issues the MySQL query SELECT * FROM cats and then displays all the rows returned. Its output is as follows:

Id	Family	Name	Age
1	Lion	Leo	4
2	Cougar	Growler	2
3	Cheetah	Charly	3

Here you can see that the *id* column has correctly auto-incremented.

Updating Data

Changing data that you have already inserted is also quite simple. Did you notice the spelling of Charly for the Cheetah's name? Let's correct that to Charlie, as in Example 10-14.

Example 10-14. Renaming Charly the Cheetah to Charlie

```php
<?php
require_once 'login.php';
$db_server = mysql_connect($db_hostname, $db_username, $db_password);
if (!$db_server) die("Unable to connect to MySQL: " . mysql_error());
mysql_select_db($db_database)
    or die("Unable to select database: " . mysql_error());

$query = "UPDATE cats SET name='Charlie' WHERE name='Charly'";

$result = mysql_query($query);
if (!$result) die ("Database access failed: " . mysql_error());
?>
```

If you run Example 10-13 again, you'll see that it now outputs the following:

```
Id Family   Name    Age
1  Lion     Leo     4
2  Cougar   Growler 2
3  Cheetah  Charlie 3
```

Deleting Data

Growler the Cougar has been transferred to another zoo, so it's time to remove him from the database—see Example 10-15.

Example 10-15. Removing Growler the Cougar from the cats table

```php
<?php
require_once 'login.php';
$db_server = mysql_connect($db_hostname, $db_username, $db_password);
if (!$db_server) die("Unable to connect to MySQL: " . mysql_error());
mysql_select_db($db_database)
    or die("Unable to select database: " . mysql_error());

$query = "DELETE FROM cats WHERE name='Growler'";

$result = mysql_query($query);
if (!$result) die ("Database access failed: " . mysql_error());
?>
```

This uses a standard DELETE FROM query, and when you run Example 10-13, you can see how the row has been removed by the following output:

```
Id Family   Name    Age
1  Lion     Leo     4
3  Cheetah  Charlie 3
```

Using AUTO_INCREMENT

When using `AUTO_INCREMENT`, you cannot know what value has been given to a column before a row is inserted. Instead, if you need to know it, you must ask MySQL afterward using the `mysql_insert_id` function. This need is common: for instance, when you process a purchase, you might insert a new customer into a *Customers* table and then refer to the newly created *CustId* when inserting a purchase into the purchase table.

Example 10-12 can be rewritten as Example 10-16 to display this value after each insert.

Example 10-16. Adding data to cats table and reporting the insertion id

```php
<?php
require_once 'login.php';
$db_server = mysql_connect($db_hostname, $db_username, $db_password);
if (!$db_server) die("Unable to connect to MySQL: " . mysql_error());
mysql_select_db($db_database)
    or die("Unable to select database: " . mysql_error());

$query = "INSERT INTO cats VALUES(NULL, 'Lynx', 'Stumpy', 5)";

$result = mysql_query($query);
echo "The Insert ID was: " . mysql_insert_id();
if (!$result) die ("Database access failed: " . mysql_error());
?>
```

The contents of the table should now look like the following (note how the previous *id* value of 2 is *not* reused, as this could cause complications in some instances):

Id	Family	Name	Age
1	Lion	Leo	4
3	Cheetah	Charlie	3
4	Lynx	Stumpy	5

Using insert IDs

It's very common to insert data in multiple tables: a book followed by its author, or a customer followed by their purchase, and so on. When doing this with an auto-increment column, you will need to retain the insert ID returned for storing in the related table.

For example, let's assume that these cats can be "adopted" by the public as a means of raising funds, and that when a new cat is stored in the *cats* table, we also want to create a key to tie it to the animal's adoptive owner. The code to do this is similar to that in Example 10-16, except that the returned insert ID is stored in the variable `$insertID`, and is then used as part of the subsequent query:

```php
$query    = "INSERT INTO cats VALUES(NULL, 'Lynx', 'Stumpy', 5)";
$result   = mysql_query($query);
$insertID = mysql_insert_id();

$query    = "INSERT INTO owners VALUES($insertID, 'Ann', 'Smith')";
$result   = mysql_query($query);
```

Now the cat is connected to its "owner" through the cat's unique ID, which was created automatically by `AUTO_INCREMENT`.

But there's a slight window of opportunity for an error to slip in. Suppose that two people visit the website at the same time and submit new information, causing the web server to run your program twice at the same time. (Web servers can run several programs at the same time to speed up response time.) The second visitor might insert a new cat just before the first visitor's program issues `mysql_insert_id`. This is a rare but serious problem, because the first person could end up being associated with the second person's cat.

So a completely safe procedure for linking tables through the insert ID is to use locks (or transactions, as described in Chapter 9). It can slow down response time a bit when there are many people submitting data to the same table, but it can also be worth it. The sequence is:

1. Lock the first table (e.g., *cats*).
2. Insert data into the first table.
3. Retrieve the unique ID from the first table through `mysql_insert_id`.
4. Unlock the first table.
5. Insert data into the second table.

The lock can safely be released before inserting data into the second table, because the insert ID has been retrieved and is stored in a program variable. A transaction can also be used instead of locking, but that slows down the MySQL server even more.

Performing Additional Queries

OK: that's enough feline fun. To explore some slightly more complex queries, we need to revert to using the *customers* and *classics* tables that you should have created in Chapter 8. There will be two customers in the *customers* table; the *classics* table holds the details of a few books. They also share a common column of ISBN numbers called *isbn* that we can use to perform additional queries.

For example, to display each of the customers along with the titles and authors of the books they have bought, you can use the code in Example 10-17.

Example 10-17. Performing a secondary query

```php
<?php
require_once 'login.php';
$db_server = mysql_connect($db_hostname, $db_username, $db_password);
if (!$db_server) die("Unable to connect to MySQL: " . mysql_error());
mysql_select_db($db_database)
    or die("Unable to select database: " . mysql_error());

$query = "SELECT * FROM customers";
```

```
$result = mysql_query($query);
if (!$result) die ("Database access failed: " . mysql_error());
$rows = mysql_num_rows($result);

for ($j = 0 ; $j < $rows ; ++$j)
{
    $row = mysql_fetch_row($result);
    echo "$row[0] purchased ISBN $row[1]:<br />";

    $subquery = "SELECT * FROM classics WHERE isbn='$row[1]'";

    $subresult = mysql_query($subquery);
    if (!$subresult) die ("Database access failed: " . mysql_error());
    $subrow = mysql_fetch_row($subresult);
    echo "  '$subrow[1]' by $subrow[0]<br />";
}
?>
```

This program uses an initial query to the *customers* table to look up all the customers and then, given the ISBN number of the book each customer purchased, makes a new query to the *classics* table to find out the title and author for each. The output from this code should be as follows:

```
Mary Smith purchased ISBN 9780582506206:
    'Pride and Prejudice' by Jane Austen
Jack Wilson purchased ISBN 9780517123201:
    'The Origin of Species' by Charles Darwin
```

 Of course, although it wouldn't illustrate performing additional queries, in this particular case you could also return the same information using a NATURAL JOIN query (see Chapter 8), like this:

```
SELECT name,isbn,title,author FROM customers
    NATURAL JOIN classics;
```

Preventing SQL Injection

It may be hard to understand just how dangerous it is to pass user input unchecked to MySQL. For example, suppose you have a simple piece of code to verify a user, and it looks like this:

```
$user  = $_POST['user'];
$pass  = $_POST['pass'];
$query = "SELECT * FROM users WHERE user='$user' AND pass='$pass'";
```

At first glance, you might think this code is perfectly fine. If the user enters values of *fredsmith* and *mypass* for $user and $pass, then the query string, as passed to MySQL, will be as follows:

```
SELECT * FROM users WHERE user='fredsmith' AND pass='mypass'
```

This is all well and good, but what if someone enters the following for $user (and doesn't even enter anything for $pass)?

```
admin' #
```

Let's look at the string that would be sent to MySQL:

```
SELECT * FROM users WHERE user='admin' #' AND pass=''
```

Do you see the problem there? In MySQL, the # symbol represents the start of a comment. Therefore the user will be logged in as *admin* (assuming there is a user *admin*), without having to enter a password. In the following, the part of the query that will be executed is shown in bold—the rest will be ignored.

```
SELECT * FROM users WHERE user='admin' #' AND pass=''
```

But you should count yourself very lucky if that's all a malicious user does to you. At least you might still be able to go into your application and undo any changes the user makes as *admin*. But what about the case in which your application code removes a user from the database? The code might look something like this:

```
$user  = $_POST['user'];
$pass  = $_POST['pass'];
$query = "DELETE FROM users WHERE user='$user' AND pass='$pass'";
```

Again, this looks quite normal at first glance, but what if someone entered the following for $user?

```
anything' OR 1=1 #
```

This would be interpreted by MySQL as:

```
DELETE FROM users WHERE user='anything' OR 1=1 #' AND pass=''
```

Ouch—that SQL query will always be true and therefore you've lost your whole *users* database! So what can you do about this kind of attack?

Well, the first thing is not to rely on PHP's built-in *magic quotes*, which automatically escape any characters such as single and double quotes by prefacing them with a backslash (\). Why? Because this feature can be turned off; many programmers do so in order to put their own security code in place. So there is no guarantee that this hasn't happened on the server you are working on. In fact, the feature was deprecated as of PHP 5.3.0 and has been removed in PHP 6.0.0.

Instead, you should always use the function mysql_real_escape_string for all calls to MySQL. Example 10-18 is a function you can use that will remove any magic quotes added to a user-inputted string and then properly sanitize it for you.

Example 10-18. How to properly sanitize user input for MySQL

```php
<?php
function mysql_fix_string($string)
{
    if (get_magic_quotes_gpc()) $string = stripslashes($string);
    return mysql_real_escape_string($string);
```

```
}
?>
```

The `get_magic_quotes_gpc` function returns TRUE if magic quotes are active. In that case, any slashes that have been added to a string have to be removed or the function `mysql_real_eascape_string` could end up double-escaping some characters, creating corrupted strings. Example 10-19 illustrates how you would incorporate `mysql_fix` within your own code.

Example 10-19. How to safely access MySQL with user input

```php
<?php
$user  = mysql_fix_string($_POST['user']);
$pass  = mysql_fix_string($_POST['pass']);
$query = "SELECT * FROM users WHERE user='$user' AND pass='$pass'";

function mysql_fix_string($string)
{
    if (get_magic_quotes_gpc()) $string = stripslashes($string);
    return mysql_real_escape_string($string);
}
?>
```

 Remember that you can use `mysql_escape_string` only when a MySQL database is actively open; otherwise, an error will occur.

Using placeholders

Another way—this one virtually bulletproof—to prevent SQL injections is to use a feature called *placeholders*. The idea is to predefine a query using ? characters where the data will appear. Then, instead of calling a MySQL query directly, you call the predefined one, passing the data to it. This has the effect of ensuring that every item of data entered is inserted directly into the database and cannot be interpreted as SQL queries. In other words, SQL injections become impossible.

The sequence of queries to execute when using MySQL's command line would be like that in Example 10-20.

Example 10-20. Using placeholders

```
PREPARE statement FROM "INSERT INTO classics VALUES(?,?,?,?,?)";

SET @author   = "Emily Brontë",
    @title    = "Wuthering Heights",
    @category = "Classic Fiction",
    @year     = "1847",
    @isbn     = "9780553212587";

EXECUTE statement USING @author,@title,@category,@year,@isbn;

DEALLOCATE PREPARE statement;
```

The first command prepares a statement called statement for inserting data into the classics table. As you can see, in place of values or variables for the data to insert, the statement contains a series of ? characters. These are the placeholders.

The next five lines assign values to MySQL variables according to the data to be inserted. Then the predefined statement is executed, passing these variables as parameters. Finally, the statement is removed, in order to return the resources it was using.

In PHP, the code for this procedure looks like Example 10-21 (assuming that you have created *login.php* with the correct details to access the database).

Example 10-21. Using placeholders with PHP

```php
<?php
require 'login.php';

$db_server = mysql_connect($db_hostname, $db_username, $db_password);
if (!$db_server) die("Unable to connect to MySQL: " . mysql_error());
mysql_select_db($db_database)
    or die("Unable to select database: " . mysql_error());

$query = 'PREPARE statement FROM "INSERT INTO classics
    VALUES(?,?,?,?,?)"';
mysql_query($query);

$query = 'SET @author = "Emily Brontë",' .
        '@title = "Wuthering Heights",' .
        '@category = "Classic Fiction",' .
        '@year = "1847",' .
        '@isbn = "9780553212587"';
mysql_query($query);

$query = 'EXECUTE statement USING @author,@title,@category,@year,@isbn';
mysql_query($query);

$query = 'DEALLOCATE PREPARE statement';
mysql_query($query);
?>
```

Once you have prepared a statement, until you deallocate it, you can use it as often as you wish. Such statements are commonly used within a loop to quickly insert data into a database by assigning values to the MySQL variables and then executing the statement. This approach is more efficient than creating the entire statement from scratch on each pass through the loop.

Preventing HTML Injection

There's another type of injection you need to concern yourself about—not for the safety of your own websites, but for your users' privacy and protection. That's Cross Site Scripting, also referred to as XSS.

This occurs when you allow HTML, or more often JavaScript code, to be input by a user and then displayed back by your website. One place this is common is in a comment form. What most often happens is that a malicious user will try to write code that steals cookies from your site's users, allowing him or her to discover username and password pairs or other information. Even worse, the malicious user might launch an attack to download a Trojan onto a user's computer.

But preventing this is as simple as calling the `htmlentities` function, which strips out all HTML markup codes and replaces them with a form that displays the characters, but does not allow a browser to act on them. For example, consider the following HTML:

```
<script src='http://x.com/hack.js'> </script><script>hack();</script>
```

This code loads in a JavaScript program and then executes malicious functions. But if it is first passed through `htmlentities`, it will be turned into the following, totally harmless string:

```
&lt;script src='http://x.com/hack.js'&gt;
  &lt;/script&gt;&lt;script&gt;hack();&lt;/script&gt;
```

Therefore, if you are ever going to display anything that your users enter, either immediately or after first storing it in database, you need to first sanitize it with `htmlentities`. To do this, I recommend you create a new function, like the first one in Example 10-22, which can sanitize for both SQL and XSS injections.

Example 10-22. Functions for preventing both SQL and XSS injection attacks

```php
<?php
function mysql_entities_fix_string($string)
{
    return htmlentities(mysql_fix_string($string));
}

function mysql_fix_string($string)
{
    if (get_magic_quotes_gpc()) $string = stripslashes($string);
    return mysql_real_escape_string($string);
}
?>
```

The `mysql_entities_fix_string` function first calls `mysql_fix_string` and then passes the result through `htmlentities` before returning the fully sanitized string. Example 10-23 shows your new "ultimate protection" version of Example 10-19.

Example 10-23. How to safely access MySQL and prevent XSS attacks

```php
<?php
$user  = mysql_entities_fix_string($_POST['user']);
$pass  = mysql_entities_fix_string($_POST['pass']);
$query = "SELECT * FROM users WHERE user='$user' AND pass='$pass'";

function mysql_entities_fix_string($string)
```

```
{
    return htmlentities(mysql_fix_string($string));
}

function mysql_fix_string($string)
{
    if (get_magic_quotes_gpc()) $string = stripslashes($string);
    return mysql_real_escape_string($string);
}
?>
```

Now that you have learned how to integrate PHP with MySQL and avoid malicious user input, the next chapter will further expand on the use of form handling, including data validation, multiple values, pattern matching, and security.

Test Your Knowledge: Questions

Question 10-1
    What is the standard PHP function for connecting to a MySQL database?

Question 10-2
    When is the `mysql_result` function not optimal?

Question 10-3
    Give one reason why using the POST form method is usually better than GET.

Question 10-4
    How can you determine the last entered value of an AUTO_INCREMENT column?

Question 10-5
    Which PHP function escapes a string, making it suitable for use with MySQL?

Question 10-6
    Which function can be used to prevent Cross Site Scripting injection attacks?

See the section "Chapter 10 Answers" on page 443 in Appendix A for the answers to these questions.

CHAPTER 11

Form Handling

The main way that website users interact with PHP and MySQL is through the use of HTML forms. These were introduced very early on in the development of the World Wide Web in 1993—even before the advent of e-commerce—and have remained a mainstay ever since, due to their simplicity and ease of use.

Of course, enhancements have been made over the years to add extra functionality to HTML form handling, so this chapter will bring you up to speed on state-of-the-art form handling and show you the best ways to implement forms for good usability and security.

Building Forms

Handling forms is a multipart process. First, a form is created into which a user can enter the required details. This data is then sent to the web server, where it is interpreted, often with some error checking. If the PHP code identifies one or more fields that require reentering, the form may be redisplayed with an error message. When the code is satisfied with the accuracy of the input, it takes some action that usually involves the database, such as entering details about a purchase.

To build a form, you must have at least the following elements:

- An opening `<form>` and closing `</form>` tag
- A submission type specifying either a **get** or **post** method
- One or more **input** fields
- The destination URL to which the form data is to be submitted

Example 11-1 shows a very simple form created using PHP. Type it in and save it as *formtest.php*.

Example 11-1. formtest.php—a simple PHP form handler

```php
<?php // formtest.php
echo <<<_END
<html>
    <head>
        <title>Form Test</title>
    </head>
    <body>
    <form method="post" action="formtest.php" />
        What is your name?
        <input type="text" name="name" />
        <input type="submit" />
    </form>
    </body>
</html>
_END;
?>
```

The first thing to notice about this example is that, as you have already seen in this book, rather than dropping in and out of PHP code, the echo <<<_END..._END construct is used whenever multiline HTML must be output.

Inside of this multiline output is some standard code for commencing an HTML document, displaying its title, and starting the body of the document. This is followed by the form, which is set to send its data using the post method to the PHP program *formtest.php*, which is the name of the program itself.

The rest of the program just closes all the items it opened: the form, the body of the HTML document, and the PHP echo <<<_END statement. The result of opening this program in a web browser can be seen in Figure 11-1.

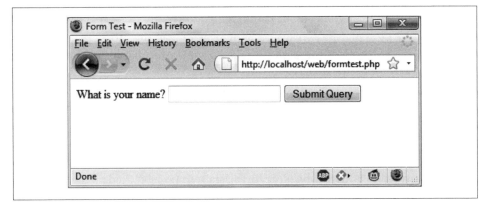

Figure 11-1. The result of opening formtest.php in a web browser

Retrieving Submitted Data

Example 11-1 is only one part of the multipart form handling process. If you enter a name and click on the Submit Query button, absolutely nothing will happen other than the form being redisplayed. So now it's time to add some PHP code to process the data submitted by the form.

Example 11-2 expands on the previous program to include data processing. Type it in, or modify *formtest.php* by adding in the new lines, save it as *formtest2.php*, and try the program for yourself. The result of running this program and entering a name can be seen in Figure 11-2.

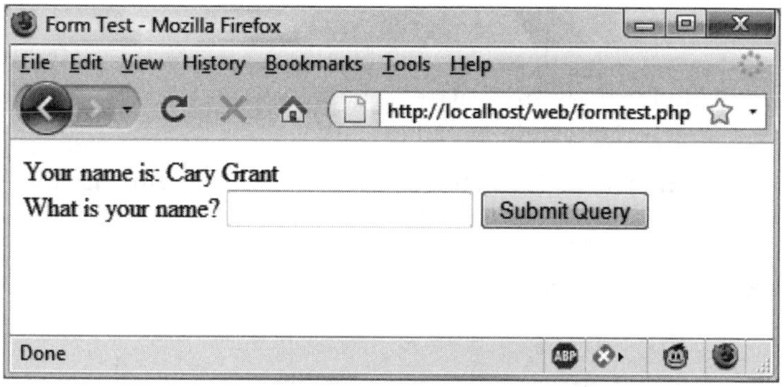

Figure 11-2. formtest.php with data handling

Example 11-2. Updated version of formtest.php

```php
<?php // formtest2.php
if (isset($_POST['name'])) $name = $_POST['name'];
else $name = "(Not entered)";

echo <<<_END
<html>
    <head>
        <title>Form Test</title>
    </head>
    <body>
    Your name is: $name<br />
    <form method="post" action="formtest2.php">
        What is your name?
        <input type="text" name="name" />
        <input type="submit" />
    </form>
    </body>
</html>
_END;
?>
```

The only changes are a couple of lines at the start that check the $_POST associative array for the field *name* having been submitted. The previous chapter introduced the $_POST associative array, which contains an element for each field in an HTML form. In Example 11-2, the input name used was *name* and the form method was post, so element name of the $_POST array contains the value in $_POST['name'].

The PHP isset function is used to test whether $_POST['name'] has been assigned a value. If nothing was posted, the program assigns the value "(Not entered)"; otherwise, it stores the value that was entered. Then a single line has been added after the <body> statement to display that value, which is stored in $name.

register_globals: An Old Solution Hangs On

Before security became such a big issue, the default behavior of PHP was to assign the $_POST and $_GET arrays directly to PHP variables. For example, there would be no need to use the instruction $name=$_POST['name']; because $name would already be given that value automatically by PHP at the program start!

Initially (prior to version 4.2.0 of PHP), this seemed a very useful idea that saved a lot of extra code-writing, but this practice has now been discontinued and the feature is disabled by default. Should you find register_globals enabled on a production web server for which you are developing, you should urgently ask your server administrator to disable it.

So why disable register_globals? It enables anyone to enter a GET input on the tail of a URL, like this: *http://myserver.com?override=1*, and if your code were ever to use the variable $override and you forgot to initialize it (for example, through $override=0;), the program could be compromised by such an exploit.

In fact, because many installations on the Web remain with this gaping hole, I advise you to always initialize every variable you use, just in case your code will ever run on such a system. Initialization is also good programming practice, because you can comment each initialization to remind yourself and other programmers what a variable is for.

 If you ever find yourself maintaining code that seems to assume values for certain variables for no apparent reason, you can make an educated guess that the programmer wrote the code using register_globals, and that these values are intended to be extracted from a POST or GET. If so, I recommend you rewrite the code to load these variables explicitly from the correct $_POST or $_GET array.

Default Values

Sometimes it's convenient to offer your site visitors a default value in a web form. For example, suppose you put up a loan repayment calculator widget on a real estate

Figure 11-3. Using default values for selected form fields

website. It could make sense to enter default values of, say, 25 years and 6 percent interest, so that the user can simply type in either the principal sum to borrow or the amount that he or she can afford to pay each month.

In this case, the HTML for those two values would be something like Example 11-3.

Example 11-3. Setting default values

```
<form method="post" action="calc.php"><pre>
      Loan Amount <input type="text" name="principle" />
Monthly Repayment <input type="text" name="monthly" />
  Number of Years <input type="text" name="years" value="25" />
    Interest Rate <input type="text" name="rate" value="6" />
                  <input type="submit" />
</pre></form>
```

> If you wish to try this (and the other HTML code samples) out, type it in and save it with a .html file extension, such as test.html, then load that file into your browser.

Take a look at the third and fourth inputs. By populating the value parameter, you display a default value in the field, which the users can then change if they wish. With sensible default values you can often make your web forms more user-friendly by min-imizing unnecessary typing. The result of the previous code looks like Figure 11-3. Of course, this was created just to illustrate default values and, because the program calc.php has not been written, the form will not do anything if submitted.

Default values are also used for hidden fields if you want to pass extra information from your web page to your program, in addition to what users enter. We'll look at hidden fields later in this chapter.

Input Types

HTML forms are very versatile and allow you to submit a wide range of different types of inputs ranging from text boxes and text areas to checkboxes, radio buttons, and more.

Text Boxes

Probably the type of input you will most often use is the text box. It accepts a wide range of alphanumeric text and other characters in a single-line box. The general format of a text box input is:

```
<input type="text" name="name" size="size" maxlength="length" value="value" />
```

We've already covered the *name* and *value* parameters, but two more are introduced here: *size* and *maxlength*. The *size* parameter specifies the width of the box, in characters of the current font, as it should appear on the screen, and *maxlength* specifies the maximum number of characters that a user is allowed to enter into the field.

The only required parameters are *type*, which tells the web browser what type of input is to be expected, and *name*, for providing a name to the input that is then used to process the field upon receipt of the submitted form.

Text Areas

When you need to accept input of more than a short line of text, use a text area. This is similar to a text box but, because it allows multiple lines, it has some different parameters. Its general format looks like this:

```
<textarea name="name" cols="width" rows="height" wrap="type">
</textarea>
```

The first thing to notice is that `<textarea>` has its own tag and is not a subtype of the `input` tag. It therefore requires a closing `</textarea>` to end input.

Instead of a default parameter, if you have default text to display, you must put it before the closing `</textarea>`, and it will then be displayed and be editable by the user, like this:

```
<textarea name="name" cols="width" rows="height" wrap="type">
This is some default text.
</textarea>
```

To control the width and height, use the `cols` and `rows` parameters. Both use the character spacing of the current font to determine the size of the area. If you omit these values, a default input box will be created that will vary in dimensions depending on the browser used, so you should always define them to be certain about how your form will appear.

Lastly, you can control how the text entered into the box will wrap (and how any such wrapping will be sent to the server) using the `wrap` parameter. Table 11-1 shows the wrap types available. If you leave out the `wrap` parameter, soft wrapping is used.

Table 11-1. The wrap types available in a textarea input

Type	Action
off	Text does not wrap and lines appear exactly as the user types them.
soft	Text wraps but is sent to the server as one long string without carriage returns and line feeds.
hard	Text wraps and is sent to the server in wrapped format with soft returns and line feeds.

Checkboxes

When you want to offer a number of different options to a user, from which he or she can select one or more items, checkboxes are the way to go. The format to use is:

```
<input type="checkbox" name="name" value="value" checked="checked" />
```

If you include the *checked* parameter, the box is already checked when the browser is displayed (the string you assign to the parameter doesn't matter; the parameter just has to be present). If you don't include the parameter, the box is shown unchecked. Here is an example of an unchecked box:

```
I Agree <input type="checkbox" name="agree" />
```

If the user doesn't check the box, no value will be submitted. But if they do, a value of "on" will be submitted for the field named *agree*. If you prefer to have your own value submitted instead of the word "on" (such as the number 1), you could use the following syntax:

```
I Agree <input type="checkbox" name="agree" value="1" />
```

On the other hand, if you wish to offer a newsletter to your readers when submitting a form, you might want to have the checkbox already checked as the default value:

```
Subscribe? <input type="checkbox" name="news" checked="checked" />
```

If you want to allow groups of items to be selected at one time, assign them all the same name. However, only the last item checked will be submitted, unless you pass an array as the name. For example, Example 11-4 allows the user to select his favorite ice creams (see Figure 11-4 for how it displays in a browser).

Example 11-4. Offering multiple checkbox choices

```
   Vanilla <input type="checkbox" name="ice" value="Vanilla" />
 Chocolate <input type="checkbox" name="ice" value="Chocolate" />
Strawberry <input type="checkbox" name="ice" value="Strawberry" />
```

If only one of the checkboxes is selected, such as the second one, only that item will be submitted (the field named *ice* would be assigned the value "Chocolate"). But if two

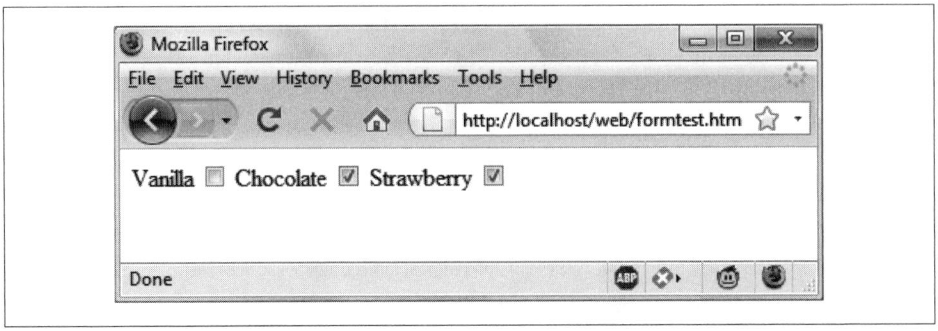

Figure 11-4. Using checkboxes to make quick selections

or more are selected, only the last value will be submitted, with prior values being ignored.

If you *want* exclusive behavior—so that only one item can be submitted—then you should use *radio buttons* (see the next section), but to allow multiple submissions, you have to slightly alter the HTML, as in Example 11-5 (note the addition of the square brackets, [ ], following the values of *ice*):

Example 11-5. Submitting multiple values with an array

```
    Vanilla <input type="checkbox" name="ice[]" value="Vanilla" />
 Chocolate <input type="checkbox" name="ice[]" value="Chocolate" />
Strawberry <input type="checkbox" name="ice[]" value="Strawberry" />
```

Now, when the form is submitted, if any of these items have been checked, an array called *ice* will be submitted that contains any and all values. In each case, you can extract either the single submitted value, or the array of values, to a variable like this:

```
    $ice = $_POST['ice'];
```

If the field *ice* has been posted as a single value, $ice will be a single string, such as "Strawberry". But if *ice* was defined in the form as an array (like Example 11-5), $ice will be an array, and its number of elements will be the number of values submitted. Table 11-2 shows the seven possible sets of values that could be submitted by this HTML for one, two, or all three selections. In each case, an array of one, two, or three items is created.

Table 11-2. The seven possible sets of values for the array $ice

One value submitted	Two values submitted	Three values submitted
$ice[0] => Vanilla	$ice[0] => Vanilla	$ice[0] => Vanilla
$ice[0] => Chocolate	$ice[1] => Chocolate	$ice[1] => Chocolate
$ice[0] => Strawberry		$ice[2] => Strawberry
	$ice[0] => Vanilla	
	$ice[1] => Strawberry	

One value submitted	Two values submitted	Three values submitted
	`$ice[0] => Chocolate`	
	`$ice[1] => Strawberry`	

If `$ice` is an array, the PHP code to display its contents is quite simple and might look like this:

```
foreach($ice as $item) echo "$item<br />";
```

This uses the standard PHP `foreach` construct to iterate through the array `$ice` and pass each element's value into the variable `$item`, which is then displayed using the `echo` command. The `<br />` is just an HTML formatting device, to force a new line after each flavor in the display.

By default, checkboxes are square.

Radio Buttons

Radio buttons are named after the push-in preset buttons found on many older radios, where any previously depressed button pops back up when another is pressed. They are used when you want only a single value to be returned from a selection of two or more options. All the buttons in a group must use the same name and, because only a single value is returned, you do not have to pass an array.

For example, if your website offers a choice of delivery times for items purchased from your store, you might use HTML like that in Example 11-6 (see Figure 11-5 to see how it displays).

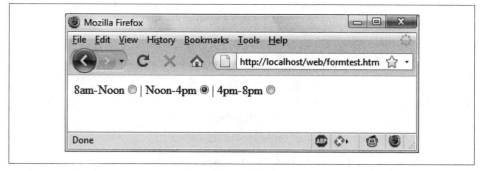

Figure 11-5. Selecting a single value with radio buttons

Example 11-6. Using radio buttons

```
8am-Noon<input type="radio" name="time" value="1" />|
Noon-4pm<input type="radio" name="time" value="2" checked="checked" />|
 4pm-8pm<input type="radio" name="time" value="3" />
```

Here the second option of *Noon-4pm* has been selected by default. This default choice ensures that at least one delivery time will be chosen by the users, which they can change to one of the other two options if they prefer. Had one of the items not been already checked, the user might forget to select an option and no value would be submitted at all for the delivery time.

By default, radio buttons are round.

Hidden Fields

Sometimes it is convenient to have hidden form fields so that you can keep track of the state of form entry. For example, you might wish to know whether a form has already been submitted. You can achieve this by adding some HTML in your PHP code, such as the following:

```
echo '<input type="hidden" name="submitted" value="yes" />'
```

This is a simple PHP `echo` statement that adds an *input* field to the HTML form. Let's assume the form was created outside the program and displayed to the user. The first time the PHP program receives the input, this line of code has not run, so there will be no field named *submitted*. The PHP program recreates the form, adding the *input* field. So when the visitor resubmits the form, the PHP program receives it with the *submitted* field set to "yes". The code can simply check whether the field is present:

```
if (isset($_POST['submitted']))
{...
```

Hidden fields can also be useful for storing other details, such as a session ID string that you might create to identify a user, and so on.

 Never treat hidden fields as secure—because they are not. The HTML containing them can easily be viewed using a browser's View Source feature.

Select

The `select` tag lets you create a drop-down list of options, offering either single or multiple selections. It conforms to the following syntax:

```
<select name="name" size="size" multiple="multiple">
```

The parameter *size* is the number of lines to display. Clicking on the display causes a list to drop down showing all the options. If you use the *multiple* parameter, multiple options can be selected from the list by pressing the Ctrl key when clicking. So to ask a user for her favorite vegetable from a choice of five, you might use HTML as in Example 11-7, which offers a single selection.

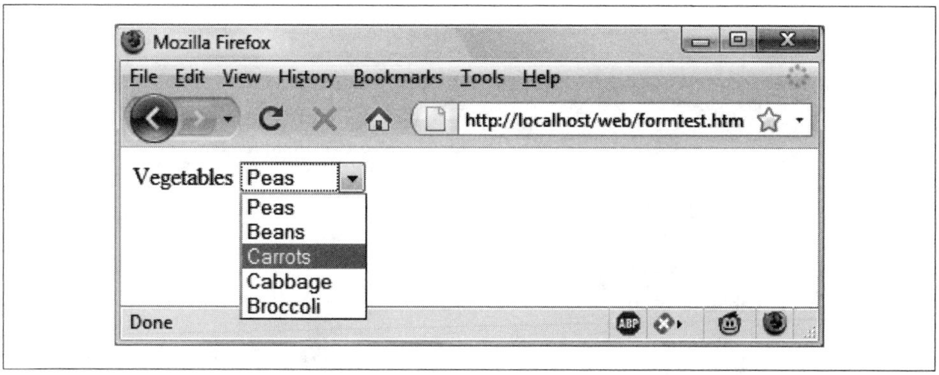

Figure 11-6. Creating a drop-down list with select

Example 11-7. Using 'select'

```
Vegetables <select name="veg" size="1">
<option value="Peas">Peas</option>
<option value="Beans">Beans</option>
<option value="Carrots">Carrots</option>
<option value="Cabbage">Cabbage</option>
<option value="Broccoli">Broccoli</option>
</select>
```

This HTML offers five choices with the first one, *Peas*, preselected (due to it being the first item). Figure 11-6 shows the output where the list has been clicked on to drop it down, and the option *Carrots* has been highlighted. If you want to have a different default option offered first (such as *Beans*), use the *selected* tag, like this:

```
<option selected="selected" value="Beans">Beans</option>
```

You can also allow for the selection of more than one item by users, as in Example 11-8.

Example 11-8. Using select with the multiple parameter

```
Vegetables <select name="veg" size="5" multiple="multiple">
<option value="Peas">Peas</option>
<option value="Beans">Beans</option>
<option value="Carrots">Carrots</option>
<option value="Cabbage">Cabbage</option>
<option value="Broccoli">Broccoli</option>
</select>
```

This HTML is not very different; only the size has been changed to "5" and the tag *multiple* has been added. But, as you can see from Figure 11-7, it is now possible to select more than one option by using the Ctrl key when clicking. You can leave out the *size* parameter if you wish, and the output will be the same, but with a larger list it might take up too much screen space, so I recommend that you pick a suitable number of rows and stick with it. I also recommend against multiple select boxes smaller than two rows in height—some browsers may not correctly display the scroll bars needed to access it.

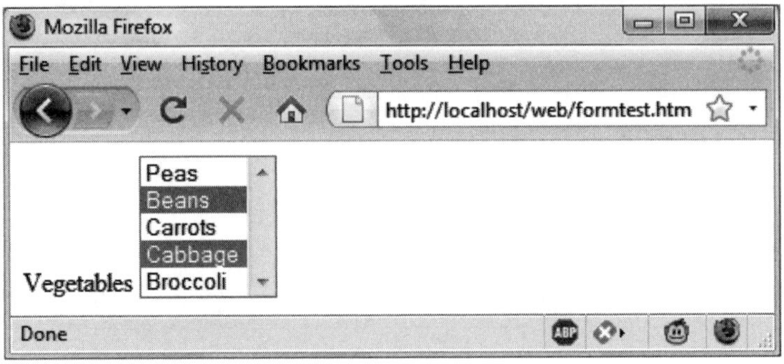

Figure 11-7. Using a select with the multiple parameter

You can also use the *selected* tag within a multiple select and can, in fact, have more than one option preselected if you wish.

Labels

You can provide an even better user experience by utilizing the *label* tag. With it, you can surround a form element, making it selectable by clicking any visible part contained between the opening and closing *label* tags.

For instance, going back to the example of choosing a delivery time, you could allow the user to click on the radio button itself *and* the associated text, like this:

```
<label>8am-Noon<input type="radio" name="time" value="1" /></label>
```

The text will not be underlined like a hyperlink when you do this, but as the mouse passes over, it will change to an arrow instead of a text cursor, indicating that the whole item is clickable.

The submit button

To match the type of form being submitted, you can change the text of the submit button to anything you like by using the *value* parameter, like this:

```
<input type="submit" value="Search" />
```

You can also replace the standard text button with a graphic image of your choice, using HTML such as this:

```
<input type="image" name="submit" src="image.gif" />
```

Sanitizing Input

Now we return to PHP programming. It can never be emphasized enough that handling user data is a security minefield, and that it is essential to learn to treat all such data with utmost caution from the word go. It's actually not that difficult to sanitize user input from potential hacking attempts, but it must be done.

The first thing to remember is that regardless of what constraints you have placed in an HTML form to limit the types and sizes of inputs, it is a trivial matter for a hacker to use their browser's *View Source* feature to extract the form and modify it to provide malicious input to your website.

Therefore you must never trust any variable that you fetch from either the `$_GET` or `$_POST` arrays until you have processed it. If you don't, users may try to inject JavaScript into the data to interfere with your site's operation, or even attempt to add MySQL commands to compromise your database.

Therefore, instead of just using code such as the following when reading in user input:

```php
$variable = $_POST['user_input'];
```

you should also use one or more of the following lines of code. For example, to prevent escape characters being injected into a string that will be presented to MySQL, you should use the following (remembering that this function takes into account the current character set of a MySQL connection, so it can be used only with an open connection):

```php
$variable = mysql_real_escape_string($variable);
```

To get rid of unwanted slashes, use:

```php
$variable = stripslashes($variable);
```

And to remove any HTML from a string, use the following:

```php
$variable = htmlentities($variable);
```

For example, this would change a string of interpretable HTML code like hi into <b>hi</b>, which displays as text, and won't be interpreted as HTML tags.

Finally, if you wish to strip HTML entirely from an input, use the following:

```php
$variable = strip_tags($variable);
```

In fact, until you know exactly what sanitization you require for a program, Example 11-9 shows a pair of functions that bring all these checks together to provide a very good level of security.

Example 11-9. The sanitizeString and sanitizeMySQL functions

```php
<?php
function sanitizeString($var)
{
    $var = stripslashes($var);
    $var = htmlentities($var);
    $var = strip_tags($var);
    return $var;
}
```

```
function sanitizeMySQL($var)
{
    $var = mysql_real_escape_string($var);
    $var = sanitizeString($var);
    return $var;
}
?>
```

Add this code to the end of your PHP programs and you can then call it for each user input to sanitize, like this:

```
$variable = sanitizeString($_POST['user_input']);
```

Or, when you have an open MySQL connection:

```
$variable = sanitizeMySQL($_POST['user_input']);
```

An Example Program

So let's look at how a real life PHP program integrates with an HTML form by creating the program *convert.php* listed in Example 11-10. Type it in as shown and try it for yourself.

Example 11-10. A program to convert values between Fahrenheit and Celsius

```
<?php // convert.php
$f = $c = "";

if (isset($_POST['f'])) $f = sanitizeString($_POST['f']);
if (isset($_POST['c'])) $c = sanitizeString($_POST['c']);

if ($f != '')
{
    $c = intval((5 / 9) * ($f - 32));
    $out = "$f °f equals $c °c";
}
elseif($c != '')
{
    $f = intval((9 / 5) * $c + 32);
    $out = "$c °c equals $f °f";
}
else $out = "";

echo <<<_END
<html><head><title>Temperature Converter</title>
</head><body><pre>
Enter either Fahrenheit or Celsius and click on Convert

<b>$out</b>
<form method="post" action="convert.php">
Fahrenheit <input type="text" name="f" size="7" />
   Celsius <input type="text" name="c" size="7" />
           <input type="submit" value="Convert" />
</form></pre></body></html>
```

```
_END;

function sanitizeString($var)
{
    $var = stripslashes($var);
    $var = htmlentities($var);
    $var = strip_tags($var);
    return $var;
}
?>
```

When you call up *convert.php* in a browser, the result should look something like the screenshot in Figure 11-8.

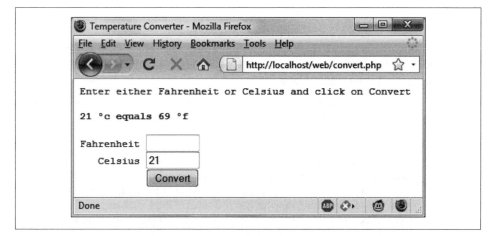

Figure 11-8. The temperature conversion program in action

To break the program down, the first line initializes the variables $c and $f in case they do not get posted to the program. The next two lines fetch the values of either the field named *f* or the one named *c*, for an input Fahrenheit or Celsius value. If the user inputs both, the Celsius is simply ignored and the Fahrenheit value is converted. As a security measure, the new function sanitizeString from Example 11-9 is also used.

So, having either submitted values or empty strings in both $f and $c, the next portion of code constitutes an if...elseif...else structure that first tests whether $f has a value. If not, it checks $c; otherwise, the variable $out is set to the empty string (more on that in a moment).

If $f is found to have a value, the variable $c is assigned a simple mathematical expression that converts the value of $f from Fahrenheit to Celsius. The formula used is *Celsius = (5 / 9) × (Fahrenheit − 32)*. The variable $out is then set to a message string explaining the conversion.

On the other hand, if $c is found to have a value, a complementary operation is performed to convert the value of $c from Celsius to Fahrenheit and assign the result to $f. The formula used is *Fahrenheit = (9 / 5) × (Celsius + 32)*. As with the previous section, the string $out is then set to contain a message about the conversion.

In both conversions, the PHP intval function is called to convert the result of the conversion to an integer value. It's not necessary, but looks better.

With all the arithmetic done, the program now outputs the HTML, which starts with the basic head and title and then contains some introductory text before displaying the value of $out. If no temperature conversion was made, $out will have a value of NULL and nothing will be displayed, which is exactly what we want when the form hasn't yet been submitted. But if a conversion was made, $out contains the result, which is displayed.

After this, we come to the form, which is set to submit using the POST method to the file *convert.php* (the program itself). Within the form, there are two inputs for either a Fahrenheit or Celsius value to be entered. A submit button with the text "Convert" is then displayed and the form is closed.

After outputting the HTML to close the document, we come finally to the function sanitizeString from Example 11-9.

 All the examples in this chapter have used the POST method to send form data. I recommend this, as the neatest and most secure method. However, the forms can easily be changed to use the GET method, as long as values are fetched from the $_GET array instead of the $_POST array. Reasons to do this might include making the result of a search bookmarkable or directly linkable from another page.

The next chapter will show you how you can use the Smarty templating engine to provide a framework for separating your application code from the way your content is presented to users.

Test Your Knowledge: Questions

Question 11-1
Form data can be submitted using either the POST or the GET method. Which associative arrays are used to pass this data to PHP?

Question 11-2
What is *register_globals* and why is it a bad idea?

Question 11-3
What is the difference between a text box and a text area?

Question 11-4

If a form has to offer three choices to a user, each of which is mutually exclusive, so that only one of the three can be selected, which input type would you use for this, given a choice between checkboxes and radio buttons?

Question 11-5

How can you submit a group of selections from a web form using a single field name?

Question 11-6

How can you submit a form field without displaying it in the browser?

Question 11-7

Which HTML tag is used to encapsulate a form element and support text or graphics, making the entire unit selectable with a mouse-click?

Question 11-8

Which PHP function converts HTML into a format that can be displayed but will not be interpreted as HTML by a browser?

See the section "Chapter 11 Answers" on page 444 in Appendix A for the answers to these questions.

CHAPTER 12

Templating with Smarty

As your projects grow more complicated, particularly when you start working with web designers, there's likely to come a time when the convenience of separating the program code from the presentation becomes apparent.

Initially PHP itself was developed as a sort of templating system with a few elements of programming and flow control. But it quickly developed into the powerful programming language we know today. Some developers still treat it a little like a templating system, though, as in the case of the WordPress blogging platform, which uses a set of template PHP files for each theme.

However, allowing presentation to become intertwined with programming can create problems, because it means that the layout designers have full access to the source code and can unwittingly make dangerous changes to it. Additionally, using a separate templating system frees up designers to modify templates to their hearts' content, safe in the knowledge that nothing they do can break your program code; it leads to much greater flexibility.

It's also an incredible boon when your boss comes along and demands a whole load of design changes, because all you have to do is modify the template files. Without a templating system, you'd very likely have to search through many files of PHP code to make the necessary modifications.

> Some programmers like to stick with just the programming language when they develop web pages, and don't use templates. If you're one of them, I still recommend that you read this chapter, as you'll learn all about templating, in case you're suddenly required to work on any projects that use it.

Why Smarty?

The Smarty templating system is probably the best known and most used on the Internet. It provides the following benefits:

- Designers can't break application code. They can modify the templates all they want, but the code stays intact. Consequently the code is tighter, more secure, and easier to maintain.

- Errors in the templates are confined to Smarty's error-handling routines, making them simple and intuitive to deal with.

- With presentation in its own layer, designers can modify or completely redesign a web layout from scratch—all without intervention from the programmer.

- Programmers can go about maintaining the application code, changing the way content is acquired, and so on, without disturbing the presentation layer.

- Templates are a close representation of what the final output will be, which is an intuitive approach.

- Smarty has many security features built in so that designers won't breach security and you won't open your server to the execution of arbitrary PHP code.

But separating the application code from the presentation layer doesn't mean that the logic is also separated, because Smarty offers comprehensive presentation logic features, too, as you'll see later.

Installation

To install Smarty, visit *http://www.smarty.net/download.php* and download the latest ZIP archive. Once it's downloaded, you need to perform the following steps:

1. Extract the contents of the downloaded file into a suitable folder.

2. Determine your web server document's root by running the following PHP snippet (if you don't already know it):

   ```
   <?php echo $_SERVER['DOCUMENT_ROOT']; ?>
   ```

3. Create a new folder called *Smarty* in this document root.

4. Open the extracted folder, navigate into the *libs* directory, and copy the entire contents (including subfolders) into the *Smarty* directory you just created. You will end up with the following directory structure in your document root:

   ```
   Smarty
       internals
           (various files...)
       plugins
           (various files...)
       Config_File.class.php
       debug.tpl
   ```

```
Smarty.class.php
Smarty_Compiler.class.php
```

That gets Smarty installed, but you also need to create four subdirectories for every application that uses it. So create the new application directory *temp* just under the same document root where you just installed Smarty. This will hold the files for a temporary application that we'll write to test Smarty.

Inside the *temp* directory, create another one called *smarty* to house the folders containing the template files. Finally, create the following subdirectories within the new *smarty* directory: *cache*, *config*, *templates*, and *templates_c*. Your directory structure is now:

```
temp
    smarty
        cache
        config
        templates
        templates_c
```

Creating Scripts

You are now ready to create some Smarty scripts. Type in the code in Example 12-1 and save it as *smarty.php*.

Example 12-1. The smarty.php program

```php
<?php // smarty.php
$path = $_SERVER['DOCUMENT_ROOT'];
require "$path/Smarty/Smarty.class.php";

$smarty = new Smarty();
$smarty->template_dir = "$path/temp/smarty/templates";
$smarty->compile_dir  = "$path/temp/smarty/templates_c";
$smarty->cache_dir    = "$path/temp/smarty/cache";
$smarty->config_dir   = "$path/temp/smarty/configs";

$smarty->assign('title', 'Test Web Page');
$smarty->display("$path/temp/index.tpl");
?>
```

This program tells Smarty where it can find the *Smarty.class.php* file, and where your Smarty templates are located. Because we will be using both *.php* and *.tpl* template files in this chapter, I have included everything you need in each file.

Example 12-1 looks up the document root and sets the variable $path to that value. It then uses $path as a prefix for fetching the Smarty class files and the template files from the *temp* folder. This saves you the maintenance hassle of hard-wiring full path names into the code.

Note the penultimate `$smarty->assign` command. This creates a Smarty variable called `title` and assigns it the string value "Test Web Page". You'll see why shortly.

Once you have typed the program in, save it using the filename *smarty.php* into the *temp* directory you created earlier.

Creating Templates

Now you need to write a simple Smarty template file to test whether everything is working, so type in Example 12-2 and save it in a file named *index.tpl* in the *temp/smarty/templates* directory you created earlier.

Example 12-2. The index.tpl template file

```
<html>
    <head>
        <title>{$title}</title>
    </head>
    <body>
        This is a Smarty Test
    </body>
</html>
```

As you can see, this is simply an HTML file with a *.tpl* file extension. But note the use of the Smarty variable {$title} on the third line. This is the same variable that was defined in Example 12-1. Smarty will substitute the value of the variable instead of the text in Example 12-2, because of the surrounding curly braces {} (see Figure 12-1).

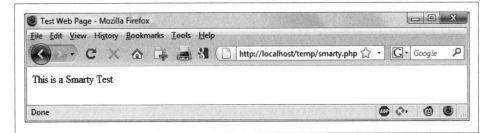

Figure 12-1. The output from index.tpl in Example 12-2

A Practical Example

Let's take the program *sqltest.php* from Example 10-8 in Chapter 10 and rewrite it to use Smarty. This will be a two-part process: one part for the program code and one for the Smarty presentation layer. Example 12-3 is the revised program. Once you have typed it in, save it into the *temp* directory that you created earlier using the filename *smartytest.php*.

Example 12-3. The sqltest.php program rewritten for Smarty as smartytest.php

```php
<?php // smartytest.php
$path = $_SERVER['DOCUMENT_ROOT'];
require "$path/Smarty/Smarty.class.php";

$smarty = new Smarty();
$smarty->template_dir = "$path/temp/smarty/templates";
$smarty->compile_dir  = "$path/temp/smarty/templates_c";
$smarty->cache_dir    = "$path/temp/smarty/cache";
$smarty->config_dir   = "$path/temp/smarty/configs";

require_once("$path/temp/login.php");
$db_server = mysql_connect($db_hostname, $db_username, $db_password);

if (!$db_server) die("Unable to connect to MySQL: " . mysql_error());

mysql_select_db($db_database)
    or die("Unable to select database: " . mysql_error());

if (isset($_POST['author']) &&
    isset($_POST['title']) &&
    isset($_POST['category']) &&
    isset($_POST['year']) &&
    isset($_POST['isbn']))
{
    $author   = get_post('author');
    $title    = get_post('title');
    $category = get_post('category');
    $year     = get_post('year');
    $isbn     = get_post('isbn');

    if (isset($_POST['delete']) && $isbn != "")
    {
        $query = "DELETE FROM classics WHERE isbn='$isbn'";

        if (!mysql_query($query))
        {
            echo "DELETE failed: $query<br>" .
            mysql_error() . "<p>";
        }
    }
    else
    {
        $query = "INSERT INTO classics VALUES" .
        "('$author', '$title', '$category', '$year', '$isbn')";

        if (!mysql_query($query))
        {
            echo "INSERT failed: $query<br>" .
            mysql_error() . "<p>";
        }
    }
}

$query = "SELECT * FROM classics";
```

```
$result = mysql_query($query);

if (!$result) die ("Database access failed: " . mysql_error());
$rows = mysql_num_rows($result);

for ($j = 0 ; $j < $rows ; ++$j)
{
    $results[] = mysql_fetch_array($result);
}

mysql_close($db_server);

$smarty->assign('results', $results);
$smarty->display("smartytest.tpl");

function get_post($var)
{
    return mysql_real_escape_string($_POST[$var]);
}
?>
```

There are a couple of things that you must have done to ensure this program will work:

- You must have worked through the examples in Chapter 8 and have the table *classics* ready-populated in the *publications* database (or another database you may have used).

- You must have copied the file *login.php* (created in Chapter 10) to the *temp* folder you created earlier, or Example 12-3 will be unable to access MySQL.

The program starts off by loading in both the Smarty class and *login.php* files from their correct places. Then it is followed by the program code from the old *sqltest.php* file, without the HTML output that it used to have. In place of the HTML, we'll use the presentation layer template that I'll show next.

The main thing remaining to note is the replacement of the `mysql_fetch_row` function with the new `mysql_fetch_array` function, just before the call to `mysql_close`. The reason for this is to fetch an entire row as an associative array.

The function `mysql_fetch_array` returns a row from the database with the value in each column as an element of the array, and the column name as the array element name. The `$results` object is an array of arrays. Each execution of `$results[] = mysql_fetch_array($result);` adds another array of results to the `$results` array.

This makes it easy to pass a lot of data directly to the Smarty template. How easy? Just a single line is used:

```
$smarty->assign('results', $results);
```

This passes an entire array of arrays using the name `results`.

The following line in Example 12-3 displays the Smarty template, then program execution ends. So now let's look at the template, which is in Example 12-4. Type it in and save it as *smartytest.tpl* in the *temp/smarty/templates* folder you created earlier.

Example 12-4. The smartytest.tpl file

```
<html><head>
<title>Smarty Test</title>
</head><body>

<form action="smartytest.php" method="post"><pre>
    Author <input type="text" name="author">
     Title <input type="text" name="title">
  Category <input type="text" name="category">
      Year <input type="text" name="year">
      ISBN <input type="text" name="isbn">
           <input type="submit" value="ADD RECORD">
</pre></form>

{section name=row loop=$results}
    <form action="smartytest.php" method="post">
    <input type="hidden" name="delete" value="yes">
    <input type="hidden" name="isbn" value="{$results[row].isbn}">
    <pre>
    Author    {$results[row].author}
    Title     {$results[row].title}
    Category  {$results[row].category}
    Year      {$results[row].year}
    ISBN      {$results[row].isbn}
              <input type="submit" value="DELETE RECORD"></form>
    </pre>
{/section}

</body></html>
```

In Figure 12-2, you can see the result of using this template file from the *smartytest.php* program. The first half of the file simply creates the form used to add more records to the MySQL database—the interesting stuff begins at the `{section` opening tag. A `{section}` tag is used for looping over arrays of data. Each time through the loop in this example, the Smarty variable `row` is assigned a value representing the iteration of the loop, starting from 0.

In the same `{section}` tag, the `loop` keyword indicates the array that must be processed. In this case, it is the `$results` array we passed to the template from the previous program. Given these parameters, it is possible to pull any data wanted from the result rows that were returned by MySQL.

For each row, any element can be accessed by its column name. For example, to output the current row's *year* field, use `{$results[row].year}`, where `row` refers to the current iteration of the loop, or the current row being processed, and `.year` tells Smarty which column to reference. It can do this because we passed an associative array from

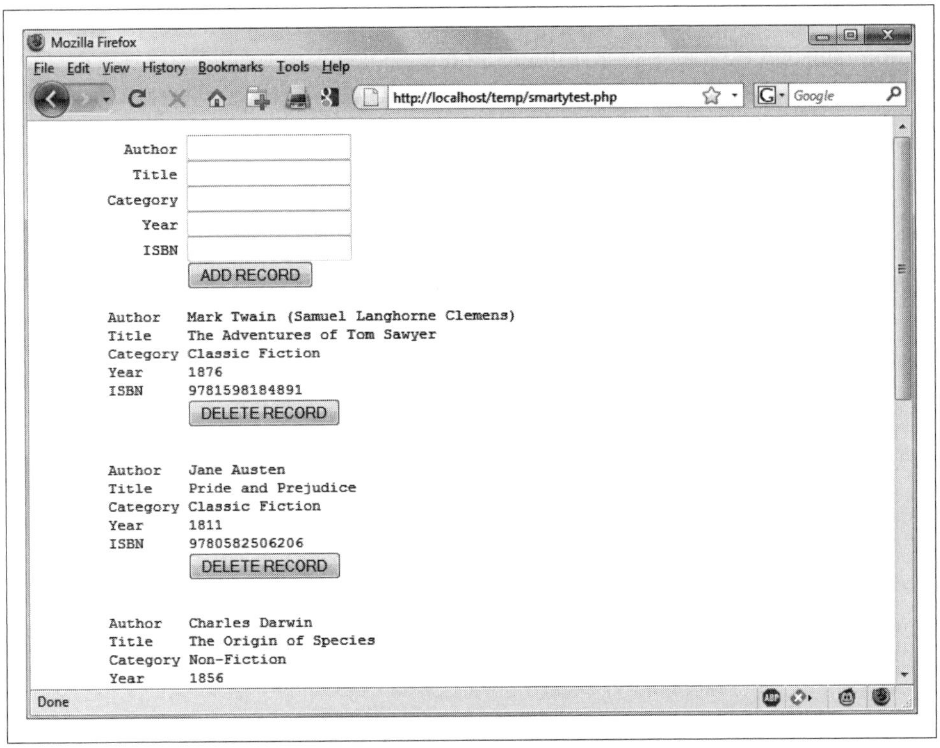

![Screenshot of Mozilla Firefox browser displaying the result of smartytest.php at http://localhost/temp/smartytest.php, showing a form with fields for Author, Title, Category, Year, ISBN and an ADD RECORD button, followed by book records with DELETE RECORD buttons.]

Figure 12-2. The result of combining smartytest.php and smartytest.tpl

smartytest.php (now you see why the program was changed from using mysql_fetch_row to mysql_fetch_array).

The loop ends with a closing {/section} tag that will cause the loop to reiterate if there are any more rows to process. Otherwise, the HTML below it is displayed.

As you can see, this leaves a tremendous amount of control over layout and design with whomever edits the template. They can place any items of data in any positions and in any order. But at no time do they have any access to your program code, and there is nothing they can do to inject bugs into your program or corrupt the MySQL database.

And as for you the programmer? If you're handing over the task of layout to a web designer, you'll never have to worry what the output is going to look like. All you need do is give them a very simple Smarty template showing all the data you are passing to it, and the form input your program will accept from it. It's up to them to then knock it all together into an award-winning design. Think of the freedom that gives you to write fast and effective code, without the dilemma of how to present its output.

You have now seen how to refer to both string and numeric variables, as well as arrays, within a Smarty template. If you think templating will be useful in your projects, you can learn what else it can do for you at *http://www.smarty.net/crashcourse.php*; the full documentation is available at *http://www.smarty.net/manual/en/*.

In the next chapter, we'll look at a range of practical PHP functions and techniques that you'll need to create efficient programs.

Test Your Knowledge: Questions

Question 12-1
    Name three benefits of using a templating system such as Smarty.

Question 12-2
    How does a PHP program pass a variable to a Smarty template?

Question 12-3
    How does a Smarty template access a variable that has been passed to it?

Question 12-4
    What Smarty programming tag is used to iterate through an array?

Question 12-5
    How do you enable Smarty templating in a PHP program?

See the section "Chapter 12 Answers" on page 445 in Appendix A for the answers to these questions.

CHAPTER 13

Cookies, Sessions, and Authentication

As your web projects grow larger and more complicated, you will find an increasing need to keep track of your users. Even if you aren't offering logins and passwords, you will still often find a need to store details about a user's current session and possibly also recognize them when they return to your site.

Several technologies support this kind of interaction, ranging from simple browser cookies to session handling and HTTP authentication. Between them, they offer the opportunity for you to configure your site to your users' preferences and ensure a smooth and enjoyable transition through it.

Using Cookies in PHP

A cookie is an item of data that a web server saves to your computer's hard disk via a web browser. It can contain almost any alphanumeric information (as long as it's under 4 KB) and can be retrieved from your computer and returned to the server. Common uses include session tracking, maintaining data across multiple visits, holding shopping cart contents, storing login details, and more.

Because of their privacy implications, cookies can be read only from the issuing domain. In other words, if a cookie is issued by, for example, *oreilly.com*, it can be retrieved only by a web server using that domain. This prevents other websites from gaining access to details to which they are not authorized.

Due to the way the Internet works, multiple elements on a web page can be embedded from multiple domains, each of which can issue its own cookies. When this happens, they are referred to as third-party cookies. Most commonly, these are created by advertising companies in order to track users across multiple websites.

Because of this, most browsers allow users to turn cookies off either for the current server's domain, third-party servers, or both. Fortunately, most people who disable cookies do so only for third-party websites.

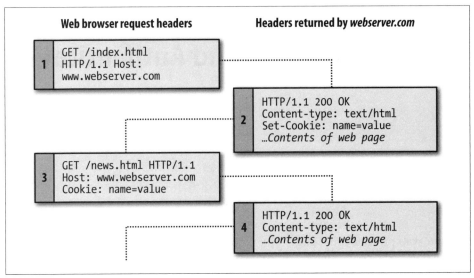

Figure 13-1. A browser/server request/response dialog with cookies

Cookies are exchanged during the transfer of headers, before the actual HTML of a web page is sent, and it is impossible to send a cookie once any HTML has been transferred. Therefore careful planning of cookie usage is important. Figure 13-1 illustrates a typical request and response dialog between a web browser and web server passing cookies.

This exchange shows a browser receiving two pages:

1. The browser issues a request to retrieve the main page, *index.html*, at the website *http://www.webserver.com*. The first header specifies the file and the second header specifies the server.

2. When the web server at *webserver.com* receives this pair of headers, it returns some of its own. The second header defines the type of content to be sent (text/html) and the third one sends a cookie of the name *name* and with the value *value*. Only then are the contents of the web page transferred.

3. Once the browser has received the cookie, it will then return it with every future request made to the issuing server until the cookie expires or is deleted. So, when the browser requests the new page */news.html*, it also returns the cookie *name* with the value *value*.

4. Because the cookie has already been set, when the server receives the request to send */news.html*, it does not have to resend the cookie, but just returns the requested page.

Setting a Cookie

To set a cookie in PHP is a simple matter. As long as no HTML has yet been transferred, you can call the setcookie function, which has the following syntax (see Table 13-1):

```
setcookie(name, value, expire, path, domain, secure, httponly);
```

Table 13-1. The setcookie parameters

Parameter	Description	Example
name	The name of the cookie. This is the name that your server will use to access the cookie on subsequent browser requests.	username
value	The value of the cookie, or the cookie's contents. This can contain up to 4 KB of alphanumeric text.	Hannah
expire	(*optional*) Unix timestamp of the expiration date. Generally, you will probably use time() plus a number of seconds. If not set, the cookie expires when the browser closes.	time() + 2592000
path	(*optional*) The path of the cookie on the server. If this is a / (forward slash), the cookie is available over the entire domain, such as *www.web-server.com*. If it is a subdirectory, the cookie is available only within that subdirectory. The default is the current directory that the cookie is being set in and this is the setting you will normally use.	/
domain	(*optional*) The Internet domain of the cookie. If this is *webserver.com*, the cookie is available to all of *webserver.com* and its subdomains, such as *www.webserver.com* and *images.webserver.com*. If it is *images.web-server.com*, the cookie is available only to *images.webserver.com* and its subdomains such as *sub.images.webserver.com*, but not, say, to *www.webserver.com*.	.webserver.com
secure	(*optional*) Whether the cookie must use a secure connection (*https://*). If this value is TRUE, the cookie can be transferred only across a secure connection. The default is FALSE.	FALSE
httponly	(*optional*; implemented since PHP version 5.2.0) Whether the cookie must use the HTTP protocol. If this value is TRUE, scripting languages such as JavaScript cannot access the cookie. (Not supported in all browsers). The default is FALSE.	FALSE

So, to create a cookie with the name *username* and the value "Hannah" that is accessible across the entire web server on the current domain, and removed from the browser's cache in seven days, use the following:

```
setcookie('username', 'Hannah', time() + 60 * 60 * 24 * 7, '/');
```

Accessing a Cookie

Reading the value of a cookie is as simple as accessing the $_COOKIE system array. For example, if you wish to see whether the current browser has the cookie called *username* already stored and, if so, to read its value, use the following:

```
if (isset($_COOKIE['username'])) $username = $_COOKIE['username'];
```

Note that you can read a cookie back only after it has been sent to a web browser. This means that when you issue a cookie, you cannot read it in again until the browser reloads the page (or another with access to the cookie) from your website and passes the cookie back to the server in the process.

Destroying a Cookie

To delete a cookie, you must issue it again and set a date in the past. It is important for all parameters in your new **setcookie** call except the timestamp to be identical to the parameters when the cookie was first issued; otherwise, the deletion will fail. Therefore, to delete the cookie created earlier, you would use the following:

```
setcookie('username', 'Hannah', time() - 2592000, '/');
```

As long as the time given is in the past, the cookie should be deleted. However, I have used a time of 2592000 seconds (one month) in the past in case the client computer's date and time are not correctly set.

HTTP Authentication

HTTP authentication uses the web server to manage users and passwords for the application. It's adequate for most applications that ask users to log in, although some applications have specialized needs or more stringent security requirements that call for other techniques.

To use HTTP authentication, PHP sends a header request asking to start an authentication dialog with the browser. The server must have this feature turned on in order for it to work, but because it's so common, your server is very likely to offer the feature.

 Although it is usually installed with Apache, HTTP authentication may not necessarily be installed on the server you use. So attempting to run these examples may generate an error telling you that the feature is not enabled, in which case you must install the module, change the configuration file to load the module, or ask your system administrator to do these fixes.

From the user's point of view, when they enter your URL into the browser or visit via a link, an "Authentication Required" prompt pops up requesting two fields: username and password (see Figure 13-2 for how this looks in Firefox).

The code to make this happen looks like Example 13-1.

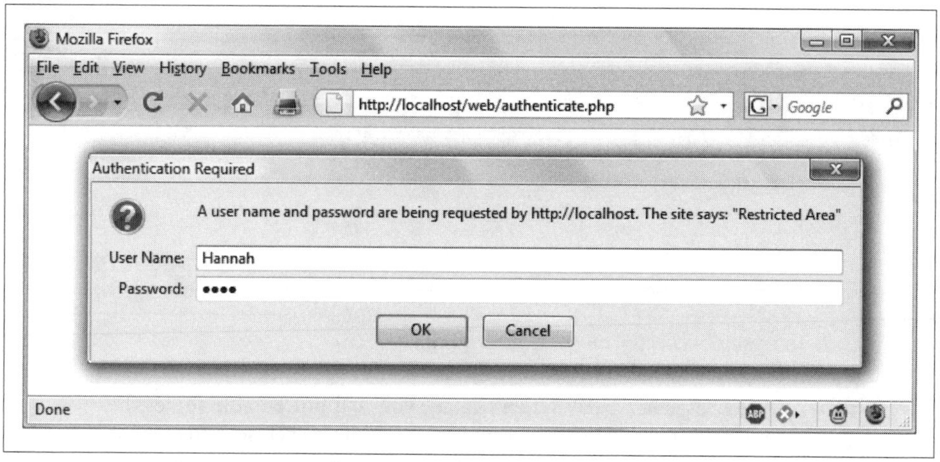

Figure 13-2. An HTTP authentication login prompt

Example 13-1. PHP authentication

```php
<?php
if (isset($_SERVER['PHP_AUTH_USER']) &&
    isset($_SERVER['PHP_AUTH_PW']))
{
    echo "Welcome User: " . $_SERVER['PHP_AUTH_USER'] .
        " Password: " .    $_SERVER['PHP_AUTH_PW'];
}
else
{
    header('WWW-Authenticate: Basic realm="Restricted Section"');
    header('HTTP/1.0 401 Unauthorized');
    die("Please enter your username and password");
}
?>
```

The first thing the program does is look for two particular values: $_SERVER['PHP_AUTH_USER'] and $_SERVER['PHP_AUTH_PW']. If they both exist, they represent the username and password entered by a user into an authentication prompt.

If either of the values do not exist, the user has not yet been authenticated and the prompt in Figure 13-2 is displayed by issuing the following header, where "Basic realm" is the name of the section that is protected and appears as part of the pop-up prompt:

```
WWW-Authenticate: Basic realm="Restricted Area"
```

If the user fills out the fields, the PHP program runs again from the top. But if the user clicks on the Cancel button, the program proceeds to the following two lines, which send the following header and an error message:

```
HTTP/1.0 401 Unauthorized
```

The die statement causes the text "Please enter your username and password" to be displayed (see Figure 13-3).

Figure 13-3. The result of clicking on the Cancel button

> Once a user has been authenticated, you will not be able to get the authentication dialog to pop up again unless the user closes and reopens all browser windows, as the web browser will keep returning the same username and password to PHP. You may need to close and reopen your browser a few times as you work through this section and try different things out.

Now let's check for a valid username and password. The code in Example 13-1 doesn't require much change to add this check, other than modifying the previous welcome message code into a test for a correct username and password, followed by issuing a welcome message. A failed authentication causes an error message to be sent (see Example 13-2).

Example 13-2. PHP Authentication with input checking

```php
<?php
$username = 'admin';
$password = 'letmein';

if (isset($_SERVER['PHP_AUTH_USER']) &&
    isset($_SERVER['PHP_AUTH_PW']))
{
    if ($_SERVER['PHP_AUTH_USER'] == $username &&
        $_SERVER['PHP_AUTH_PW']   == $password)
        echo "You are now logged in";
    else die("Invalid username / password combination");
}
else
{
    header('WWW-Authenticate: Basic realm="Restricted Section"');
    header('HTTP/1.0 401 Unauthorized');
    die ("Please enter your username and password");
}
?>
```

Incidentally, take a look at the wording of the error message: "Invalid username / password combination." It doesn't say whether the username or the password or both were wrong—the less information you can give to a potential hacker, the better.

A mechanism is now in place to authenticate users, but only for a single username and password. Also, the password appears in clear text within the PHP file, and if someone managed to hack into your server, they would instantly know it. So let's look at a better way to handle usernames and passwords.

Storing Usernames and Passwords

Obviously MySQL is the natural way to store usernames and passwords. But again, we don't want to store the passwords as clear text, because our website could be compromised if the database were accessed by a hacker. Instead, we'll use a neat trick called a *one-way function*.

This type of function is easy to use and converts a string of text into a seemingly random string. Due to their one-way nature, such functions are virtually impossible to reverse, so their output can be safely stored in a database—and anyone who steals it will be none the wiser as to the passwords used.

The particular function we'll use is called md5. You pass it a string to hash and it returns a 32-character hexadecimal number. Use it like this:

```
$token = md5('mypassword');
```

That example happens to give $token the value:

```
34819d7beeabb9260a5c854bc85b3e44
```

Also available is the similar sha1 function, which is considered to be more secure, as it has a better algorithm and also returns a 40-character hexadecimal number.

Salting

Unfortunately, md5 on its own is not enough to protect a database of passwords, because it could still be susceptible to a brute force attack that uses another database of known 32-character hexadecimal md5 tokens. Such databases do exist, as a quick Google search will verify.

Thankfully, though, we can put a spanner in the works of any such attempts by *salting* all the passwords before they are sent to md5. Salting is simply a matter of adding some text that only we know about to each parameter to be encrypted, like this:

```
$token = md5('saltstringmypassword');
```

In this example, the text "saltstring" has been prepended to the password. Of course, the more obscure you can make the salt, the better. I like to use salts such as this:

```
$token = md5('hqb%$tmypasswordcg*l');
```

Here some random characters have been placed both before and after the password. Given just the database, and without access to your PHP code, it should now be next to impossible to work out the stored passwords.

All you have to do when verifying someone's login password is to add these same random strings back in before and after it, and then check the resulting token from an md5 call against the one stored in the database for that user.

Let's create a MySQL table to hold some user details and add a couple of accounts. So type in and save the program in Example 13-3 as *setupusers.php*, then open it in your browser.

Example 13-3. Creating a users table and adding two accounts

```php
<?php // setupusers.php
require_once 'login.php';
$db_server = mysql_connect($db_hostname, $db_username, $db_password);
if (!$db_server) die("Unable to connect to MySQL: " . mysql_error());
mysql_select_db($db_database)
    or die("Unable to select database: " . mysql_error());

$query = "CREATE TABLE users (
          forename VARCHAR(32) NOT NULL,
          surname  VARCHAR(32) NOT NULL,
          username VARCHAR(32) NOT NULL UNIQUE,
          password VARCHAR(32) NOT NULL
       )";

$result = mysql_query($query);
if (!$result) die ("Database access failed: " . mysql_error());

$salt1 = "qm&h*";
$salt2 = "pg!@";

$forename = 'Bill';
$surname  = 'Smith';
$username = 'bsmith';
$password = 'mysecret';
$token    = md5("$salt1$password$salt2");
add_user($forename, $surname, $username, $token);

$forename = 'Pauline';
$surname  = 'Jones';
$username = 'pjones';
$password = 'acrobat';
$token    = md5("$salt1$password$salt2");
add_user($forename, $surname, $username, $token);

function add_user($fn, $sn, $un, $pw)
{
    $query = "INSERT INTO users VALUES('$fn', '$sn', '$un', '$pw')";
    $result = mysql_query($query);
    if (!$result) die ("Database access failed: " . mysql_error());
```

```
}
?>
```

This program will create the table **users** within your **publications** database (or which-ever database you set up for the *login.php* file in Chapter 10). In this table, it will create two users: Bill Smith and Pauline Jones. They have the usernames and passwords of *bsmith/mysecret* and *pjones/acrobat*, respectively.

Using the data in this table, we can now modify Example 13-2 to properly authenticate users, and Example 13-4 shows the code needed to do this. Type it in, save it as *authenticate.php*, and call it up in your browser.

Example 13-4. PHP authentication using MySQL

```php
<?php // authenticate.php
require_once 'login.php';
$db_server = mysql_connect($db_hostname, $db_username, $db_password);
if (!$db_server) die("Unable to connect to MySQL: " . mysql_error());
mysql_select_db($db_database)
    or die("Unable to select database: " . mysql_error());

if (isset($_SERVER['PHP_AUTH_USER']) &&
    isset($_SERVER['PHP_AUTH_PW']))
{
    $un_temp = mysql_entities_fix_string($_SERVER['PHP_AUTH_USER']);
    $pw_temp = mysql_entities_fix_string($_SERVER['PHP_AUTH_PW']);

    $query = "SELECT * FROM users WHERE username='$un_temp'";
    $result = mysql_query($query);
    if (!$result) die("Database access failed: " . mysql_error());
    elseif (mysql_num_rows($result))
    {
        $row = mysql_fetch_row($result);
        $salt1 = "qm&h*";
        $salt2 = "pg!@";
        $token = md5("$salt1$pw_temp$salt2");

        if ($token == $row[3]) echo "$row[0] $row[1] :
            Hi $row[0], you are now logged in as '$row[2]'";
        else die("Invalid username/password combination");
    }
    else die("Invalid username/password combination");
}
else
{
    header('WWW-Authenticate: Basic realm="Restricted Section"');
    header('HTTP/1.0 401 Unauthorized');
    die ("Please enter your username and password");
}

function mysql_entities_fix_string($string)
{
    return htmlentities(mysql_fix_string($string));
}
```

```
function mysql_fix_string($string)
{
    if (get_magic_quotes_gpc()) $string = stripslashes($string);
    return mysql_real_escape_string($string);
}
?>
```

As you might expect at this point in the book, some of the examples are starting to get quite a bit longer. But don't be put off. The final 10 lines are simply Example 10-31 from Chapter 10. They are there to sanitize the user input—very important.

The only lines to really concern yourself with at this point start with the assigning of two variables $un_temp and $pw_temp using the submitted username and password, highlighted in bold text. Next, a query is issued to MySQL to look up the user $un_temp and, if a result is returned, to assign the first row to $row. (Because usernames are unique, there will be only one row.) Then the two salts are created in $salt1 and $salt2, which are then added before and after the submitted password $pw_temp. This string is then passed to the md5 function, which returns a 32-character hexadecimal value in $token.

Now all that's necessary is to check $token against the value stored in the database, which happens to be in the fourth column—which is column 3 when starting from 0. So $row[3] contains the previous token calculated for the salted password. If the two match, a friendly welcome string is output, calling the user by his or her first name (see Figure 13-4). Otherwise, an error message is displayed. As mentioned before, the error message is the same regardless of whether such a username exists, as this provides minimal information to potential hackers or password guessers.

Figure 13-4. Bill Smith has now been authenticated

You can try this out for yourself by calling up the program in your browser and entering a username of "bsmith" and password of "mysecret" (or "pjones" and "acrobat"), the values that were saved in the database by Example 13-3.

Using Sessions

Because your program can't tell what variables were set in other programs—or even what values the same program set the previous time it ran—you'll sometimes want to track what your users are doing from one web page to another. You can do this by setting hidden fields in a form, as seen in Chapter 10, and checking the value of the fields after the form is submitted, but PHP provides a much more powerful and simpler solution in the form of *sessions*. These are groups of variables that are stored on the server but relate only to the current user. To ensure that the right variables are applied to the right users, a cookie is saved in their web browsers to uniquely identify them.

This cookie has meaning only to the web server and cannot be used to ascertain any information about a user. You might ask about those users who have their cookies turned off. Well, that's not a problem since PHP 4.2.0, because it will identify when this is the case and place a cookie token in the GET portion of each URL request instead. Either way, sessions provide a solid way of keeping track of your users.

Starting a Session

Starting a session requires calling the PHP function `session_start` before any HTML has been output, similarly to how cookies are sent during header exchanges. Then, to begin saving session variables, you just assign them as part of the `$_SESSION` array, like this:

```
$_SESSION['variable'] = $value;
```

They can then be read back just as easily in later program runs, like this:

```
$variable = $_SESSION['variable'];
```

Now assume that you have an application that always needs access to the username, password, forename, and surname of each user, as stored in the table *users*, which you should have created a little earlier. So let's further modify *authenticate.php* from Example 13-4 to set up a session once a user has been authenticated.

Example 13-5 shows the changes needed. The only difference is the contents of the `if` (`$token == $row[3]`) section, which now starts by opening a session and saving these four variables into it. Type this program in (or modify Example 13-4) and save it as *authenticate2.php*. But don't run it in your browser yet, as you will also need to create a second program in a moment.

Example 13-5. Setting a session after successful authentication

```php
<?php //authenticate2.php
require_once 'login.php';
$db_server = mysql_connect($db_hostname, $db_username, $db_password);
if (!$db_server) die("Unable to connect to MySQL: " . mysql_error());
mysql_select_db($db_database)
    or die("Unable to select database: " . mysql_error());
```

```php
if (isset($_SERVER['PHP_AUTH_USER']) &&
    isset($_SERVER['PHP_AUTH_PW']))
{
    $un_temp = mysql_entities_fix_string($_SERVER['PHP_AUTH_USER']);
    $pw_temp = mysql_entities_fix_string($_SERVER['PHP_AUTH_PW']);

    $query = "SELECT * FROM users WHERE username='$un_temp'";
    $result = mysql_query($query);
    if (!$result) die("Database access failed: " . mysql_error());
    elseif (mysql_num_rows($result))
    {
        $row = mysql_fetch_row($result);
        $salt1 = "qm&h*";
        $salt2 = "pg!@";
        $token = md5("$salt1$pw_temp$salt2");

        if ($token == $row[3])
        {
            session_start();
            $_SESSION['username'] = $un_temp;
            $_SESSION['password'] = $pw_temp;
            $_SESSION['forename'] = $row[0];
            $_SESSION['surname']  = $row[1];
            echo "$row[0] $row[1] : Hi $row[0],
                you are now logged in as '$row[2]'";
            die ("<p><a href=continue.php>Click here to continue</a></p>");
        }
        else die("Invalid username/password combination");
    }
    else die("Invalid username/password combination");
}
else
{
    header('WWW-Authenticate: Basic realm="Restricted Section"');
    header('HTTP/1.0 401 Unauthorized');
    die ("Please enter your username and password");
}

function mysql_entities_fix_string($string)
{
    return htmlentities(mysql_fix_string($string));
}

function mysql_fix_string($string)
{
    if (get_magic_quotes_gpc()) $string = stripslashes($string);
    return mysql_real_escape_string($string);
}
?>
```

One other addition to the program is the "Click here to continue" link with a destination URL of *continue.php*. This will be used to illustrate how the session will transfer to another program or PHP web page. So create *continue.php* by typing in the program in Example 13-6 and saving it.

Example 13-6. Retrieving session variables

```php
<?php // continue.php
session_start();

if (isset($_SESSION['username']))
{
    $username = $_SESSION['username'];
    $password = $_SESSION['password'];
    $forename = $_SESSION['forename'];
    $surname  = $_SESSION['surname'];

    echo "Welcome back $forename.<br />
          Your full name is $forename $surname.<br />
          Your username is '$username'
          and your password is '$password'.";
}
else echo "Please <a href=authenticate2.php>click here</a> to log in.";
?>
```

Now you are ready to call up *authenticate2.php* into your browser, enter a username of "bsmith" and password of "mysecret", (or "pjones" and "acrobat") when prompted, and click on the link to load in *continue.php*. When your browser calls it up, the result should be something like Figure 13-5.

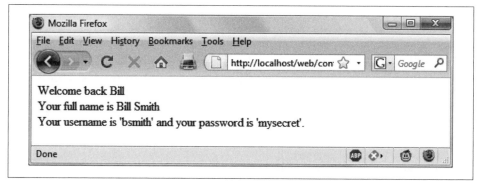

Figure 13-5. Maintaining user data with sessions

Sessions neatly confine to a single program the extensive code required to authenticate and log in a user. Once a user has been authenticated, and you have created a session, your program code becomes very simple indeed. You need only to call up `session_start` and look up any variables to which you need access from `$_SESSION`.

In Example 13-6, a quick test of whether `$_SESSION['username']` has a value is enough to let you know that the current user is authenticated, because session variables are stored on the server (unlike cookies, which are stored on the web browser) and can therefore be trusted.

If `$_SESSION['username']` has not been assigned a value, no session is active, so the last line of code in Example 13-6 directs users to the login page at *authenticate2.php*.

The *continue.php* program prints back the value of the user's password to show you how session variables work. In practice, you already know that the user is logged in, so it should not be necessary to keep track of (or display) any passwords, and doing so would be a security risk.

Ending a Session

When the time comes to end a session, usually when a user requests to log out from your site, you can use the `session_destroy` function in association with the `unset` function, as in Example 13-7. That example provides a useful function for totally destroying a session, logging a user out, and unsetting all session variables.

Example 13-7. A handy function to destroy a session and its data

```php
<?php
function destroy_session_and_data()
{
    session_start();
    $_SESSION = array();
    if (session_id() != "" || isset($_COOKIE[session_name()]))
        setcookie(session_name(), '', time() - 2592000, '/');
    session_destroy();
}
?>
```

To see this in action, you could modify *continue.php* as in Example 13-8.

Example 13-8. Retrieving session variables, then destroying the session

```php
<?php
session_start();

if (isset($_SESSION['username']))
{
    $username = $_SESSION['username'];
    $password = $_SESSION['password'];
    $forename = $_SESSION['forename'];
    $surname  = $_SESSION['surname'];

    echo "Welcome back $forename.<br />
          Your full name is $forename $surname.<br />
          Your username is '$username'
          and your password is '$password'.";

    destroy_session_and_data();
}
else echo "Please <a href=authenticate2.php>click here</a> to log in.";

function destroy_session_and_data()
{
    $_SESSION = array();
    if (session_id() != "" || isset($_COOKIE[session_name()]))
        setcookie(session_name(), '', time() - 2592000, '/');
```

```
    session_destroy();
}
?>
```

The first time you surf from *authenticate2.php* to *continue.php*, it will display all the session variables. But, because of the call to `destroy_session_and_data`, if you then click on your browser's Reload button, the session will have been destroyed and you'll be prompted to return to the login page.

Setting a timeout

There are other times when you might wish to close a user's session yourself, such as when the user has forgotten or neglected to log out, and you wish the program to do it for them for their own security. The way to do this is to set the timeout, after which a logout will automatically occur if there has been no activity.

To do this, use the `ini_set` function as follows. This example sets the timeout to exactly one day:

```
ini_set('session.gc_maxlifetime', 60 * 60 * 24);
```

If you wish to know what the current timeout period is, you can display it using the following:

```
echo ini_get('session.gc_maxlifetime');
```

Session Security

Although I mentioned that once you had authenticated a user and set up a session you could safely assume that the session variables were trustworthy, this isn't exactly the case. The reason is that it's possible to use packet sniffing (sampling of data) to discover session IDs passing across a network. Additionally, if the session ID is passed in the GET part of a URL, it might appear in external site server logs. The only truly secure way of preventing these from being discovered is to implement a Secure Socket Layer (SSL) and run HTTPS instead of HTTP web pages. That's beyond the scope of this book, although you may like to take a look at *http://www.apache-ssl.org* for details on setting up a secure web server.

Preventing session hijacking

When SSL is not a possibility, you can further authenticate users by storing their IP address along with their other details by adding a line such as the following when you store their session:

```
$_SESSION['ip'] = $_SERVER['REMOTE_ADDR'];
```

Then, as an extra check, whenever any page loads and a session is available, perform the following check. It calls the function `different_user` if the stored IP address doesn't match the current one:

```
        if ($_SESSION['ip'] != $_SERVER['REMOTE_ADDR']) different_user();
```

What code you place in your `different_user` function is up to you. I recommend that you simply delete the current session and ask the user to log in again due to a technical error. Don't say any more than that or you're giving away potentially useful information.

Of course, you need to be aware that users on the same proxy server, or sharing the same IP address on a home or business network, will have the same IP address. Again, if this is a problem for you, use SSL. You can also store a copy of the browser user agent string (a string that developers put in their browsers to identify them by type and version), which might also distinguish users due to the wide variety of browser types, versions, and computer platforms. Use the following to store the user agent:

```
        $_SESSION['ua'] = $_SERVER['HTTP_USER_AGENT'];
```

And use this to compare the current agent string with the saved one:

```
        if ($_SESSION['ua'] != $_SERVER['HTTP_USER_AGENT']) different_user();
```

Or, better still, combine the two checks like this and save the combination as an `md5` hexadecimal string:

```
        $_SESSION['check'] = md5($_SERVER['REMOTE_ADDR'] .
            $_SERVER['HTTP_USER_AGENT']);
```

And this to compare the current and stored strings:

```
        if ($_SESSION['check'] != md5($_SERVER['REMOTE_ADDR'] .
            $_SERVER['HTTP_USER_AGENT'])) different_user();
```

Preventing session fixation

Session fixation happens when a malicious user tries to present a session ID to the server rather than letting the server create one. It can happen when a user takes advantage of the ability to pass a session ID in the GET part of a URL, like this:

```
        http://yourserver.com/authenticate.php?PHPSESSID=123456789
```

In this example, the made-up session ID of 123456789 is being passed to the server. Now, consider Example 13-9, which is susceptible to session fixation. To see how, type it in and save it as *sessiontest.php*.

Example 13-9. A session susceptible to session fixation

```
<?php // sessiontest.php
session_start();

if (!isset($_SESSION['count'])) $_SESSION['count'] = 0;
else ++$_SESSION['count'];
echo $_SESSION['count'];
?>
```

Once saved, call it up in your browser using the following URL (prefacing it with the correct pathname, such as *http://localhost/web/*):

```
sessiontest.php?PHPSESSID=1234
```

Press Reload a few times and you'll see the counter increase. Now try browsing to:

```
sessiontest.php?PHPSESSID=5678
```

Press Reload a few times here and you should see it count up again from zero. Leave the counter on a different number than the first URL and then go back to the first URL and see how the number changes back. You have created two different sessions of your own choosing here, and you could easily create as many as you needed.

The reason this approach is so dangerous is that a malicious attacker could try to distribute these types of URLs to unsuspecting users, and if any of them followed these links, the attacker would be able to come back and take over any sessions that had not been deleted or expired!

To prevent this, add a simple additional check to change the session ID using `session_regenerate_id`. This function keeps all current session variable values, but replaces the session ID with a new one that an attacker cannot know. To do this, you can check for a special session variable's existence. If it doesn't exist, you know that this is a new session, so you simply change the session ID and set the special session variable to note the change.

Example 13-10 shows what the code might look like using the session variable `initiated`.

Example 13-10. Session regeneration

```php
<?php
session_start();
if (!isset($_SESSION['initiated']))
{
    session_regenerate_id();
    $_SESSION['initiated'] = 1;
}

if (!isset($_SESSION['count'])) $_SESSION['count'] = 0;
else ++$_SESSION['count'];
echo $_SESSION['count'];
?>
```

This way, an attacker can come back to your site using any of the session IDs that he generated, but none of them will call up another user's session, as they will all have been replaced with regenerated IDs. If you want to be ultra-paranoid, you can even regenerate the session ID on each request.

Forcing cookie-only sessions

If you are prepared to require your users to enable cookies on your website, you can use the `ini_set` function like this:

```
ini_set('session.use_only_cookies', 1);
```

With that setting, the `?PHPSESSID=` trick will be completely ignored. If you use this security measure, I also recommend you inform your users that your site requires cookies, so they know what's wrong if they don't get the results they want.

Using a shared server

On a server shared with other accounts, you will not want to have all your session data saved into the same directory as theirs. Instead, you should choose a directory to which only your account has access (and that is not web-visible) to store your sessions, by placing an `ini_set` call near the start of a program, like this:

```
ini_set('session.save_path', '/home/user/myaccount/sessions');
```

The configuration option will keep this new value only during the program's execution, and the original configuration will be restored at the program's ending.

This sessions folder can fill up quickly; you may wish to periodically clear out older sessions according to how busy your server gets. The more it's used, the less time you will want to keep a session stored.

 Remember that your websites can and will be subject to hacking attempts. There are automated bots running riot around the Internet trying to find sites vulnerable to exploits. So whatever you do, whenever you are handling data that is not 100 percent generated within your own program, you should always treat it with the utmost caution.

At this point, you should now have a very good grasp of both PHP and MySQL, so in the next chapter it's time to introduce the third major technology covered by this book, JavaScript.

Test Your Knowledge: Questions

Question 13-1
> Why must a cookie be transferred at the start of a program?

Question 13-2
> Which PHP function stores a cookie on a web browser?

Question 13-3
> How can you destroy a cookie?

Question 13-4
  Where are the username and password stored in a PHP program when using HTTP authentication?

Question 13-5
  Why is the md5 function a powerful security measure?

Question 13-6
  What is meant by "salting" a string?

Question 13-7
  What is a PHP session?

Question 13-8
  How do you initiate a PHP session?

Question 13-9
  What is session hijacking?

Question 13-10
  What is session fixation?

See the section "Chapter 13 Answers" on page 445 in Appendix A for the answers to these questions.

CHAPTER 14

Exploring JavaScript

JavaScript brings a dynamic functionality to your websites. Every time you see something pop up when you mouse over an item in the browser, or see new text, colors, or images appear on the page in front of your eyes, or grab an object on the page and drag it to a new location—all those things are done through JavaScript. It offers effects that are not otherwise possible, because it runs inside the browser and has direct access to all the elements in a web document.

JavaScript first appeared in the Netscape Navigator browser in 1995, coinciding with the addition of support for Java technology in the browser. Because of the initial incorrect impression that JavaScript was a spin-off of Java, there has been some long-term confusion over their relationship. However, the naming was just a marketing ploy to help the new scripting language benefit from the popularity of the Java programming language.

JavaScript gained new power when the HTML elements of the web page got a more formal, structured definition in what is called the Document Object Model or DOM. DOM makes it relatively easy to add a new paragraph or focus on a piece of text and change it.

Because both JavaScript and PHP support much of the structured programming syntax used by the C programming language, they look very similar to each other. They are both fairly high-level languages, too; for instance, they are weakly typed, so it's easy to change a variable to a new type just by using it in a new context.

Now that you have learned PHP, you should find JavaScript even easier. And you'll be glad you did, because it's at the heart of the Web 2.0 Ajax technology that provides the fluid web front-ends that savvy Web users expect these days.

JavaScript and HTML Text

JavaScript is a client-side scripting language that runs entirely inside the web browser. To call it up, you place it between opening `<script>` and closing `</script>` HTML tags.

A typical HTML 4.01 "Hello World" document using JavaScript might look like Example 14-1.

Example 14-1. "Hello World" displayed using JavaScript

```
<html>
    <head><title>Hello World</title></head>
    <body>
        <script type="text/javascript">
            document.write("Hello World")
        </script>
        <noscript>
            Your browser doesn't support or has disabled JavaScript
        </noscript>
    </body>
</html>
```

 You may have seen web pages that use the HTML tag `<script language="javascript">`, but that usage has now been deprecated. This example uses the more recent and preferred `<script type="text/javascript">`.

Within the script tags is a single line of JavaScript code that uses its equivalent of the PHP `echo` or `print` commands, `document.write`. As you'd expect, it simply outputs the supplied string to the current document, where it is displayed.

You may also have noticed that, unlike PHP, there is no trailing semicolon (`;`). This is because a new line acts the same way as a semicolon in JavaScript. However, if you wish to have more than one statement on a single line, you do need to place a semicolon after each command except the last one. Of course, if you wish, you can add a semicolon to the end of every statement and your JavaScript will work fine.

The other thing to note in this example is the `<noscript>` and `</noscript>` pair of tags. These are used when you wish to offer alternative HTML to users whose browser does not support JavaScript or who have it disabled. The use of these tags is up to you, as they are not required, but you really ought to use them, because it's usually not that difficult to provide static HTML alternatives to the operations you provide using JavaScript. However the remaining examples in this book will omit `<noscript>` tags, because we're focusing on what you can do with JavaScript, not what you can do without it.

When Example 14-1 is loaded, a web browser with JavaScript enabled will output the following (see Figure 14-1):

```
Hello World
```

One with JavaScript disabled will display this (see Figure 14-2):

```
Your browser doesn't support or has disabled JavaScript
```

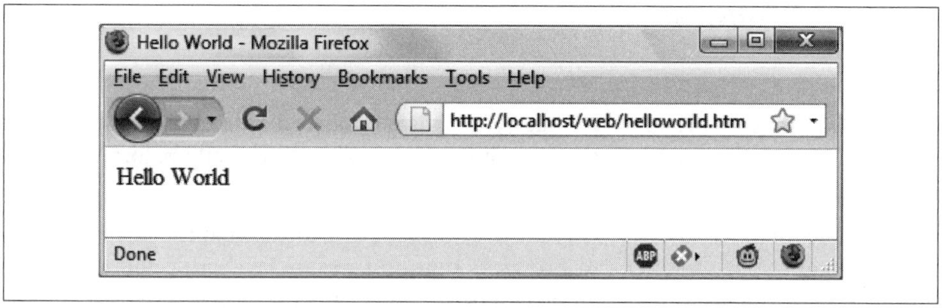

Figure 14-1. JavaScript, enabled and working

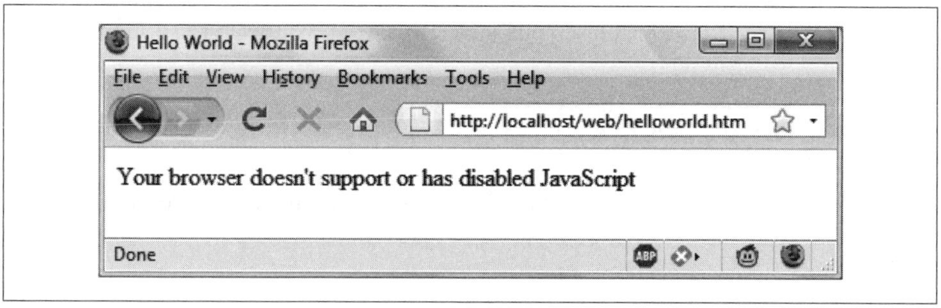

Figure 14-2. JavaScript has been disabled

Using Scripts Within a Document Head

In addition to placing a script within the body of a document, you can put it in the `<head>` section, which is the ideal place if you wish to execute a script when a page loads. If you place critical code and functions there, you can also ensure that they are ready to use immediately by any other script sections in the document that rely on them.

Another reason for placing a script in the head is to enable JavaScript to write things such as meta tags into the head section, because the location of your script is the part of the document it writes to by default.

Older and Nonstandard Browsers

If you need to support browsers that do not offer scripting, you will need to use the HTML comment tags (`<!--` and `-->`) to prevent them from encountering script code that they should not see. Example 14-2 shows how you add them to your script code.

Example 14-2. The "Hello World" example modified for non-JavaScript browsers

```
<html>
    <head><title>Hello World</title></head>
    <body>
        <script type="text/javascript"><!--
            document.write("Hello World")
```

```
        // --></script>
    </body>
</html>
```

Here an opening HTML comment tag (`<!--`) has been added directly after the opening `<script ...>` statement and a closing comment tag (`// -->`) directly before the script is closed with `</script>`.

The double forward slash (`//`) is used by JavaScript to indicate that the rest of the line is a comment. It is there so that browsers that *do* support JavaScript will ignore the following `-->`, but non-JavaScript browsers will ignore the preceding `//`, and act on the `-->` by closing the HTML comment.

Although the solution is a little convoluted, all you really need to remember is to use the two following lines to enclose your JavaScript when you wish to support very old or nonstandard browsers:

```
<script type="text/javascript"><!--
  (Your JavaScript goes here...)
// --></script>
```

However, the use of these comments is unnecessary for any browser released over the past several years.

 There are a couple of other scripting languages you should know about. These include Microsoft's VBScript, which is based on the Visual Basic programming language, and Tcl, a rapid prototyping language. They are called up in a similar way to JavaScript, except they use types of *text/vbscript* and *text/tcl*, respectively. VBScript works only in Internet Explorer; use of it in other browsers requires a plug-in. Tcl always needs a plug-in. So both should be considered nonstandard and neither is covered in this book.

Including JavaScript Files

In addition to writing JavaScript code directly in HTML documents, you can include files of JavaScript code either from your website or from anywhere on the Internet. The syntax for this is:

```
<script type="text/javascript" src="script.js"></script>
```

Or, to pull a file in from the Internet, use:

```
<script type="text/javascript" src="http://someserver.com/script.js">
</script>
```

As for the script files themselves, they must *not* include any `<script>` or `</script>` tags, because they are unnecessary: the browser already knows that a JavaScript file is being loaded. Putting them in the JavaScript files will cause an error.

Including script files is the preferred way for you to use third-party JavaScript files on your website.

 It is possible to leave out the `type="text/javascript"` parameters; all modern browsers default to assuming that the script contains JavaScript.

Debugging JavaScript Errors

When learning JavaScript, it's important to be able to track typing or other coding errors. Unlike PHP, which displays error messages in the browser, JavaScript error messages are handled differently, and in a way that changes according to the browser used. Table 14-1 lists how to access JavaScript error messages in each of the five most commonly used browsers.

Table 14-1. Accessing JavaScript error messages in different browsers

Browser	How to access JavaScript error messages
Apple Safari	Safari does not have an Error Console enabled by default, so the Firebug Lite JavaScript module will do what you need. To use it, add the following line of code somewhere before the `<body>` tag in a document: `<script src='http://tinyurl.com/fblite'></script>`
Google Chrome	Click the menu icon that looks like a page with a corner turned, then select Developer→JavaScript Console. You can also use the following shortcut: Ctrl-Shift-J on a PC or Command-Shift-J on a Mac.
Microsoft Internet Explorer	Select Tools→Internet Options→Advanced, then uncheck the Disable Script Debugging box and check the Display a Notification about Every Script Error box.
Mozilla Firefox	Select Tools→Error Console or use this shortcut: Ctrl-Shift-J on a PC or Command-Shift-J on a Mac.
Opera	Select Tools→Advanced→Error Console.

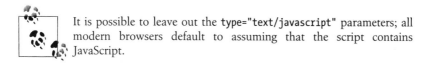 Safari Users: although I have shown a way for you to create an Error Console for JavaScript, I strongly recommend that you use a different browser, if at all possible, as this method is little more than a work-around. On a PC, you could try Google Chrome, which uses the same WebKit engine as Safari. On a Mac, until Chrome has been ported to Mac OS (a project that is still underway as I write), I suggest that you try Firefox for debugging your JavaScript.

To try out whichever Error Console you are using, let's create a script with a small error. Example 14-3 is much the same as Example 14-1, but the final double quotation mark has been left off the end of the string "Hello World"—a common syntax error.

Example 14-3. A JavaScript "Hello World" script with an error

```
<html>
    <head><title>Hello World</title></head>
    <body>
        <script type="text/javascript">
            document.write("Hello World)
        </script>
    </body>
</html>
```

Type the example in and save it as *test.html*, then call it up in your browser. It should succeed only in displaying the title, not anything in the main browser window. Now call up the Error Console in your browser and you should see a message such as the one in Example 14-4 (if using Firefox).

Example 14-4. A Mozilla Firefox Error Console message

```
unterminated string literal
document.write("Hello World)
---------------^
```

Note the handy arrow pointing to the start of the incorrect part of code. You will also be told that the offending code is at line 5.

In Microsoft Internet Explorer, the error message will look like Example 14-5.

Example 14-5. A Microsoft Internet Explorer Error Console message

```
unterminated string constant
```

There's no helpful arrow, but you are told that the problem is in line 5 at position 32.

Google Chrome will give the message in Example 14-6.

Example 14-6. A Google Chrome Error Console message

```
Uncaught SyntaxError: Unexpected token ILLEGAL
```

You'll be told that the error is in line 5, but not the exact location.

Opera will supply the message in Example 14-7.

Example 14-7. An Opera Error Console message

```
Syntax error while loading line 2 of inline script
expected statement
                    document.write("Hello World)
------------------------------^
```

Note how Opera differs from the other browsers by reporting the error to be on line 2 of the inline script, rather than referring to the line number of the entire HTML file. Also Opera tries to point to the start of the problem, but gets only close to the first double quote.

Two browsers do quite well at pinpointing the error, though. Firefox highlights the opening double quote, which gives a big clue, and Internet Explorer says the error is at position 32, which is exactly where the closing double quote should be placed—but, because there's no arrow pointing to this position, it's necessary to count along to find it.

So, as you can see, on the whole Firefox probably provides the easiest to read and most accurate messages, and for that reason I would recommend it as the best browser for debugging JavaScript.

However, as you will learn, there are some major compatibility issues with Microsoft Internet Explorer, the browser of choice for two-thirds of the entire market as I write. So, as a developer, you'll need to test your programs with various versions of this browser before you release them on a production server.

The Firebug plug-in for Firefox (*http://getfirebug.com*) is very popular among JavaScript developers, and is also worth a look.

 If you will be typing in the following code snippets to try them out, don't forget to surround them with `<script>` and `</script>` tags.

Using Comments

Due to their shared inheritance from the C programming language, PHP and JavaScript share many similarities, one of which is commenting. First there's the single line comment, like this:

```
// This is a comment
```

This style uses a pair of forward slash characters (//) to inform JavaScript that everything following is to be ignored. And then you also have multiline comments, like this:

```
/* This is a section
   of multiline comments
   that will not be
   interpreted */
```

Here you start a multiline comment with the sequence /* and end it with */. Just remember that you cannot nest multiline comments, so make sure that you don't comment out large sections of code that already contain multiline comments.

Semicolons

Unlike PHP, semicolons are not generally required by JavaScript if you have only one statement on a line. Therefore the following is valid:

```
x += 10
```

However, when you wish to place more than one statement on a line, they must be separated with semicolons, like this:

```
x += 10; y -= 5; z = 0
```

You can normally leave the final semicolon off, because the new line terminates the final statement.

 There are exceptions to the semicolon rule. If you write JavaScript bookmarklets, or end a statement with a variable or function reference *and* the first character of the line below is a left parenthesis or bracket, you *must* remember to append a semicolon or the JavaScript will fail. So, if in doubt, use a semicolon.

Variables

No particular character identifies a variable in JavaScript as the dollar sign does in PHP. Instead, variables use the following naming rules:

- A variable may include only the letters a-z, A-Z, 0-9, the $ symbol, and the underscore (_).
- No other characters such as spaces or punctuation are allowed in a variable name.
- The first character of a variable name can be only a-z, A-Z, $, or _ (no numbers).
- Names are case-sensitive. Count, count, and COUNT are all different variables.
- There is no set limit on variable name lengths.

And yes, you're right, that is the $ sign there in that list. It *is* allowed by JavaScript and *may* be the first character of a variable or function name. Although I don't recommend keeping the $ signs, it means that you can port a lot of PHP code more quickly to JavaScript that way.

String Variables

JavaScript string variables should be enclosed in either single or double quotation marks, like this:

```
greeting = "Hello there"
warning  = 'Be careful'
```

You may include a single quote within a double-quoted string or a double quote within a single-quoted string. But a quote of the same type must be escaped using the backslash character, like this:

```
greeting = "\"Hello there\" is a greeting"
warning  = '\'Be careful\' is a warning'
```

To read from a string variable, you can assign it to another one, like this:

```
newstring = oldstring
```

or you can use it in a function, like this:

```
status = "All systems are working"
document.write(status)
```

Numeric Variables

Creating a numeric variable is as simple as assigning a value, like these examples:

```
count       = 42
temperature = 98.4
```

Like strings, numeric variables can be read from and used in expressions and functions.

Arrays

JavaScript arrays are also very similar to those in PHP, in that an array can contain string or numeric data, as well as other arrays. To assign values to an array, use the following syntax (which in this case creates an array of strings):

```
toys = ['bat', 'ball', 'whistle', 'puzzle', 'doll']
```

To create a multidimensional array, nest smaller arrays within a larger one. So, to create a two-dimensional array containing the colors of a single face of a scrambled Rubik's Cube (where the colors red, green, orange, yellow, blue, and white are represented by their capitalized initial letters), you could use the following code.

```
face =
[
    ['R', 'G', 'Y'],
    ['W', 'R', 'O'],
    ['Y', 'W', 'G']
]
```

The previous example has been formatted to make it obvious what is going on, but it could also be written like this:

```
face = [['R', 'G', 'Y'], ['W', 'R', 'O'], ['Y', 'W', 'G']]
```

or even like this:

```
top = ['R', 'G', 'Y']
mid = ['W', 'R', 'O']
bot = ['Y', 'W', 'G']

face = [top, mid, bot]
```

To access the element two down and three along in this matrix, you would use the following (because array elements start at position zero):

```
document.write(face[1][2])
```

This statement will output the letter O for orange.

JavaScript arrays are powerful storage structures, so Chapter 16 discusses them in much greater depth.

Operators

Operators in JavaScript, as in PHP, can involve mathematics, changes to strings, and comparison and logical operations (**and**, **or**, etc.). JavaScript mathematical operators look a lot like plain arithmetic; for instance, the following statement outputs 16:

```
document.write(14 + 2)
```

The following sections teach you about the various operators.

Arithmetic Operators

Arithmetic operators are used to perform mathematics. You can use them for the main four operations (addition, subtraction, multiplication, and division) as well as to find the modulus (the remainder after a division) and to increment or decrement a value (see Table 14-2).

Table 14-2. Arithmetic operators

Operator	Description	Example
+	Addition	j + 12
-	Subtraction	j - 22
*	Multiplication	j * 7
/	Division	j / 3.14
%	Modulus (division remainder)	j % 6
++	Increment	++j
--	Decrement	--j

Assignment Operators

The assignment operators are used to assign values to variables. They start with the very simple, =, and move on to +=, -=, and so on. The operator += adds the value on the right side to the variable on the left, instead of totally replacing the value on the left. Thus, if count starts with the value 6, the statement:

```
count += 1
```

sets count to 7, just like the more familiar assignment statement:

```
count = count + 1
```

Table 14-3 lists the various assignment operators available.

Table 14-3. Assignment operators

Operator	Example	Equivalent to
=	j = 99	j = 99
+=	j += 2	j = j + 2
+=	j += 'string'	j = j + 'string'
-=	j -= 12	j = j - 12
*=	j *= 2	j = j * 2
/=	j /= 6	j = j / 6
%=	j %= 7	j = j % 7

Comparison Operators

Comparison operators are generally used inside a construct such as an `if` statement where you need to compare two items. For example, you may wish to know whether a variable you have been incrementing has reached a specific value, or whether another variable is less than a set value, and so on (see Table 14-4).

Table 14-4. Comparison operators

Operator	Description	Example
==	Is **equal** to	j == 42
!=	Is **not equal** to	j != 17
>	Is **greater than**	j > 0
<	Is **less than**	j < 100
>=	Is **greater than or equal** to	j >= 23
<=	Is **less than or equal** to	j <= 13
===	Is **equal** to (and of the same type)	j === 56
!==	Is **not equal** to (and of the same type)	j !== '1'

Logical Operators

Unlike PHP, JavaScript's logical operators do not include **and** and **or** equivalents to `&&` and `||`, and there is no `xor` operator (see Table 14-5).

Table 14-5. Logical operators

Operator	Description	Example
&&	And	j == 1 && k == 2
||	Or	j < 100 || j > 0
!	Not	! (j == k)

Variable Incrementing and Decrementing

The following forms of post- and preincrementing and decrementing you learned to use in PHP are also supported by JavaScript:

```
++x
--y
x += 22
y -= 3
```

String Concatenation

JavaScript handles string concatenation slightly differently from PHP. Instead of the . (period) operator, it uses the plus sign (+), like this:

```
document.write("You have " + messages + " messages.")
```

Assuming that the variable `messages` is set to the value 3, the output from this line of code will be:

```
You have 3 messages.
```

Just as you can add a value to a numeric variable with the += operator, you can also append one string to another the same way:

```
name =  "James"
name += " Dean"
```

Escaping Characters

Escape characters, which you've seen used to insert quotation marks in strings, can also insert various special characters such as tabs, new lines, and carriage returns. Here is an example using tabs to lay out a heading; it is included here merely to illustrate escapes, because in web pages, there are better ways to do layout:

```
heading = "Name\tAge\tLocation"
```

Table 14-6 details the escape characters available.

Table 14-6. JavaScript's escape characters

Character	Meaning
\b	Backspace
\f	Form feed
\n	New line
\r	Carriage return
\t	Tab
\'	Single quote (or apostrophe)
\"	Double quote

Character	Meaning
\\	Backslash
\XXX	An octal number between 000 and 377 that represents the Latin-1 character equivalent (such as \251 for the © symbol)
\xXX	A hexadecimal number between 00 and FF that represents the Latin-1 character equivalent (such as \xA9 for the © symbol)
\uXXXX	A hexadecimal number between 0000 and FFFF that represents the Unicode character equivalent (such as \u00A9 for the © symbol)

Variable Typing

Like PHP, JavaScript is a very loosely typed language; the *type* of a variable is determined only when a value is assigned and can change as the variable appears in different contexts. Usually, you don't have to worry about the type; JavaScript figures out what you want and just does it.

Take a look at Example 14-8, in which:

1. The variable n is assigned the string value "838102050", the next line prints out its value, and the typeof operator is used to look up the type.

2. n is given the value returned when the numbers 12345 and 67890 are multiplied together. This value is also 838102050, but it is a number, not a string. The type of variable is then looked up and displayed.

3. Some text is appended to the number n and the result is displayed.

Example 14-8. Setting a variable's type by assignment

```
<script>
n = '838102050'       // Set 'n' to a string
document.write('n = ' + n + ', and is a ' + typeof n + '<br />')

n = 12345 * 67890;    // Set 'n' to a number
document.write('n = ' + n + ', and is a ' + typeof n + '<br />')

n += ' plus some text' // Change 'n' from a number to a string
document.write('n = ' + n + ', and is a ' + typeof n + '<br />')
</script>
```

The output from this script looks like:

```
n = 838102050, and is a string
n = 838102050, and is a number
n = 838102050 plus some text, and is a string
```

If there is ever any doubt about the type of a variable, or you need to ensure a variable has a particular type, you can force it to that type using statements such as the following (which respectively turn a string into a number and a number into a string):

```
n = "123"
n *= 1     // Convert 'n' into a number

n = 123
n += ""    // Convert 'n' into a string
```

Or, of course, you can always look up a variable's type using the **typeof** operator.

Functions

As with PHP, JavaScript functions are used to separate out sections of code that perform a particular task. To create a function, declare it in the manner shown in Example 14-9.

Example 14-9. A simple function declaration

```
<script>
function product(a, b)
{
    return a*b
}
</script>
```

This function takes the two parameters passed, multiplies them together, and returns the product.

Global Variables

Global variables are ones defined outside of any functions (or within functions, but defined without the **var** keyword). They can be defined in the following ways:

```
    a = 123               // Global scope
    var b = 456           // Global scope
    if (a == 123) var c = 789 // Global scope
```

Regardless of whether you are using the **var** keyword, as long as a variable is defined outside of a function, it is global in scope. This means that every part of a script can have access to it.

Local Variables

Parameters passed to a function automatically have local scope. That is, they can be referenced only from within that function. However, there is one exception. Arrays are passed to a function by reference, so if you modify any elements in an array parameter, the elements of the original array will be modified.

To define a local variable that has scope only within the current function, and has not been passed as a parameter, use the **var** keyword. Example 14-10 shows a function that creates one variable with global scope and two with local scope.

Example 14-10. A function creating variables with global and local scope

```
<script>
function test()
{
      a = 123                 // Global scope
   var b = 456                 // Local scope
   if (a == 123) var c = 789 // Local scope
}
</script>
```

To test whether scope setting has worked in PHP, we can use the `isset` function. But in JavaScript there isn't one, so let's make our own—it's sure to come in handy in the future—with Example 14-11.

Example 14-11. A version of the isset function for JavaScript

```
<script>
function isset(varname)
{
   return typeof varname != 'undefined'
}
</script>
```

This function makes use of the **typeof** operator, which returns the string "undefined" when a variable is not defined. So let's use it to test our **isset** function in Example 14-12.

Example 14-12. Checking the scope of the variables defined in function test

```
<script>
test()

if (isset(a)) document.write('a = "' + a + '"<br />')
if (isset(b)) document.write('b = "' + b + '"<br />')
if (isset(c)) document.write('c = "' + c + '"<br />')

function test()
{
      a = 123
   var b = 456
   if (a == 123) var c = 789
}

function isset(varname)
{
   return typeof varname != 'undefined'
}
</script>
```

The output from this script is the following single line:

```
a = "123"
```

This shows that only the variable a was given global scope, which is exactly what we would expect, given that the variables b and c were given local scope by prefacing them with the var keyword.

If your browser issues a warning about b being undefined, the warning is correct but can be ignored.

The Document Object Model

The designers of JavaScript were very smart. Rather than just creating yet another scripting language (which would have still been a pretty good improvement at the time), they had the vision to build it around the Document Object Model or DOM. This breaks down the parts of an HTML document into discrete *objects*, each with its own *properties* and *methods*, and each subject to JavaScript's control.

JavaScript separates objects, properties, and methods using a period (one good reason why + is the string concatenation operator in JavaScript, rather than the period). For example, let's consider a business card as an object we'll call card. This object contains properties such as a name, address, phone number, and so on. In the syntax of JavaScript, these properties would look like this:

```
card.name
card.phone
card.address
```

Its methods are functions that retrieve, change, and otherwise act on the properties. For instance, to invoke a method that displays the properties of object card, you might use syntax such as:

```
card.display()
```

Have a look at some of the earlier examples in this chapter and look at where the statement document.write is used. Now that you understand how JavaScript is based around objects, you will see that write is actually a method of the document object.

Within JavaScript, there is a hierarchy of parent and child objects. This is what is known as the Document Object Model (see Figure 14-3).

The figure uses HTML tags that you are already familiar with to illustrate the parent/child relationship between the various objects in a document. For example, a URL within a link is part of the body of an HTML document. In JavaScript, it is referenced like this:

```
url = document.links.linkname.href
```

Notice how this follows the central column down. The first part, document, refers to the <html> and <body> tags, links.linkname to the <a ...> tag and href to the href=... element.

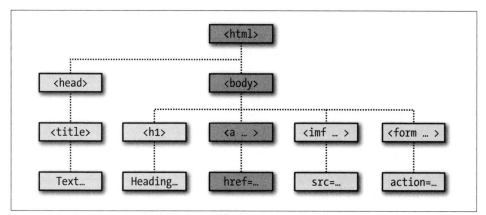

Figure 14-3. Example of DOM object hierarchy

Let's turn this into some HTML and a script to read a link's properties. Type in Example 14-13 and save it as *linktest.html*, then call it up in your browser.

 If you are using Microsoft Internet Explorer as your main development browser, please just read through this section, then read the section titled "Browser Incompatibilities" on page 316 and then come back and try the example with the getElementById modification discussed there. Without it, this example will not work for you.

Example 14-13. Reading a link URL with JavaScript

```html
<html>
    <head>
        <title>Link Test</title>
    </head>
    <body>
        <a id="mylink" href="http://mysite.com">Click me</a><br />
        <script>
            url = document.links.mylink.href
            document.write('The URL is ' + url)
        </script>
    </body>
</html>
```

Note the short form of the script tags where I have omitted the parameter type="text/JavaScript" to save you some typing. If you wish, just for the purposes of testing this (and other examples), you could also omit everything outside of the <script> and </script> tags. The output from this example is:

```
Click me
The URL is http://mysite.com
```

The second line of output comes from the `document.write` method. Notice how the code follows the document tree down from `document` to `links` to `mylink` (the `id` given to the link) to `href` (the URL destination value).

There is also a short form that works equally well, which starts with the value in the `id` attribute: `mylink.href`. So you can replace this:

```
url = document.links.mylink.href
```

with the following:

```
url = mylink.href
```

Browser Incompatibilities

If you tried Example 14-13 in Safari, Firefox, Opera, or Chrome, it will have worked just great. But in Internet Explorer (even version 8) it will fail, because Microsoft's implementation of JavaScript, called JScript, has many subtle differences from the recognized standards. Welcome to the world of advanced web development!

So what can we do about this? Well, in this case, instead of using the `links` child object of the parent `document` object, which Internet Explorer balks at when used this way, you have to replace it with a method to fetch the element by its `id`. Therefore, the following line:

```
url = document.links.mylink.href
```

can be replaced with this one:

```
url = document.getElementById('mylink').href
```

And now the script will work in all major browsers. Incidentally, when you don't have to look the element up by `id`, the short form that follows will still work in Internet Explorer, as well as the other browsers:

```
url = mylink.href
```

Another use for the $ sign

As mentioned earlier, the $ symbol is allowed in JavaScript variable and function names. Because of this, you may sometimes encounter some strange-looking code, like this:

```
url = $('mylink').href
```

Some enterprising programmers have decided that the `getElementById` function is so prevalent in JavaScript that they have written a function to replace it called $, shown in Example 14-14.

Example 14-14. A replacement function for the getElementById method

```
<script>
function $(id)
{
    return document.getElementById(id)
```

```
}
</script>
```

Therefore, as long as you have included the $ function in your code, syntax such as:

```
$('mylink').href
```

can replace code such as:

```
document.getElementById('mylink').href
```

Using the DOM

The links object is actually an array of URLs, so the mylink URL in Example 14-13 can also be safely referred to on all browsers in the following way (because it's the first, and only, link):

```
url = document.links[0].href
```

If you want to know how many links there are in an entire document, you can query the length property of the links object like this:

```
numlinks = document.links.length
```

You can therefore extract and display all links in a document like this:

```
for (j=0 ; j < document.links.length ; ++j)
    document.write(document.links[j].href + '<br />')
```

The length of something is a property of every array, and many objects as well. For example, the number of items in your browser's web history can be queried like this:

```
document.write(history.length)
```

However, to stop websites from snooping on your browsing history, the history object stores only the number of sites in the array: you cannot read from or write to these values. But you can replace the current page with one from the history, if you know what position it has within the history. This can be very useful in cases in which you know that certain pages in the history came from your site, or you simply wish to send the browser back one or more pages, which is done with the go method of the history object. For example, to send the browser back three pages, issue the following command:

```
history.go(-3)
```

You can also use the following methods to move back or forward a page at a time:

```
history.back()
history.forward()
```

In a similar manner, you can replace the currently loaded URL with one of your choosing, like this:

```
document.location.href = 'http://google.com'
```

Of course, there's a whole lot more to the DOM than reading and modifying links. As you progress through the following chapters on JavaScript, you'll become quite familiar with the DOM and how to access it.

Test Your Knowledge: Questions

Question 14-1
Which tags do you use to enclose JavaScript code?

Question 14-2
By default, to which part of a document will JavaScript code output?

Question 14-3
How can you include JavaScript code from another source in your documents?

Question 14-4
Which JavaScript function is the equivalent of echo or print in PHP?

Question 14-5
How can you create a comment in JavaScript?

Question 14-6
What is the JavaScript string concatenation operator?

Question 14-7
Which keyword can you use within a JavaScript function to define a variable that has local scope?

Question 14-8
Give two cross-browser methods to display the URL assigned to the link with an id of thislink.

Question 14-9
Which two JavaScript commands will make the browser load the previous page in its history array?

Question 14-10
What JavaScript command would you use to replace the current document with the main page at the *oreilly.com* website?

See the section "Chapter 14 Answers" on page 446 in Appendix A for the answers to these questions.

CHAPTER 15

Expressions and Control Flow in JavaScript

In the last chapter I introduced the basics of JavaScript and DOM. Now it's time to look at how to construct complex expressions in JavaScript and how to control the program flow of your scripts using conditional statements.

Expressions

JavaScript expressions are very similar to those in PHP. As you learned in Chapter 4, an expression is a combination of values, variables, operators, and functions that results in a value; the result can be a number, a string, or a Boolean value (which evaluates to either **true** or **false**).

Example 15-1 shows some simple expressions. For each line, it prints out a letter between a and d, followed by a colon and the result of the expressions (the **
** tag is there to create a line break and separate the output into four lines).

Example 15-1. Four simple Boolean expressions

```
<script>
document.write("a: " + (42 > 3) + "<br />")
document.write("b: " + (91 < 4) + "<br />")
document.write("c: " + (8 == 2) + "<br />")
document.write("d: " + (4 < 17) + "<br />")
</script>
```

The output from this code is as follows:

```
a: true
b: false
c: false
d: true
```

Notice that both expressions a: and d: evaluate to **true**. But b: and c: evaluate to **false**. Unlike PHP (which would print the number 1 and nothing, respectively), actual strings of "true" and "false" are displayed.

In JavaScript, when checking whether a value is true or false, all values evaluate to true with the exception of the following, which evaluate to false: the string false itself, 0, –0, the empty string, null, undefined, and NaN (Not a Number, a computer engineering concept for an illegal floating-point operation such as division by zero).

Note how I am referring to true and false in lowercase. This is because, unlike in PHP, these values *must* be in lowercase in JavaScript. Therefore only the first of the two following statements will display, printing the lowercase word "true," because the second will cause a "'TRUE' is not defined" error:

```
if (1 == true) document.write('true') // True
if (1 == TRUE) document.write('TRUE') // Will cause an error
```

 Remember that any code snippets you wish to type in and try for yourself in an HTML file need to be enclosed within <script> and </script> tags.

Literals and Variables

The simplest form of an expression is a *literal*, which means something that evaluates to itself, such as the number 22 or the string "Press Enter". An expression could also be a variable, which evaluates to the value that has been assigned to it. They are both types of expressions, because they return a value.

Example 15-2 shows five different literals, all of which return values, albeit of different types.

Example 15-2. Five types of literals

```
<script>
myname = "Peter"
myage  = 24
document.write("a: " + 42     + "<br />") // Numeric literal
document.write("b: " + "Hi"   + "<br />") // String literal
document.write("c: " + true   + "<br />") // Constant literal
document.write("d: " + myname + "<br />") // Variable string literal
document.write("e: " + myage  + "<br />") // Variable numeric literal
</script>
```

And, as you'd expect, you see a return value from all of these in the following output:

```
a: 42
b: Hi
c: true
d: Peter
e: 24
```

Operators let you create more complex expressions that evaluate to useful results. When you combine assignment or control-flow construct with expressions, the result is a *statement*.

Example 15-3 shows one of each. The first assigns the result of the expression `366 - day_number` to the variable `days_to_new_year`, and the second outputs a friendly message only if the expression `days_to_new_year < 30` evaluates to `true`.

Example 15-3. Two simple JavaScript statements

```
<script>
days_to_new_year = 366 - day_number;
if (days_to_new_year < 30) document.write("It's nearly New Year")
</script>
```

Operators

JavaScript offers a lot of powerful operators that range from arithmetic, string, and logical operators to assignment, comparison, and more (see Table 15-1).

Table 15-1. JavaScript operator types

Operator	Description	Example
Arithmetic	Basic mathematics	`a + b`
Array	Array manipulation	`a + b`
Assignment	Assign values	`a = b + 23`
Bitwise	Manipulate bits within bytes	`12 ^ 9`
Comparison	Compare two values	`a < b`
Increment/Decrement	Add or subtract one	`a++`
Logical	Boolean	`a && b`
String	Concatenation	`a + 'string'`

Each operator takes a different number of operands:

- *Unary* operators, such as incrementing (`a++`) or negation (`-a`) take a single operand.
- *Binary* operators, which represent the bulk of JavaScript operators, including addition, subtraction, multiplication, and division.
- One *ternary* operator, which takes the form `? x : y`. It's a terse single-line `if` statement that chooses between two expressions depending on a third one.

Operator Precedence

As with PHP, JavaScript utilizes operator precedence, in which some operators in an expression are considered more important than others and are therefore evaluated first. Table 15-2 lists JavaScript's operators and their precedences.

Table 15-2. The precedence of JavaScript operators (high to low)

Operator(s)	Type(s)
() [] .	Parentheses, call, and member
++ --	Increment/decrement
+ - ~ !	Unary, bitwise, and logical
* / %	Arithmetic
+ -	Arithmetic and string
<< >> >>>	Bitwise
< > <= >=	Comparison
== != === !==	Comparison
&&	Logical
||	Logical
? :	Ternary
= += -= *= /= %= <<= >>= >>>= &= ^= |=	Assignment
,	Sequential evaluation

Associativity

Most JavaScript operators are processed in order from left to right in an equation. But some operators require processing from right to left instead. The direction of processing is called the operator's *associativity*.

This associativity becomes important in cases where you do not explicitly force precedence. For example, look at the following assignment operators, by which three variables are all set to the value 0:

```
level = score = time = 0
```

This multiple assignment is possible only because the rightmost part of the expression is evaluated first and then processing continues in a right-to-left direction. Table 15-3 lists all the operators that have right-to-left associativity.

Table 15-3. Operators with right-to-left associativity

Operator	Description
New	Create a new object
++ --	Increment and decrement
+ - ~ !	Unary and bitwise
? :	Conditional
= *= /= %= += -= <<= >>= >>>= &= ^= |=	Assignment

Relational Operators

Relational operators test two operands and return a Boolean result of either `true` or `false`. There are three types of relational operators: *equality*, *comparison*, and *logical*.

Equality operators

The equality operator is `==` (which should not be confused with the `=` assignment operator). In Example 15-4, the first statement assigns a value and the second tests it for equality. As it stands, nothing will be printed out, because `month` is assigned the string value "July" and therefore the check for it having a value of "October" will fail.

Example 15-4. Assigning a value and testing for equality

```
<script>
month = "July"
if (month == "October") document.write("It's the Fall")
</script>
```

If the two operands of an equality expression are of different types, JavaScript will convert them to whatever type makes best sense to it. For example, any strings composed entirely of numbers will be converted to numbers whenever compared with a number. In Example 15-5, `a` and `b` are two different values (one is a number and the other is a string), and we would therefore normally expect neither of the `if` statements to output a result.

Example 15-5. The equality and identity operators

```
<script>
a = 3.1415927
b = "3.1415927"
if (a == b) document.write("1")
if (a === b) document.write("2")
</script>
```

However, if you run the example, you will see that it outputs the number 1, which means that the first `if` statement evaluated to `true`. This is because the string value of `b` was first temporarily converted to a number, and therefore both halves of the equation had a numerical value of 3.1415927.

In contrast, the second `if` statement uses the *identity* operator, three equals signs in a row, which prevents JavaScript from automatically converting types. This means that `a` and `b` are therefore found to be different, so nothing is output.

As with forcing operator precedence, whenever you feel there may be doubt about how JavaScript will convert operand types, you can use the identity operator to turn this behavior off.

Comparison operators

Using comparison operators, you can test for more than just equality and inequality. JavaScript also gives you > (is greater than), < (is less than), >= (is greater than or equal to), and <= (is less than or equal to) to play with. Example 15-6 shows these operators in use.

Example 15-6. The four comparison operators

```
<script>
a = 7; b = 11
if (a > b)  document.write("a is greater than b<br />")
if (a < b)  document.write("a is less than b<br />")
if (a >= b) document.write("a is greater than or equal to b<br />")
if (a <= b) document.write("a is less than or equal to b<br />")
</script>
```

In this example, where a is 7 and b is 11, the following is output:

```
a is less than b
a is less than or equal to b
```

Logical operators

Logical operators produce true-or-false results, and are also known as *Boolean* operators. There are three of them in JavaScript (see Table 15-4).

Table 15-4. JavaScript's logical operators

Logical operator	Description
&& *(and)*	true if both operands are true
|| *(or)*	true if either operand is true
! *(not)*	true if the operand is false or false if the operand is true

You can see how these can be used in Example 15-7, which outputs 0, 1, and true.

Example 15-7. The logical operators in use

```
<script>
a = 1; b = 0
document.write((a && b) + "<br />")
document.write((a || b) + "<br />")
document.write((  !b  ) + "<br />")
</script>
```

The && statement requires both operands to be true if it is going to return a value of true, the || statement will be true if either value is true, and the third statement performs a NOT on the value of b, turning it from 0 into a value of true.

The || operator can cause unintentional problems, because the second operand will not be evaluated if the first is evaluated as `true`. In Example 15-8, the function `getnext` will never be called if `finished` has a value of 1.

Example 15-8. A statement using the || operator

```
<script>
if (finished == 1 || getnext() == 1) done = 1
</script>
```

If you *need* `getnext` to be called at each `if` statement, you should rewrite the code as shown in Example 15-9.

Example 15-9. The if...or statement modified to ensure calling of getnext

```
<script>
gn = getnext()
if (finished == 1 OR gn == 1) done = 1;
</script>
```

In this case, the code in function `getnext` will be executed and its return value stored in gn before the `if` statement.

Table 15-5 shows all the possible variations of using the logical operators. You should also note that `!true` equals `false` and `!false` equals `true`.

Table 15-5. All possible logical expressions

Inputs		Operators & results	
a	b	&&	||
true	true	true	true
true	false	false	true
false	true	false	true
false	false	false	false

The with Statement

The `with` statement is not one that you've seen in earlier chapters on PHP, because it's exclusive to JavaScript. With it (if you see what I mean), you can simplify some types of JavaScript statements by reducing many references to an object to just one reference. References to properties and methods within the `with` block are assumed to apply to that object.

For example, take the code in Example 15-10, in which the `document.write` function never references the variable `string` by name.

Example 15-10. Using the with statement

```
<script>
string = "The quick brown fox jumps over the lazy dog"

with (string)
{
    document.write("The string is " + length + " characters<br />")
    document.write("In upper case it's: " + toUpperCase())
}
</script>
```

Even though **string** is never directly referenced by **document.write**, this code still manages to output the following:

```
The string is 43 characters
In upper case it's: THE QUICK BROWN FOX JUMPS OVER THE LAZY DOG
```

This is how the code works: the JavaScript interpreter recognizes that the **length** property and **toUpperCase()** method have to be applied to some object. Because they stand alone, the interpreter assumes they apply to the **string** object that you specified in the **with** statement.

Using onError

Here are more constructs not available in PHP. Using either the **onError** event, or a combination of the **try** and **catch** keywords, you can catch JavaScript errors and deal with them yourself.

Events are actions that can be detected by JavaScript. Every element on a web page has certain events that can trigger JavaScript functions. For example, the **onClick** event of a button element can be set to call a function and make it run whenever a user clicks on the button.

Example 15-11 illustrates how to use the **onError** event.

Example 15-11. A script employing the onError event

```
<script>
onerror = errorHandler
document.writ("Welcome to this website") // Deliberate error

function errorHandler(message, url, line)
{
    out  = "Sorry, an error was encountered.\n\n";
    out += "Error: " + message + "\n";
    out += "URL: "   + url + "\n";
    out += "Line: "  + line + "\n\n";
    out += "Click OK to continue.\n\n";
    alert(out);
    return true;
}
</script>
```

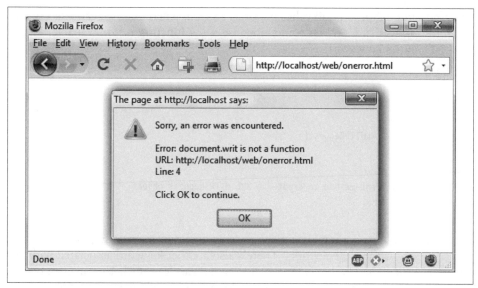

Figure 15-1. Using the onError event with an alert method pop up

The first line of this script tells the error event to use the new errorHandler function from now on. This function takes three parameters, a message, a url and a line number, so it's a simple matter to display all these in an alert pop up.

Then, to test the new function, a syntax error is deliberately placed in the code with a call to document.writ instead of document.write (the final e is missing). Figure 15-1 shows the result of running this script in a browser. Using onError this way can also be quite useful during the debugging process.

Unfortunately, only Firefox and Internet Explorer appear to support this event so you will not be able to test this particular example in the Opera, Safari, or Chrome browsers.

Using try...catch

The try and catch keywords are more standard and more flexible than the onError technique shown in the previous section. These keywords let you trap errors for a selected section of code, rather than all scripts in a document. However, they do not catch syntax errors, for which you need onError.

The try...catch construct is supported by all major browsers and is handy when you want to catch a certain condition that you are aware could occur in a specific part of your code.

For example, in Chapter 18 we'll be exploring Ajax techniques that make use of the XMLHttpRequest object. Unfortunately, this isn't available in the Internet Explorer browser (although it is in all other major browsers). Therefore, we can use try and catch to trap this case and do something else if the function is not available. Example 15-12 shows how.

Example 15-12. Trapping an error with try and catch

```
<script>
try
{
    request = new XMLHTTPRequest()
}
catch(err)
{
    // Use a different method to create an XML HTTP Request object
}
</script>
```

I won't go into how we implement the missing object in Internet Explorer here, but you can see how the system works. There's also another keyword associated with try and catch called finally that is always executed, regardless of whether an error occurs in the try clause. To use it, just add something like the following statements after a catch statement:

```
finally
{
    alert("The 'try' clause was encountered")
}
```

Conditionals

Conditionals alter program flow. They enable you to ask questions about certain things and respond to the answers you get in different ways. There are three types of non-looping conditionals: the if statement, the switch statement, and the ? operator.

The if Statement

Several examples in this chapter have already made use of if statements. The code within such a statement is executed only if the given expression evaluates to true. Multiline if statements require curly braces around them, but as in PHP, you can omit the braces for single statements. Therefore, the following statements are valid:

```
if (a > 100)
{
    b=2
    document.write("a is greater than 100")
}

if (b == 10) document.write("b is equal to 10")
```

The else statement

When a condition has not been met, you can execute an alternative using an `else` statement, like this:

```
if (a > 100)
{
    document.write("a is greater than 100")
}
else
{
    document.write("a is less than or equal to 100")
}
```

Unlike, PHP there is no `elseif` statement, but that's not a problem, because you can use an `else` followed by another `if` to form the equivalent of an `elseif` statement, like this:

```
if (a > 100)
{
    document.write("a is greater than 100")
}
else if(a < 100)
{
    document.write("a is less than 100")
}
else
{
    document.write("a is equal to 100")
}
```

As you can see, you can use another `else` after the new `if`, which could equally be followed by another `if` statement and so on. Although I have shown braces on the statements, because each is a single line the whole previous example could be written as follows:

```
if (a > 100) document.write("a is greater than 100")
else if(a < 100) document.write("a is less than 100")
else document.write("a is equal to 100")
```

The switch Statement

The `switch` statement is useful when one variable or the result of an expression can have multiple values, for each of which you want to perform a different function.

For example, the following code takes the PHP menu system we put together in Chapter 4 and converts it to JavaScript. It works by passing a single string to the main menu code according to what the user requests. Let's say the options are Home, About, News, Login, and Links, and we set the variable **page** to one of these according to the user's input.

The code for this written using `if...else if...` might look like Example 15-13.

Example 15-13. A multiline if...else if... statement

```
<script>
if      (page == "Home")  document.write("You selected Home")
else if (page == "About") document.write("You selected About")
else if (page == "News")  document.write("You selected News")
else if (page == "Login") document.write("You selected Login")
else if (page == "Links") document.write("You selected Links")
</script>
```

But using a `switch` construct, the code could look like Example 15-14.

Example 15-14. A switch construct

```
<script>
switch (page)
{
    case "Home":  document.write("You selected Home")
        break
    case "About": document.write("You selected About")
        break
    case "News":  document.write("You selected News")
        break
    case "Login": document.write("You selected Login")
        break
    case "Links": document.write("You selected Links")
        break
}
</script>
```

The variable `page` is mentioned only once at the start of the `switch` statement. Thereafter the `case` command checks for matches. When one occurs, the matching conditional statement is executed. Of course, a real program would have code here to display or jump to a page, rather than simply telling the user what was selected.

Breaking out

As you can see in the Example 15-14, just as with PHP, the `break` command allows your code to break out of the `switch` statement once a condition has been satisfied. Remember to include the `break` unless you want to continue executing the statements under the next `case`.

Default action

When no condition is satisfied, you can specify a default action for a `switch` statement using the `default` keyword. Example 15-15 shows a code snippet that could be inserted into Example 15-14.

Example 15-15. A default statement to add to Example 15-12

```
default: document.write("Unrecognized selection")
        break
```

The ? Operator

The *ternary* operator (?), combined with the : character, provides a quick way of doing if...else tests. With it you can write an expression to evaluate, then follow it with a ? symbol and the code to execute if the expression is **true**. After that, place a : and the code to execute if the expression evaluates to **false**.

Example 15-16 shows a ternary operator being used to print out whether the variable a is less than or equal to 5, and prints something either way.

Example 15-16. Using the ternary operator

```
<script>
document.write(
        a <= 5 ?
        "a is less than or equal to 5" :
        "a is greater than 5"
        )
</script>
```

The statement has been broken up into several lines for clarity, but you would be more likely to use such a statement on a single line, in this manner:

```
    size = a <= 5 ? "short" : "long"
```

Looping

Again, you will find many close similarities between JavaScript and PHP when it comes to looping. Both languages support **while**, **do...while**, and **for** loops.

while Loops

A JavaScript **while** loop first checks the value of an expression and starts executing the statements within the loop only if that expression is **true**. If it is **false**, execution skips over to the next JavaScript statement (if any).

Upon completing an iteration of the loop, the expression is again tested to see if it is **true** and the process continues until such a time as the expression evaluates to **false**, or until execution is otherwise halted. Example 15-17 shows such a loop.

Example 15-17. A while loop

```
<script>
counter=0

while (counter < 5)
{
    document.write("Counter: " + counter + "<br />")
    ++counter
}
</script>
```

This script outputs the following:

```
Counter: 0
Counter: 1
Counter: 2
Counter: 3
Counter: 4
```

 If the variable counter were not incremented within the loop, it is quite possible that some browsers could become unresponsive due to a never-ending loop, and the page may not even be easy to terminate with Escape or the Stop button. So be careful with your JavaScript loops.

do...while Loops

When you require a loop to iterate at least once before any tests are made, use a do...while loop, which is similar to a while loop, except that the test expression is checked only after each iteration of the loop. So, to output the first seven results in the seven times table, you could use code such as that in Example 15-18.

Example 15-18. A do...while loop

```
<script>
count = 1
do
{
    document.write(count + " times 7 is " + count * 7 + "<br />")
} while (++count <= 7)
</script>
```

As you might expect, this loop outputs the following:

```
1 times 7 is 7
2 times 7 is 14
3 times 7 is 21
4 times 7 is 28
5 times 7 is 35
6 times 7 is 42
7 times 7 is 49
```

for Loops

A for loop combines the best of all worlds into a single looping construct that allows you to pass three parameters for each statement:

- An initialization expression
- A condition expression
- A modification expression

These are separated by semicolons, like this: for (*expr1*; *expr2*; *expr3*). At the start of the first iteration of the loop, the initialization expression is executed. In the case of the

---

code for the multiplication table for 7, count would be initialized to the value 1. Then, each time round the loop, the condition expression (in this case count <= 7) is tested, and the loop is entered only if the condition is true. Finally, at the end of each iteration, the modification expression is executed. In the case of the multiplication table for 7, the variable count is incremented. Example 15-19 shows what the code would look like.

Example 15-19. Using a for loop

```
<script>
for (count = 1 ; count <= 7 ; ++count)
{
    document.write(count + "times 7 is " + count * 7 + "<br />");
}
</script>
```

As in PHP, you can assign multiple variables in the first parameter of a for loop by separating them with a comma, like this:

```
for (i = 1, j = 1 ; i < 10 ; i++)
```

Likewise, you can perform multiple modifications in the last parameter, like this:

```
for (i = 1 ; i < 10 ; i++, --j)
```

Or you can do both at the same time:

```
for (i = 1, j = 1 ; i < 10 ; i++, --j)
```

Breaking Out of a Loop

The break command, which you saw to be important inside a switch statement, is also available within for loops. You might need to use this, for example, when searching for a match of some kind. Once the match is found, you know that continuing to search will only waste time and make your visitor wait. Example 15-20 shows how to use the break command.

Example 15-20. Using the break command in a for loop

```
<script>
haystack = new Array()
haystack[17] = "Needle"

for (j = 0 ; j < 20 ; ++j)
{
    if (haystack[j] == "Needle")
    {
        document.write("<br />- Found at location " + j)
        break
    }
    else document.write(j + ", ")
}
</script>
```

This script outputs the following:

```
0, 1, 2, 3, 4, 5, 6, 7, 8, 9, 10, 11, 12, 13, 14, 15, 16,
- Found at location 17
```

The continue Statement

Sometimes you don't want to entirely exit from a loop, but instead wish to skip the remaining statements just for this iteration of the loop. In such cases, you can use the `continue` command. Example 15-21 shows this in use.

Example 15-21. Using the continue command in a for loop

```
<script>
haystack = new Array()
haystack[4]  = "Needle"
haystack[11] = "Needle"
haystack[17] = "Needle"

for (j = 0 ; j < 20 ; ++j)
{
    if (haystack[j] == "Needle")
    {
        document.write("<br />- Found at location " + j + "<br />")
        continue
    }

    document.write(j + ", ")
}
</script>
```

Notice how the second `document.write` call does not have to be enclosed in an `else` statement (which it did before), because the `continue` command will skip it if a match has been found. The output from this script is as follows:

```
0, 1, 2, 3,
- Found at location 4
5, 6, 7, 8, 9, 10,
- Found at location 11
12, 13, 14, 15, 16,
- Found at location 17
18, 19,
```

Explicit Casting

Unlike PHP, JavaScript has no explicit casting of types such as (`int`) or (`float`). Instead, when you need a value to be of a certain type, use one of JavaScript's built-in functions, shown in Table 15-6.

Table 15-6. JavaScript's type-changing functions

Change to type	Function to use
Int, Integer	parseInt()
Bool, Boolean	Boolean()
Float, Double, Real	parseFloat()
String	String()
Array	split()

So, for example, to change a floating-point number to an integer, you could use code such as the following (which displays the value 3):

```
n = 3.1415927
i = parseInt(n)
document.write(i)
```

Or you can use the compound form:

```
document.write(parseInt(3.1415927))
```

That's it for control flow and expressions. The next chapter focuses on the use of functions, objects, and arrays in JavaScript.

Test Your Knowledge: Questions

Question 15-1
> How are Boolean values handled differently by PHP and JavaScript?

Question 15-2
> What character is used to define a JavaScript variable name?

Question 15-3
> What is the difference between unary, binary, and ternary operators?

Question 15-4
> What is the best way to force your own operator precedence?

Question 15-5
> When would you use the === (identity) operator?

Question 15-6
> What are the simplest two forms of expressions?

Question 15-7
> Name the three conditional statement types.

Question 15-8
> How do if and while statements interpret conditional expressions of different data types?

Question 15-9

Why is a `for` loop more powerful than a `while` loop?

Question 15-10

What is the purpose of the `with` statement?

See the section "Chapter 15 Answers" on page 447 in Appendix A for the answers to these questions.

CHAPTER 16

JavaScript Functions, Objects, and Arrays

Just like PHP, JavaScript offers access to functions and objects. In fact, JavaScript is actually based on objects, because—as you've seen—it has to access the DOM, which makes every element of an HTML document available to manipulate as an object.

The usage and syntax are also quite similar to those of PHP, so you should feel right at home as I take you through using functions and objects in JavaScript, as well as conducting an in-depth exploration of array handling.

JavaScript Functions

In addition to having access to dozens of built-in functions (or methods) such as `write`, which you have already seen being used in `document.write`, you can easily create your own functions. Whenever you have a more complex piece of code that is likely to be reused, you have a candidate for a function.

Defining a Function

The general syntax for a function is:

```
function function_name([parameter [, ...]])
{
    statements
}
```

The first line of the syntax indicates that:

- A definition starts with the word `function`.
- A name follows that must start with a letter or underscore, followed by any number of letters, digits, dollar symbols, or underscores.

- The parentheses are required.
- One or more parameters, separated by commas, are optional (indicated by the square brackets, which are not part of the function syntax).

Function names are case-sensitive, so all of the following strings refer to different functions: `getInput`, `GETINPUT`, and `getinput`.

In JavaScript there is a general naming convention for functions: the first letter of each word in a name is capitalized except for the very first letter, which is lowercase. Therefore, of the previous examples, `getInput` would be the preferred name used by most programmers. The convention is commonly referred to as *bumpyCaps*.

The opening curly brace starts the statements that will execute when you call the function; a matching curly brace must close it. These statements may include one or more `return` statements, which force the function to cease execution and return to the calling code. If a value is attached to the `return` statement, the calling code can retrieve it.

The arguments array

The `arguments` array is a member of every function. With it, you can determine the number of variables passed to a function and what they are. Take the example of a function called `displayItems`. Example 16-1 shows one way of writing it.

Example 16-1. Defining a function

```
<script>
displayItems("Dog", "Cat", "Pony", "Hamster", "Tortoise")

function displayItems(v1, v2, v3, v4, v5)
{
    document.write(v1 + "<br />")
    document.write(v2 + "<br />")
    document.write(v3 + "<br />")
    document.write(v4 + "<br />")
    document.write(v5 + "<br />")
}
</script>
```

When you call this script in your browser, it will display the following:

```
Dog
Cat
Pony
Hamster
Tortoise
```

All of this is fine, but what if you wanted to pass more than five items to the function? Also, reusing the `document.write` call multiple times instead of employing a loop is wasteful programming. Luckily, the `arguments` array gives you the flexibility to handle a variable number of arguments. Example 16-2 shows how you can use it to rewrite the example in a much more efficient manner.

Example 16-2. Modifying the function to use the arguments array

```
<script>
function displayItems()
{
    for (j = 0 ; j < displayItems.arguments.length ; ++j)
        document.write(displayItems.arguments[j] + "<br />")
}
</script>
```

Note the use of the `length` property, which you already encountered in the previous chapter, and also how the array `displayItems.arguments` is referenced using the variable j as an offset into it. I also chose to keep the function short and sweet by not surrounding the contents of the `for` loop in curly braces, as it contains only a single statement.

Using this technique you now have a function that can take as many (or as few) arguments as you like and act on each argument as you desire.

Returning a Value

Functions are not used just to display things. In fact, they are mostly used to perform calculations or data manipulation and then return a result. The function `fixNames` in Example 16-3 uses the `arguments` array (discussed in the previous section) to take a series of strings passed to it and return them as a single string. The "fix" it performs is to convert every character in the arguments to lowercase except for the first character of each argument, which is set to a capital letter.

Example 16-3. Cleaning up a full name

```
<script>
document.write(fixNames("the", "DALLAS", "CowBoys"))

function fixNames()
{
    var s = ""

    for (j = 0 ; j < fixNames.arguments.length ; ++j)
        s += fixNames.arguments[j].charAt(0).toUpperCase() +
            fixNames.arguments[j].substr(1).toLowerCase() + " "

    return s.substr(0, s.length-1)
}
</script>
```

When called with the parameters "the", "DALLAS", and "CowBoys", for example, the function returns the string "The Dallas Cowboys". Let's walk through the function.

The function first initializes the temporary (and local) variable s to the empty string. Then a `for` loop iterates through each of the passed parameters, isolating the parameter's first character using the `charAt` method and converting it to uppercase with the `toUpperCase` method. The various methods shown in this example are all built-in to JavaScript and available by default.

Then the `substr` method is used to fetch the rest of each string, which is converted to lowercase using the `toLowerCase` method. A fuller version of the `substr` method here would specify how many characters are part of the substring as a second argument:

```
substr(1, (arguments[j].length) - 1 )
```

In other words, this `substr` method says, "Start with the character at position 1 (the second character) and return the rest of the string (the length minus one)." As a nice touch, though, the `substr` method assumes that you want the rest of the string if you omit the second argument.

After the whole argument is converted to our desired case, a space character is added to the end and the result is appended to the temporary variable `s`.

Finally, the `substr` method is used again to return the contents of the variable `s`, except for the final space—which is unwanted. This is removed by using `substr` to return the string up to, but not including, the final character.

This example is particularly interesting in that it illustrates the use of multiple properties and methods in a single expression. For example:

```
fixNames.arguments[j].substr(1).toLowerCase()
```

You have to interpret the statement by mentally dividing it into parts at the periods. JavaScript evaluates these elements of the statement from left to right as follows:

1. Start with the name of the function itself: `fixNames`.
2. Extract element `j` from the array `arguments` representing `fixNames` arguments.
3. Invoke `substr` with a parameter of 1 to the extracted element. This passes all but the first character to the next section of the expression.
4. Apply the method `toLowerCase` to the string that has been passed this far.

This practice is often referred to as *method chaining*. So, for example, if the string "mixedCASE" is passed to the example expression, it will go through the following transformations:

```
mixedCase
ixedCase
ixedcase
```

One final reminder: the `s` variable created inside the function is local, and therefore cannot be accessed outside the function. By returning `s` in the `return` statement, we made its value available to the caller, which could store or use it any way it wanted. But `s` itself disappears at the end of the function. Although we could make a function operate on global variables (and sometimes that's necessary), it's much better to just return the values you want to preserve and let JavaScript clean up all the other variables used by the function.

Returning an Array

In Example 16-3, the function returned only one parameter, but what if you need to return multiple parameters? This can be done by returning an array, as in Example 16-4.

Example 16-4. Returning an array of values

```
<script>
words = fixNames("the", "DALLAS", "CowBoys")

for (j = 0 ; j < words.length ; ++j)
    document.write(words[j] + "<br />")

function fixNames()
{
    var s = new Array()

    for (j = 0 ; j < fixNames.arguments.length ; ++j)
        s[j] = fixNames.arguments[j].charAt(0).toUpperCase() +
                fixNames.arguments[j].substr(1).toLowerCase()

    return s
}
</script>
```

Here the variable words is automatically defined as an array and populated with the returned result of a call to the function fixNames. Then a for loop iterates through the array and displays each member.

As for the fixNames function, it's almost identical to Example 16-3, except that the variable s is now an array, and after each word has been processed it is stored as an element of this array, which is returned by the return statement.

This function enables the extraction of individual parameters from its returned values, like the following (the output from which is simply "The Cowboys"):

```
words = fixNames("the", "DALLAS", "CowBoys")
document.write(words[0] + " " + words[2])
```

JavaScript Objects

A JavaScript object is a step up from a variable, which can contain only one value at a time, in that objects can contain multiple values and even functions. An object groups data together with the functions needed to manipulate it.

Declaring a Class

When creating a script to use objects, you need to design a composite of data and code called a *class*. Each new object based on this class is called an *instance* (or *occurrence*) of that class. As you've already seen, the data associated with an object are called its *properties*, while the functions it uses are called *methods*.

Let's look at how to declare the class for an object called User that will contain details about the current user. To create the class, just write a function named after the class. This function can accept arguments (I'll show later how it's invoked) and can create properties and methods for the objects in that class. The function is called a *constructor*.

Example 16-5 shows a constructor for the class User with three properties: forename, username, and password. The class also defines the method showUser.

Example 16-5. Declaring the User class and its method

```
<script>
function User(forename, username, password)
{
    this.forename = forename
    this.username = username
    this.password = password

    this.showUser = function()
    {
        document.write("Forename: " + this.forename + "<br />")
        document.write("Username: " + this.username + "<br />")
        document.write("Password: " + this.password + "<br />")
    }
}
</script>
```

The function is different from other functions we've seen so far in two ways:

- It refers to an object named this. When the program creates an instance of User by running this function, this refers to the instance being created. The same function can be called over and over with different arguments, and will create a new User each time with different values for the properties forename, and so on.
- A new function named showUser is created within the function. The syntax shown here is new and rather complicated, but its purpose is to tie showUser to the User class. Thus, showUser comes into being as a method of the User class.

The naming convention I have used is to keep all properties in lowercase and to use at least one uppercase character in method names, following the bumpyCaps convention mentioned earlier in the chapter.

Example 16-5 follows the recommended way to write a class constructor, which is to include methods in the constructor function. However, you can also refer to functions defined outside the constructor, as in Example 16-6.

Example 16-6. Separately defining a class and method

```
<script>
function User(forename, username, password)
{
```

```
    this.forename = forename
    this.username = username
    this.password = password
    this.showUser = showUser
}

function showUser()
{
    document.write("Forename: " + this.forename + "<br />")
    document.write("Username: " + this.username + "<br />")
    document.write("Password: " + this.password + "<br />")
}
</script>
```

I show you this form because you are certain to encounter it when perusing other programmers' code.

Creating an Object

To create an instance of the class User, you can use a statement such as the following:

```
details = new User("Wolfgang", "w.a.mozart", "composer")
```

Or you can create an empty object, like this:

```
details = new User()
```

and then populate it later, like this:

```
details.forename = "Wolfgang"
details.username = "w.a.mozart"
details.password = "composer"
```

You can also add new properties to an object, like this:

```
details.greeting = "Hello"
```

You can verify that adding such new properties works with the following statement:

```
document.write(details.greeting)
```

Accessing Objects

To access an object, you can refer to its properties, as in the following two unrelated example statements:

```
name = details.forename
if (details.username == "Admin") loginAsAdmin()
```

So to access the showUser method of an object of class User, you would use the following syntax, in which the object details has already been created and populated with data:

```
details.showUser()
```

Assuming the data supplied earlier, this code would display:

```
Forename: Wolfgang
Username: w.a.mozart
Password: composer
```

The prototype Keyword

The prototype keyword can save you a lot of memory. In the User class, every instance will contain the three properties and the method. Therefore, if you have 1,000 of these objects in memory, the method showUser will also be replicated 1,000 times. However, because the method is identical in every case, you can specify that new objects should refer to a single instance of the method instead of creating a copy of it. So, instead of using the following in a class constructor:

```
this.showUser = function()
```

you could replace it with this:

```
User.prototype.showUser = function()
```

Example 16-7 shows what the new constructor would look like.

Example 16-7. Declaring a class using the prototype keyword for a method

```
<script>
function User(forename, username, password)
{
    this.forename = forename
    this.username = username
    this.password = password

    User.prototype.showUser = function()
    {
        document.write("Forename: " + this.forename + "<br />")
        document.write("Username: " + this.username + "<br />")
        document.write("Password: " + this.password + "<br />")
    }
}
</script>
```

This works because all functions have a **prototype** property, designed to hold properties and methods that are not replicated in any objects created from a class. Instead, they are passed to its objects by reference.

This means that you can add a **prototype** property or method at any time and all objects (even those already created) will inherit it, as the following statements illustrate:

```
User.prototype.greeting = "Hello"
document.write(details.greeting)
```

The first statement adds the **prototype** property of **greeting** with a value of "Hello" to the class User. In the second line, the object **details**, which has already been created, correctly displays this new property.

You can also add to or modify methods in a class, as the following statements illustrate:

```
User.prototype.showUser = function() { document.write("Name " +
this.forename + " User " + this.username + " Pass " + this.password) }
details.showUser()
```

You might add these lines to your script in a conditional statement (such as `if`), so they run if user activities cause you to decide you need a different `showUser` method. After these lines run, even if the object `details` has been created already, further calls to `details.showUser` will run the new function. The old definition of `showUser` has been erased.

Static methods and properties

When reading about PHP objects, you learned that classes can have static properties and methods as well as properties and methods associated with a particular instance of a class. JavaScript also supports static properties and methods, which you can conveniently store and retrieve from the class's **prototype**. Thus, the following statements set and read a static string from `User`:

```
User.prototype.greeting = "Hello"
document.write(User.prototype.greeting)
```

Extending JavaScript objects

The `prototype` keyword even lets you add functionality to a built-in object. For example, suppose that you would like to add the ability to replace all spaces in a string with nonbreaking spaces in order to prevent it from wrapping around. This can be done by adding a prototype method to JavaScript's default **String** object definition, like this:

```
String.prototype.nbsp =
    function() { return this.replace(/ /g, ' ') }
```

Here the `replace` method is used with a regular expression (see Chapter 17) to find and replace all single spaces with the string " ". If you then enter the following command:

```
document.write("The quick brown fox".nbsp())
```

It will output the string "The quick brown fox". Or here's a method you can add that will trim leading and trailing spaces from a string (once again using a regular expression):

```
String.prototype.trim =
    function() { return this.replace(/^\s+|\s+$/g, '') }
```

If you issue the following statement the output will be the string "Please trim me" (with the leading and trailing spaces removed).

```
document.write("  Please trim me    ".trim())
```

JavaScript Arrays

Array handling in JavaScript is very similar to PHP, although the syntax is a little different. Nevertheless, given all you have already learned about arrays, this section should be relatively straightforward for you.

Numeric Arrays

To create a new array, use the following syntax:

```
arrayname = new Array()
```

Or you can use the shorthand form, as follows:

```
arrayname = []
```

Assigning element values

In PHP, you could add a new element to an array by simply assigning it without specifying the element offset, like this:

```
$arrayname[] = "Element 1";
$arrayname[] = "Element 2";
```

But in JavaScript you use the push method to achieve the same thing, like this:

```
arrayname.push("Element 1")
arrayname.push("Element 2")
```

This allows you to keep adding items to an array without having to keep track of the number of items. When you need to know how many elements are in an array, you can use the length property, like this:

```
document.write(arrayname.length)
```

Alternatively, if you wish to keep track of the element locations yourself and place them in specific locations, you can use syntax such as this:

```
arrayname[0] = "Element 1"
arrayname[1] = "Element 2"
```

Example 16-8 shows a simple script that creates an array, loads it with some values, and then displays them.

Example 16-8. Creating, building, and printing an array

```
<script>
numbers = []
numbers.push("One")
numbers.push("Two")
numbers.push("Three")

for (j = 0 ; j < numbers.length ; ++j)
    document.write("Element " + j + " = " + numbers[j] + "<br />")
</script>
```

The output from this script is:

```
Element 0 = One
Element 1 = Two
Element 2 = Three
```

Assignment using the array keyword

You can also create an array together with some initial elements using the `Array` keyword, like this:

```
numbers = Array("One", "Two", "Three")
```

There is nothing stopping you from adding more elements afterward as well.

So now you have a couple of ways you can add items to an array, and one way of referencing them, but JavaScript offers many more, which I'll get to shortly. But first we'll look at another type of array.

Associative Arrays

An associative array is one in which its elements are referenced by name rather than by numeric offset. To create an associative array, define a block of elements within curly braces. For each element, place the key on the left and the contents on the right of a colon (:). Example 16-9 shows how you might create an associative array to hold the contents of the balls section of an online sports equipment retailer.

Example 16-9. Creating and displaying an associative array

```
<script>
balls = {"golf":    "Golf balls, 6",
         "tennis":  "Tennis balls, 3",
         "soccer":  "Soccer ball, 1",
         "ping":    "Ping Pong balls, 1 doz"}

for (ball in balls)
    document.write(ball + " = " + balls[ball] + "<br />")
</script>
```

To verify that the array has been correctly created and populated, I have used another kind of `for` loop using the `in` keyword. This creates a new variable to use only within the array (`ball` in this example) and iterates through all elements of the array to the right of the `in` keyword (`balls` in this example). The loop acts on each element of `balls`, placing the key value into `ball`.

Using this key value stored in `ball`, you can also get the value of the current element of `balls`. The result of calling up the example script in a browser is as follows:

```
golf = Golf balls, 6
tennis = Tennis balls, 3
soccer = Soccer ball, 1
ping = Ping Pong balls, 1 doz
```

To get a specific element of an associative array, you can specify a key explicitly, in the following manner (in this case outputting the value "Soccer ball, 1"):

```
document.write(balls['soccer'])
```

Multidimensional Arrays

To create a multidimensional array in JavaScript, just place arrays inside other arrays. For example, to create an array to hold the details of a two dimensional checkerboard (8×8 squares), you could use the code in Example 16-10.

Example 16-10. Creating a multidimensional numeric array

```
<script>
checkerboard = Array(
    Array(' ', 'o', ' ', 'o', ' ', 'o', ' ', 'o'),
    Array('o', ' ', 'o', ' ', 'o', ' ', 'o', ' '),
    Array(' ', 'o', ' ', 'o', ' ', 'o', ' ', 'o'),
    Array(' ', ' ', ' ', ' ', ' ', ' ', ' ', ' '),
    Array(' ', ' ', ' ', ' ', ' ', ' ', ' ', ' '),
    Array('O', ' ', 'O', ' ', 'O', ' ', 'O', ' '),
    Array(' ', 'O', ' ', 'O', ' ', 'O', ' ', 'O'),
    Array('O', ' ', 'O', ' ', 'O', ' ', 'O', ' '))

document.write("<pre>")
for (j = 0 ; j < 8 ; ++j)
{
    for (k = 0 ; k < 8 ; ++k)
        document.write(checkerboard[j][k] + " ")
    document.write("<br />")
}
document.write("</pre>")
</script>
```

In this example, the lowercase letters represent black pieces and the uppercase white. A pair of nested **for** loops walk through the array and display its contents.

The outer loop contains two statements, so curly braces enclose them. The inner loop then processes each square in a row, outputting the character at location [j][k], followed by a space (to square up the printout). This loop contains a single statement, so curly braces are not required to enclose it. The **<pre>** and **</pre>** tags ensure that the output displays correctly, like this:

```
   o   o   o   o
 o   o   o   o
   o   o   o   o


 O   O   O   O
   O   O   O   O
 O   O   O   O
```

You can also directly access any element within this array using square brackets, as follows:

```
document.write(checkerboard[7][2])
```

This statement outputs the uppercase letter O, the eighth element down and the third along—remember that array indexes start at 0, not 1.

Using Array Methods

Due to the power of arrays, JavaScript comes ready-made with a number of methods for manipulating them and their data. Here is a selection of the most useful ones.

concat

The concat method concatenates two arrays, or a series of values with an array. For example, the following code outputs "Banana,Grape,Carrot,Cabbage":

```
fruit = ["Banana", "Grape"]
veg   = ["Carrot", "Cabbage"]
document.write(fruit.concat(veg))
```

You can specify multiple arrays as arguments, in which case concat adds all their elements in the order that the arrays are specified.

Here's another way to use concat, This time plain values are concatenated with the array pets, which outputs "Cat,Dog,Fish,Rabbit,Hamster":

```
pets      = ["Cat", "Dog", "Fish"]
more_pets = pets.concat("Rabbit", "Hamster")
document.write(more_pets)
```

forEach: For non-IE browsers

The forEach method in JavaScript is another way of achieving functionality similar to the PHP foreach keyword, but *only for browsers other than Internet Explorer*. To use it you pass it the name of a function, which will be called for each element within the array. Example 16-11 shows how.

Example 16-11. Using the forEach method

```
<script>
pets = ["Cat", "Dog", "Rabbit", "Hamster"]
pets.forEach(output)

function output(element, index, array)
{
    document.write("Element at index " + index + " has the value " +
        element + "<br />")
}
</script>
```

In this case, the function passed to forEach is called output. It takes three parameters: the element, its index, and the array. These can be used as required by your function. In this example, just the element and index values are displayed using the function document.write.

Once an array has been populated, the method is called up like this:

```
pets.forEach(output)
```

The output from which is:

```
Element 0 has the value Cat
Element 1 has the value Dog
Element 2 has the value Rabbit
Element 3 has the value Hamster
```

forEach: A cross-browser solution

Of course, as is its way, Microsoft chose not to support the forEach method, so the previous example will work only on non-Internet Explorer browsers. Therefore until IE does support it, and to ensure cross-browser compatibility, you should use a statement such as the following instead of pets.forEach(output):

```
for (j = 0 ; j < pets.length ; ++j) output(pets[j], j)
```

join

With the join method, you can convert all the values in an array to strings and then join them together into one large string, placing an optional separator between them. Example 16-12 shows three ways of using this method.

Example 16-12. Using the join method

```
<script>
pets = ["Cat", "Dog", "Rabbit", "Hamster"]
document.write(pets.join()      + "<br />")
document.write(pets.join(' ')   + "<br />")
document.write(pets.join(' : ') + "<br />")
</script>
```

Without a parameter, join uses a comma to separate the elements; otherwise, the string passed to join is inserted between each element. The output of Example 16-12 looks like this:

```
Cat,Dog,Rabbit,Hamster
Cat Dog Rabbit Hamster
Cat : Dog : Rabbit : Hamster
```

push and pop

You already saw how the push method can be used to insert a value into an array. The inverse method is pop. It deletes the most recently inserted element from an array and returns it. Example 16-13 shows an example of its use.

Example 16-13. Using the push and pop methods

```
<script>
sports = ["Football", "Tennis", "Baseball"]
document.write("Start = "        + sports +  "<br />")
sports.push("Hockey")
document.write("After Push = " + sports +  "<br />")
removed = sports.pop()
document.write("After Pop = "    + sports +  "<br />")
document.write("Removed = "      + removed + "<br />")
</script>
```

The three main statements of this script are shown in bold type. First the script creates an array called **sports** with three elements and then **pushes** a fourth element into the array. After that it **pops** that element back off. In the process, the various current values are displayed using **document.write**. The script outputs the following:

```
Start = Football,Tennis,Baseball
After Push = Football,Tennis,Baseball,Hockey
After Pop = Football,Tennis,Baseball
Removed = Hockey
```

The **push** and **pop** functions are useful in situations where you need to divert from some activity to do another, then return, as in Example 16-14.

Example 16-14. Using push and pop inside and outside of a loop

```
<script>
numbers = []

for (j=0 ; j<3 ; ++j)
{
    numbers.push(j);
    document.write("Pushed " + j + "<br />")
}

// Perform some other activity here
document.write("<br />")

document.write("Popped " + numbers.pop() + "<br />")
document.write("Popped " + numbers.pop() + "<br />")
document.write("Popped " + numbers.pop() + "<br />")
</script>
```

The output from this example is:

```
Pushed 0
Pushed 1
Pushed 2

Popped 2
Popped 1
Popped 0
```

Using reverse

The **reverse** method simply reverses the order of all elements in an array. Example 16-15 shows this in action.

Example 16-15. Using the reverse method

```
<script>
sports = ["Football", "Tennis", "Baseball", "Hockey"]
sports.reverse()
document.write(sports)
</script>
```

The original array is modified and the output from this script is:

```
Hockey,Baseball,Tennis,Football
```

sort

With the **sort** method, you can place all the elements of an array in alphabetical or other order, depending upon the parameters used. Example 16-16 shows four types of sort.

Example 16-16. Using the sort method

```
<script>
// Alphabetical sort
sports = ["Football", "Tennis", "Baseball", "Hockey"]
sports.sort()
document.write(sports + "<br />")

// Reverse alphabetical sort
sports = ["Football", "Tennis", "Baseball", "Hockey"]
sports.sort().reverse()
document.write(sports + "<br />")

// Ascending numerical sort
numbers = [7, 23, 6, 74]
numbers.sort(function(a,b){return a - b})
document.write(numbers + "<br />")

// Descending numerical sort
numbers = [7, 23, 6, 74]
numbers.sort(function(a,b){return b - a})
document.write(numbers + "<br />")
</script>
```

The first of the four example sections is the default **sort** method, *alphabetical sort*, while the second uses the default **sort** and then applies the **reverse** method to get a *reverse alphabetical sort*.

The third and fourth sections are a little more complicated by using a function to compare the relationships between a and b. The function doesn't have a name, because it's used just in the sort. You have already seen the function named function to create an anonymous function; we used it to define a method in a class (the showUser method).

Here, function creates an anonymous function meeting the needs of the sort method. If the function returns a value greater than zero, the sort assumes that a comes before b. If the function returns a value less than zero, the sort assumes that b comes before a. The sort runs this function across all the values in the array to determine their order.

By manipulating the value returned (a - b in contrast to b - a), the third and fourth sections of Example 16-16 choose between an *ascending numerical sort* and a *descending numerical sort*.

And, believe it or not, this represents the end of your introduction to JavaScript. You should therefore now have a core knowledge of the three main technologies covered in this book. The next chapter will look at some advanced techniques used across these technologies, such as pattern matching and input validation.

Test Your Knowledge: Questions

Question 16-1
Are JavaScript functions and variable names case-sensitive or -insensitive?

Question 16-2
How can you write a function that accepts and processes an unlimited number of parameters?

Question 16-3
Name a way to return multiple values from a function.

Question 16-4
When defining a class, what keyword is used to refer to the current object?

Question 16-5
Do all the methods of a class have to be defined within the class definition?

Question 16-6
What keyword is used to create an object?

Question 16-7
How can a property or method be made available to all objects in a class without replicating the property or method within the object?

Question 16-8
How can you create a multidimensional array?

Question 16-9

What syntax is used to create an associative array?

Question 16-10

Write a statement to sort an array of numbers in descending numerical order.

See the section "Chapter 16 Answers" on page 448 in Appendix A for the answers to these questions.

CHAPTER 17

JavaScript and PHP Validation and Error Handling

With your solid foundation in both PHP and JavaScript, it's time to bring these technologies together to create web forms that are as user-friendly as possible.

We'll be using PHP to create the forms and JavaScript to perform client-side validation to ensure that the data is as complete and correct as it can be before it is submitted. Final validation of the input will then be made by the PHP, which will, if necessary, present the form again to the user for further modification.

In the process, this chapter will cover validation and regular expressions in both JavaScript and PHP.

Validating User Input with JavaScript

JavaScript validation should be considered an assistance more to your users than to your websites because, as I have already stressed many times, you cannot trust any data submitted to your server, even if it has supposedly been validated with JavaScript. This is because hackers can quite easily simulate your web forms and submit any data of their choosing.

Another reason you cannot rely on JavaScript to perform all your input validation is that some users disable JavaScript, or use browsers that don't support it.

So the best types of validation to do in JavaScript are checking that fields have content if they are not to be left empty, ensuring that email addresses conform to the proper format, and ensuring that values entered are within expected bounds.

The validate.html Document (Part One)

So let's take a general sign-up form, common on most sites that offer memberships or registered users. The inputs being requested will be *forename*, *surname*, *username*, *password*, *age*, and *email address*. Example 17-1 provides a good template for such a form.

Example 17-1. A form with JavaScript validation (part one)

```
<html><head><title>An Example Form</title>
<style>.signup { border: 1px solid #999999;
    font: normal 14px helvetica; color:#444444; }</style>

<script>
function validate(form) {
    fail  = validateForename(form.forename.value)
    fail += validateSurname(form.surname.value)
    fail += validateUsername(form.username.value)
    fail += validatePassword(form.password.value)
    fail += validateAge(form.age.value)
    fail += validateEmail(form.email.value)
    if (fail == "") return true
    else { alert(fail); return false }
}
</script></head><body>

<table class="signup" border="0" cellpadding="2"
    cellspacing="5" bgcolor="#eeeeee">
<th colspan="2" align="center">Signup Form</th>
<form method="post" action="adduser.php"
    onSubmit="return validate(this)">
    <tr><td>Forename</td><td><input type="text" maxlength="32"
    name="forename" /></td>
</tr><tr><td>Surname</td><td><input type="text" maxlength="32"
    name="surname" /></td>
</tr><tr><td>Username</td><td><input type="text" maxlength="16"
    name="username" /></td>
</tr><tr><td>Password</td><td><input type="text" maxlength="12"
    name="password" /></td>
</tr><tr><td>Age</td><td><input type="text" maxlength="3"
    name="age" /></td>
</tr><tr><td>Email</td><td><input type="text" maxlength="64"
    name="email" /></td>
</tr><tr><td colspan="2" align="center">
    <input type="submit" value="Signup" /></td>
</tr></form></table>
```

As it stands, this form will display correctly but will not self-validate, because the main validation functions have not yet been added. Even so, if you type it in and save it as *validate.html*, when you call it up in your browser, it will look like Figure 17-1.

Figure 17-1. The output from Example 17-1

How it works

Let's look at how this document is made up. The first three lines set up the document and use a little CSS to make the form look a little less plain. The parts of the document related to JavaScript come next and are show in bold.

Between the `<script ...>` and `</script>` tags lies a single function called `validate` that itself calls up six other functions to validate each of the form's input fields. We'll get to these functions shortly. For now I'll just explain that they return either an empty string if a field validates, or an error message if it fails. If there are any errors, the final line of the script pops up an alert box to display them.

Upon passing validation, the `validate` function returns a value of `true`; otherwise, it returns `false`. The return values from `validate` are important, because if it returns `false`, the form is prevented from being submitted. This allows the user to close the alert pop up and make changes. If `true` is returned, no errors were encountered in the form's fields and so the form is allowed to be submitted.

The second part of this example features the HTML for the form with each field and its name placed within its own row of a table. This is pretty straightforward HTML, with the exception of the `onSubmit="return validate(this)"` statement within the opening `<form ...>` tag. Using `onSubmit`, you can cause a function of your choice to be called when a form is submitted. That function can perform some checking and return a value of either `true` or `false` to signify whether the form should be allowed to be submitted.

The this parameter is the current object (i.e., this form) and is passed to the validate function just discussed. The validate function receives this parameter as the object form.

As you can see, the only JavaScript used within the form's HTML is the call to return buried in the onSubmit attribute. Browsers with JavaScript disabled or not available will simply ignore the onSubmit attribute, and the HTML will display just fine.

The validate.html Document (Part Two)

Now we come to Example 17-2, a set of six functions that do the actual form field validation. I suggest that you type all of this second part in and append it to the first half, which you should already have saved as *validate.html*. It's fine to include multiple <script> sections in a single HTML file. If you prefer, you can incorporate the additional code into the first <script> section from Example 17-1.

Example 17-2. Part two of the JavaScript validation form

```
<script>
function validateForename(field) {
    if (field == "") return "No Forename was entered.\n"
    return ""
}

function validateSurname(field) {
    if (field == "") return "No Surname was entered.\n"
    return ""
}

function validateUsername(field) {
    if (field == "") return "No Username was entered.\n"
    else if (field.length < 5)
        return "Usernames must be at least 5 characters.\n"
    else if (/[^a-zA-Z0-9_-]/.test(field))
        return "Only a-z, A-Z, 0-9, - and _ allowed in Usernames.\n"
    return ""
}

function validatePassword(field) {
    if (field == "") return "No Password was entered.\n"
    else if (field.length < 6)
        return "Passwords must be at least 6 characters.\n"
    else if (!/[a-z]/.test(field) || ! /[A-Z]/.test(field) ||
            !/[0-9]/.test(field))
        return "Passwords require one each of a-z, A-Z and 0-9.\n"
    return ""
}

function validateAge(field) {
    if (isNaN(field)) return "No Age was entered.\n"
    else if (field < 18 || field > 110)
        return "Age must be between 18 and 110.\n"
```

```
        return ""
}

function validateEmail(field) {
    if (field == "") return "No Email was entered.\n"
        else if (!((field.indexOf(".") > 0) &&
                   (field.indexOf("@") > 0)) ||
                  /[^a-zA-Z0-9.@_-]/.test(field))
        return "The Email address is invalid.\n"
    return ""
}
</script></body></html>
```

We'll go through each of these functions in turn, starting with `validateForename` so you can see how validation works.

Validating the forename

`validateForename` is quite a short function that accepts the parameter `field`, which is the value of the *forename* passed to it by the `validate` function.

If this value is an empty string, an error message is returned; otherwise, an empty string is returned to signify that no error was encountered.

If the user entered spaces in this field, it would be accepted by `validateForename`, even though it's empty for all intents and purposes. You can fix this by adding an extra statement to trim whitespace from the field before checking whether it's empty, use a regular expression to make sure there's something besides whitespace in the field, or—as I do here—just let the user make the mistake and allow the PHP program to catch it on the server.

Validating the surname

The `validateSurname` function is almost identical to `validateForename` in that an error is returned only if the *surname* supplied was the empty string. I chose not to limit the characters allowed in either of the name fields to allow for non-English and accented characters, etc.

Validating the username

The `validateUsername` function is a little more interesting, because it has a more complicated job. It has to allow only the characters `a-z`, `A-Z`, `0-9`, `_` and `-`, and ensure that *username*s are at least five characters long.

The `if...else` statements commence by returning an error if `field` has not been filled in. If it's not the empty string, but is less than five characters in length, another error message is returned.

Then the JavaScript `test` function is called, passing a regular expression (which matches any character that is *not* one of those allowed) to be matched against `field` (see the section "Regular Expressions" on page 361). If even one character that isn't one of the acceptable ones is encountered, the `test` function returns `false` and so `validateUser name` returns an error string. Otherwise, an empty string is returned to signify that no error was found.

Validating the password

Similar techniques are used in the `validatePassword` function. First the function checks whether `field` is empty, and an error is returned if it is. Next, an error message is returned if a password is shorter than six characters.

One of the requirements we're imposing on *passwords* is that they must have at least one each of a lowercase, uppercase, and numerical character, so the `test` function is called three times, once for each of these cases. If any one of them returns `false`, one of the requirements was not met and so an error message is returned. Otherwise, the empty string is returned to signify that the password was OK.

Validating the age

`validateAge` returns an error message if `field` is not a number (determined by a call to the `isNaN` function), or if the age entered is lower than 18 or greater than 110. Your applications may well have different or no age requirements. Again, upon successful validation the empty string is returned.

Validating the email

Last, and most complicated, the *email* address is validated with `validateEmail`. After checking whether anything was actually entered, and returning an error message if it wasn't, the function calls the JavaScript `indexOf` function twice. The first time a check is made to ensure there is a period (`.`) somewhere from at least the second character of the field, and the second checks that an `@` symbol appear somewhere at or after the second character.

If those two checks are satisfied, the `test` function is called to see whether any disallowed characters appear in the field. If any of these tests fail, an error message is returned. The allowed characters in an email address are uppercase and lowercase letters, numbers, and the _, -, period, and @ characters, as detailed in the regular expression passed to the `test` method. If no errors are found the empty string is returned to indicate successful validation. On the last line, the script and document are closed.

Figure 17-2 shows the result of clicking on the Signup button without having completed any fields.

Using a separate JavaScript file

Of course, because they are generic in construction and could apply to many types of validations you might require, these six functions make ideal candidates for moving

---

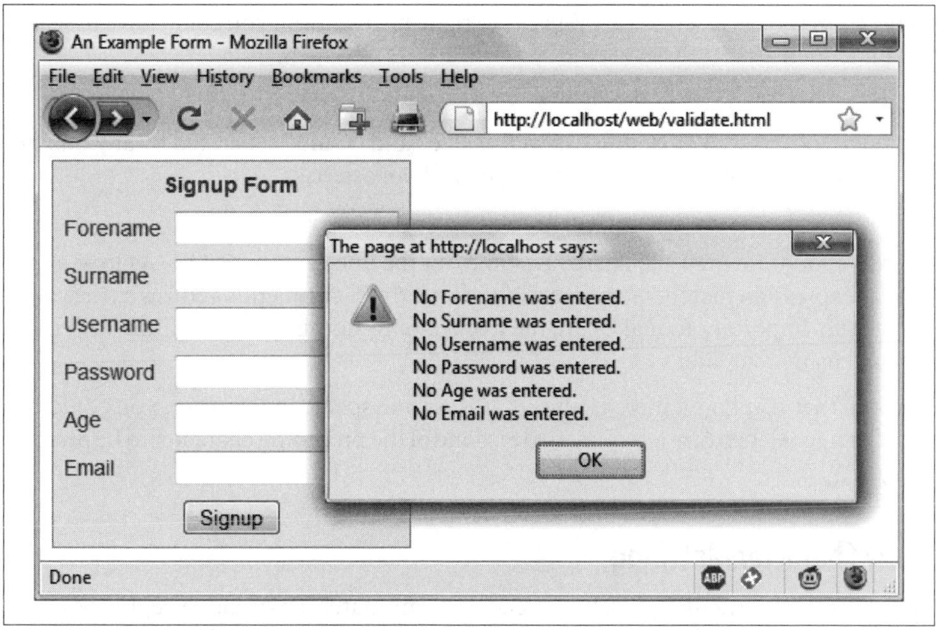

Figure 17-2. JavaScript form validation in action

out into a separate JavaScript file, remembering to remove any `<script>` or `</script>` tags. You could name the file something like *validate_functions.js* and include it right after the initial script section in Example 17-1, using the following statement:

```
<script src="validate_functions.js"></script>
```

Regular Expressions

Let's look a little more closely at the pattern matching we have been doing. This has been achieved using *regular expressions*, which are supported by both JavaScript and PHP. They make it possible to construct the most powerful of pattern-matching algorithms within a single expression.

Matching Through Metacharacters

Every regular expression must be enclosed in slashes. Within these slashes, certain characters have special meanings; there are called *metacharacters*. For instance, an asterisk (*) has a meaning similar to what you have seen if you use a shell or Windows Command prompt (but not quite the same). An asterisk means, "the text you're trying to match may have any number of the preceding character—or none at all."

For instance, let's say you're looking for the name "Le Guin" and know that someone might spell it with or without a space. Because the text is laid out strangely (for instance, someone may have inserted extra spaces to right-justify lines), you could have to search for a line such as:

```
The    difficulty  of    classifying Le      Guin's     works
```

So you need to match "LeGuin," as well as "Le" and "Guin" separated by any number of spaces. The solution is to follow a space with an asterisk:

```
/Le *Guin/
```

There's a lot more than the name "Le Guin" in the line, but that's OK. As long as the regular expression matches some part of the line, the **test** function returns a true value. What if it's important to make sure the line contains nothing but "Le Guin"? I'll show how to ensure that later.

Suppose that you know there is always at least one space. In that case, you could use the plus sign (+), because it requires at least one of the preceding character to be present:

```
/Le +Guin/
```

Fuzzy Character Matching

The dot (.) is particularly useful, because it can match anything except a newline. Suppose that you are looking for HTML tags, which start with "<" and end with ">". A simple way to do so is:

```
/<.*>/
```

The dot matches any character and the * expands it to match zero or more characters, so this is saying, "match anything that lies between < and >, even if there's nothing." You will match <>, <em>, <br /> and so on. But if you don't want to match the empty case, <>, you should use the + sign instead of *, like this:

```
/<.+>/
```

The plus sign expands the dot to match one or more characters, saying, "match anything that lies between < and > as long as there's at least one character between them." You will match <em> and </em>, <h1> and </h1>, and tags with attributes such as:

```
<a href="www.mozilla.org">
```

Unfortunately, the plus sign keeps on matching up to the last > on the line, so you might end up with:

```
<h1><b>Introduction</b></h1>
```

A lot more than one tag! I'll show a better solution later in this section.

 If you use the dot on its own between the angle brackets, without following it with either a + or *, then it matches a single character; you will match <b> and <i> but *not* <em> or <textarea>.

If you want to match the dot character itself (.), you have to escape it by placing a backslash (\) before it, because otherwise it's a metacharacter and matches anything. As an example, suppose you want to match the floating-point number "5.0". The regular expression is:

```
/5\.0/
```

The backslash can escape any metacharacter, including another backslash (in case you're trying to match a backslash in text). However, to make things a bit confusing, you'll see later how backslashes sometimes give the following character a special meaning.

We just matched a floating-point number. But perhaps you want to match "5." as well as "5.0", because both mean the same thing as a floating-point number. You also want to match "5.00", "5.000", and so forth—any number of zeros is allowed. You can do this by adding an asterisk, as you've seen:

```
/5\.0*/
```

Grouping Through Parentheses

Suppose you want to match powers of increments of units, such as kilo, mega, giga, and tera. In other words, you want all the following to match:

```
1,000
1,000,000
1,000,000,000
1,000,000,000,000
...
```

The plus sign works here, too, but you need to group the string ",000" so the plus sign matches the whole thing. The regular expression is:

```
/1(,000)+ /
```

The parentheses mean "treat this as a group when you apply something such as a plus sign." 1,00,000 and 1,000,00 won't match because the text must have a 1 followed by one or more complete groups of a comma followed by three zeros.

The space after the + character indicates that the match must end when a space is encountered. Without it, 1,000,00 would incorrectly match, because only the first 1,000 would be taken into account, and the remaining 00 would be ignored. Requiring a space afterward ensures that matching will continue right through to the end of a number.

Character Classes

Sometimes you want to match something fuzzy, but not so broad that you want to use a dot. Fuzziness is the great strength of regular expressions: they allow you to be as precise or vague as you want.

One of the key features supporting fuzzy matching is the pair of square brackets, [ ]. It matches a single character, like a dot, but inside the brackets you put a list of things that can match. If any of those characters appears, the text matches. For instance, if you wanted to match both the American spelling "gray" and the British spelling "grey," you could specify:

```
/gr[ae]y/
```

After the gr in the text you're matching, there can be either an a or an e. But there must be only one of them: whatever you put inside the brackets matches exactly one character. The group of characters inside the brackets is called a *character class*.

Indicating a Range

Inside the brackets, you can use a hyphen (-) to indicate a range. One very common task is matching a single digit, which you can do with a range as follows:

```
/[0-9]/
```

Digits are such a common item in regular expressions that a single character is provided to represent them: \d. You can use it in the place of the bracketed regular expression to match a digit:

```
/\d/
```

Negation

One other important feature of the square brackets is *negation* of a character class. You can turn the whole character class on its head by placing a caret (^) after the opening bracket. Here it means, "Match any characters *except* the following." So let's say you want to find instances of "Yahoo" that lack the following exclamation point. (The name of the company officially contains an exclamation point!) You could do it as follows:

```
/Yahoo[^!]/
```

The character class consists of a single character—an exclamation point—but it is inverted by the preceding ^. This is actually not a great solution to the problem—for instance, it fails if "Yahoo" is at the end of the line, because then it's not followed by *anything*, whereas the brackets must match a character. A better solution involves negative look-ahead (matching something that is not followed by anything else), but that's beyond the scope of this book.

Some More Complicated Examples

With an understanding of character classes and negation, you're ready now to see a better solution to the problem of matching an HTML tag. This solution avoids going past the end of a single tag, but still matches tags such as <em> and </em> as well as tags with attributes such as:

```
<a href="www.mozilla.org">
```

One solution is:

```
/<[^>]+>/
```

That regular expression may look like I dropped my teacup on the keyboard, but it is perfectly valid and very useful. Let's break it apart. Figure 17-3 shows the various elements, which I'll describe one by one.

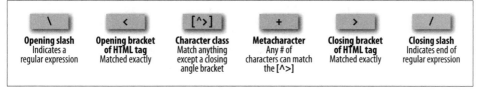

Figure 17-3. Breakdown of a typical regular expression

The elements are:

/

Opening slash that indicates this is a regular expression.

<

Opening bracket of an HTML tag. This is matched exactly; it is not a metacharacter.

[^>]

Character class. The embedded ^> means "match anything except a closing angle bracket."

+

Allows any number of characters to match the previous [^>], as long as there is at least one of them.

>

Closing bracket of an HTML tag. This is matched exactly.

/

Closing slash that indicates the end of the regular expression.

 Another solution to the problem of matching HTML tags is to use a nongreedy operation. By default, pattern matching is greedy, returning the longest match possible. Nongreedy matching finds the shortest possible match and its use is beyond the scope of this book, but there are more details at *http://oreilly.com/catalog/regex/chapter/ch04.html*.

We are going to look now at one of the expressions from Example 17-1, where the `validateUsername` function used:

```
/[^a-zA-Z0-9_]/
```

Figure 17-4 shows the various elements.

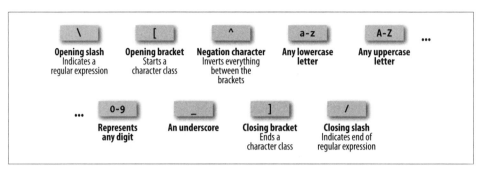

Figure 17-4. Breakdown of the validateUsername regular expression

Let's look at these elements in detail:

/

Opening slash that indicates this is a regular expression.

[

Opening bracket that starts a character class.

^

Negation character: inverts everything else between the brackets.

a-z

Represents any lowercase letter.

A-Z

Represents any uppercase letter.

0-9

Represents any digit.

_

An underscore.

]

Closing bracket that ends a character class.

/

Closing slash that indicates the end of the regular expression.

There are two other important metacharacters. They "anchor" a regular expression by requiring that it appear in a particular place. If a caret (^) appears at the beginning of the regular expression, the expression has to appear at the beginning of a line of text—otherwise, it doesn't match. Similarly, if a dollar sign ($) appears at the end of the regular expression, the expression has to appear at the end of a line of text.

It may be somewhat confusing that ^ can mean "negate the character class" inside square brackets and "match the beginning of the line" if it's at the beginning of the regular expression. Unfortunately, the same character is used for two different things, so take care when using it.

We'll finish our exploration of regular expression basics by answering a question raised earlier: suppose you want to make sure there is nothing extra on a line besides the regular expression? What if you want a line that has "Le Guin" and nothing else? We can do that by amending the earlier regular expression to anchor the two ends:

    /^Le *Guin$/

Summary of Metacharacters

Table 17-1 shows the metacharacters available in regular expressions.

Table 17-1. Regular expression metacharacters

Metacharacters	Description
/	Begins and ends the regular expression
.	Matches any single character except the newline
element*	Matches *element* zero or more times
element+	Matches *element* one or more times
element?	Matches *element* zero or one time
[characters]	Matches a character out of those contained within the brackets
[^characters]	Matches a single character that is not contained within the brackets
(regex)	Treats the *regex* as a group for counting or a following *, +, or ?
left|right	Matches either *left* or *right*
l-r	Matches a range of characters between *l* and *r* (only within brackets)
^	Requires match to be at the string's start
$	Requires match to be at the string's end
\b	Matches a word boundary
\B	Matches where there is not a word boundary
\d	Matches a single digit
\D	Matches a single nondigit
\n	Matches a newline character
\s	Matches a whitespace character
\S	Matches a nonwhitespace character
\t	Matches a tab character
\w	Matches a word character (a-z, A-Z, 0-9, and _)

Metacharacters	Description
\W	Matches a nonword character (anything but a-z, A-Z, 0-9, and _)
\x	x (useful if x is a metacharacter, but you really want x)
{n}	Matches exactly n times
{n,}	Matches n times or more
{min,max}	Matches at least min and at most max times

Provided with this table, and looking again at the expression /[^a-zA-Z0-9_]/, you can see that it could easily be shortened to /[^\w]/ because the single metacharacter \w (with a lowercase w) specifies the characters a-z, A-Z, 0-9, and _.

In fact, we can be more clever than that, because the metacharacter \W (with an uppercase W) specifies all characters *except* for a-z, A-Z, 0-9, and _. Therefore we could also drop the ^ metacharacter and simply use /[\W]/ for the expression.

To give you more ideas of how this all works, Table 17-2 shows a range of expressions and the patterns they match.

Table 17-2. Some example regular expressions

Example	Matches
r	The first r in *The quick brown*
rec[ei][ei]ve	Either of *receive* or *recieve* (but also *receeve* or *reciive*)
rec[ei]{2}ve	Either of *receive* or *recieve* (but also *receeve* or *reciive*)
rec(ei)|(ie)ve	Either of *receive* or *recieve* (but not *receeve* or *reciive*)
cat	The word *cat* in *I like cats and dogs*
cat|dog	Either of the words *cat* or *dog* in *I like cats and dogs*
\.	. (the \ is necessary because . is a metacharacter)
5\.0*	*5., 5.0, 5.00, 5.000*, etc.
a-f	Any of the characters *a, b, c, d, e* or *f*
cats$	Only the final *cats* in *My cats are friendly cats*
^my	Only the first *my* in *my cats are my pets*
\d{2,3}	Any two or three digit number (*00* through *999*)
7(,000)+	*7,000; 7,000,000; 7,000,000,000; 7,000,000,000,000;* etc.
[\w]+	Any word of one or more characters
[\w]{5}	Any five-letter word

General Modifiers

Some additional modifiers are available for regular expressions:

- /g enables "global" matching. When using a replace function, specify this modifier to replace all matches, rather than only the first one.
- /i makes the regular expression match case-insensitive. Thus, instead of /[a-zA-Z]/ you could specify /[a-z]/i or /[A-Z]/i.
- /m enables multiline mode, in which the caret (^) and dollar ($) match before and after any newlines in the subject string. Normally, in a multiline string, ^ matches only at the start of the string and $ matches only at the end of the string.

For example, the expression /cats/g will match both occurrences of the word *cats* in the sentence "I like cats and cats like me". Similarly, /dogs/gi will match both occurrences of the word dogs (Dogs and dogs) in the sentence "Dogs like other dogs", because you can use these specifiers together.

Using Regular Expressions in JavaScript

In JavaScript you will use regular expressions mostly in two methods: test (which you have already seen) and replace. Whereas test just tells you whether its argument matches the regular expression, replace takes a second parameter: the string to replace the text that matches. Like most functions, replace generates a new string as a return value; it does not change the input.

To compare the two methods, the following statement just returns true to let us know that the word "cats" appears at least once somewhere within the string:

```
document.write(/cats/i.test("Cats are fun. I like cats."))
```

But the following statement replaces both occurrences of the word *cats* with the word *dogs*, printing the result. The search has to be global (/g) to find all occurrences, and case-insensitive (/i) to find the capitalized "Cats":

```
document.write("Cats are fun. I like cats.".replace(/cats/gi,"dogs"))
```

If you try out the statement, you'll see a limitation of replace: because it replaces text with exactly the string you tell it to use, the first word "Cats" is replaced by "dogs" instead of "Dogs".

Using Regular Expressions in PHP

The most common regular expression functions that you are likely to use in PHP are preg_match, preg_match_all, and preg_replace.

To test whether the word *cats* appears anywhere within a string, in any combination of upper- and lowercase, you could use `preg_match` like this:

```
$n = preg_match("/cats/i", "Cats are fun. I like cats.");
```

Because PHP uses 1 for TRUE and 0 for FALSE, the preceding statement sets `$n` to 1. The first argument is the regular expression and the second is the text to match. But `preg_match` is actually a good deal more powerful and complicated, because it takes a third argument that shows what text matched:

```
$n = preg_match("/cats/i", "Cats are fun. I like cats.", $match);
echo "$n Matches: $match[0]";
```

The third argument is an array (here given the name `$match`). The function puts the text that matches into the first element, so if the match is successful you can find the text that matched in `$match[0]`. In this example, the output lets us know that the matched text was capitalized:

```
1 Matches: Cats
```

If you wish to locate all matches, you use the `preg_match_all` function, like this:

```
$n = preg_match_all("/cats/i", "Cats are fun. I like cats.", $match);
echo "$n Matches: ";
for ($j=0 ; $j < $n ; ++$j) echo $match[0][$j]." ";
```

As before, `$match` is passed to the function and the element `$match[0]` is assigned the matches made, but this time as a subarray. To display the subarray, this example iterates through it with a `for` loop.

When you want to replace part of a string, you can use `preg_replace` as shown here. This example replaces all occurrences of the word *cats* with the word *dogs*, regardless of case:

```
echo preg_replace("/cats/i", "dogs", "Cats are fun. I like cats.");
```

 The subject of regular expressions is a large one and entire books have been written about it. If you would like further information I suggest the Wikipedia entry at *http://wikipedia.org/wiki/Regular_expression*, or the excellent book *Mastering Regular Expressions* by Jeffrey E.F. Friedl (O'Reilly).

Redisplaying a Form After PHP Validation

OK, back to form validation. So far we've created the HTML document *validate.html*, which will post through to the PHP program *adduser.php*, but only if JavaScript validates the fields, or if JavaScript is disabled or unavailable.

So now it's time to create *adduser.php* to receive the posted form, perform its own validation, and then present the form again to the visitor if the validation fails. Example 17-3 contains the code that you should type in and save.

Example 17-3. The adduser.php program

```php
<?php // adduser.php

// Start with the PHP code

$forename = $surname = $username = $password = $age = $email = "";

if (isset($_POST['forename']))
    $forename = fix_string($_POST['forename']);
if (isset($_POST['surname']))
    $surname = fix_string($_POST['surname']);
if (isset($_POST['username']))
    $username = fix_string($_POST['username']);
if (isset($_POST['password']))
    $password = fix_string($_POST['password']);
if (isset($_POST['age']))
    $age = fix_string($_POST['age']);
if (isset($_POST['email']))
    $email = fix_string($_POST['email']);

$fail  = validate_forename($forename);
$fail .= validate_surname($surname);
$fail .= validate_username($username);
$fail .= validate_password($password);
$fail .= validate_age($age);
$fail .= validate_email($email);

echo "<html><head><title>An Example Form</title>";

if ($fail == "") {
    echo "</head><body>Form data successfully validated: $forename,
        $surname, $username, $password, $age, $email.</body></html>";

    // This is where you would enter the posted fields into a database

    exit;
}

// Now output the HTML and JavaScript code

echo <<<_END

<!-- The HTML section -->

<style>.signup { border: 1px solid #999999;
    font: normal 14px helvetica; color:#444444; }</style>
<script type="text/javascript">
function validate(form)
{
    fail  = validateForename(form.forename.value)
    fail += validateSurname(form.surname.value)
    fail += validateUsername(form.username.value)
    fail += validatePassword(form.password.value)
    fail += validateAge(form.age.value)
    fail += validateEmail(form.email.value)
```

```
        if (fail == "") return true
        else { alert(fail); return false }
}
</script></head><body>
<table class="signup" border="0" cellpadding="2"
    cellspacing="5" bgcolor="#eeeeee">
<th colspan="2" align="center">Signup Form</th>

<tr><td colspan="2">Sorry, the following errors were found<br />
in your form: <p><font color=red size=1><i>$fail</i></font></p>
</td></tr>

<form method="post" action="adduser.php"
    onSubmit="return validate(this)">
    <tr><td>Forename</td><td><input type="text" maxlength="32"
    name="forename" value="$forename" /></td>
</tr><tr><td>Surname</td><td><input type="text" maxlength="32"
    name="surname" value="$surname" /></td>
</tr><tr><td>Username</td><td><input type="text" maxlength="16"
    name="username" value="$username" /></td>
</tr><tr><td>Password</td><td><input type="text" maxlength="12"
    name="password" value="$password" /></td>
</tr><tr><td>Age</td><td><input type="text" maxlength="3"
    name="age" value="$age" /></td>
</tr><tr><td>Email</td><td><input type="text" maxlength="64"
    name="email" value="$email" /></td>
</tr><tr><td colspan="2" align="center">
    <input type="submit" value="Signup" /></td>
</tr></form></table>

<!-- The JavaScript section -->

<script type="text/javascript">
function validateForename(field) {
    if (field == "") return "No Forename was entered.\\n"
    return ""
}

function validateSurname(field) {
    if (field == "") return "No Surname was entered.\\n"
    return ""
}

function validateUsername(field) {
    if (field == "") return "No Username was entered.\\n"
    else if (field.length < 5)
        return "Usernames must be at least 5 characters.\\n"
    else if (/[^a-zA-Z0-9_-]/.test(field))
        return "Only a-z, A-Z, 0-9, - and _ allowed in Usernames.\\n"
    return ""
}

function validatePassword(field) {
    if (field == "") return "No Password was entered.\\n"
    else if (field.length < 6)
```

```
        return "Passwords must be at least 6 characters.\\n"
    else if (!/[a-z]/.test(field) || ! /[A-Z]/.test(field) ||
            ! /[0-9]/.test(field))
        return "Passwords require one each of a-z, A-Z and 0-9.\\n"
    return ""
}

function validateAge(field) {
    if (isNaN(field)) return "No Age was entered.\\n"
    else if (field < 18 || field > 110)
        return "Age must be between 18 and 110.\\n"
    return ""
}

function validateEmail(field) {
    if (field == "") return "No Email was entered.\\n"
        else if (!((field.indexOf(".") > 0) &&
                    (field.indexOf("@") > 0)) ||
                /[^a-zA-Z0-9.@_-]/.test(field))
        return "The Email address is invalid.\\n"
    return ""
}
</script></body></html>
_END;

// Finally, here are the PHP functions

function validate_forename($field) {
    if ($field == "") return "No Forename was entered<br />";
    return "";
}

function validate_surname($field) {
    if ($field == "") return "No Surname was entered<br />";
    return "";
}

function validate_username($field) {
    if ($field == "") return "No Username was entered<br />";
    else if (strlen($field) < 5)
        return "Usernames must be at least 5 characters<br />";
    else if (preg_match("/[^a-zA-Z0-9_-]/", $field))
        return "Only letters, numbers, - and _ in usernames<br />";
    return "";
}

function validate_password($field) {
    if ($field == "") return "No Password was entered<br />";
    else if (strlen($field) < 6)
        return "Passwords must be at least 6 characters<br />";
    else if ( !preg_match("/[a-z]/", $field) ||
            !preg_match("/[A-Z]/", $field) ||
            !preg_match("/[0-9]/", $field))
        return "Passwords require 1 each of a-z, A-Z and 0-9<br />";
    return "";
```

```php
}

function validate_age($field) {
    if ($field == "") return "No Age was entered<br />";
    else if ($field < 18 || $field > 110)
        return "Age must be between 18 and 110<br />";
    return "";
}

function validate_email($field) {
    if ($field == "") return "No Email was entered<br />";
        else if (!((strpos($field, ".") > 0) &&
                   (strpos($field, "@") > 0)) ||
                   preg_match("/[^a-zA-Z0-9.@_-]/", $field))
            return "The Email address is invalid<br />";
    return "";
}

function fix_string($string) {
    if (get_magic_quotes_gpc()) $string = stripslashes($string);
    return htmlentities ($string);
}
?>
```

The result of submitting the form with JavaScript disabled (and two fields incorrectly completed) can be seen in Figure 17-5.

Figure 17-5. The form as represented after PHP validation fails

---

I have put the PHP section of this code (and changes to the HTML section) in a bold typeface so that you can more clearly see the difference between this and Examples 17-1 and 17-2.

If you browsed through this example (or, hopefully, typed it in or downloaded it from the *http://lpmj.net* website), you'll have seen that the PHP code is almost a clone of the JavaScript code; the same regular expressions are used to validate each field in very similar functions.

But there are a couple of things to note. First, the `fix_string` function (right at the end) is used to sanitize each field and prevent any attempts at code injection from succeeding.

Also, you will see that the HTML from Example 17-1 has been repeated in the PHP code within a `<<<_END... _END;` structure, displaying the form with the values that the visitor entered the previous time. This is done by simply adding an extra `value` parameter to each `<input ...>` tag (such as `value="$forename"`). This courtesy is highly recommended so that the user has to edit only the previously entered values, and doesn't have to type the fields in all over again.

> In the real world, you probably wouldn't start with an HTML form such as the one in Example 17-1. Instead, you'd be more likely to go straight ahead and write the PHP program in Example 17-3, which incorporates all the HTML. And, of course, you'd also need to make a minor tweak for the case when it's the first time the program is called up, to prevent it displaying errors when all the fields are empty. You also might drop the six JavaScript functions into their own *.js* file for separate inclusion.

Now that you've seen how to bring all of PHP, HTML, and JavaScript together, the next chapter will introduce Ajax (Asynchronous JavaScript And XML), which uses JavaScript calls to the server in the background to seamlessly update portions of a web page, without having to resubmit the entire page to the web server.

Test Your Knowledge: Questions

Question 17-1
What JavaScript method can you use to send a form for validation prior to submitting it?

Question 17-2
What JavaScript method is used to match a string against a regular expression?

Question 17-3
Write a regular expression to match any characters that are *not* in a *word*, as defined by regular expression syntax.

Question 17-4

Write a regular expression to match either of the words *fox* or *fix*.

Question 17-5

Write a regular expression to match any single word followed by any nonword character.

Question 17-6

Using regular expressions, write a JavaScript function to test whether the word *fox* exists in the string "The quick brown fox".

Question 17-7

Using regular expressions, write a PHP function to replace all occurrences of the word *the* in "The cow jumps over the moon" with the word *my*.

Question 17-8

What HTML keyword is used to precomplete form fields with a value?

See the section "Chapter 17 Answers" on page 449 in Appendix A for the answers to these questions.

CHAPTER 18

Using Ajax

The term "Ajax" was first coined in 2005. It stands for Asynchronous JavaScript and XML, which, in simple terms, means using a set of methods built into JavaScript to transfer data between the browser and a server in the background. An excellent example of this technology is Google Maps (see Figure 18-1), in which new sections of a map are downloaded from the server when needed, without requiring a page refresh.

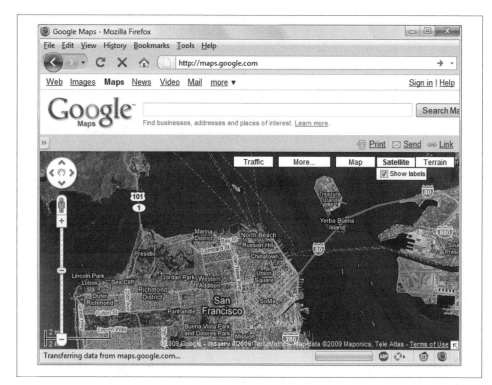

Figure 18-1. Google Maps is an excellent example of Ajax in action

Using Ajax not only substantially reduces the amount of data that must be sent back and forth, it also makes web pages seamlessly dynamic—allowing them to behave more like self-contained applications. The results are a much improved user interface and better responsiveness.

What Is Ajax?

The beginnings of Ajax as used today started with the release of Internet Explorer 5 in 1999, which introduced a new ActiveX object, XMLHttpRequest. ActiveX is Microsoft's technology for signing plug-ins that add additional software to your computer. Other browser developers later followed suit, but rather than using ActiveX, they all implemented the feature as a native part of the JavaScript interpreter.

However, even before then, an early form of Ajax had already surfaced that used hidden frames on a page that interacted with the server in the background. Chat rooms were early adopters of this technology, using it to poll for and display new message posts without requiring page reloads.

Nowadays, though, XMLHttpRequest is the way to go, and there have been numerous frameworks written to simplify its use. In fact, Chapter 19 introduces the powerful Yahoo! User Interface (YUI) JavaScript framework. But first, let's see how to implement Ajax with raw JavaScript. This will help you understand what your program and the browser are doing as you code with YUI or another library of your choice.

Using XMLHttpRequest

Due to the differences between browser implementations of XMLHttpRequest, it's necessary to create a special function in order to ensure that your code will work on all major browsers.

To do this, you must understand the three ways of creating an XMLHttpRequest object:

- IE 5: request = new ActiveXObject("Microsoft.XMLHTTP")
- IE 6+: request = new ActiveXObject("Msxml2.XMLHTTP")
- All others: request = new XMLHttpRequest()

This is the case because Microsoft chose to implement a change with the release of Internet Explorer 6. Therefore, the code in Example 18-1 will work for all the following browsers and newer versions:

- Windows Internet Explorer 5.0
- Mozilla Firefox 1.0
- Netscape 7.1
- Apple Safari 1.2

- Konqueror 3.0
- Nokia S60
- Google Chrome 1.0
- Opera 8.0

Example 18-1. A cross-browser Ajax function

```
<script>
function ajaxRequest()
{
    try // Non IE Browser?
    {
        var request = new XMLHttpRequest()
    }
    catch(e1)
    {
        try // IE 6+?
        {
            request = new ActiveXObject("Msxml2.XMLHTTP")
        }
        catch(e2)
        {
            try // IE 5?
            {
                request = new ActiveXObject("Microsoft.XMLHTTP")
            }
            catch(e3) // There is no Ajax Support
            {
                request = false
            }
        }
    }
    return request
}
</script>
```

You may remember the introduction to error handling in the previous chapter, using the `try...catch` construct. Example 18-1 is a perfect illustration of its utility, because it uses the `try` keyword to execute the non-IE Ajax command, and upon success, jumps on to the final `return` statement, where the new object is returned.

Otherwise, a `catch` traps the error and the subsequent command is executed. Again, upon success, the new object is returned; otherwise, the final of the three commands is tried. If that attempt fails, then the browser doesn't support Ajax and the `request` object is set to `false`; otherwise, the object is returned. So there you have it—a cross-browser Ajax request function that you may wish to add to your library of useful Java-Script functions.

OK, so now you have a means of creating an `XMLHttpRequest` object, but what can you do with these objects? Well, each one comes with a set of properties (variables) and methods (functions), which are detailed in Tables 18-1 and 18-2.

Table 18-1. An XMLHttpRequest object's properties

Properties	Description
onreadystatechange	Specifies an event handling function to be called whenever the readyState property of an object changes.
readyState	An integer property that reports on the status of a request. It can have any of these values: 0 = Uninitialized, 1 = Loading, 2 = Loaded, 3 = Interactive, and 4 = Completed.
responseText	The data returned by the server in text format.
responseXML	The data returned by the server in XML format.
status	The HTTP status code returned by the server.
statusText	The HTTP status text returned by the server.

Table 18-2. An XMLHttpRequest object's methods

Methods	Description
abort()	Aborts the current request.
getAllResponseHeaders()	Returns all headers as a string.
getResponseHeader(*param*)	Returns the value of *param* as a string.
open('*method*', '*url*', '*asynch*')	Specifies the HTTP method to use (GET or POST), the target URL, and whether the request should be handled asynchronously (true or false).
send(*data*)	Sends *data* to the target server using the specified HTTP method.
setRequestHeader('*param*', '*value*')	Sets a header with a parameter/value pair.

These properties and methods give you control over what data you send to the server and receive back, as well as a choice of send and receive methods. For example, you can choose whether to request plain text (which could include HTML and other tags) or data in XML format. You can also decide whether you wish to use the POST or GET method to send to the server.

Let's look at the POST method first by creating a very simple pair of documents: a combination of HTML and JavaScript, and a PHP program to interact via Ajax with the first. Hopefully you'll enjoy these examples, because they illustrate just what Web 2.0 and Ajax are all about. With a few lines of JavaScript, they request a web document from a third-party web server, which is then returned to the browser by your server and placed within a section of the current document.

Your First Ajax Program

Type in and save the code in Example 18-2 as *urlpost.html*, but don't load it into your browser yet.

Example 18-2. urlpost.html

```html
<html><head><title>Ajax Example</title>
</head><body><center />
<h1>Loading a web page into a DIV</h1>
<div id='info'>This sentence will be replaced</div>
<script>

params = "url=oreilly.com"
request = new ajaxRequest()
request.open("POST", "urlpost.php", true)
request.setRequestHeader("Content-type",
    "application/x-www-form-urlencoded")
request.setRequestHeader("Content-length", params.length)
request.setRequestHeader("Connection", "close")

request.onreadystatechange = function()
{
    if (this.readyState == 4)
    {
        if (this.status == 200)
        {
            if (this.responseText != null)
            {
                document.getElementById('info').innerHTML =
                    this.responseText
            }
            else alert("Ajax error: No data received")
        }
        else alert( "Ajax error: " + this.statusText)
    }
}

request.send(params)

function ajaxRequest()
{
    try
    {
        var request = new XMLHttpRequest()
    }
    catch(e1)
    {
        try
        {
            request = new ActiveXObject("Msxml2.XMLHTTP")
        }
        catch(e2)
        {
            try
            {
                request = new ActiveXObject("Microsoft.XMLHTTP")
            }
            catch(e3)
            {
                request = false
```

```
            }
        }
    }
    return request
}
</script></body></html>
```

Let's go through this document and look at what it does, starting with the first three lines, which simply set up an HTML document and display a heading. The next line creates an HTML DIV tag with the ID "info", containing the text "This sentence will be replaced" by default. Later on, the text returned from the Ajax call will be inserted here.

The next six lines are required for making an HTTP POST Ajax request. The first sets the variable params to a *parameter=value* pair, which is what we'll send to the server. Then the Ajax object request is created. After this, the open method is called to set the object to make a POST request to *geturl.php* in asynchronous mode. The last three lines in this group set up headers that are required for the receiving server to know that a POST request is coming.

The readyState property

Now we get to the nitty-gritty of an Ajax call, which all hangs on the readyState property. The "asynchronous" aspect of Ajax allows the browser to keep accepting user input and changing the screen, while our program sets the onreadystatechange property to call a function of our choice each time readyState changes. In this case, a nameless (or anonymous) inline function has been used, as opposed to a separate, named function. This type of function is known as a *callback* function, as it is called back each time readyState changes.

The syntax to set up the callback function using an inline, anonymous function is as follows:

```
request.onreadystatechange = function()
{
    if (this.readyState == 4)
    {
        // do something
    }
}
```

If you wish to use a separate, named function, the syntax is slightly different:

```
request.onreadystatechange = ajaxCallback

function ajaxCallback()
{
    if (this.readyState == 4)
    {
        // do something
    }
}
```

Looking at Table 18-1, you'll see that `readyState` can have five different values. But only one of them concerns us: value 4, which represents a completed Ajax call. Therefore, each time the new function gets called, it returns without doing anything until `readyState` has a value of 4. When our function detects that value, it next inspects the `status` of the call to ensure it has a value of 200, which means that the call succeeded. If it's not 200, an alert pop up is displayed containing the error message contained in `statusText`.

> You will notice that all of these object properties are referenced using `this.readyState`, `this.status`, and so on, rather than the object's current name, `request`, as in `request.readyState` or `request.status`. This is so that you can easily copy and paste the code and it will work with any object name, because the `this` keyword always refers to the current object.

So, having ascertained that the `readyState` is 4 and the status is 200, the `responseText` value is tested to see whether it contains a value. If not, an error message is displayed in an alert box. Otherwise, the inner HTML of the DIV is assigned the value of `responseText`, like this:

```
document.getElementById('info').innerHTML = this.responseText
```

What happens in this line is that the element "info" is referenced using the `getElementByID` method and then its `innerHTML` property is assigned the value that was returned by the Ajax call.

After all this setting up and preparation, the Ajax request is finally sent to the server using the following command, which passes the parameters already defined in the variable `params`:

```
request.send(params)
```

After that, all the preceding code is activated each time `readyState` changes.

The remainder of the document is the `ajaxRequest` method from Example 18-1, and the closing script and HTML tags.

The server half of the Ajax process

Now we get to the PHP half of the equation, which you can see in Example 18-3. Type it in and save it as *urlpost.php*.

Example 18-3. urlpost.php

```php
<?php // urlpost.php
if (isset($_POST['url'])) {
    echo file_get_contents("http://".SanitizeString($_POST['url']));
}

function SanitizeString($var) {
```

```
    $var = strip_tags($var);
    $var = htmlentities($var);
    return stripslashes($var);
}
?>
```

As you can see, this is short and sweet, and also makes use of the ever-important SanitizeString function, as should always be done with all posted data.

What the program does is use the file_get_contents PHP function to load in the web page at the URL supplied to it in the POST variable $_POST['url']. The file_get_contents function is versatile, in that it loads in the entire contents of a file or web page from either a local or a remote server—it even takes into account moved pages and other redirects.

Once you have typed the program in, you are ready to call up *urlpost.html* into your web browser and, after a few seconds, you should see the contents of the *oreilly.com* front page loaded into the DIV that we created for that purpose. It won't be as fast as directly loading the web page, because it is transferred twice: once to the server and again from the server to your browser. The result should look like Figure 18-2.

Figure 18-2. The oreilly.com front page has been loaded into a DIV

Not only have we succeeded in making an Ajax call and having a response returned back to JavaScript, we also harnessed the power of PHP to enable the merging in of a totally unrelated web object. Incidentally, if we had tried to find a way to fetch the *oreilly.com* web page directly via Ajax (without recourse to the PHP server-side module), we wouldn't have succeeded, because there are security blocks preventing cross-domain Ajax. So this little example also illustrates a handy solution to a very practical problem.

Using GET Instead of POST

As with submitting any form data, you have the option of submitting your data in the form of GET requests, and you will save a few lines of code if you do so. However, there is a downside: some browsers may cache GET requests, whereas POST requests will never be cached. You don't want to cache a request because the browser will just redisplay what it got last time instead of going to the server for fresh input. The solution to this is to use a workaround that adds a random parameter to each request, ensuring that each URL requested is unique.

Example 18-4 shows how you would achieve the same result as with Example 18-2, but using an Ajax GET request instead of POST.

Example 18-4. urlget.html

```
<html><head><title>Ajax GET Example</title>
</head><body><center />
<h1>Loading a web page into a DIV</h1>
<div id='info'>This sentence will be replaced</div>
<script>

nocache = "&nocache=" + Math.random() * 1000000
request = new ajaxRequest()
request.open("GET", "urlget.php?url=oreilly.com" + nocache, true)

request.onreadystatechange = function()
{
    if (this.readyState == 4)
    {
        if (this.status == 200)
        {
            if (this.responseText != null)
            {
                document.getElementById('info').innerHTML =
                    this.responseText
            }
            else alert("Ajax error: No data received")
        }
        else alert( "Ajax error: " + this.statusText)
    }
}

request.send(null)
```

```
function ajaxRequest()
{
    try
    {
        var request = new XMLHttpRequest()
    }
    catch(e1)
    {
        try
        {
            request = new ActiveXObject("Msxml2.XMLHTTP")
        }
        catch(e2)
        {
            try
            {
                request = new ActiveXObject("Microsoft.XMLHTTP")
            }
            catch(e3)
            {
                request = false
            }
        }
    }
    return request
}
</script></body></html>
```

The differences to note between the two documents are highlighted in bold, and are as follows:

- It is not necessary to send headers for a GET request.
- The open method is called using a GET request, supplying a URL with a string comprising a ? symbol followed by the parameter/value pair url=oreilly.com.
- A second parameter/value pair is started using an & symbol, followed by setting the value of the parameter nocache to a random value between 0 and a million. This is used to ensure that each URL requested is different, and therefore that no requests will be cached.
- The call to send now contains only a parameter of null as no parameters are being passed via a POST request. Note that leaving the parameter out is not an option, as it would result in an error.

To accompany this new document, it is necessary to modify the PHP program to respond to a GET request, as in Example 18-5, *urlget.php*.

Example 18-5. urlget.php

```php
<?php
if (isset($_GET['url'])) {
    echo file_get_contents("http://".sanitizeString($_GET['url']));
}
```

```
function sanitizeString($var) {
    $var = strip_tags($var);
    $var = htmlentities($var);
    return stripslashes($var);
}
?>
```

All that's different between this and Example 18-3 is that the references to $_POST have been replaced with $_GET. The end result of calling up *urlget.html* in your browser is identical to loading in *urlpost.html*.

Sending XML Requests

Although the objects we've been creating are called XMLHttpRequest objects, so far we have made absolutely no use of XML. This is where the Ajax term is a bit of a misnomer, because the technology actually allows you to request any type of textual data, only one of which is XML. As you have seen, we have requested an entire HTML document via Ajax, but we could equally have asked for a text page, a string or number, or even spreadsheet data.

So let's modify the previous example document and PHP program to fetch some XML data. To do this, take a look at the PHP program first, *xmlget.php*, shown in Example 18-6.

Example 18-6. xmlget.php

```
<?php
if (isset($_GET['url'])) {
    header('Content-Type: text/xml');
    echo file_get_contents("http://".sanitizeString($_GET['url']));
}

function sanitizeString($var) {
    $var = strip_tags($var);
    $var = htmlentities($var);
    return stripslashes($var);
}
?>
```

This program has been very slightly modified (shown in bold highlighting) to first output the correct XML header before returning a fetched document. No checking is made here, as it is assumed the calling Ajax will request an actual XML document.

Now on to the HTML document, *xmlget.html*, shown in Example 18-7.

Example 18-7. xmlget.html

```
<html><head><title>Ajax XML Example</title>
</head><body>
<h2>Loading XML content into a DIV</h2>
<div id='info'>This sentence will be replaced</div>
```

```
<script>

nocache = "&nocache=" + Math.random() * 1000000
url = "rss.news.yahoo.com/rss/topstories"
request = new ajaxRequest()
request.open("GET", "xmlget.php?url=" + url + nocache, true)
out = "";

request.onreadystatechange = function()
{
    if (this.readyState == 4)
    {
        if (this.status == 200)
        {
            if (this.responseXML != null)
            {
                titles = this.responseXML.getElementsByTagName('title')

                for (j = 0 ; j < titles.length ; ++j)
                {
                    out += titles[j].childNodes[0].nodeValue + '<br />'
                }
                document.getElementById('info').innerHTML = out
            }
            else alert("Ajax error: No data received")
        }
        else alert( "Ajax error: " + this.statusText)
    }
}

request.send(null)

function ajaxRequest() {
    try
    {
        var request = new XMLHttpRequest()
    }
    catch(e1)
    {
        try
        {
            request = new ActiveXObject("Msxml2.XMLHTTP")
        }
        catch(e2)
        {
            try
            {
                request = new ActiveXObject("Microsoft.XMLHTTP")
            }
            catch(e3)
            {
                request = false
            }
        }
    }
```

```
      return request
}
</script></body></html>
```

Again, the differences have been highlighted in bold, so you can see that this code is substantially similar to previous versions, except that the URL now being requested, *rss.news.yahoo.com/rss/topstories*, contains an XML document, the Yahoo! News Top Stories feed.

The other big change is the use of the `responseXML` property, which replaces the `responseText` property. Whenever a server returns XML data, `responseText` will return a `null` value, and `responseXML` will contain the XML returned instead.

However, `responseXML` doesn't simply contain a string of XML text: it is actually a complete XML document object that can be examined and parsed using DOM tree methods and properties. This means it is accessible, for example, by the JavaScript `getElementsByTagName` method.

About XML

An XML document will generally take the form of the RSS feed shown in Example 18-8. However, the beauty of XML is that this type of structure can be stored internally in a DOM tree (see Figure 18-3) to make it quickly searchable.

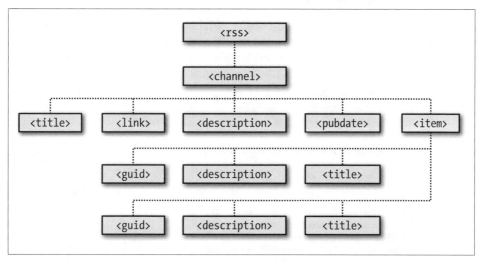

Figure 18-3. The DOM tree of Example 18-8

Example 18-8. An XML document

```
<?xml version="1.0" encoding="UTF-8"?>
<rss version="2.0">
    <channel>
        <title>RSS Feed</title>
```

```
        <link>http://website.com</link>
        <description>website.com's RSS Feed</description>
        <pubDate>Mon, 16 May 2011 00:00:00 GMT</pubDate>
        <item>
            <title>Headline</title>
            <guid>http://website.com/headline</guid>
            <description>This is a headline</description>
        </item>
        <item>
            <title>Headline 2</title>
            <guid>http://website.com/headline2</guid>
            <description>The 2nd headline</description>
        </item>
    </channel>
</rss>
```

Therefore, using the `getElementsByTagName` method, you can quickly extract the values associated with various tags without a lot of string searching. This is exactly what we do in Example 18-7, where the following command is issued:

```
titles = this.responseXML.getElementsByTagName('title')
```

This single command has the effect of placing all the values of the "title" elements into the array `titles`. From there, it is a simple matter to extract them with the following expression (where j is the title to access):

```
titles[j].childNodes[0].nodeValue
```

All the titles are then appended to the string variable **out** and, once all have been processed, the result is inserted into the empty DIV at the document start. When you call up *xmlget.html* in your browser, the result will be something like Figure 18-4.

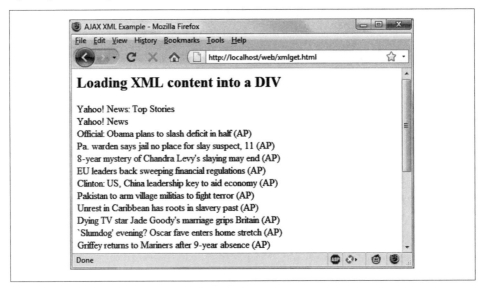

Figure 18-4. Fetching a Yahoo! XML news feed via Ajax

As with all form data, you can use either the POST or the GET method when requesting XML data—your choice will make little difference to the result.

Why use XML?

You may ask why you would use XML other than for fetching XML documents such as RSS feeds. Well, the simple answer is that you don't have to, but if you wish to pass structured data back to your Ajax applications, it could be a real pain to send a simple, unorganized jumble of text that would need complicated processing in JavaScript.

Instead, you can create an XML document and pass that back to the Ajax function, which will automatically place it into a DOM tree as easily accessible as the HTML DOM object with which you are now familiar.

Now that you've learned how Ajax works in raw form, in the next chapter we'll look at the popular YUI library, which is a framework that makes Ajax and other JavaScript even easier to use.

Test Your Knowledge: Questions

Question 18-1
> Why is it necessary to write a function for creating new XMLHttpRequest objects?

Question 18-2
> What is the purpose of the try...catch construct?

Question 18-3
> How many properties and how many methods does an XMLHttpRequest object have?

Question 18-4
> How can you tell when an Ajax call has completed?

Question 18-5
> How do you know whether an Ajax call completed successfully?

Question 18-6
> What XMLHttpRequest object's property returns an Ajax text response?

Question 18-7
> What XMLHttpRequest object's property returns an Ajax XML response?

Question 18-8
> How can you specify a callback function to handle Ajax responses?

Question 18-9
> What XMLHttpRequest method is used to initiate an Ajax request?

Question 18-10
   What are the main differences between an Ajax GET and POST request?

See the section "Chapter 18 Answers" on page 450 in Appendix A for the answers to these questions.

CHAPTER 19

Using YUI for Ajax and More

Let's face it: JavaScript isn't the easiest programming language to master, particularly if you've never come across such an object-oriented approach before. And this is true also because Microsoft has, until relatively recently, steadfastly ignored web standards, resulting in the need to spend a lot of time writing cross-browser-compatible code.

Thankfully, though, several organizations have set about trying to make JavaScript a much simpler and even more powerful language by creating frameworks for it. What they do is write wrappers around the JavaScript to break down complex tasks into small, more easily manageable ones. At the same time, they ensure that their framework methods are fully cross-browser compatible.

Choosing a Framework

The new difficulty now is choosing among the bewildering variety of frameworks. Some of the more popular of which are listed in Table 19-1.

Table 19-1. Some popular JavaScript frameworks

Framework	Web address
ASP.NET Ajax Framework	*http://asp.net/ajax*
Clean Ajax Framework	*http://sourceforge.net/projects/clean-ajax*
Dojo Toolkit	*http://dojotoolkit.org*
jQuery	*http://jquery.com*
MochiKit	*http://mochikit.com*
MooTools	*http://mootools.net*
OpenJS	*http://openjs.com*
Prototype	*http://prototypejs.org*
Rialto	*http://rialto.improve-technologies.com/wiki*
script.aculo.us	*http://script.aculo.us*

Framework	Web address
Spry Framework	*http://labs.adobe.com/technologies/spry*
YUI	*http://developer.yahoo.com/yui*

Because each of these frameworks works differently, I have opted to settle on just one of them—the YUI framework—for this chapter. I made this decision because it was originally written by programmers at Yahoo!, which since then has allowed the JavaScript community as a whole to contribute code to the project. As a result, it's a solid framework used across all the Yahoo! properties and also by tens of thousands of developers around the world.

What's more, you can download the entire framework and an extensive collection of more than 300 example programs, along with a comprehensive amount of documentation, amounting to over 70 MB of data once uncompressed. But although I say "you can," you don't *have* to, because all of these scripts and the documentation appear on the YUI developer website, and you are permitted to simply link to each YUI script directly from Yahoo's servers.

Using YUI

To get started with YUI, visit the following URL to download the complete distribution to your hard disk, where you can work on it locally:

http://developer.yahoo.com/yui/download

The download is about 11 MB in size and is supplied as a ZIP file that you will need to decompress. Once this is done, you will have a folder with a name such as *yui_2.7.0b*, depending on the version downloaded, inside of which will be another folder simply called *yui*.

Navigate to this folder and load up the *index.html* file that you'll find there into your browser to see a web page like that shown in Figure 19-1.

In the same directory where *index.html* resides, you'll also see a number of others. In particular I'd like to point you in the direction of the *build* folder, which contains about 60 subfolders that hold all the framework scripts (see Figure 19-2). You can copy the ones you need from here directly to your website, or access the ones on Yahoo's website by referencing *http://yui.yahooapis.com/2.7.0/build/* followed by the folder and script name. (Without the latter two names, this URL will call up an error page.)

For example, you could copy the file *yahoo.js* from the *build/yahoo* folder to your website and link to it like this:

```
<script src="yahoo.js"></script>
```

Or you could link directly to Yahoo's copy, like this:

```
<script src="http://yui.yahooapis.com/2.7.0/build/yahoo/yahoo.js"></script>
```

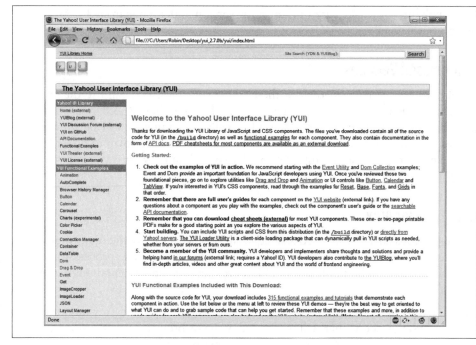

Figure 19-1. The YUI documentation main page

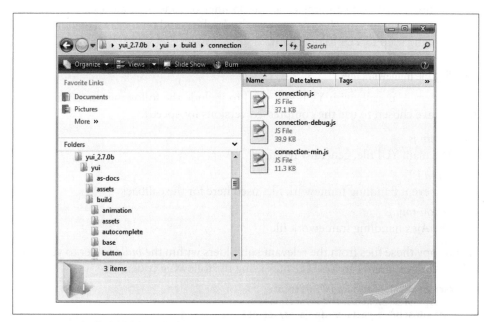

Figure 19-2. The build folder, which contains the .js framework files

If you link directly, make sure to change the version folder name from *2.7.0* if you are using a newer version of YUI.

Compressed Versions

If you wish to speed up loading of these framework files, you can use the alternate "min" versions Yahoo! supplies. For example, *yahoo.js* is about 33 KB in size, but there is a file called *yahoo-min.js* that acts identically; by simply removing unnecessary whitespace and other text, the developers have compressed it down to under 6 KB in size. (There are tools on the Internet that let you minimize your own scripts, in case you think doing so will speed up loading significantly.)

Using YUI for Ajax

In the previous chapter, we used `XMLHttpRequest` objects to provide Ajax connectivity between the web browser, a server, and a third-party server. The process wasn't too difficult, but it was a bit fiddly due to differences between implementations in different browsers.

With YUI, handling Ajax becomes a whole lot easier, because it provides a range of cross-browser methods that will work on any major browser. What's more, they remove the need for you to output headers and perform other bits and pieces for `POST` requests, and so on.

The upshot is that you can replace about 35 lines of code with a dozen or less. This makes your programs much easier to write and debug, and removes all the lower-level stuff, leaving it up to YUI to deal with.

Including the framework files

To perform Ajax calls with YUI, you need to include the following three framework files (I have chosen to use the compressed versions for speed):

yahoo-min.js
> The main YUI file, generally required

event-min.js
> The event handling framework file, used here for the callback

connection-min.js
> The Ajax handling framework file

If you copy those files from the relevant subfolders within the *build* folder to your web folder, your program can load the files using the following code:

```
<script src="yahoo-min.js"></script>
<script src="event-min.js"></script>
<script src="connection-min.js"></script>
```

Or you can fetch them directly from Yahoo's website using the following code:

```
<script src="http://yui.yahooapis.com/2.7.0/build/yahoo/yahoo-min.js"></script>
<script src="http://yui.yahooapis.com/2.7.0/build/event/event-min.js"></script>
<script src="http://yui.yahooapis.com/2.7.0/build/connection/connection-min.js">
</script>
```

The YUI asyncRequest method

Now all you need to do is call `asyncRequest`, Yahoo's version of the `ajaxRequest` function we created in the last chapter. The syntax is:

```
YAHOO.util.Connect.asyncRequest('method', 'url', callback [, 'parameters...'])
```

The *method* to use is either POST or GET; the *url* should be a PHP script on your server. If you're using the GET method, the name of the script should be followed by a ? and the parameter/value pairs you wish to send. The *callback* needs to point to a pair of functions to handle either successful completion or failure, and the *parameters* are passed only when you are using the POST method and the target server requires parameters for the request.

So an Ajax GET request might look like this:

```
YAHOO.util.Connect.asyncRequest('GET', 'program.php', callback)
```

The callback object should be created like this:

```
callback = { success:successHandler, failure:failureHandler }
```

The `successHandler` and `failureHandler` functions should contain instructions for your program to execute according to the intention of your project.

An Ajax GET example using YUI

Let's take Example 18-4 from the previous chapter and see what it looks like when modified to use YUI (see Example 19-1, *yuiurlget.html*).

Example 19-1. yuiurlget.html

```
<html><head><title>YUI GET Example</title>
</head><body><center />
<h2>Loading a web page into a DIV with YUI</h2>
<div id='info'>This sentence will be replaced</div>
<script src="yahoo-min.js"></script>
<script src="event-min.js"></script>
<script src="connection-min.js"></script>
<script>
url = "yahoo.com"
callback = { success:successHandler, failure:failureHandler }
request = YAHOO.util.Connect.asyncRequest('GET',
    'urlget.php?url=' + url, callback)

function successHandler(o) {
    document.getElementById('info').innerHTML = o.responseText
}
```

```
function failureHandler(o) {
    document.getElementById('info').innerHTML =
        o.status + " " + o.statusText
}
</script></body></html>
```

I'm sure you'll agree that this is very simple indeed. After setting up the web page, displaying a heading, and creating the DIV in which to place the Ajax response, the program loads three YUI framework files. The rest of the document (less than 10 lines of code) is the Ajax, which does the following:

1. Place the URL to fetch, *yahoo.com*, in the variable `url`.

2. Create the `callback` object. This is an associative array that points to the handlers to be called in case of the success or failure of the call.

3. Place the Ajax call, which is a GET request to the URL *urlget.php?url=yahoo.com*.

You may recall that we wrote *urlget.php* in the previous chapter (Example 18-5) and, as it doesn't require modifying, I won't repeat it here. Suffice it to say that the program fetches the HTML page at *http://yahoo.com* and returns it to the Ajax method.

All that remains are the two functions for success or failure of the call. The success function, `successHandler`, simply places the Ajax response text into the DIV that we prepared for it, and `failureHandler` displays an appropriate message upon error.

The result of calling up this new document in your browser can be seen in Figure 19-3.

Figure 19-3. The result of calling up yuiurlget.html in a browser

An Ajax XML example using YUI

Now let's see how you can use the `asyncRequest` method with XML by calling up the Yahoo! RSS weather feed for Washington, D.C., using Example 19-2, *yuixmlget.html*.

Example 19-2. yuixmlget.html

```
<html><head><title>YUI XML Example</title>
</head><body>
<h2>Loading XML content into a DIV with YUI</h2>
<div id='info'>This sentence will be replaced</div>
<script src="yahoo-min.js"></script>
<script src="event-min.js"></script>
<script src="connection-min.js"></script>
<script>
url = encodeURI("xml.weather.yahoo.com/forecastrss?p=20500")
callback = { success:successHandler, failure:failureHandler }
request = YAHOO.util.Connect.asyncRequest('GET',
    'xmlget.php?url=' + url, callback)

function successHandler(o) {
    root = o.responseXML.documentElement;
    title = root.getElementsByTagName('description')[0].
        firstChild.nodeValue
    date = root.getElementsByTagName('lastBuildDate')[0].
        firstChild.nodeValue
    text = root.getElementsByTagName('description')[1].
        firstChild.nodeValue

    document.getElementById('info').innerHTML =
        title + "<br />" + date + "<br />" + text
}

function failureHandler(o) {
    document.getElementById('info').innerHTML =
        o.status + " " + o.statusText
}
</script></body></html>
```

This document is fairly similar to the previous one, in that the same YUI framework scripts are included, but right away, you'll notice that the `url` is different. Because the weather feed itself takes `GET` parameters using a ? symbol, we have to URI-encode it as follows:

```
url = encodeURI("xml.weather.yahoo.com/forecastrss?p=20500")
```

This encoding has the effect of turning any special characters into a form that will not confuse the PHP program into thinking that additional parameters have been passed.

Next, you'll see that the `callback` object is the same as before, so we'll gloss over that and move on to the request, which has only a name change from *urlget.php* to *xmlget.php* in order to call the correct PHP program for XML. The *xmlget.php* program is the same one we created in the previous chapter (see Example 18-6) and thus doesn't need repeating here.

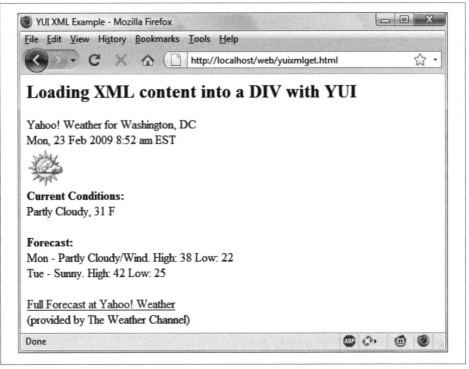

Figure 19-4. The result of calling up yuixmlget.html in a browser

You'll also notice that the function `failureHandler` is identical. So the main remaining change is in `successHandler`. This function refers to `responseXML` instead of `responseText`, from which it extracts the `title`, `date`, and `text` from the RSS feed and then inserts them into the DIV we prepared. The result of calling up *yuixmlget.html* into a browser can be seen in Figure 19-4.

Other Uses for YUI

The YUI framework offers support in a wide range of areas, including animation, buttons, calendars, charts, colors, cookies, drag and drop, fonts, imaging, menus, styles, uploading, and a great deal more as well.

To find features you need, check out the examples down the left of the main *index.html* page in the downloaded distribution or at *http://developer.yahoo.com/yui* and click on ones that interest you.

A Simple YUI Calendar

For example, clicking through to the *calendar* link reveals how you can make your own calendars, a common feature needed by many websites. Here's how you can recreate the calendar example shown at:

> *http://developer.yahoo.com/yui/examples/calendar/multi.html*

To do so, locate all the following files in the *build* folder of the downloaded YUI distribution on your hard disk, and copy them to your web folder (bearing in mind that *assets* is a folder, not a file):

- *fonts/fonts-min.css*
- *calendar/assets*
- *yahoo-dom-event /yahoo-dom-event.js*
- *calendar/calendar-min.js*

Now you can type in the document in Example 19-3, *calendar.html*, which, when you call it up in your browser, will look like Figure 19-5.

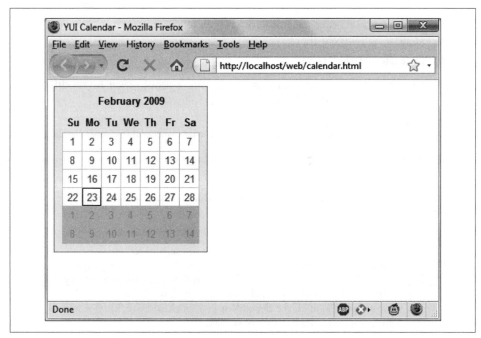

Figure 19-5. A YUI calendar

Example 19-3. calendar.html—a multiselect calendar

```
<html><head><title>YUI Calendar</title>
<link rel="stylesheet"
    type="text/css" href="fonts-min.css" />
<link rel="stylesheet"
    type="text/css" href="assets/skins/sam/calendar.css" />
<script src="yahoo-dom-event.js"></script>
<script src="calendar-min.js"></script>
</head><body class="yui-skin-sam">
<div id="cal1Container"></div>

<script>
YAHOO.namespace("example.calendar")
YAHOO.example.calendar.init = function() {
    YAHOO.example.calendar.cal1 =
        new YAHOO.widget.Calendar("cal1", "cal1Container",
            { MULTI_SELECT: true } )
    YAHOO.example.calendar.cal1.render()
}
YAHOO.util.Event.onDOMReady(YAHOO.example.calendar.init)
</script>
</body></html>
```

All that remains to do is place the following DIV where you want it on your web page, and the calendar will appear there:

```
<div id="cal1Container"></div>
```

You can also link directly to the various files on the Yahoo! server by modifying the three lines that link to the YUI libraries to read as follows:

```
<link rel="stylesheet" type="text/css"
 href="http://yui.yahooapis.com/2.7.0/build/calendar/assets/skins/sam/calendar.css" />

<script src="http://yui.yahooapis.com/2.7.0/build/yahoo-dom-event/yahoo-dom-event.js">
</script>

<script src="http://yui.yahooapis.com/2.7.0/build/calendar/calendar-min.js">
</script>
```

> All the other YUI features are just as easy to use, and require you only to carefully read the accompanying documentation before copying and pasting the supplied code. There's even a link to the YUI Dependency Configurator supplied with each example, which will build a copy-and-paste script to load all the dependent JavaScript and CSS files for any feature, directly from the Yahoo! servers.

I hope you have a lot of fun using the resources supplied by YUI (and any of the other frameworks you try). If you do, you'll find yourself saved from reinventing the wheel time and time again.

In the next and final chapter I'll bring everything you've learned so far together into a social networking application.

Test Your Knowledge: Questions

Question 19-1
What is YUI's method of implementing an Ajax connection?

Question 19-2
Write a callback object for YUI called `callback` to reference a success handler called `succeeded` and a failure handler called `failed`.

Question 19-3
Write a `GET` call to `asyncRequest` that references the program *getdata.php* and a `callback` object.

Question 19-4
How can you encode the URL *mysite.com/message?m=123*, which contains the ? symbol, so that if sent as a `GET` request it will be treated just as a string and not interpreted?

See the section "Chapter 19 Answers" on page 451 in Appendix A for the answers to these questions.

CHAPTER 20

Bringing It All Together

Now that you've reached the end of your journey into learning the hows, whys, and wherefores of dynamic web programming, I want to leave you with a real example that you can sink your teeth into. In fact, it's 10 examples, because I've put together a simple social networking project comprising all the main features you'd expect from such a site.

Across the various files, there are examples of MySQL table creation and database access, file inclusion, session control, DOM access, Ajax calls, event and error handling, file uploading, image manipulation, and a whole lot more.

Each example file is complete and self-contained, yet works with all the others to build a fully working social networking site. I have deliberately left styling and design to an absolute minimum to keep the examples short and easy to follow. This means that, as it stands, the end product is particularly usable on mobile platforms such as the iPhone, where reducing the file size and dimensions of web documents is important.

I leave it up to you to take any pieces of code you think you can use and expand on them for your own purposes. Perhaps you may even wish to build on these files to create a social networking site of your own.

Designing a Social Networking Site

Before writing any code, I sat down and came up with several things that I decided were essential to such a site. These included:

- A sign-up process
- A login form
- A logout facility
- Session control
- User profiles with uploaded thumbnails
- A member directory

- Adding members as friends
- Public and private messaging between members

That's 8 main elements, but in the end it turned out that because the project would require a main *index.html* page and a separate include file for the main functions, 10 PHP program files were required.

I decided to name the project *Robin's Nest*, but you have to modify only one line of code to change this to a name of your choice. Also, all the filenames (except *index.html*) start with the letters *rn* to separate them from any other files you have saved from this book. If you change these names, make sure you also change all references across all the files.

About Third-Party Add-Ons

For reasons of simplicity and size, and so that you don't have to install add-ons to your server if you don't wish to, I have deliberately not used either PEAR (see Appendix E) or Smarty (see Chapter 12) in these examples. But if you plan on extending the code, I strongly recommend you consider them, as PEAR can make the programming process simpler. Furthermore, if you will be working with separate designers, Smarty can remove the programming layer from the presentation layer, leaving them free to create at their heart's content.

However, where I have implemented an Ajax call, I have also included an alternative YUI version, as you can use it without installing any software on your server.

On the Website

All the examples in this chapter can be found on the companion website located at *http://lpmj.net*, where the code syntax is color-highlighted, making it easier to follow. You can also download the examples from there to your computer by clicking on the "Examples" link. This will download an archive file called *examples.zip*, which you should extract to a suitable location on your computer.

Of particular interest to this chapter, within the ZIP file there's a folder called *robinsnest*, in which all the following examples have been saved using the correct filenames required by this sample application. So you can easily copy them all to your web development folder to try them out.

rnfunctions.php

So let's jump right into the project, starting with Example 20-1, *rnfunctions.php*, the include file of main functions. This file contains a little more than just the functions, though, because I have added the database login details here instead of using yet another

---

separate file. So the first half-dozen lines of code define the host, database name, username, and password of the database to use.

It doesn't matter what you call the database, as long as it already exists (see Chapter 8 for how to create a new database). Also make sure to correctly assign a MySQL username and password to $dbuser and $dbpass. With correct values, the subsequent two lines will open a connection to MySQL and select the database. The last of the initial instructions sets the name of the social networking site by assigning the value "Robin's Nest" to the variable $appname. If you want to change the name, here's the place to do so.

The Functions

The project uses six main functions:

createTable
: Checks whether a table already exists and, if not, creates it.

tableExists
: Returns a value of 1 if a table already exists, otherwise 0.

queryMysql
: Issues a query to MySQL, outputting an error message if it fails.

destroySession
: Destroys a PHP session and clears its data to log users out.

sanitizeString
: Removes potentially malicious code or tags from user input.

showProfile
: Displays a user's image and "about me" if they have one.

All of these should be obvious in their action to you by now, with the possible exception of showProfile, which looks for an image of the name *user.jpg* (where *user* is the username of the current user), and if found, displays it. It also displays any "about me" text the user may have saved.

I have ensured that error handling is in place for all the functions that need it, so that they can catch any typographical or other errors you may introduce. However, if you use any of this code on a production server, you will probably want to provide your own error-handling routines to make the code more user-friendly.

So type this file in and save it as *rnfunctions.php* and you'll be ready to move on to the next section.

Example 20-1. rnfunctions.php

```php
<?php // rnfunctions.php
$dbhost = 'localhost';    // Unlikely to require changing
$dbname = 'publications'; // Modify these...
$dbuser = 'username';     // ...variables according
```

```php
$dbpass = 'password';     // ...to your installation
$appname = "Robin's Nest"; // ...and preference

mysql_connect($dbhost, $dbuser, $dbpass) or die(mysql_error());
mysql_select_db($dbname) or die(mysql_error());

function createTable($name, $query)
{
    if (tableExists($name))
    {
        echo "Table '$name' already exists<br />";
    }
    else
    {
        queryMysql("CREATE TABLE $name($query)");
        echo "Table '$name' created<br />";
    }
}

function tableExists($name)
{
    $result = queryMysql("SHOW TABLES LIKE '$name'");
    return mysql_num_rows($result);
}

function queryMysql($query)
{
    $result = mysql_query($query) or die(mysql_error());
    return $result;
}

function destroySession()
{
    $_SESSION=array();

    if (session_id() != "" || isset($_COOKIE[session_name()]))
        setcookie(session_name(), '', time()-2592000, '/');

    session_destroy();
}

function sanitizeString($var)
{
    $var = strip_tags($var);
    $var = htmlentities($var);
    $var = stripslashes($var);
    return mysql_real_escape_string($var);
}

function showProfile($user)
{
    if (file_exists("$user.jpg"))
        echo "<img src='$user.jpg' border='1' align='left' />";

    $result = queryMysql("SELECT * FROM rnprofiles WHERE user='$user'");
```

```
    if (mysql_num_rows($result))
    {
        $row = mysql_fetch_row($result);
        echo stripslashes($row[1]) . "<br clear=left /><br />";
    }
}
?>
```

rnheader.php

For uniformity, each page of the project needs to have the same overall design and layout. Therefore I placed these things in Example 20-2, *rnheader.php*. This is the file that is actually included by the other files and it, in turn, includes *rnfunctions.php*. This means that only a single include is required in each file.

rnheader.php starts by calling the function `session_start`. As you'll recall from Chapter 13, this sets up a session that will remember certain values we want stored across different PHP files.

With the session started, the program then checks whether the session variable `'user'` is currently assigned a value. If so, a user has logged in and the variable `$loggedin` is set to TRUE.

Using the value of `$loggedin`, an `if` block displays one of two sets of menus. The non-logged-in set simply offers options of *Home*, *Sign up*, and *Log in*, whereas the logged-in version offers full access to the project's features. Additionally, if a user is logged in, his or her username is appended in brackets to the page title and placed before the menu options. We can freely refer to `$user` wherever we want to put in the name, because if the user is not logged in, that variable is empty and will have no effect on the output.

The only styling applied in this file is to set the default font to Verdana at a size of 2 via a `<font...>` tag. For a more comprehensive design and layout, you'll probably wish to apply CSS styling to the HTML.

Example 20-2. rnheader.php

```
<?php // rnheader.php
include 'rnfunctions.php';
session_start();

if (isset($_SESSION['user']))
{
    $user = $_SESSION['user'];
    $loggedin = TRUE;
}
else $loggedin = FALSE;

echo "<html><head><title>$appname";
if ($loggedin) echo " ($user)";
```

```
echo "</title></head><body><font face='verdana' size='2'>";
echo "<h2>$appname</h2>";

if ($loggedin)
{
    echo "<b>$user</b>:
        <a href='rnmembers.php?view=$user'>Home</a> |
        <a href='rnmembers.php'>Members</a> |
        <a href='rnfriends.php'>Friends</a> |
        <a href='rnmessages.php'>Messages</a> |
        <a href='rnprofile.php'>Profile</a> |
        <a href='rnlogout.php'>Log out</a>";
}
else
{
    echo "<a href='index.php'>Home</a> |
        <a href='rnsignup.php'>Sign up</a> |
        <a href='rnlogin.php'>Log in</a>";
}
?>
```

rnsetup.php

With the pair of included files written, it's now time to set up the MySQL tables they will use. This is done with Example 20-3, *rnsetup.php*, which you should type in and load into your browser before calling up any other files—otherwise you'll get numerous MySQL errors.

The tables created are kept short and sweet, and have the following names and columns:

rnmembers
> username *user* (indexed), password *pass*

rnmessages
> ID *id* (indexed), author *auth* (indexed), recipient *recip*, message type *pm*, message *message*

rnfriends
> username *user* (indexed), friend's username *friend*

rnprofiles
> username *user* (indexed), "about me" *text*

Because the function `createTable` first checks whether a table already exists, this program can be safely called multiple times without generating any errors.

It is very likely that you will need to add many more columns to these tables if you choose to expand on this project. If so, you may need to issue a MySQL `DROP TABLE` command before recreating a table.

Example 20-3. rnsetup.php

```php
<?php // rnsetup.php
include_once 'rnfunctions.php';
echo '<h3>Setting up</h3>';

createTable('rnmembers', 'user VARCHAR(16), pass VARCHAR(16),
            INDEX(user(6))');

createTable('rnmessages',
            'id INT UNSIGNED AUTO_INCREMENT PRIMARY KEY,
             auth VARCHAR(16), recip VARCHAR(16), pm CHAR(1),
             time INT UNSIGNED, message VARCHAR(4096),
            INDEX(auth(6)), INDEX(recip(6))');

createTable('rnfriends', 'user VARCHAR(16), friend VARCHAR(16),
            INDEX(user(6)), INDEX(friend(6))');

createTable('rnprofiles', 'user VARCHAR(16), text VARCHAR(4096),
            INDEX(user(6))');
?>
```

index.php

This file is a trivial file but necessary nonetheless to give the project a home page. All it does is display a simple welcome message. In a finished application, this would be where you sell the virtues of your site to encourage signups.

Incidentally, seeing as all the MySQL tables have been created and the include files saved, you can now load Example 20-4, *index.php*, into your browser to get your first peek at the new application. It should look like Figure 20-1.

Figure 20-1. The main page of the site

Example 20-4. index.php

```php
<?php // index.php
include_once 'rnheader.php';

echo "<h3>Home page</h3>
    Welcome, please Sign up and/or Log in to join in.";
?>
```

rnsignup.php

Now we need a module to enable users to join the new network, and that's Example 20-5, *rnsignup.php*. This is a slightly longer program, but you've seen all its parts before.

Let's start by looking at the end block of HTML. This is a simple form that allows a username and password to be entered. But note the use of the empty span given the id of 'info'. This will be the destination of the Ajax call in this program that checks whether a desired username is available. See Chapter 18 for a complete description of how this works.

Checking for Username Availability

Now go back to the program start and you'll see a block of JavaScript that starts with the function checkUser. This is called by the JavaScript onBlur event when focus is removed from the username field of the form. First it sets the contents of the span I mentioned (with the id of 'info') to an empty string, which clears it in case it previously had a value.

Next a request is made to the program *rnchecker.php*, which reports whether the username *user* is available. The returned result of the Ajax call, a friendly message, is then placed in the 'info' span.

After the JavaScript section comes some PHP code that you should recognize from the Chapter 17 section of form validation. This section also uses the sanitizeString function to remove potentially malicious characters before looking up the username in the database and, if it's not already taken, inserting the new username $user and password $pass.

Upon successfully signing up, the user is then prompted to log in. A more fluid response at this point might be to automatically log in a newly created user but, as I don't want to overly complicate the code, I have kept the sign-up and login modules separate from each other.

When loaded into a browser (and in conjunction with *rncheckuser.php*, shown later) this program will look like Figure 20-2, where you can see that the Ajax call has identified that the username *Robin* is available.

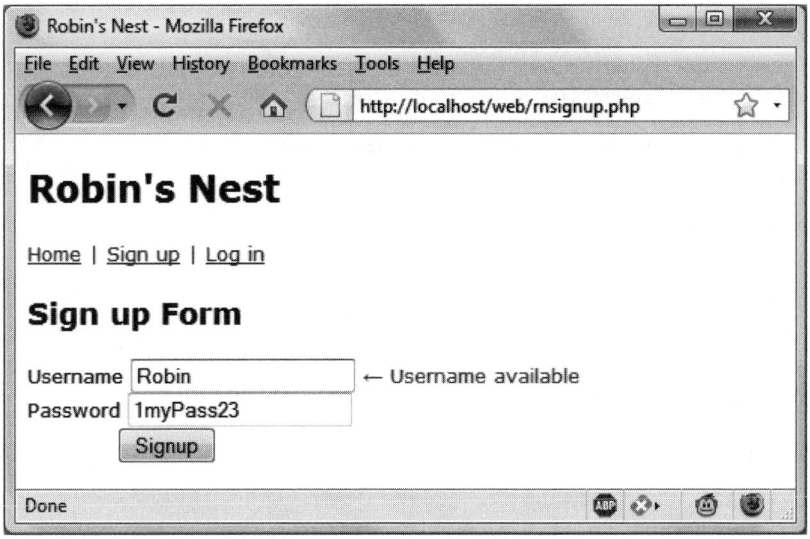

Figure 20-2. The sign-up page

Example 20-5. rnsignup.php

```php
<?php // rnsignup.php
include_once 'rnheader.php';

echo <<<_END
<script>
function checkUser(user)
{
    if (user.value == '')
    {
        document.getElementById('info').innerHTML = ''
        return
    }

    params  = "user=" + user.value
    request = new ajaxRequest()
    request.open("POST", "rncheckuser.php", true)
    request.setRequestHeader("Content-type",
        "application/x-www-form-urlencoded")
    request.setRequestHeader("Content-length", params.length)
    request.setRequestHeader("Connection", "close")

    request.onreadystatechange = function()
    {
        if (this.readyState == 4)
        {
            if (this.status == 200)
            {
                if (this.responseText != null)
```

```
                {
                    document.getElementById('info').innerHTML =
                        this.responseText
                }
                else alert("Ajax error: No data received")
            }
            else alert( "Ajax error: " + this.statusText)
        }
    }
    request.send(params)
}

function ajaxRequest()
{
    try
    {
        var request = new XMLHttpRequest()
    }
    catch(e1)
    {
        try
        {
            request = new ActiveXObject("Msxml2.XMLHTTP")
        }
        catch(e2)
        {
            try
            {
                request = new ActiveXObject("Microsoft.XMLHTTP")
            }
            catch(e3)
            {
                request = false
            }
        }
    }
    return request
}
</script>
<h3>Sign up Form</h3>
_END;

$error = $user = $pass = "";
if (isset($_SESSION['user'])) destroySession();

if (isset($_POST['user']))
{
    $user = sanitizeString($_POST['user']);
    $pass = sanitizeString($_POST['pass']);

    if ($user == "" || $pass == "")
    {
        $error = "Not all fields were entered<br /><br />";
    }
    else
```

```
    {
        $query = "SELECT * FROM rnmembers WHERE user='$user'";

        if (mysql_num_rows(queryMysql($query)))
        {
            $error = "That username already exists<br /><br />";
        }
        else
        {
            $query = "INSERT INTO rnmembers VALUES('$user', '$pass')";
            queryMysql($query);
            die("<h4>Account created</h4>Please Log in.");
        }
    }
}

echo <<<_END
<form method='post' action='rnsignup.php'>$error
Username <input type='text' maxlength='16' name='user' value='$user'
    onBlur='checkUser(this)'/><span id='info'></span><br />
Password <input type='text' maxlength='16' name='pass'
    value='$pass' /><br />
           
<input type='submit' value='Signup' />
</form>
_END;
?>
```

 On a production server, I wouldn't recommend storing user passwords in the clear as I've done here (for reasons of space and simplicity). Instead, you should salt them and store them as MD5 or other one-way hash strings. See Chapter 13 for more details on how to do this.

rnsignup.php (YUI version)

If you prefer to use YUI, here's an alternative version of *rnsignup.php* (see Example 20-6). I have highlighted the main differences in bold type and, as you can see, it's substantially shorter. Please refer to Chapter 19 for details on how the YUI Ajax implementation works.

Example 20-6. rnsignup.php (YUI version)

```
<?php // rnsignup.php (YUI version)
include_once 'rnheader.php';

echo <<<_END
<script src="yahoo-min.js"></script>
<script src="event-min.js"></script>
<script src="connection-min.js"></script>
<script>
function checkUser(user)
{
    if (user.value == '')
```

```
    {
        document.getElementById('info').innerHTML = ''
        return
    }

    params = "user=" + user.value
    callback = { success:successHandler, failure:failureHandler }
    request = YAHOO.util.Connect.asyncRequest('POST',
        'rncheckuser.php', callback, params);
}

function successHandler(o)
{
    document.getElementById('info').innerHTML = o.responseText;
}

function failureHandler(o)
{
    document.getElementById('info').innerHTML =
        o.status + " " + o.statusText;
}

</script>
<h3>Sign up Form</h3>
_END;

$error = $user = $pass = "";
if (isset($_SESSION['user'])) destroySession();

if (isset($_POST['user']))
{
    $user = sanitizeString($_POST['user']);
    $pass = sanitizeString($_POST['pass']);

    if ($user == "" || $pass == "")
    {
        $error = "Not all fields were entered<br /><br />";
    }
    else
    {
        $query = "SELECT * FROM rnmembers WHERE user='$user'";

        if (mysql_num_rows(queryMysql($query)))
        {
            $error = "That username already exists<br /><br />";
        }
        else
        {
            $query = "INSERT INTO rnmembers VALUES('$user', '$pass')";
            queryMysql($query);
        }

        die("<h4>Account created</h4>Please Log in.");
    }
}
```

```
echo <<<_END
<form method='post' action='rnsignup.php'>$error
Username <input type='text' maxlength='16' name='user' value='$user'
    onBlur='checkUser(this)'/><span id='info'></span><br />
Password <input type='text' maxlength='16' name='pass'
    value='$pass' /><br />
           
<input type='submit' value='Signup' />
</form>
_END;
?>
```

rncheckuser.php

To go with *rnsignup.php*, here's Example 20-7, *rncheckuser.php*, the program that looks up a username in the database and returns a string indicating whether it has already been taken. Because it relies on the functions `sanitizeString` and `queryMysql`, the program first includes the file *rnfunctions.php*.

Then, if the `$_POST` variable `'user'` has a value, the function looks it up in the database and, depending on whether it exists as a username, outputs either "Sorry, already taken" or "Username available." Just checking the function `mysql_num_rows` against the result is sufficient for this, as it will return 0 for not found, or 1 if it is found.

The HTML entity `&larr;` is also used to preface the string with a little left-pointing arrow.

Example 20-7. rncheckuser.php

```
<?php // rncheckuser.php
include_once 'rnfunctions.php';

if (isset($_POST['user']))
{
    $user = sanitizeString($_POST['user']);
    $query = "SELECT * FROM rnmembers WHERE user='$user'";

    if (mysql_num_rows(queryMysql($query)))
        echo "<font color=red> &larr;
            Sorry, already taken</font>";
    else echo "<font color=green> &larr;
            Username available</font>";
}
?>
```

rnlogin.php

With users now able to sign up to the site, Example 20-8, *rnlogin.php*, provides the code needed to let them log in. Like the sign-up page, it features a simple HTML form and some basic error checking, as well as using `sanitizeString` before querying the MySQL database.

The main thing to note here is that, upon successful verification of the username and password, the session variables `'user'` and `'pass'` are given the username and password values. As long as the current session remains active these variables will be accessible by all the programs in the project, allowing them to automatically provide access to logged-in users.

You may be interested in the use of the `die` function upon successfully logging in. This is used because it combines an `echo` and an `exit` command in one, thus saving a line of code.

When you call this program up in your browser, it should look like Figure 20-3. Note how the `<input...>` type of `password` has been used here to mask the password with asterisks to prevent it from being viewed by anyone looking over the user's shoulder.

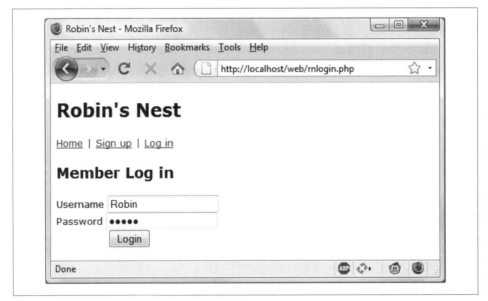

Figure 20-3. The login page

Example 20-8. rnlogin.php

```php
<?php // rnlogin.php
include_once 'rnheader.php';
echo "<h3>Member Log in</h3>";
$error = $user = $pass = "";

if (isset($_POST['user']))
{
    $user = sanitizeString($_POST['user']);
    $pass = sanitizeString($_POST['pass']);
```

```
    if ($user == "" || $pass == "")
    {
        $error = "Not all fields were entered<br />";
    }
    else
    {
        $query = "SELECT user,pass FROM rnmembers
                WHERE user='$user' AND pass='$pass'";

        if (mysql_num_rows(queryMysql($query)) == 0)
        {
            $error = "Username/Password invalid<br />";
        }
        else
        {
            $_SESSION['user'] = $user;
            $_SESSION['pass'] = $pass;
            die("You are now logged in. Please
                <a href='rnmembers.php?view=$user'>click here</a>.");
        }
    }
}

echo <<<_END
<form method='post' action='rnlogin.php'>$error
Username <input type='text' maxlength='16' name='user'
    value='$user' /><br />
Password <input type='password' maxlength='16' name='pass'
    value='$pass' /><br />
             
<input type='submit' value='Login' />
</form>
_END;
?>
```

rnprofile.php

One of the first things that new users may want to do after signing up and logging in is to create a profile, which can be done via Example 20-9, *rnprofile.php*. I think you'll find some interesting code here, such as routines to upload, resize, and sharpen images.

Let's start by looking at the main HTML at the end of the code. This is like the forms you've just seen, but this time it has the parameter enctype='multipart/form-data'. This allows us to send more than one type of data at a time, enabling the posting of an image as well as some text. There's also an <input...> type of file, which creates a browse button that a user can press to select a file to be uploaded.

When the form is submitted, the code at the start of the program is executed. The first thing it does is ensure that a user is logged in before allowing program execution to proceed. Only then is the page heading displayed.

Adding the "About Me" Text

Then the POST variable 'text' is checked to see whether some text was posted to the program. If so, it is sanitized and all long whitespace sequences (including returns and line feeds) are replaced with a single space. This function incorporates a double security check, ensuring that the user actually exists in the database and that no attempted hacking can succeed before inserting this text into the database, where it will become the user's "about me" details.

If no text was posted, the database is queried to see whether any already exists in order to prepopulate the textarea for the user to edit it.

Adding a Profile Image

Next we move on to the section where the $_FILES system variable is checked to see whether an image has been uploaded. If so, a string variable called $saveto is created, based on the user's username followed by the extension *.jpg*. For example, user Jill will cause $saveto to have the value *Jill.jpg*. This is the file where the uploaded image will be saved for use in the user's profile.

Following this, the uploaded image type is examined and is only accepted if it is a *jpeg*, *png*, or *gif* image. Upon success, the variable $src is populated with the uploaded image using one of the imagecreatefrom functions according to the image type uploaded. The image is now in a raw format that PHP can process. If the image is not of an allowed type, the flag $typeok is set to FALSE, preventing the final section of image upload code from being processed.

Processing the Image

First, the image's dimensions are stored in $w and $h using the following statement, which is a quick way of assigning values from an array to separate variables:

```
list($w, $h) = getimagesize($saveto);
```

Then, using the value of $max (which is set to 100), new dimensions are calculated that will result in a new image of the same ratio, but with no dimension greater than 100 pixels. This results in giving the variables $tw and $th the new values needed. If you want smaller or larger thumbnails, simply change the value of $max accordingly.

Next, the function imagecreatetruecolor is called to create a new, blank canvas $tw wide and $th high in $tmp. Then imagecopyresampled is called to resample the image from $src, to the new $tmp. Sometimes resampling images can result in a slightly blurred copy, so the next piece of code uses the imageconvolution function to sharpen the image up a bit.

Finally the image is saved as a *jpeg* file in the location defined by the variable $saveto, after which both the original and the resized image canvases are removed from memory using the imagedestroy function, returning the memory that was used.

Displaying the Current Profile

Last but not least, so that the user can see what the current profile looks like before editing it, the showProfile function from *rnfunctions.php* is called prior to outputting the form HTML. If no profile exists yet, nothing will be displayed.

The result of loading Example 20-9 into a browser is shown in Figure 20-4, where you can see that the textarea has been prepopulated with the "about me" text.

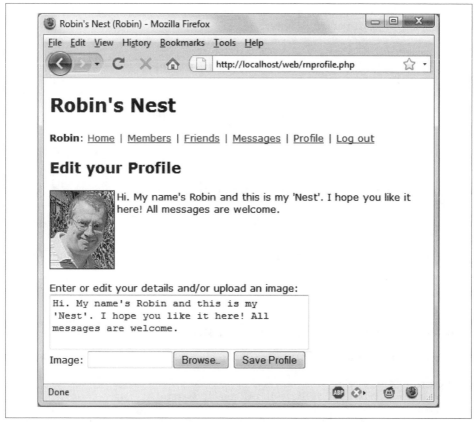

Figure 20-4. Editing a user profile

Example 20-9. rnprofile.php

```php
<?php // rnprofile.php
include_once 'rnheader.php';

if (!isset($_SESSION['user']))
    die("<br /><br />You need to login to view this page");
$user = $_SESSION['user'];

echo "<h3>Edit your Profile</h3>";

if (isset($_POST['text']))
{
    $text = sanitizeString($_POST['text']);
    $text = preg_replace('/\s\s+/', ' ', $text);

    $query = "SELECT * FROM rnprofiles WHERE user='$user'";
    if (mysql_num_rows(queryMysql($query)))
    {
        queryMysql("UPDATE rnprofiles SET text='$text'
                where user='$user'");
    }
    else
    {
        $query = "INSERT INTO rnprofiles VALUES('$user', '$text')";
        queryMysql($query);
    }
}
else
{
    $query  = "SELECT * FROM rnprofiles WHERE user='$user'";
    $result = queryMysql($query);

    if (mysql_num_rows($result))
    {
        $row  = mysql_fetch_row($result);
        $text = stripslashes($row[1]);
    }
    else $text = "";
}

$text = stripslashes(preg_replace('/\s\s+/', ' ', $text));

if (isset($_FILES['image']['name']))
{
    $saveto = "$user.jpg";
    move_uploaded_file($_FILES['image']['tmp_name'], $saveto);
    $typeok = TRUE;

    switch($_FILES['image']['type'])
    {
        case "image/gif":   $src = imagecreatefromgif($saveto); break;

        case "image/jpeg":  // Both regular and progressive jpegs
        case "image/pjpeg":   $src = imagecreatefromjpeg($saveto); break;
```

```
        case "image/png":    $src = imagecreatefrompng($saveto); break;

        default:             $typeok = FALSE; break;
    }

    if ($typeok)
    {
        list($w, $h) = getimagesize($saveto);
        $max = 100;
        $tw  = $w;
        $th  = $h;

        if ($w > $h && $max < $w)
        {
            $th = $max / $w * $h;
            $tw = $max;
        }
        elseif ($h > $w && $max < $h)
        {
            $tw = $max / $h * $w;
            $th = $max;
        }
        elseif ($max < $w)
        {
            $tw = $th = $max;
        }

        $tmp = imagecreatetruecolor($tw, $th);
        imagecopyresampled($tmp, $src, 0, 0, 0, 0, $tw, $th, $w, $h);
        imageconvolution($tmp, array( // Sharpen image
                            array(-1, -1, -1),
                            array(-1, 16, -1),
                            array(-1, -1, -1)
                            ), 8, 0);
        imagejpeg($tmp, $saveto);
        imagedestroy($tmp);
        imagedestroy($src);
    }
}

showProfile($user);

echo <<<_END
<form method='post' action='rnprofile.php'
    enctype='multipart/form-data'>
Enter or edit your details and/or upload an image:<br />
<textarea name='text' cols='40' rows='3'>$text</textarea><br />
Image: <input type='file' name='image' size='14' maxlength='32' />
<input type='submit' value='Save Profile' />
</pre></form>
_END;
?>
```

rnmembers.php

Using Example 20-10, *rnmembers.php*, your users will be able to find other members and choose to add them as friends (or drop them if they are already friends). This program has two modes. The first lists all members and their relationships to you, and the second shows a user's profile.

Viewing a User's Profile

The code for the latter mode comes first, where a test is made for the GET variable `'view'`. If it exists, a user wants to view someone's profile, so the program does that using the `showProfile` function, along with providing a couple of links to the user's friends and messages.

Adding and Dropping Friends

After that the two GET variables `'add'` and `'remove'` are tested. If one or the other has a value, it will be the username of a user to either add or drop as a friend. This is achieved by looking the user up in the MySQL `rnfriends` table and either inserting a friend username or removing it from the table.

And, of course, every posted variable is first passed through `sanitizeString` to ensure it is safe to use with MySQL.

Listing All Members

The final section of code issues a SQL query to list all usernames. The code places the number returned in the variable `$num` before outputting the page heading.

A `for` loop then iterates through each and every member, fetching their details and then looking them up in the `rnfriends` table to see if they are either being followed by or a follower of the user. If someone is both a follower and a followee, they are classed as a mutual friend. By the way, this section of code is particularly amenable to a template solution such as Smarty.

The variable `$t1` is nonzero when the user is following another member, and `$t2` is nonzero when another member is following the user. Depending on these values, text is displayed after each username showing their relationship (if any) to the current user.

Icons are also displayed to show the relationships. A double pointing arrow means that the users are mutual friends. A left-pointing arrow indicates the user is following another member. And a right-pointing arrow indicates that another member is following the user.

Finally, depending on whether the user is following another member, a link is provided to either add or drop that member as a friend.

When you call Example 20-10 up in a browser, it will look like Figure 20-5. See how the user is invited to "follow" a nonfollowing member, but if the member is already following the user, a "recip" link to reciprocate the friendship is offered. In the case of a user already following another member, the user can select "drop" to stop the following.

Figure 20-5. Using the members module

Example 20-10. rnmembers.php

```php
<?php // rnmembers.php
include_once 'rnheader.php';

if (!isset($_SESSION['user']))
    die("<br /><br />You must be logged in to view this page");
$user = $_SESSION['user'];

if (isset($_GET['view']))
{
    $view = sanitizeString($_GET['view']);

    if ($view == $user) $name = "Your";
    else $name = "$view's";

    echo "<h3>$name Page</h3>";
    showProfile($view);
    echo "<a href='rnmessages.php?view=$view'>$name Messages</a><br />";
    die("<a href='rnfriends.php?view=$view'>$name Friends</a><br />");
}
```

```php
if (isset($_GET['add']))
{
    $add = sanitizeString($_GET['add']);
    $query = "SELECT * FROM rnfriends WHERE user='$add'
            AND friend='$user'";

    if (!mysql_num_rows(queryMysql($query)))
    {
        $query = "INSERT INTO rnfriends VALUES ('$add', '$user')";
        queryMysql($query);
    }
}
elseif (isset($_GET['remove']))
{
    $remove = sanitizeString($_GET['remove']);
    $query = "DELETE FROM rnfriends WHERE user='$remove'
            AND friend='$user'";
    queryMysql($query);
}

$result = queryMysql("SELECT user FROM rnmembers ORDER BY user");
$num = mysql_num_rows($result);
echo "<h3>Other Members</h3><ul>";

for ($j = 0 ; $j < $num ; ++$j)
{
    $row = mysql_fetch_row($result);
    if ($row[0] == $user) continue;

    echo "<li><a href='rnmembers.php?view=$row[0]'>$row[0]</a>";
    $query = "SELECT * FROM rnfriends WHERE user='$row[0]'
            AND friend='$user'";
    $t1 = mysql_num_rows(queryMysql($query));

    $query = "SELECT * FROM rnfriends WHERE user='$user'
            AND friend='$row[0]'";
    $t2 = mysql_num_rows(queryMysql($query));
    $follow = "follow";

    if (($t1 + $t2) > 1)
    {
        echo " &harr; is a mutual friend";
    }
    elseif ($t1)
    {
        echo " &larr; you are following";
    }
    elseif ($t2)
    {
        $follow = "recip";
        echo " &rarr; is following you";
    }

    if (!$t1)
    {
```

```
        echo " [<a href='rnmembers.php?add=".$row[0] . "'>$follow</a>]";
    }
    else
    {
        echo " [<a href='rnmembers.php?remove=".$row[0] . "'>drop</a>]";
    }
}
?>
```

 On a production server, there could be thousands or even hundreds of thousands of users, so you would probably substantially modify this program to include searching the "about me" text, and support paging of the output a screen at a time.

rnfriends.php

The module that shows a user's friends and followers is Example 20-11, *rnfriends.php*. This interrogates the **rnfriends** table just like the *rnmembers.php* program, but only for a single user. It then shows all of that user's mutual friends and followers along with the people they are following.

All the followers are saved into an array called **$followers** and all the people being followed are placed in an array called **$following**. Then a neat piece of code is used to extract all those that are both following and followed by the user, like this:

```
$mutual = array_intersect($followers, $following);
```

The **array_intersect** function extracts all members common to both arrays and returns a new array containing only those people. This array is then stored in **$mutual**. Now it's possible to use the **array_diff** function for each of the **$followers** and **$following** arrays to keep only those people who are *not* mutual friends, like this:

```
$followers = array_diff($followers, $mutual);
$following = array_diff($following, $mutual);
```

This results in the array **$mutual** containing only mutual friends, **$followers** containing only followers (and no mutual friends), and **$following** containing only people being followed (and no mutual friends).

Armed with these arrays, it's a simple matter to separately display each category of members, as can be seen in Figure 20-6. The PHP **sizeof** function returns the number of elements in an array; here I use it just to trigger code when the size is nonzero (that is, friends of that type exist). Note how, by using the variables **$name1**, **$name2**, and **$name3** in the relevant places, the code can tell when you're looking at your own friends list, using the words *Your* and *You are*, instead of simply displaying the username.

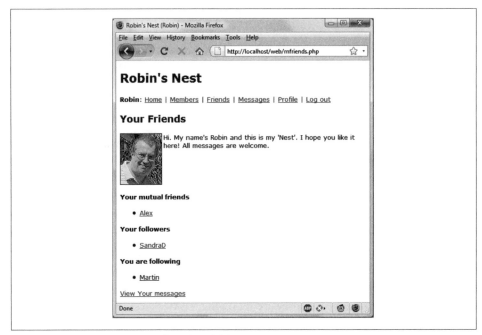

Figure 20-6. Displaying a user's friends and followers

Example 20-11. rnfriends.php

```php
<?php // rnfriends.php
include_once 'rnheader.php';

if (!isset($_SESSION['user']))
    die("<br /><br />You need to login to view this page");
$user = $_SESSION['user'];

if (isset($_GET['view'])) $view = sanitizeString($_GET['view']);
else $view = $user;

if ($view == $user)
{
    $name1 = "Your";
    $name2 = "Your";
    $name3 = "You are";
}
else
{
    $name1 = "<a href='rnmembers.php?view=$view'>$view</a>'s";
    $name2 = "$view's";
    $name3 = "$view is";
}

echo "<h3>$name1 Friends</h3>";
showProfile($view);
$followers = array(); $following = array();
```

```php
$query   = "SELECT * FROM rnfriends WHERE user='$view'";
$result = queryMysql($query);
$num     = mysql_num_rows($result);

for ($j = 0 ; $j < $num ; ++$j)
{
    $row = mysql_fetch_row($result);
    $followers[$j] = $row[1];
}

$query   = "SELECT * FROM rnfriends WHERE friend='$view'";
$result = queryMysql($query);
$num     = mysql_num_rows($result);

for ($j = 0 ; $j < $num ; ++$j)
{
    $row = mysql_fetch_row($result);
    $following[$j] = $row[0];
}

$mutual     = array_intersect($followers, $following);
$followers = array_diff($followers, $mutual);
$following = array_diff($following, $mutual);
$friends    = FALSE;

if (sizeof($mutual))
{
    echo "<b>$name2 mutual friends</b><ul>";
    foreach($mutual as $friend)
        echo "<li><a href='rnmembers.php?view=$friend'>$friend</a>";
    echo "</ul>";
    $friends = TRUE;
}

if (sizeof($followers))
{
    echo "<b>$name2 followers</b><ul>";
    foreach($followers as $friend)
        echo "<li><a href='rnmembers.php?view=$friend'>$friend</a>";
    echo "</ul>";
    $friends = TRUE;
}

if (sizeof($following))
{
    echo "<b>$name3 following</b><ul>";
    foreach($following as $friend)
        echo "<li><a href='rnmembers.php?view=$friend'>$friend</a>";
    $friends = TRUE;
}

if (!$friends) echo "<ul><li>None yet";
```

```
echo "</ul><a href='rnmessages.php?view=$view'>View $name2 messages</a>";
?>
```

rnmessages.php

The last of the main modules is Example 20-12, *rnmessages.php*. The program starts by checking whether a message has been posted in the POST variable 'text'. If so, it is inserted into the rnmessages table. At the same time, the value of 'pm' is also stored. This indicates whether a message is private or public. A 0 represents a public message and 1 is private.

Next, the user's profile and a form for entering a message are displayed, along with radio buttons to choose between a private or public message. After this, all the messages are shown, depending on whether they are private or public. If they are public, all users can see them, but private messages are visible only to the sender and recipient. This is all handled by a couple of queries to the MySQL database. Additionally, when a message is private, it is introduced by the word "whispered" and shown in italic.

Finally, the program displays a couple of links to refresh the messages, in case another user has posted one in the meantime, and to view the user's friends. The trick using the variables $name1 and $name2 is again used so that when you view your own profile the word *Your* is displayed instead of the username.

You can see the result of viewing this program with a browser in Figure 20-7. Note how users viewing their own messages are provided with links to erase any they don't want.

Figure 20-7. The messaging module

Example 20-12. rnmessages.php

```php
<?php // rnmessages.php
include_once 'rnheader.php';

if (!isset($_SESSION['user']))
    die("<br /><br />You need to login to view this page");
$user = $_SESSION['user'];

if (isset($_GET['view'])) $view = sanitizeString($_GET['view']);
else $view = $user;

if (isset($_POST['text']))
{
    $text = sanitizeString($_POST['text']);

    if ($text != "")
    {
        $pm = substr(sanitizeString($_POST['pm']),0,1);
        $time = time();
        queryMysql("INSERT INTO rnmessages VALUES(NULL,
                    '$user', '$view', '$pm', $time, '$text')");
    }
}

if ($view != "")
{
    if ($view == $user)
    {
        $name1 = "Your";
        $name2 = "Your";
    }
    else
    {
        $name1 = "<a href='rnmembers.php?view=$view'>$view</a>'s";
        $name2 = "$view's";
    }

    echo "<h3>$name1 Messages</h3>";
    showProfile($view);

    echo <<<_END
<form method='post' action='rnmessages.php?view=$view'>
Type here to leave a message:<br />
<textarea name='text' cols='40' rows='3'></textarea><br />
Public<input type='radio' name='pm' value='0' checked='checked' />
Private<input type='radio' name='pm' value='1' />
<input type='submit' value='Post Message' /></form>
_END;

    if (isset($_GET['erase']))
    {
        $erase = sanitizeString($_GET['erase']);
        queryMysql("DELETE FROM rnmessages WHERE id=$erase
                    AND recip='$user'");
    }
```

```
$query = "SELECT * FROM rnmessages WHERE recip='$view'
        ORDER BY time DESC";
$result = queryMysql($query);
$num = mysql_num_rows($result);

for ($j = 0 ; $j < $num ; ++$j)
{
    $row = mysql_fetch_row($result);

    if ($row[3] == 0 ||
        $row[1] == $user ||
        $row[2] == $user)
    {
        echo date('M jS \'y g:sa:', $row[4]);
        echo " <a href='rnmessages.php?";
        echo "view=$row[1]'>$row[1]</a> ";

        if ($row[3] == 0)
        {
            echo "wrote: &quot;$row[5]&quot; ";
        }
        else
        {
            echo "whispered: <i><font
            color='#006600'>&quot;$row[5]&quot;</font></i> ";
        }

        if ($row[2] == $user)
        {
            echo "[<a href='rnmessages.php?view=$view";
            echo "&erase=$row[0]'>erase</a>]";
        }
        echo "<br>";
    }
}
}

if (!$num) echo "<li>No messages yet</li><br />";

echo "<br><a href='rnmessages.php?view=$view'>Refresh messages</a>";
echo " | <a href='rnfriends.php?view=$view'>View $name2 friends</a>";
?>
```

rnlogout.php

The final ingredient in our social networking recipe is Example 20-13, *rnlogout.php*, the logout page that closes a session and deletes any associated data and cookies. The result of calling up this program can be seen in Figure 20-8, where the user is now asked to click on a link which will take them to the un-logged-in home page and remove the logged-in links from the top of the screen. Of course, you could write a JavaScript or

PHP redirect to do this, and this is probably a good idea in order to keep logging out looking clean.

Figure 20-8. The logout page

Example 20-13. rnlogout.php

```php
<?php // rnlogout.php
include_once 'rnheader.php';
echo "<h3>Log out</h3>";

if (isset($_SESSION['user']))
{
    destroySession();
    echo "You have been logged out. Please
    <a href='index.php'>click here</a> to refresh the screen.";
}
else echo "You are not logged in";
?>
```

And that, as they say, is that. If you write anything based on this code, or any other examples in this book, or have gained in any other way from it, then I'm glad to have been of help, and thank you for reading this book.

But before you go out and try out your newly learned skills on the Web at large, please take a browse through the appendices that follow, as there's a lot of additional information there you should find useful.

Solutions to the Chapter Questions

Chapter 1 Answers

Question 1-1

A web server (such as Apache), a server-side scripting language (PHP), a database (MySQL), and a client-side scripting language (JavaScript).

Question 1-2

HyperText Markup Language: the web page itself, including text and markup commands.

Question 1-3

Like nearly all database engines, MySQL accepts commands in Structured Query Language (SQL). SQL is the way that every user (including a PHP program) communicates with MySQL.

Question 1-4

PHP runs on the server, whereas JavaScript runs on the client. PHP can communicate with the database to store and retrieve data, but it can't alter the user's web page quickly and dynamically. JavaScript has the opposite benefits and drawbacks.

Question 1-5

Some of these technologies are controlled by companies that accept bug reports and fix the errors like any software company. But open source software also depends on a community, so your bug report may be handled by any user who understands the code well enough. You may someday fix bugs in an open source tool yourself.

Chapter 2 Answers

Question 2-1
> WAMP stands for "Windows, Apache, MySQL, and PHP," whereas the first M in MAMP stands for Mac instead of Windows. They both refer to a complete solution for hosting dynamic web pages.

Question 2-2
> Both *127.0.0.1* and *http://localhost* are ways of referring to the local computer. When a WAMP or MAMP is properly configured, you can type either into a browser's address bar to call up the default page on the local server.

Question 2-3
> FTP stands for File Transfer Protocol. An FTP program is used to transfer files back and forth between a client and a server.

Question 2-4
> It is necessary to FTP files to a remote server in order to update it, which can substantially increase development time if this action is carried out many times in a session.

Question 2-5
> Dedicated program editors are smart and can highlight problems in your code before you even run it.

Chapter 3 Answers

Question 3-1
> The tag used to start PHP interpreting code is `<?php ... ?>`, which can be shortened to `<? ... ?>`.

Question 3-2
> You can use `//` for a single line comment or `/* ... */` to span multiple lines.

Question 3-3
> All PHP statements must end with a semicolon (`;`).

Question 3-4
> With the exception of constants, all PHP variables must begin with `$`.

Question 3-5
> Variables hold a value that can be a string, a number, or other data.

Question 3-6
> `$variable = 1` is an assignment statement, whereas `$variable == 1` is a comparison operator. Use `$variable = 1` to set the value of `$variable`. Use `$variable == 1` to find out later in the program whether `$variable` equals 1. If you mistakenly use `$variable = 1` where you meant to do a comparison, it will do two things you probably don't want: set `$variable` to 1 and return a `true` value all the time, no matter what its previous value was.

Question 3-7

A hyphen is reserved for the subtraction operators. A construct like `$current-user` would be harder to interpret if hyphens were also allowed in variable names and, in any case, would lead programs to be ambiguous.

Question 3-8

Variable names are case-sensitive. `$This_Variable` is not the same as `$this_variable`.

Question 3-9

You cannot use spaces in variable names, as this would confuse the PHP parser. Instead try using the _ (underscore).

Question 3-10

To convert one variable type to another, reference it and PHP will automatically convert it for you.

Question 3-11

There is no difference between `++$j` and `$j++` unless the value of `$j` is being tested, assigned to another variable, or passed as a parameter to a function. In such cases, `++$j` increments `$j` before the test or other operation is performed, whereas `$j++` performs the operation and then increments `$j`.

Question 3-12

Generally, the operators `&&` and `and` are interchangeable except where precedence is important, in which case `&&` has a high precedence while `and` has a low one.

Question 3-13

You can use multiple lines within quotations marks or the `<<< _END ... _END` construct to create a multiline `echo` or assignment.

Question 3-14

You cannot redefine constants because, by definition, once defined they retain their value until the program terminates.

Question 3-15

You can use `\'` or `\"` to escape either a single or double quote.

Question 3-16

The `echo` and `print` commands are similar, except that `print` is a PHP function and takes a single argument and `echo` is a construct that can take multiple arguments.

Question 3-17

The purpose of functions is to separate discrete sections of code into their own, self-contained sections that can be referenced by a single function name.

Question 3-18

You can make a variable accessible to all parts of a PHP program by declaring it as `global`.

Question 3-19

If you generate data within a function, you can convey the data to the rest of the program by returning a value or modifying a global variable.

Question 3-20

When you combine a string with a number, the result is another string.

Chapter 4 Answers

Question 4-1

In PHP `TRUE` represents the value 1 and `FALSE` represents `NULL`, which can be thought of as "nothing" and is output as the empty string.

Question 4-2

The simplest forms of expressions are literals (such as numbers and strings) and variables, which simply evaluate to themselves.

Question 4-3

The difference between unary, binary and ternary operators is the number of operands each requires (one, two, and three, respectively).

Question 4-4

The best way to force your own operator precedence is to place parentheses around subexpressions to which you wish to give high precedence.

Question 4-5

Operator associativity refers to the direction of processing (left-to-right or right-to-left).

Question 4-6

You use the identity operator when you wish to bypass PHP's automatic operand type changing (also called *type casting*).

Question 4-7

The three conditional statement types are `if`, `switch`, and the `?` operator.

Question 4-8

To skip the current iteration of a loop and move on to the next one, use a `continue` statement.

Question 4-9

Loops using `for` statements are more powerful than `while` loops, because they support two additional parameters to control the loop handling.

Question 4-10

Most conditional expressions in `if` and `while` statements are literal (or Boolean) and therefore trigger execution when they evaluate to `TRUE`. Numeric expressions trigger execution when they evaluate to a nonzero value. String expressions trigger execution when they evaluate to a nonempty string. A `NULL` value is evaluated as false and therefore does not trigger execution.

Chapter 5 Answers

Question 5-1

Using functions avoids the need to copy or rewrite similar code sections many times over by combining sets of statements together so that they can be called by a simple name.

Question 5-2

By default, a function can return a single value. But by utilizing arrays, references, and global variables, any number of values can be returned.

Question 5-3

When you reference a variable by name, such as by assigning its value to another variable or by passing its value to a function, its value is copied. The original does not change when the copy is changed. But if you reference a variable, only a pointer (or reference) to its value is used, so that a single value is referenced by more than one name. Changing the value of the reference will change the original as well.

Question 5-4

Scope refers to which parts of a program can access a variable. For example, a variable of global scope can be accessed by all parts of a PHP program.

Question 5-5

To incorporate one file within another, you can use the `include` or `require` directives, or their safer variants, `include_once` and `require_once`.

Question 5-6

A function is a set of statements referenced by a name that can receive and return values. An object may contain zero or many functions (which are then called methods) as well as variables (which are called properties) all combined in a single unit.

Question 5-7

To create a new object in PHP, use the `new` keyword like this: `$object = new Class`.

Question 5-8

To create a subclass, use the `extends` keyword with syntax such as this: `class Sub class extends Parentclass`.

Question 5-9

To call a piece of initializing code when an object is created, create a constructor method called `__construct` within the class and place your code there.

Question 5-10

Explicitly declaring properties within a class is unnecessary, as they will be implicitly declared upon first use. But it is considered good practice as it helps with code readability and debugging, and is especially useful to other people who may have to maintain your code.

Chapter 6 Answers

Question 6-1

A numeric array can be indexed numerically using numbers or numeric variables. An associative array uses alphanumeric identifiers to index elements.

Question 6-2

The main benefit of the **array** keyword is that it enables you to assign several values at a time to an array without repeating the array name.

Question 6-3

Both the **each** function and the **foreach...as** loop construct return elements from an array; both start at the beginning and increment a pointer to make sure the next element is returned each time; and both return **FALSE** when the end of the array is reached. The difference is that the **each** function returns just a single element, so it is usually wrapped in a loop. The **foreach...as** construct is already a loop, executing repeatedly until the array is exhausted or you explicitly break out of the loop.

Question 6-4

To create a multidimensional array, you need to assign additional arrays to elements of the main array.

Question 6-5

You can use the **count** function to count the number of elements in an array.

Question 6-6

The purpose of the **explode** function is to extract sections from a string that are separated by an identifier, such as extracting words separated by spaces within a sentence.

Question 6-7

To reset PHP's internal pointer into an array back to the first element, call the **reset** function.

Chapter 7 Answers

Question 7-1

The conversion specifier you would use to display a floating-point number is **%f**.

Question 7-2

To take the input string "Happy Birthday" and output the string "**Happy", you could use a **printf** statement such as `printf("%'*7.5s", "Happy Birthday");`.

Question 7-3

To send the output from **printf** to a variable instead of to a browser, you would use **sprintf** instead.

Question 7-4

To create a Unix timestamp for 7:11am on May 2nd 2016, you could use the command `$timestamp = mktime(7, 11, 0, 5, 2, 2016);`.

Question 7-5

You would use the "w+" file access mode with **fopen** to open a file in write and read mode, with the file truncated and the file pointer at the start.

Question 7-6

The PHP command for deleting the file *file.txt* is `unlink('file.txt');`.

Question 7-7

The PHP function `file_get_contents` is used to read in an entire file in one go. It will also read them from across the Internet if provided with a URL.

Question 7-8

The PHP associative array `$_FILES` contains the details about uploaded files.

Question 7-9

The PHP **exec** function enables the running of system commands.

Question 7-10

In XHTML 1.0, the tag `<input type=file name=file size=10>` should be replaced with the following correct syntax `<input type="file" name="file" size="10" />`, because all parameters must be quoted, and tags without closing tags must be self closed using `/>`.

Chapter 8 Answers

Question 8-1

The semicolon is used by MySQL to separate or end commands. If you forget to enter it, MySQL will issue a prompt and wait for you to enter it. (In the answers in this section, I've left off the semicolon, because it looks strange in the text. But it must terminate every statement.)

Question 8-2

To see the available databases, type `SHOW databases`. To see tables within a database that you are using, type `SHOW tables`. (These commands are case-insensitive.)

Question 8-3

To create this new user, use the `GRANT` command like this:

```
GRANT PRIVILEGES ON newdatabase.* TO 'newuser'
    IDENTIFIED BY 'newpassword';
```

Question 8-4

To view the structure of a table, type `DESCRIBE tablename`.

Question 8-5

The purpose of a MySQL index is to substantially decrease database access times by maintaining indexes of one or more key columns, which can then be quickly searched to locate rows within a table.

Question 8-6

A FULLTEXT index enables natural language queries to find keywords, wherever they are in the FULLTEXT column(s), in much the same way as using a search engine.

Question 8-7

A stopword is a word that is so common that it is considered not worth including in a FULLTEXT index or using in searches. However, it does participate in a search when it is part of a larger string bounded by double quotes.

Question 8-8

SELECT DISTINCT essentially affects only the display, choosing a single row and eliminating all the duplicates. GROUP BY does not eliminate rows, but combines all the rows that have the same value in the column. Therefore, GROUP BY is useful for performing an operation such as COUNT on groups of rows. SELECT DISTINCT is not useful for that purpose.

Question 8-9

To return only those rows containing the word *Langhorne* somewhere in the column *author* of the table *classics*, use a command such as:

```
SELECT * FROM classics WHERE author LIKE "%Langhorne%";
```

Question 8-10

When joining two tables together, they must share at least one common column such as an ID number or, as in the case of the *classics* and *customers* tables, the *isbn* column.

Question 8-11

To correct the years in the classics table you could issue the following three commands:

```
UPDATE classics SET year='1813' WHERE title='Pride and Prejudice';
UPDATE classics SET year='1859' WHERE title='The Origin of Species';
UPDATE classics SET year='1597' WHERE title='Romeo and Juliet';
```

Chapter 9 Answers

Question 9-1

The term *relationship* refers to the connection between two pieces of data that have some association, such as a book and its author, or a book and the customer who bought the book. A relational database such as MySQL specializes in storing and retrieving such relations.

Question 9-2

The process of removing duplicate data and optimizing tables is called *normalization*.

Question 9-3

The three rules of First Normal Form are: (1) There should be no repeating columns containing the same kind of data; (2) All columns should contain a single value; and (3) There should be a primary key to uniquely identify each row.

Question 9-4

To satisfy Second Normal Form, columns whose data repeats across multiple rows should be removed to their own tables.

Question 9-5

In a one-to-many relationship, the primary key from the table on the "one" side must be added as a separate column (a foreign key) to the table on the "many" side.

Question 9-6

To create a database with a many-to-many relationship, you create an intermediary table containing keys from two other tables. The other tables can then reference each other via the third.

Question 9-7

To initiate a MySQL transaction, use either the `BEGIN` or the `START TRANSACTION` command. To terminate a transaction and cancel all actions, issue a `ROLLBACK` command. To terminate a transaction and commit all actions, issue a `COMMIT` command.

Question 9-8

To examine how a query will work in detail, you can use the `EXPLAIN` command.

Question 9-9

To back up the database *publications* to a file called *publications.sql*, you would use a command such as:

```
mysqldump -u user -ppassword publications > publications.sql
```

Chapter 10 Answers

Question 10-1

The standard MySQL function used for connecting to a MySQL database is `mysql_connect`.

Question 10-2

The `mysql_result` function is not optimal when more than one cell is being requested, because it fetches only a single cell from a database and therefore has to be called multiple times, whereas `mysql_fetch_row` will fetch an entire row.

Question 10-3

The `POST` form method is generally better than `GET`, because the fields are posted directly, rather than appending them to the URL. This has several advantages, particularly in removing the possibility to enter spoof data at the browser's address bar. (It is not a complete defense against spoofing, however.)

Question 10-4

To determine the last entered value of an `AUTO_INCREMENT` column, use the `mysql_insert_id` function.

Question 10-5

The PHP function that escapes a string, making it suitable for use with MySQL, is `mysql_real_escape_string`.

Question 10-6

Cross Site Scripting injection attacks can be prevented using the function `htmlentities`.

Chapter 11 Answers

Question 11-1

The associative arrays used to pass submitted form data to PHP are `$_GET` for the `GET` method and `$_POST` for the `POST` method.

Question 11-2

The *register_globals* setting was the default in versions of PHP prior to 4.2.0. It was not a good idea, because it automatically assigned submitted form field data to PHP variables, thus opening up a security hole for potential hackers, who could attempt to break into PHP code by initializing variables to values of their choice.

Question 11-3

The difference between a text box and a text area is that although they both accept text for form input, a text box is a single line, whereas a text area can be multiple lines and include word wrapping.

Question 11-4

To offer three mutually exclusive choices in a web form, you should use radio buttons, because checkboxes allow multiple selections.

Question 11-5

Submit a group of selections from a web form using a single field name by using an array name with square brackets such as `choices[]`, instead of a regular field name. Each value is then placed into the array, whose length will be the number of elements submitted.

Question 11-6

To submit a form field without the user seeing it, place it in a hidden field using the parameter `type="hidden"`.

Question 11-7

You can encapsulate a form element and supporting text or graphics, making the entire unit selectable with a mouse-click, by using the `<label>` and `</label>` tags.

Question 11-8

To convert HTML into a format that can be displayed but will not be interpreted as HTML by a browser, use the PHP `htmlentities` function.

Chapter 12 Answers

Question 12-1

There are several benefits to using a templating system such as Smarty. They include but are not limited to:

- Separating the program code from the presentation layer.
- Preventing template editors from modifying program code.
- Removing the need for programmers to design page layout.
- Allowing the redesign of a web page without modifying any program code.
- Enabling multiple "skin" designs with little recourse to modifying program code.

Question 12-2

To pass a variable to a Smarty template, a PHP program uses the `$smarty->assign` function.

Question 12-3

Smarty templates access variables passed to them by prefacing them with a dollar sign $ and enclosing them with curly braces {}.

Question 12-4

To iterate through an array in a Smarty template, you use the opening `{section}` and closing `{/section}` tags.

Question 12-5

If Smarty has been installed, you can enable it in a PHP program by including the *Smarty.class.php* file from its correct location (normally in a folder called *Smarty*, just under the document root).

Chapter 13 Answers

Question 13-1

Cookies should be transferred before a web page's HTML, because they are sent as part of the headers.

Question 13-2

To store a cookie on a web browser, use the `set_cookie` function.

Question 13-3

To destroy a cookie, reissue it with `set_cookie` but set its expiration date in the past.

Question 13-4

Using HTTP authentication, the username and password are stored in `$_SERVER['PHP_AUTH_USER']` and `$_SERVER['PHP_AUTH_PW']`.

Question 13-5

The md5 function is a powerful security measure, because it is a one-way function that converts a string to a 32-character hexadecimal number that cannot be converted back, and is therefore almost uncrackable.

Question 13-6

When a string is salted, extra characters (known only by the programmer) are added to it before md5 conversion. This makes it nearly impossible for a brute force dictionary attack to succeed.

Question 13-7

A PHP session is a group of variables unique to the current user.

Question 13-8

To initiate a PHP session, use the `session_start` function.

Question 13-9

Session hijacking is where a hacker somehow discovers an existing session ID and attempts to take it over.

Question 13-10

Session fixation is the attempt to force your own session ID onto a server rather than letting it create its own.

Chapter 14 Answers

Question 14-1

To enclose JavaScript code, you use `<script>` and `</script>` tags.

Question 14-2

By default, JavaScript code will output to the part of the document in which it resides. If the head it will output to the head; if the body then the body.

Question 14-3

You can include JavaScript code from other source in your documents by either copying and pasting them or, more commonly, including them as part of a `<script src='filename.js'>` tag.

Question 14-4

The equivalent of the `echo` and `print` commands used in PHP is the JavaScript `document.write` function (or method).

Question 14-5

To create a comment in JavaScript, preface it with `//` for a single-line comment or surround it with `/*` and `*/` for a multiline comment.

Question 14-6

The JavaScript string concatenation operator is the + symbol.

Question 14-7

Within a JavaScript function, you can define a variable that has local scope by preceding it with the **var** keyword upon first assignment.

Question 14-8

To display the URL assigned to the link ID `thislink` in all main browsers, you can use the two following commands:

```
document.write(document.getElementById('thislink').href)
document.write(thislink.href)
```

Question 14-9

The commands to change to the previous page in the browser's history array are:

```
history.back()
history.go(-1)
```

Question 14-10

To replace the current document with the main page at the *oreilly.com* website, you could use the following command:

```
document.location.href = 'http://oreilly.com'
```

Chapter 15 Answers

Question 15-1

The most noticeable difference between Boolean values in PHP and JavaScript is that PHP recognizes the keywords TRUE, true, FALSE, and false, whereas only true and false are supported in JavaScript. Additionally, in PHP TRUE has a value of 1 and FALSE is NULL; in JavaScript they are represented by true and false, which can be returned as string values.

Question 15-2

Unlike PHP, no character is used (such as $) to define a JavaScript variable name. JavaScript variable names can start with and contain any uppercase and lowercase letters as well as underscores; names can also include digits, but not as the first character.

Question 15-3

The difference between unary, binary, and ternary operators is the number of operands each requires (one, two, and three, respectively).

Question 15-4

The best way to force your own operator precedence is to surround the parts of an expression to be evaluated first with parentheses.

Question 15-5

You use the identity operator when you wish to bypass JavaScript's automatic operand type changing.

Question 15-6

The simplest forms of expressions are literals (such as numbers and strings) and variables, which simply evaluate to themselves.

Question 15-7

The three conditional statement types are `if`, `switch`, and the ? operator.

Question 15-8

Most conditional expressions in `if` and `while` statements are literal or Boolean and therefore trigger execution when they evaluate to TRUE. Numeric expressions trigger execution when they evaluate to a nonzero value. String expressions trigger execution when they evaluate to a nonempty string. A NULL value is evaluated as false and therefore does not trigger execution.

Question 15-9

Loops using `for` statements are more powerful than `while` loops, because they support two additional parameters to control loop handling.

Question 15-10

The `with` statement takes an object as its parameter. Using it, you specify an object once, then for each statement within the `with` block, that object is assumed.

Chapter 16 Answers

Question 16-1

JavaScript functions and variable names are case-sensitive. The variables `Count`, `count`, and `COUNT` are all different.

Question 16-2

To write a function that accepts and processes an unlimited number of parameters, access parameters through the `arguments` array, which is a member of all functions.

Question 16-3

One way to return multiple values from a function is to place them all inside an array and return the array.

Question 16-4

When defining a class, use the `this` keyword to refer to the current object.

Question 16-5

The methods of a class do not have to be defined within a class definition. If a method is defined outside the constructor, the method name must be assigned to the `this` object within the class definition.

Question 16-6

New objects are created using the `new` keyword.

Question 16-7

A property or method can be made available to all objects in a class without replicating the property or method within the object by using the `prototype` keyword

---

to create a single instance, which is then passed by reference to all the objects in a class.

Question 16-8

To create a multidimensional array, place subarrays inside the main array.

Question 16-9

The syntax you would use to create an associative array is `key : value`, within curly braces, as in the following:

```
assocarray = {"forename" : "Paul", "surname" : "McCartney",
"group" : "Beatles"}
```

Question 16-10

A statement to sort an array of numbers into descending numerical order would look like this:

```
numbers.sort(function(a,b){return b - a})
```

Chapter 17 Answers

Question 17-1

You can send a form for validation prior to submitting it by adding the JavaScript `onSubmit` method to the `<form ...>` tag. Make sure that your function returns `true` if the form is to be submitted and `false` otherwise.

Question 17-2

To match a string against a regular expression in JavaScript, use the `test` method.

Question 17-3

Regular expressions to match characters not in a word could be any of `/[^\w]/`, `/[\W]/`, `/[^a-zA-Z0-9_]/`, and so on.

Question 17-4

A regular expression to match either of the words *fox* or *fix* could be `/f[oi]x/`.

Question 17-5

A regular expression to match any single word followed by any non-word character could be `/\w+\W/g`.

Question 17-6

A JavaScript function using regular expressions to test whether the word *fox* exists in the string "The quick brown fox" could be:

```
document.write(/fox/.test("The quick brown fox"))
```

Question 17-7

A PHP function using a regular expression to replace all occurrences of the word *the* in "The cow jumps over the moon" with the word *my* could be:

```
$s=preg_replace("/the/i", "my", "The cow jumps over the moon");
```

Question 17-8

The HTML keyword used to precomplete form fields with a value is the `value` keyword, which is placed within an `<input ...>` tag and takes the form `value="value"`.

Chapter 18 Answers

Question 18-1

It's necessary to write a function for creating new `XMLHTTPRequest` objects, because Microsoft browsers use two different methods of creating them, while all other major browsers use a third. By writing a function to test the browser in use, you can ensure that code will work on all major browsers.

Question 18-2

The purpose of the `try...catch` construct is to set an error trap for the code inside the `try` statement. If the code causes an error, the `catch` section will be executed instead of a general error being issued.

Question 18-3

An `XMLHTTPRequest` object has six properties and six methods (see Tables 18-1 and 18-2).

Question 18-4

You can tell that an Ajax call has completed when the `readyState` property of an object has a value of 4.

Question 18-5

When an Ajax call successfully completes, the object's `status` will have a value of 200.

Question 18-6

The `responseText` property of an `XMLHTTPRequest` object contains the value returned by a successful Ajax call.

Question 18-7

The `responseXML` property of an `XMLHTTPRequest` object contains a DOM tree created from the XML returned by a successful Ajax call.

Question 18-8

To specify a callback function to handle Ajax responses, assign the function name to the `XMLHTTPRequest` object's `onreadystatechange` property. You can also use an unnamed, inline function.

Question 18-9

To initiate an Ajax request, an `XMLHTTPRequest` object's `send` method is called.

Question 18-10

The main differences between an Ajax GET and POST request are that GET requests append the data to the URL and not as a parameter of the send method, and POST requests pass the data as a parameter of the send method and require the correct form headers to be sent first.

Chapter 19 Answers

Question 19-1

To implement an Ajax connection, YUI uses a method called asyncRequest, which is referenced as YAHOO.util.Connect.asyncRequest.

Question 19-2

A callback object called callback for YUI, referring to a success handler called succeeded and a failure handler called failed, would be written like this:

```
callback = { success:succeeded, failure:failed }
```

Question 19-3

A GET call to asyncRequest that refers to the program getdata.php and a callback object would look like this:

```
request = YAHOO.util.Connect.asyncRequest('GET', 'getdata.php', callback);
```

Question 19-4

To encode the URL *mysite.com/message?m=123*, which contains the ? symbol, so that if sent as a GET request, it will be treated just as a string and not interpreted, use the encodeURI method, like this:

```
url = encodeURI("mysite.com/message?m=123")
```

Online Resources

This appendix lists useful websites where you can get material used in this book, or other resources that will enhance your web programs.

PHP Resource Sites

- *http://codewalkers.com*
- *http://developer.yahoo.com/php/*
- *http://forums.devshed.com*
- *http://free-php.net*
- *http://hotscripts.com/category/php/*
- *http://htmlgoodies.com/beyond/php/*
- *http://php.net*
- *http://php.resourceindex.com*
- *http://php-editors.com*
- *http://phpbuilder.com*
- *http://phpfreaks.com*
- *http://phpunit.de*
- *http://w3schools.com/php/*
- *http://zend.com*

MySQL Resource Sites

- *http://code.google.com/edu/tools101/mysql.html*
- *http://launchpad.net/mysql/*
- *http://mysql.com*
- *http://php.net/mysql*
- *http://planetmysql.org*
- *http://sun.com/software/products/mysql/*
- *http://sun.com/systems/solutions/mysql/resources.jsp*
- *http://w3schools.com/PHP/php_mysql_intro.asp*

JavaScript Resource Sites

- *http://developer.mozilla.org/en/JavaScript*
- *http://dynamicdrive.com*
- *http://javascript.about.com*
- *http://javascript.internet.com*
- *http://javascript.com*
- *http://javascriptkit.com*
- *http://w3schools.com/JS/*
- *http://www.webreference.com/js/*

Ajax Resource Sites

- *http://ajax.asp.net*
- *http://ajaxian.com*
- *http://ajaxmatters.com*
- *http://developer.mozilla.org/en/AJAX*
- *http://dojotoolkit.org*
- *http://jquery.com*
- *http://mochikit.com*
- *http://mootools.net*
- *http://openjs.com*
- *http://prototypejs.org*

- *http://sourceforge.net/projects/clean-ajax*
- *http://w3schools.com/Ajax/*

Miscellaneous Resource Sites

- *http://apachefriends.org*
- *http://easyphp.org*
- *http://eclipse.org*
- *http://editra.org*
- *http://fireftp.mozdev.org*
- *http://sourceforge.net/projects/glossword/*
- *http://mamp.info/en/*
- *http://pear.php.net*
- *http://programmingforums.org*
- *http://putty.org*
- *http://smarty.net*
- *http://wampserver.com/en/*

O'Reilly Resource Sites

- *http://onlamp.com*
- *http://onlamp.com/php/*
- *http://onlamp.com/onlamp/general/mysql.csp*
- *http://oreilly.com/ajax/*
- *http://oreilly.com/javascript/*
- *http://oreilly.com/mysql/*
- *http://oreilly.com/php/*
- *http://oreillynet.com/javascript/*

MySQL's FULLTEXT Stopwords

This appendix contains the more than 500 *stopwords* referred to in the section "Using a FULLTEXT Index" in Chapter 7. Stopwords are words that are considered so common as to not be worth searching for, or storing, in a FULLTEXT index. Theoretically, ignoring these words makes little difference to the results of most FULLTEXT searches, but makes MySQL databases considerably smaller and more efficient. The words are shown here in lowercase but apply to uppercase and mixed-case versions, too:

A

a's, able, about, above, according, accordingly, across, actually, after, afterwards, again, against, ain't, all, allow, allows, almost, alone, along, already, also, although, always, am, among, amongst, an, and, another, any, anybody, anyhow, anyone, anything, anyway, anyways, anywhere, apart, appear, appreciate, appropriate, are, aren't, around, as, aside, ask, asking, associated, at, available, away, awfully

B

be, became, because, become, becomes, becoming, been, before, beforehand, behind, being, believe, below, beside, besides, best, better, between, beyond, both, brief, but, by

C

c'mon, c's, came, can, can't, cannot, cant, cause, causes, certain, certainly, changes, clearly, co, com, come, comes, concerning, consequently, consider, considering, contain, containing, contains, corresponding, could, couldn't, course, currently

D

definitely, described, despite, did, didn't, different, do, does, doesn't, doing, don't, done, down, downwards, during

E

each, edu, eg, eight, either, else, elsewhere, enough, entirely, especially, et, etc, even, ever, every, everybody, everyone, everything, everywhere, ex, exactly, example, except

F

far, few, fifth, first, five, followed, following, follows, for, former, formerly, forth, four, from, further, furthermore

G

get, gets, getting, given, gives, go, goes, going, gone, got, gotten, greetings

H

had, hadn't, happens, hardly, has, hasn't, have, haven't, having, he, he's, hello, help, hence, her, here, here's, hereafter, hereby, herein, hereupon, hers, herself, hi, him, himself, his, hither, hopefully, how, howbeit, however

I

i'd, i'll, i'm, i've, ie, if, ignored, immediate, in, inasmuch, inc, indeed, indicate, indicated, indicates, inner, insofar, instead, into, inward, is, isn't, it, it'd, it'll, it's, its, itself

J

just

K

keep, keeps, kept, know, knows, known

L

last, lately, later, latter, latterly, least, less, lest, let, let's, like, liked, likely, little, look, looking, looks, ltd

M

mainly, many, may, maybe, me, mean, meanwhile, merely, might, more, moreover, most, mostly, much, must, my, myself

N

name, namely, nd, near, nearly, necessary, need, needs, neither, never, nevertheless, new, next, nine, no, nobody, non, none, noone, nor, normally, not, nothing, novel, now, nowhere

O

obviously, of, off, often, oh, ok, okay, old, on, once, one, ones, only, onto, or, other, others, otherwise, ought, our, ours, ourselves, out, outside, over, overall, own

P

particular, particularly, per, perhaps, placed, please, plus, possible, presumably, probably, provides

Q

que, quite, qv

R

rather, rd, re, really, reasonably, regarding, regardless, regards, relatively, respectively, right

S

said, same, saw, say, saying, says, second, secondly, see, seeing, seem, seemed, seeming, seems, seen, self, selves, sensible, sent, serious, seriously, seven, several, shall, she, should, shouldn't, since, six, so, some, somebody, somehow, someone, something, sometime, sometimes, somewhat, somewhere, soon, sorry, specified, specify, specifying, still, sub, such, sup, sure

T

t's, take, taken, tell, tends, th, than, thank, thanks, thanx, that, that's, thats, the, their, theirs, them, themselves, then, thence, there, there's, thereafter, thereby, therefore, therein, theres, thereupon, these, they, they'd, they'll, they're, they've, think, third, this, thorough, thoroughly, those, though, three, through, throughout, thru, thus, to, together, too, took, toward, towards, tried, tries, truly, try, trying, twice, two

U

un, under, unfortunately, unless, unlikely, until, unto, up, upon, us, use, used, useful, uses, using, usually

V

value, various, very, via, viz, vs

W

want, wants, was, wasn't, way, we, we'd, we'll, we're, we've, welcome, well, went, were, weren't, what, what's, whatever, when, whence, whenever, where, where's, whereafter, whereas, whereby, wherein, whereupon, wherever, whether, which, while, whither, who, who's, whoever, whole, whom, whose, why, will, willing, wish, with, within, without, won't, wonder, would, would, wouldn't

Y

yes, yet, you, you'd, you'll, you're, you've, your, yours, yourself, yourselves

Z

zero

MySQL Functions

By having functions built into MySQL, the speed of performing complex queries is substantially reduced, as is their complexity. If you wish to learn more about the available functions you can visit the following URLs:

- String functions: *http://dev.mysql.com/doc/refman/5.0/en/string-functions.html*
- Date and time: *http://dev.mysql.com/doc/refman/5.0/en/date-and-time-functions.html*

But, for easy reference, here are some of the most commonly used MySQL functions.

String Functions

CONCAT()

CONCAT(*str1*, *str2*, ...)

Returns the result of concatenating *str1*, *str2*, and any other parameters (or NULL if any argument is NULL). If any of the arguments are binary, then the result is a binary string; otherwise, the result is a nonbinary string. The code returns the string "MySQL":

```
SELECT CONCAT('My', 'S', 'QL');
```

CONCAT_WS()

CONCAT_WS(*separator*, *str1*, *str2*, ...)

This works in the same way as CONCAT except it inserts a separator between the items being concatenated. If the separator is NULL the result will be NULL, but NULL values can be used as other arguments, which will then be skipped. This code returns the string "Truman,Harry,S":

```
SELECT CONCAT_WS(',' 'Truman', 'Harry', 'S');
```

LEFT()

LEFT(*str*, *len*)

Returns the leftmost *len* characters from the string *str* (or NULL if any argument is NULL). The following code returns the string "Chris":

```
SELECT LEFT('Christopher Columbus', '5');
```

RIGHT()

RIGHT(*str*, *len*)

Returns the rightmost *len* characters from the string *str* (or NULL if any argument is NULL). This code returns the string "Columbus":

```
SELECT RIGHT('Christopher Columbus', '8');
```

MID()

MID(*str*, *pos*, *len*)

Returns up to *len* characters from the string *str* starting at position *pos*. If *len* is omitted, then all characters up to the end of the string are returned. You may use a negative value for *pos*, in which case it represents the character *pos* places from the end of the string. The first position in the string is 1. This code returns the string "stop":

```
SELECT MID('Christopher Columbus', '6', '4');
```

LENGTH()

LENGTH(*str*)

Returns the length in bytes of the string *str*. Note that multibyte characters count as multiple bytes. If you need to know the actual number of characters in a string use the CHAR_LENGTH function. This code returns the value 10:

```
SELECT LENGTH('Tony Blair');
```

LPAD()

LPAD(*str*, *len*, *padstr*)

Returns the string *str* padded to a length of *len* characters by prepending the string with *padstr* characters. If *str* is longer than *len* then the string returned will be truncated to *len* characters. The example code returns the following strings:

```
January
February
```

```
      March
      April
        May
```

Notice how all the strings have been padded to be eight characters long.

```
SELECT LPAD('January', '8', ' ');
SELECT LPAD('February', '8', ' ');
SELECT LPAD('March', '8', ' ');
SELECT LPAD('April', '8', ' ');
SELECT LPAD('May', '8', ' ');
```

RPAD

RPAD(*str*, *len*, *padstr*)

This is the same as the LPAD function except that the padding takes place on the right of the returned string. This code returns the string "Hi!!!":

```
SELECT RPAD('Hi', '5', '!');
```

LOCATE()

LOCATE(*substr*, *str*, *pos*)

Returns the position of the first occurrence of *substr* in the string *str*. If the parameter *pos* is passed, the search begins at position *pos*. If *substr* is not found in *str*, a value of zero is returned. This code returns the values 5 and 11, because the first function call returns the first encounter of the word "unit", while the second one only starts to search at the seventh character, and so returns the second instance:

```
SELECT LOCATE('unit', 'Community unit');
SELECT LOCATE('unit', 'Community unit' 7);
```

LOWER()

LOWER(*str*)

This is the inverse of UPPER. Returns the string *str* with all the characters changed to lowercase. This code returns the string "queen elizabeth ii":

```
SELECT LOWER('Queen Elizabeth II');
```

UPPER()

UPPER(*str*)

This is the inverse of LOWER. It returns the string *str* with all the characters changed to upper-case. This code returns the string "I CAN'T HELP SHOUTING":

```
SELECT UPPER('I can't help shouting');
```

QUOTE()

QUOTE(*str*)

Returns a quoted string that can be used as a properly escaped value in a SQL statement. The returned string is enclosed in single quotes with all instances of single quotes, backslashes, the ASCII NUL character, and Control-Z preceded by a backslash. If the argument *str* is NULL, the return value is the word NULL without enclosing quotes. The example code returns the following string:

```
'I\'m hungry'
```

Note how the " symbol has been replaced with \".

```
SELECT QUOTE("I'm hungry");
```

REPEAT()

REPEAT(*str*, *count*)

Returns a string comprising *count* copies of the string *str*. If *count* is less than 1, an empty string is returned. If either parameter is NULL then NULL is returned. This code returns the strings "Ho Ho Ho" and "Merry Christmas":

```
SELECT REPEAT('Ho', 3), 'Merry Christmas';
```

REPLACE()

REPLACE(*str*, *from*, *to*)

Returns the string *str* with all occurrences of the string *from* replaced with the string *to*. The search and replace is case-sensitive when searching for *from*. This code returns the string "Cheeseburger and Coke":

```
SELECT REPLACE('Cheeseburger and Fries', 'Fries', 'Coke');
```

TRIM()

TRIM([*specifier remove* FROM] *str*)

Returns the string *str* with all remove prefixes or suffixes removed. The *specifier* can be one of BOTH, LEADING, or TRAILING. If no *specifier* is supplied, then BOTH is assumed. The *remove* string is optional and, if omitted, spaces are removed. This code returns the strings "No Padding" and "Hello__":

```
SELECT TRIM('   No Padding   ');
SELECT TRIM(LEADING '_' FROM '__Hello__');
```

LTRIM() and RTRIM()

LTRIM(*str*)

RTRIM(*str*)

The function RTRIM returns the string *str* with any leading spaces removed, while the function RTRIM performs the same action on the string's tail. This code returns the strings "No Padding " and " No Padding":

```
SELECT LTRIM('   No Padding   ');
SELECT RTRIM('   No Padding   ');
```

Date Functions

Dates are an important part of most databases. Whenever financial transactions take place, the date has to be recorded, expiry dates of credit cards need to be noted for repeat billing purposes, and so on. So, as you might expect, MySQL comes with a wide variety of functions to make handling dates a breeze.

CURDATE()

CURDATE()

Returns the current date in YYYY-MM-DD or YYYMMDD format, depending on whether the function is used in a numeric or string context. On the date May 2, 2010, the following code returns the values 2010-05-02 and 20100502:

```
SELECT CURDATE();
SELECT CURDATE() + 0;
```

DATE()

DATE(*expr*)

Extracts the date part of the date for a DATETIME expression *expr*. This code returns the value "1961-05-02":

```
SELECT DATE('1961-05-02 14:56:23');
```

DATE_ADD()

DATE_ADD(*date*, INTERVAL *expr unit*)

Returns the result of adding the expression *expr* using units *unit* to the *date*. The *date* argument is the starting date or DATETIME value and *expr* may start with a - symbol for negative intervals. Table D-1 shows the interval types supported and the expected *expr* values. Note the examples in this table that show where it is necessary to surround the *expr* value with quotes for MySQL to correctly interpret them. Although if you are ever in doubt, adding the quotes will always work.

Table D-1. Expected expr values

Type	Expected expr value	Example
MICROSECOND	MICROSECONDS	111111
SECOND	SECONDS	11
MINUTE	MINUTES	11
HOUR	HOURS	11
DAY	DAYS	11
WEEK	WEEKS	11
MONTH	MONTHS	11
QUARTER	QUARTERS	1
YEAR	YEARS	11
SECOND_MICROSECOND	'SECONDS.MICROSECONDS'	11.22
MINUTE_MICROSECOND	'MINUTES.MICROSECONDS'	11.22
MINUTE_SECOND	'MINUTES:SECONDS'	'11:22'
HOUR_MICROSECOND	'HOURS.MICROSECONDS'	11.22
HOUR_SECOND	'HOURS:MINUTES:SECONDS'	'11:22:33'
HOUR_MINUTE	'HOURS:MINUTES'	'11:22'
DAY_MICROSECOND	'DAYS.MICROSECONDS'	11.22
DAY_SECOND	'DAYS HOURS:MINUTES:SECONDS'	'11 22:33:44'
DAY_MINUTE	'DAYS HOURS:MINUTES'	'11 22:33'
DAY_HOUR	'DAYS HOURS'	'11 22'
YEAR_MONTH	'YEARS-MONTHS'	'11-2'

You can also use the DATE_SUB function to subtract date intervals. However it's not actually necessary for you to use the DATE_ADD or DATE_SUB functions, as you can use date arithmetic directly in MySQL. This code:

```
SELECT DATE_ADD('1975-01-01', INTERVAL 77 DAY);
SELECT DATE_SUB('1982-07-04', INTERVAL '3-11' YEAR_MONTH);
SELECT '2010-12-31 23:59:59' + INTERVAL 1 SECOND;
SELECT '2000-01-01' - INTERVAL 1 SECOND;
```

returns the following values:

```
1975-03-19
1978-08-04
```

```
2011-01-01 00:00:00
1999-12-31 23:59:59
```

Notice how the last two commands use direct date arithmetic without recourse to functions.

DATE_FORMAT()

DATE_FORMAT(*date*, *format*)

This returns the *date* value formatted according to the *format* string. Table D-2 shows the specifiers that can be used in the *format* string. Note that the % character is required before each specifier, as shown. This code returns the given date and time as "Thursday May 4th 2006 03:02 AM":

```
SELECT DATE_FORMAT('2006-05-04 03:02:01', '%W %M %D %Y %h:%i %p');
```

Table D-2. DATE_FORMAT specifiers

Specifier	Description
%a	Abbreviated weekday name (Sun–Sat)
%b	Abbreviated month name (Jan–Dec)
%c	Month, numeric (0–12)
%D	Day of the month with English suffix (0th, 1st, 2nd, 3rd, ...)
%d	Day of the month, numeric (00–31)
%e	Day of the month, numeric (0–31)
%f	Microseconds (000000–999999)
%H	Hour (00–23)
%h	Hour (01–12)
%I	Hour (01–12)
%i	Minutes, numeric (00–59)
%j	Day of year (001–366)
%k	Hour (0–23)
%l	Hour (1–12)
%M	Month name (January–December)
%m	Month, numeric (00–12)
%p	AM or PM
%r	Time, 12-hour (hh:mm:ss followed by AM or PM)
%S	Seconds (00–59)
%s	Seconds (00–59)
%T	Time, 24-hour (hh:mm:ss)

Specifier	Description
%U	Week (00–53), where Sunday is the first day of the week
%u	Week (00–53), where Monday is the first day of the week
%V	Week (01–53), where Sunday is the first day of the week; used with %X
%v	Week (01–53), where Monday is the first day of the week; used with %x
%W	Weekday name (Sunday–Saturday)
%w	Day of the week (0=Sunday–6=Saturday)
%X	Year for the week where Sunday is the first day of the week, numeric, four digits; used with %V
%x	Year for the week, where Monday is the first day of the week, numeric, four digits; used with %v
%Y	Year, numeric, four digits
%y	Year, numeric, two digits
%%	A literal % character

DAY()

DAY(*date*)

Returns the day of the month for *date*, in the range 1 to 31 or 0 for dates that have a zero day part such as "0000-00-00" or "2010-00-00". You can also use the function DAYOFMONTH to return the same value. This code returns the value 3:

```
SELECT DAY('2001-02-03');
```

DAYNAME()

DAYNAME(*date*)

Returns the name of the weekday for the *date*. This code returns the string "Saturday":

```
SELECT DAYNAME('2001-02-03');
```

DAYOFWEEK()

DAYOFWEEK(*date*)

Returns the weekday index for *date* between 1 for Sunday through 7 for Saturday. This code returns the value 7:

```
SELECT DAYOFWEEK('2001-02-03');
```

DAYOFYEAR()

DAYOFYEAR(*date*)

Returns the day of the year for *date* in the range 1 to 366. This code returns the value 34:

```
SELECT DAYOFYEAR('2001-02-03');
```

LAST_DAY()

LAST_DAY(*date*)

Returns the last day of the month for the given DATETIME value *date*. If the argument is invalid it returns NULL. This code:

```
SELECT LAST_DAY('2011-02-03');
SELECT LAST_DAY('2011-03-11');
SELECT LAST_DAY('2011-04-26');
```

returns the following values:

```
2011-02-28
2011-03-31
2011-04-30
```

As you'd expect, it correctly returns the 28th day of February, the 31st of March, and the 30th of April 2011.

MAKEDATE()

MAKEDATE(*year, dayofyear*)

Returns a date given *year* and *dayofyear* values. If *dayofyear* is zero, the result is NULL. This code returns the date "2011-10-01":

```
SELECT MAKEDATE(2011,274);
```

MONTH()

MONTH(*date*)

Returns the month for *date* in the range 1 through 12 for January through December. Dates that have a zero month part, such as "0000-00-00" or "2012-00-00", return zero. This code returns the value 7:

```
SELECT MONTH('2012-07-11');
```

MONTHNAME()

MONTHNAME(*date*)

Returns the full name of the month for *date*. This code returns the string "July":

```
SELECT MONTHNAME('2012-07-11');
```

SYSDATE()

```
SYSDATE()
```

Returns the current date and time as a value in either YYYY-MM-DD HH:MM:SS or YYYYMMDDHHMMSS format, depending on whether the function is used in a string or numeric context. The function NOW works in a similar manner, except that it returns the time and date only at the start of the current statement, whereas SYSDATE returns the time and date at the exact moment the function itself is called. On December 19, 2011, this code returns the values 2011-12-19 19:11:13 and 20111219191113:

```
SELECT SYSDATE();
SELECT SYSDATE() + 0;
```

YEAR()

```
YEAR(date)
```

Returns the year for *date* in the range 1000 to 9999, or 0 for the zero date. This code returns the year 1999:

```
SELECT YEAR('1999-08-07');
```

WEEK()

```
WEEK(date [, mode])
```

Returns the week number for *date*. If passed the optional *mode* parameter, the week number returned will be modified according to Table D-3. You can also use the function WEEKOFYEAR, which is equivalent to using the WEEK function with a *mode* of 3. This code returns the week number 14:

```
SELECT WEEK('2006-04-04', 1);
```

Table D-3. The modes supported by the WEEK function

Mode	First day of week	Range	Where week 1 is the first week ...
0	Sunday	0–53	with a Sunday in this year
1	Monday	0–53	with more than 3 days this year
2	Sunday	1–53	with a Sunday in this year
3	Monday	1–53	with more than 3 days this year
4	Sunday	0–53	with more than 3 days this year
5	Monday	0–53	with a Monday in this year
6	Sunday	1–53	with more than 3 days this year
7	Monday	1–53	with a Monday in this year

WEEKDAY()

WEEKDAY(*date*)

Returns the weekday index for *date* where 0=Monday through 6=Sunday. This code returns the value 1:

```
SELECT WEEKDAY('2006-04-04');
```

Time Functions

Sometimes you need to work with the time, rather than the date, and MySQL provides plenty of functions for you to do so.

CURTIME()

CURTIME()

Returns the current time as a value in the format HH:MM::SS or HHMMSS.uuuuuu, depending on whether the function is used in a string or numeric context. The value is expressed using the current time zone. When the current time is 11:56:23, this code returns the values 11:56:23 and 11:56:23.000000:

```
SELECT CURTIME() + 0;
```

HOUR()

HOUR(*time*)

Returns the hour for *time*. This code returns the value 11:

```
SELECT HOUR('11:56:23');
```

MINUTE()

MINUTE(*time*)

Returns the minute for *time*. This code returns the value 56:

```
SELECT MINUTE('11:56:23');
```

SECOND()

SECOND(*time*)

Returns the second for *time*. This code returns the value 23:

```
SELECT SECOND('11:56:23');
```

MAKETIME()

MAKETIME(*hour, minute, second*)

Returns a time value calculated from the *hour*, *minute*, and *second* arguments. This code returns the time 11:56:23:

```
SELECT MAKETIME(11, 56, 23);
```

TIMEDIFF()

TIMEDIFF(*expr1, expr2*)

Returns the difference between *expr1* and *expr2* (*expr1 – expr2*) as a time value. Both *expr1* and *expr2* must be TIME or DATETIME expressions of the same type. This code returns the value 01:37:38:

```
SELECT TIMEDIFF('2000-01-01 01:02:03', '1999-12-31 23:24:25');
```

UNIX_TIMESTAMP()

UNIX_TIMESTAMP([*date*])

If called without the optional *date* argument, this function returns the number of seconds since 1970-01-01 00:00:00 UTC as an unsigned integer. If the *date* parameter is passed, then the value returned is the number of seconds since the 1970 start date until the given date. This code will return the value 946684800 (the number of seconds up to the start of the new millennium) followed by a TIMESTAMP representing the current Unix time at the moment you run it:

```
SELECT UNIX_TIMESTAMP('2000-01-01');
SELECT UNIX_TIMESTAMP();
```

FROM_UNIXTIME()

FROM_UNIXTIME(*unix_timestamp* [, *format*])

Returns the *unix_timestamp* parameter as either a string in YYYY-MM-DD HH:MM:SS or YYYYMMDDHHMMSS.uuuuuu format, depending on whether the function is used in a string or numeric context. If the optional *format* parameter is provided, the result is formatted according to the specifiers in Table 8-17. This code returns the strings "2000-01-01 00:00:00" and "Saturday January 1st 2000 12:00 AM":

```
SELECT FROM_UNIXTIME(946684800);
SELECT FROM_UNIXTIME(946684800, '%W %M %D %Y %h:%i %p');
```

Using PEAR and PHPUnit

If you're going to use PHP as a web development language, why not make use of the wealth of packages that have already been written for it? The community has turned out in force to write an enormous amount of add-ons, a whole host of which have been combined in PEAR (the PHP Extension and Application Repository). Among these submissions is MDB2, a powerful package that makes it easier to access MySQL. Table E-1 lists some of the PEAR packages.

Table E-1. Categories of PEAR packages (number in each category)

Authentication (8)	Filesystem (5)	Math (19)	Streams (2)
Caching (2)	Gtk Components (4)	Networking (55)	Structures (30)
Console (7)	Gtk2 Components (7)	Numbers (2)	System (8)
Database (31)	HTML (40)	Payment (4)	Text (19)
Date and Time (22)	HTTP (14)	PEAR (18)	Tools & Utilities (9)
Encryption (13)	Images (19)	PEAR Website (5)	Validate (29)
Event (2)	Internationalization (6)	PHP (20)	Web Services (40)
File Formats (33)	Mail (8)	Semantic Web (5)	XML (32)

Installation

Installation of PEAR will vary according to which operating system you are using. A Linux/Unix machine (especially if XAMPP has been installed on it as described in Chapter 2) will generally be ready to go after issuing just a couple of commands. But Windows and Mac OS X require a little more work.

Windows

The EasyPHP setup that you installed in Chapter 2 comes packaged with a version of PEAR that you can install by selecting Start→Programs→Accessories and then right-clicking on the Command Prompt and choosing the "Run as Administrator" option. You must have administrative privileges to install PEAR.

Now navigate to *C:\Program Files\EasyPHP 3.0\php*, then run the batch file *go-pear.bat* by typing the following (and then pressing Return):

```
go-pear
```

During installation, accept the defaults by pressing Return whenever you're asked to do something. Figure E-1 shows the installation process.

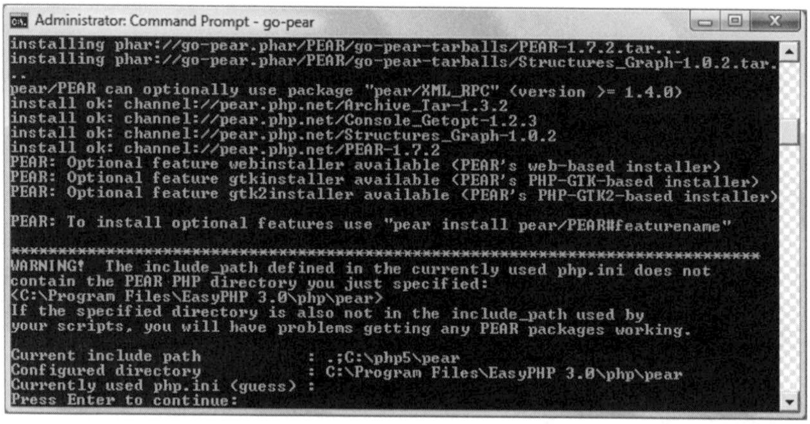

Figure E-1. Installing PEAR on Windows

Next you need to install PEAR's database helper package, called MDB2, by typing in the following (see Figure E-2):

```
pear install MDB2
```

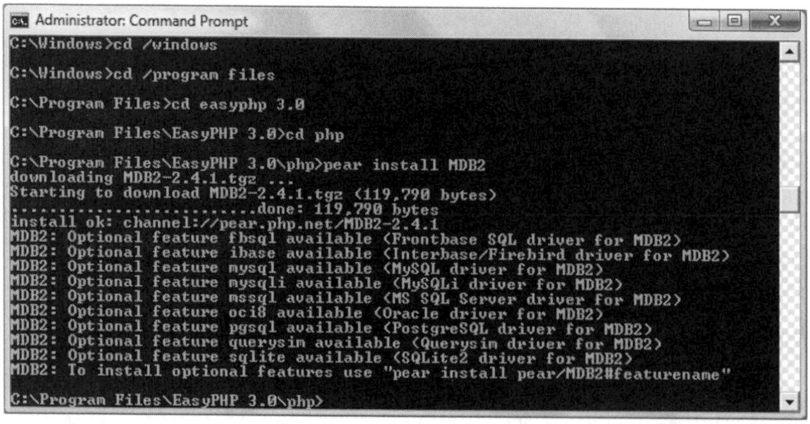

Figure E-2. Installing the PEAR MDB2 package

To finish your installation, install the MDB2 add-on driver that understands how to interact with MySQL. To do this, type in the following (see Figure E-3):

```
pear install -f MDB2_Driver_mysql
```

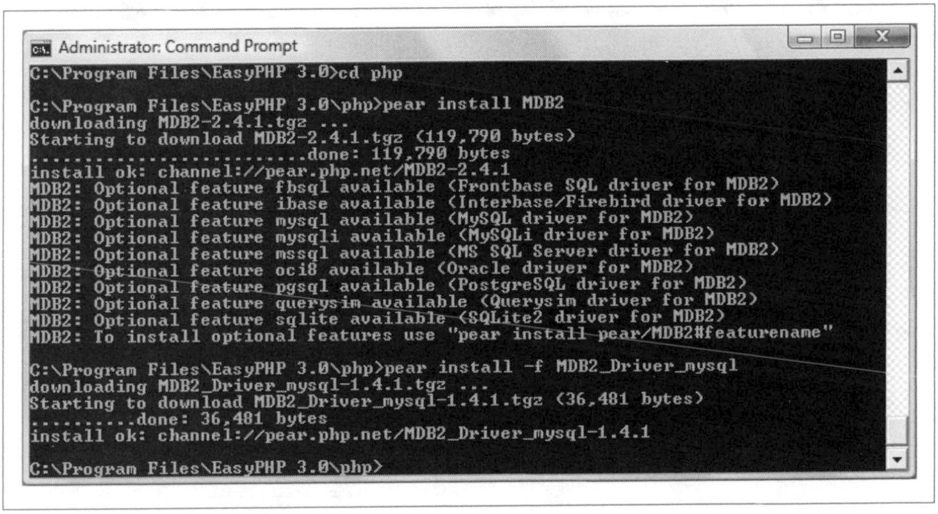

Figure E-3. Installing the PEAR MySQL MDB2 driver

If you receive an error message at any point from a pop-up window that says "Invalid configuration directive" while installing PEAR or MDB2, you should be able to safely ignore it by clicking the OK button.

Finally, as there appears to be a problem with file and path locations in EasyPHP 3.0, you need to type the following command to copy the PEAR files to a location where they can be found by PHP:

```
xcopy /E pear\*.* includes
```

Mac OS

Most Macs come supplied with a version of PEAR, but often it's out of date. The safest bet is to ensure that you have the latest version by visiting *http://pear.php.net/go-pear* in your browser and then using Save As to save the file that loads into your browser as *go-pear.php* in your MAMP *htdocs* folder. Once saved, ensure that you have MAMP running and enter the following into your browser's address bar:

```
http://localhost/go-pear.php
```

Now all you have to do is click on the Next >> button to see the main installation screen (see Figure E-4). Ensure that the MDB2 checkbox is checked and then edit the Installation prefix field to read:

```
/Applications/MAMP
```

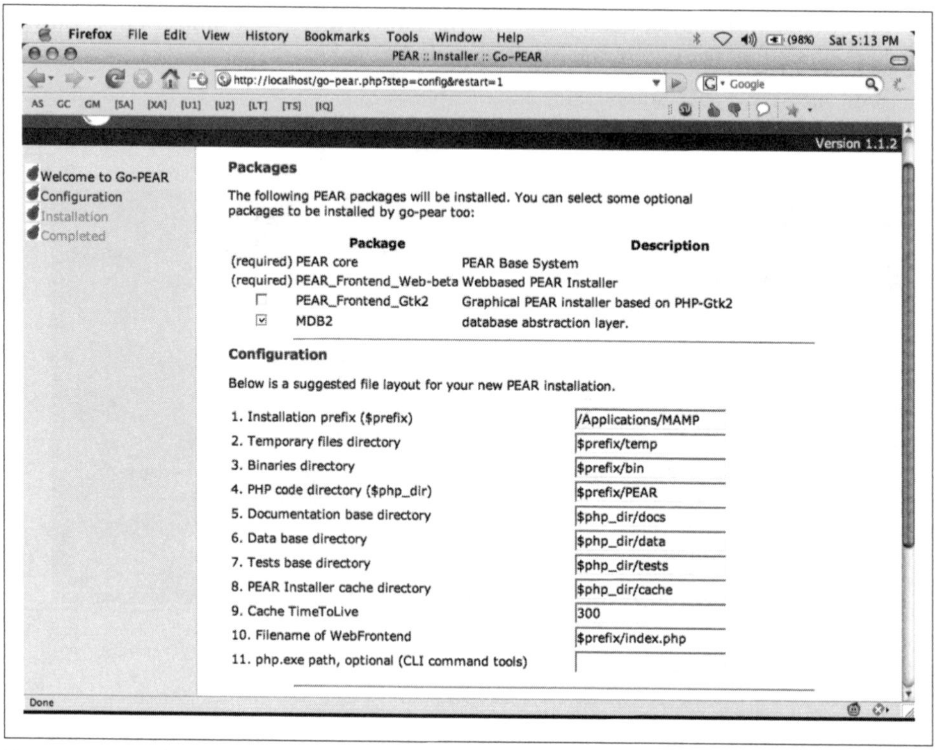

Figure E-4. Installing Pear and MDB2

Finally, scroll to the bottom of the page and click the Install button. You can now sit back and watch the installation as it progresses.

Once the installation completes, you will need to add the PEAR installation path to your include path. To do this, open up the file */Applications/MAMP/conf/php5/ php.ini* in a text or program editor and locate the line that reads:

```
include_path = ".:/Applications/MAMP/bin/PHP5/lip/php"
```

Now change the string after `include_path` = to read:

```
".:/Applications/MAMP/bin/PHP5/lip/php:/Applications/MAMP/PEAR"
```

Once you have done this, pull up the MAMP control panel and stop and restart the servers. If prompted, you may also have to enter your Mac password, too.

The last part of the installation involves downloading and adding the MySQL driver to PEAR. To do this, call up the Terminal and type the following. The output on the Terminal will look like Figure E-5.

```
/Applications/MAMP/bin/pear install MDB2_Driver_mysql
```

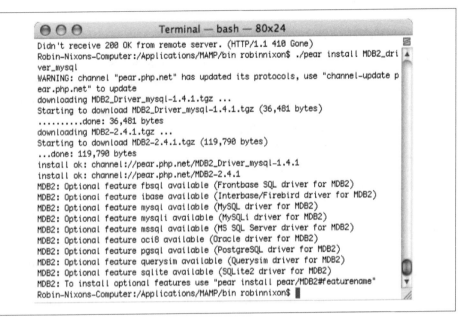

Figure E-5. Installing the PEAR MySQL MDB2 driver

Linux/Unix

If you installed the XAMPP package in Chapter 2, you already have PEAR installed. However, you will need to install the MDB2 database access package and the MySQL driver for it. To do this, you should need to issue only the following two commands:

```
pear install MDB2
pear install MDB2_Driver_mysql
```

Creating a Connect Instance

With all of PEAR, the MDB2 package, and the MySQL driver installed, you can start to take advantage of these new additions. But to do so, you need to understand what MDB2 is providing you with: a layer of abstraction.

In other words, MDB2 knows everything about accessing any major brand of database program you may have installed. You simply use a common set of commands and tell MDB2 which database to access. This means you can migrate to another SQL database such as PostgreSQL and will only have to install the new MDB2 driver and change a single line of code in your PHP file to be up and running again.

You connect to a MySQL database using MDB2 with code such as the following, where $db_username and the other $db_ variables have already been read in from the *login.php* file:

```
require_once 'MDB2.php';

$dsn  = "$db_username:$db_password@$db_hostname/$db_database";
$mdb2 = MDB2::connect("mysql://$dsn");
```

The require_once line loads MDB2. In the next line, the variable $dsn stands for *data source name* and is an identifier for the database. It comprises *username:password@hostname/database*. The variable $mdb2 is an object returned by calling the connect method within the MDB2 class. Recall that as mentioned in Chapter 5, the double colon (::) token indicates a class to be used on the left and a method to call from that class to the right.

The full string passed to the connect method is as follows:

```
mysql://username:password@hostname/database
```

The *mysql://* at the head of the string identifies the MDB2 driver to use and hence the type of database to access. If, for example, you were using a PostgreSQL database you would replace the head with *pgsql://*. The possible database types supported (as long as you install the drivers) are *fbsql*, *ibase*, *mssql*, *mysql*, *mysqli*, *oci8*, *pgsql*, *querysim*, and *sqlite*.

To check whether the program successfully connected to the database, you can issue a call to the PEAR isError method, like this:

```
if (PEAR::isError($mdb2))
    die("Unable to connect to MySQL: " . $mdb2->getMessage());
```

Here the $mdb2 object is passed to the isError method, which returns TRUE if there is an error. In that case the die function is called, and an error message is issued before calling the getMessage method from within the $mdb2 object to output the last message, describing the error encountered.

Querying

Once you have an MDB2 object in $mdb2, you can use it to query the database. Instead of calling the mysql_query function, call the query method of the $mdb2 object as follows (assuming that the variable $query has already been assigned a query string):

```
$result = $mdb2->query($query);
```

Fetching a Row

The variable $result, returned by the query method, is another object. To fetch a row from the database, just call the object's fetchRow method like this:

```
$row = $result->fetchRow();
```

You can also determine the number of rows in $result using the numRows method like this:

```
$rows = $result->numRows();
```

Closing a Connection

To close an MDB2 database connection, call the disconnect method of the $mdb2 object:

```
$mdb2->disconnect();
```

Rewriting Example 10-8 to Use PEAR

Hopefully you now have the hang of this new object-oriented approach to accessing MySQL. So let's look at how the *sqltest.php* program in Example 10-8 can be rewritten using PEAR's MDB2 package (see Example E-1, *sqltest_mdb2.php*).

Example E-1. Inserting and deleting using MDB2: sqltest_mdb2.php

```php
<?php // sqltest_mdb2.php
require_once 'login.php';
require_once 'MDB2.php';

$dsn = "mysql://$db_username:$db_password@$db_hostname/$db_database";
$options = array('debug' => 2);
$mdb2 = MDB2::connect($dsn,$options);

if (PEAR::isError($mdb2))
    die("Unable to connect to MySQL: " . $mdb2->getMessage());

if (isset($_POST['author']) &&
    isset($_POST['title']) &&
    isset($_POST['category']) &&
    isset($_POST['year']) &&
    isset($_POST['isbn']))
{
    $author   = get_post('author');
    $title    = get_post('title');
    $category = get_post('category');
    $year     = get_post('year');
    $isbn     = get_post('isbn');

    if (isset($_POST['delete']) && $isbn != "")
    {
        $query = "DELETE FROM classics WHERE isbn='$isbn'";

        if (!$mdb2->query($query))
            echo "DELETE failed: $query<br />" .
            $mdb2->getMessage() . "<br /><br />";
    }
    else
    {
        $query = "INSERT INTO classics VALUES" .
        "('$author', '$title', '$category', '$year', '$isbn')";

        if (!$mdb2->query($query))
            echo "INSERT failed: $query<br />" .
            $mdb2->getMessage() . "<br /><br />";
    }
```

```
}

echo <<<_END
<form action="sqltest_mdb2.php" method="post"><pre>
  Author <input type="text" name="author" />
   Title <input type="text" name="title"/ >
Category <input type="text" name="category" />
    Year <input type="text" name="year" />
    ISBN <input type="text" name="isbn" />
         <input type="submit" value="ADD RECORD" />
</pre></form>
_END;

$query = "SELECT * FROM classics";
$result = $mdb2->query($query);

if (!$result)     die ("Database access failed: " . $mdb2->getMessage());
$rows = $result->numRows();

for ($j = 0 ; $j < $rows ; ++$j)
{
    $row = $result->fetchRow();
    echo <<<_END
<pre>
  Author $row[0]
   Title $row[1]
Category $row[2]
    Year $row[3]
    ISBN $row[4]
</pre>
<form action="sqltest_mdb2.php" method="post">
<input type="hidden" name="delete" value="yes" />
<input type="hidden" name="isbn" value="$row[4]" />
<input type="submit" value="DELETE RECORD" /></form>
_END;
}

$mdb2->disconnect();

function get_post($var)
{
    return mysql_real_escape_string(@$_POST[$var]);
}
?>
```

Looking through this code, you should see that very little has been changed from the
nonobject-oriented version of the program, other than replacing the database accessing
functions with calls to methods contained within the $mdb2 object, and objects returned
from them. The differences have been highlighted in bold.

I recommend that you try modifying *sqltest.php* for yourself to use MDB2, as in the
example, and then save it as *sqltest_mdb2.php* to test it.

Using PEAR, you can save yourself a considerable amount of work, but if you still prefer not to use it, at least you will now recognize PEAR packages when you see them used in other programs and will know how to work with them.

Adding Other PEAR Packages

With PEAR properly installed on your system, you are able to install additional packages from the command line by using one of the commands in Table E-2, where *package* is the name of a PEAR package, as listed at the web page *http://pear.php.net/packages.php*.

Table E-2. Installing PEAR packages on different systems

System	Command
Windows	`"C:\Program Files\EasyPHP 3.0\php\pear" install package`
Mac OS X	`/Applications/MAMP/bin/pear install package`
Linux Unix	`pear install package`

To determine which packages are installed, replace `install package` in Table E-2 with the word `list` and the output should be similar to the following:

```
INSTALLED PACKAGES, CHANNEL PEAR.PHP.NET:
=========================================
PACKAGE            VERSION STATE
Archive_Tar        1.3.2   stable
Console_Getopt     1.2.3   stable
MDB2               2.4.1   stable
MDB2_Driver_mysql  1.4.1   stable
PEAR               1.7.2   stable
Structures_Graph   1.0.2   stable
```

Unit Testing with PHPUnit

Now that you are familiar with object-oriented programming, it's a good idea to get a taste of *unit testing*. This is a method of code testing that verifies whether individual units of source code are working correctly.

Unit testing provides the following benefits:

- It allows for automation of the testing process.
- It reduces the difficulty of discovering errors within more complex code.
- Testing is often enhanced because attention is given to each unit.

Install PHPUnit with the PEAR installer. To do this, go to a Command or Terminal prompt, ensure that you have Administrator or Superuser privileges, and issue the two lines of code in Table E-3, according to your operating system. (On Windows systems, ignore and close any pop-up "Invalid configuration directive" alerts that may appear.)

Table E-3. Commands for Installing PHPUnit on different systems

System	Instructions to type from an Administrator Command prompt or a Terminal window
XP/Vista	`cd \Program Files\EasyPHP 3.0\php`
(4 instructions)	`pear channel-discover pear.phpunit.de`
	`pear install phpunit/PHPUnit`
	`Xcopy /E pear\*.* includes`
Mac OS X	`cd /Applications/MAMP/bin`
(3 instructions)	`pear channel-discover pear.phpunit.de`
	`pear install phpunit/PHPUnit`
Linux/Unix	`pear channel-discover pear.phpunit.de`
(2 instructions)	`pear install phpunit/PHPUnit`

The two main commands register the PEAR channel on your system, download PHPUnit, and install it. On Windows, you need the additional XCOPY command to resolve a file and path bug in EasyPHP 3.0. Press the A key if prompted to "Overwrite (Yes/No/All)?".

You are then ready to take on some powerful bug testing. But first, let's look at how you might perform testing without PHPUnit. So, for example, consider the case of testing PHP's in-built `array` and the function `sizeof` and its alias `count`. For a newly created array, `sizeof` should return a value of 0 and then increase by 1 for every new element added, as in Example E-2.

Example E-2. Testing array and sizeof

```
$names = array();
echo sizeof($names) . "<br />";
$names[] = 'Bob';
echo count($names) . "<br />";  // count is an alias of sizeof
```

As you would expect, the output from this code is:

```
0
1
```

In Example E-3, this code is expanded to support automatic interpretation by writing the comparison of the expected and actual values, outputting "OK" if the value is correct and "Not OK" if it isn't.

Example E-3. Modified Example E-2 to output OK/Not OK

```
$names = array();
echo sizeof($names) == 0 ? "OK<br />" : "Not OK<br />";
$names[] = 'Bob';
echo sizeof($names) == 1 ? "OK<br />" : "Not OK<br />";
```

Helpful as this code is, there's an even better way to handle errors, which is to display a message only when a value is incorrect. Example E-4 uses function `assertTrue` to do this by throwing an exception.

Example E-4. Modified Example E-2 to throw an exception

```
$names = array();
assertTrue(sizeof($names) == 0);
$names[] = 'Bob';
assertTrue(sizeof($names) == 1);

function assertTrue($condition)
{
    if (!$condition) throw new Exception('Assertion failed.');
}
```

Now we've arrived at a fully automated test, let's look at how we would rewrite it using PHPUnit (see Example E-5).

Example E-5. PHPUnit testing in action

```
require_once 'PHPUnit/Framework.php';

class ArrayTest extends PHPUnit_Framework_TestCase
{
    public function testNewArrayIsEmpty()
    {
        $names = array();
        $this->assertEquals(0, sizeof($names));
    }

    public function testArrayContainsAnElement()
    {
        $names = array();
        $names[] = 'Bob';
        $this->assertEquals(1, sizeof($names));
    }
}

$testObject = new ArrayTest;
$testObject->testNewArrayIsEmpty();
$testObject->testArrayContainsAnElement();
```

The first thing to notice is that *PHPUnit/Framework.php* has been included in order to make the PHPUnit classes available to the program. After that, the program defines a new class that extends the `PHPUnit_Framework_TestCase` class. This new class contains two methods: one for testing a newly created array and another for testing an array containing an element.

The rules for writing PHPUnit tests are:

- The tests for a class called *Class* go into a class with the name *Class*Test.
- *Class*Test usually inherits from `PHPUnit_Framework_TestCase`.
- The tests are public methods that are named test*SomethingDescriptive*.
- Inside the test methods, assertion methods such as `assertEquals` are used to assert that an actual value matches an expected value.

And there you have it. The three lines of code at the end of Example E-5 create a new test object called `$testObject` and then call each of the object's methods in turn. All being well, this program will display nothing, so to see the output from PHPUnit, try changing the 0 or 1 parameters in the `assertEquals` calls to other values.

A comprehensive and easy-to-follow manual on PHPUnit is available at *http://www .phpunit.de*. Click "Read the documentation" to view it in either HTML or PDF format.

Index

Symbols

! (exclamation mark)
  != (not equal) operator, 43, 65, 68, 309,
    321
  !== (not identical) operator, 65, 68, 309,
    321
  logical not operator, 44, 309, 321, 324
    precedence in PHP, 65
  NOT operator, 69
" " (quotation marks, double)
  escaping in JavaScript strings, 310
  in multiline PHP strings, 47
  in MySQL search strings, 189
  in PHP strings, 38, 46
  in JavaScript strings, 306
$ (dollar sign)
  $ function in JavaScript, 316
  end-of-line matching in regular expressions,
    366, 367
  preceding PHP variable names, 37
    omitting when using -> operator, 105
% (percent sign)
  %= (modulus assignment) operator, 43, 65,
    308, 321
  modulus operator, 42, 65, 308, 321
& (ampersand)
  && (logical and) operator, 44, 309, 321,
    324
    precedence of, 321
  && (logical and) operator/precedence in
    PHP, 65
  &= (bitwise and assignment) operator, 65,
    321
  bitwise and operator, 65

variables passed by reference, 94
' ' (quotation marks, single)
  enclosing PHP array items, 40
  escaping in JavaScript strings, 310
  in PHP strings, 46
  in JavaScript strings, 306
( ) (parentheses)
  forcing operator precedence, 65
  function call in JavaScript, 321
  function call in PHP, 90
  grouping in regular expressions, 363, 367
  implied, indicating operator precedence,
    65
  precedence in PHP, 65
* (asterisk)
  *= (multiplication assignment) operator, 43,
    65, 308, 321
  multiplication operator, 42, 65, 308, 321
  regular expression metacharacter, 361, 367
  wildcard character, use with SELECT
    command, 183
+ (plus sign)
  ++ (increment) operator, 42, 45, 308, 310,
    321
    precedence in PHP, 65
    using in while loop, 80
  += (addition assignment) operator, 43, 45,
    65, 308, 321
  addition and string concatenation operator
    in JavaScript, 321
  addition operator, 42, 65, 308
  Boolean mode in MySQL searches, 189
  regular expression metacharacter, 362, 367
  string concatenation operator in JavaScript,
    310, 321

We'd like to hear your suggestions for improving our indexes. Send email to *index@oreilly.com*.

combining with expressions in PHP, 63
to PHP arrays, using array keyword, 118
variable type, setting in JavaScript, 311
assignment operators
JavaScript, 308
PHP, 43
associative arrays
in JavaScript, 347
in PHP, 117
$_FILES array, 145
multidimensional, 121
walking through, using foreach . . . as, 119
walking through, using list and each functions, 120
associativity, operator, 66
in JavaScript, 322
authentication, 279
(see also HTTP authentication)
login page for social networking site project, 418
simplifying with sessions, 291
starting session after, 289
storing user IP addresses, 293
AUTO_INCREMENT data type, 172
using in MySQL table from PHP, 243

B

\b (backspace character) in JavaScript strings, 310
\B (nonword boundary) in regular expressions, 367
\b (word boundary) in regular expressions, 367
backups and restores in MySQL, 219–223
creating backup file, 220
planning backups, 223
restoring from backup file, 222
using mysqldump, 219
BEGIN command, 216
Berners-Lee, Tim, 1
BIGINT data type, 171
BINARY data type, 169
binary operators, 64
bitwise operators, 63
BLOB data type, 170
blogging platform, WordPress, 86
Boolean expressions in JavaScript, 319

Boolean mode in MATCH . . . AGAINST queries, 189
break command
using in JavaScript loops, 333
using in JavaScript switch statement, 330
using in PHP for loop, 83
using in PHP switch statement, 76
browser/server request/response dialog with cookies, 279
browsers, 1
basic request/response procedure, 2
catching JavaScript errors with try . . . catch, 327
dynamic request/response procedure, 3
forEach method, cross-browser solution, 350
JavaScript, 299
JavaScript error messages, accessing, 303
JavaScript implementations, differences in, 7
older and nonstandard, not supporting scripting, 301
reading link URL in JavaScript, 316
user agent string, 294
XMLHttpRequest object, cross-browser function, 378
browsing history (JavaScript history object), 317
bumpyCaps convention, 338, 342
BYTE data type, 169

C

calendar (YUI), 400–403
callbacks, YUI asyncRequest method, 397
carriage return (\r)
in JavaScript strings, 310
in PHP strings, 47
Cascading Style Sheets (CSS), manipulation with JavaScript, 5
case commands in switch statement, 76
case-insensitive matching in regular expressions (/i), 369
case-insensitivity, function names in PHP, 92
casting
explicit, JavaScript and, 334
implicit and explicit in PHP, 84
CERN (European Laboratory for Particle Physics), 1

example XML document, DOM tree of, 389

DOUBLE data type, 171

DROP keyword, 176

DROP TABLE command, issuing from PHP, 240

duplication of data
across multiple database columns, 204
across multiple database rows, 206

dynamic linking (PHP), 85
use by WordPress blogging platform, 86

dynamic web content, 1–11
Apache web server, 8
benefits of PHP, MySQL, and JavaScript, 5–8
combination of PHP, MySQL, and JavaScript, 9
HTTP and HTML, 2

E

each function, using with list function to walk through associative array, 120

EasyPHP, 14–18
downloading and installing, 14
overcoming installation problems, 14
testing installation, 16

echo <<< construct, 252

echo command (PHP), print command versus, 51

Editra program editor, 29

else statements
in JavaScript, 329
in PHP, 72
closing if . . . else or if . . . elseif . . . else statements, 74

elseif statements (PHP), 73
positioning and number of, 74

email address, validating in form input, 360

empty object, creating in JavaScript, 343

encapsulation, 100

end function, using with PHP arrays, 128

endswitch command, replacing final curly brace in switch statement, 77

equality operators
in JavaScript, 323
in PHP, 67

ereg_replace function (PHP), 149

errors

error text from last called MySQL function in PHP, 227

JavaScript
catching using onError, 326
catching using try . . . catch, 327
debugging, 303
trapping in for loop using break statement, 83
trapping in for loop using continue statement, 84

escape characters
backslash (\) in regular expressions, 363
in JavaScript, 310
in PHP, 47
preventing in strings for submission to MySQL, 263

escapeshellcmd function (PHP), 150

European Laboratory for Particle Physics (CERN), 1

event-min.js file, 396

exclusive or (xor) operator, 44

exec system call (PHP), 149
arguments, 150

execution (` `) operator, 63

EXPLAIN tool (MySQL), 217

explicit casting, 85
JavaScript and, 334

explode function, using to create PHP arrays, 125

expressions
JavaScript, 319–321
literals and variables, 320
operators, 321–325
PHP, 61
literals and variables, 62
operators, 63–70

extends operator (PHP), 109

Extensible Hypertext Markup Language (see XHTML)

extract function, using with PHP arrays, 125

F

\f (form feed) in JavaScript strings, 310

fclose function (PHP), 138

fgets function (PHP), 138, 141
reading from files, 139

file handling in PHP, 137–149
checking if file exists, 137
copying files, 139

functions
  defined, 89
  JavaScript, 312, 337–341
    defining, 337
    prototype property, 344
    returning a value, 339
    returning an array, 341
  MySQL, 194
    commonly used, reference listing, 461–
      472
  PHP, 52, 90–96
    array functions, 123–128
    defining, 91
    passing by reference, 94
    returning a value, 92
    returning an array, 93
    version compatibility, 98
  social networking site project, 407–409
fwrite function (PHP), 138

G

/g (global matching) in regular expressions,
  369
$_GET and $_POST arrays, sanitizing user
  input, 263
GET method, 380, 397
  Ajax GET example using YUI, 397
  using instead of Ajax POST, 385–387
getElementById function (JavaScript), 316
get_post function (PHP), 234
global matching in regular expressions (/g),
  369
global variables
  JavaScript, 312
  PHP, 55
    returning from function calls, 95
Glossword WAMP, 18
Gmail, use of Ajax to check for username
  availability, 10
Google Chrome
  accessing JavaScript error messages, 303
  Error Console message for JavaScript error,
    304
Google Maps, 377
GRANT command, example parameters for,
  165
GROUP BY command, 191

H

head section of HTML document, using
  JavaScript within, 301
heredoc (<<<) operator, 48
hexadecimals, escaping in JavaScript strings,
  310
hidden fields in forms, 260
history object (JavaScript), 317
HTML, 2, 151
  (see also XHTML)
  basic knowledge of, xiii
  DOM (Document Object Model) in
    JavaScript, 314–318
  incorporating PHP within, 33
  JavaScript and, 300
    comment tags for older and nonstandard
      browsers, 301
    debugging JavaScript errors, 303
    including JavaScript files, 302
    using scripts within document head,
      301
  left arrow (← entity), 417
  manipulation with JavaScript, 7
  multiline output, creating in PHP, 252
  program editors for, 29
  sanitizing in form input, 263
HTML 4.01 document types, 153
HTML injections, 248
<html> tag, xmlns attribute, 153
htmlentities function (PHP), 57, 249
HTTP, 2
  request/response procedure, 2
HTTP authentication, 282–288
  checking for valid username and password
    using PHP, 284
  login prompt, 282
  storing usernames and passwords, 285
    creating users table in MySQL using
      PHP, 286
    PHP authentication using MySQL, 287
    salting passwords, 285
  user clicks Cancel before logging in, 283
HTTPS, 293

I

identity operator (see ===, under symbols)
IDEs (Integrated Development Environments),
  30

regeneration, session, 295
register_globals function (PHP), 254
regular expressions, 361–370
  breakdown of typical regular expression, 365
  breakdown of validateUsername regular expression (example), 366
  character classes, 363
  examples of, 368
  general modifiers, 369
  grouping through parentheses, 363
  metacharacters, 361
    summary of, 367
  negation of character class, 364
  ranges in, 364
  using in JavaScript, 369
  using in PHP, 369
  using to validate username in a form, 360
  using with ereg_replace function in PHP, 149
relational databases, 158
  (see also MySQL)
  normalization, 203
relational operators
  in JavaScript, 323–325
  in PHP, 67–70
relationships in database data, 211–214
  many-to-many, 213
  one-to-many, 212
  one-to-one, 211
  privacy and, 214
remote server, accessing MySQL on, 162
RENAME command, 175
rename function (PHP), 140
replace method (JavaScript), 369
request/response process, 2
  for dynamic web pages, 3
require statements (PHP), 97
require_once (PHP), 97, 227
reset function, using with PHP arrays, 127
results from PHP query of MySQL database, 229
  fetching a row, 231
return statements, 92
reverse method (JavaScript), 352
Robin's Nest project (see social networking site, creating)
ROLLBACK command, 216
rows

defined, 158
deleting from table, 184
preventing duplicates, using AUTO_INCREMENT type, 172

S

\S (nonwhitespace character) in regular expressions, 367
\s (whitespace character) in regular characters, 367
Safari, accessing JavaScript error messages, 303
salting passwords, 285
sanitizeString and sanitizeMySQL functions (PHP), 263
sanitizing user input, PHP authentication using MySQL, 288
scope of variables
  global and local variables in JavaScript, 312
  PHP, 53–58, 96
scope resolution operator (::), 106
<script> </script> tags, 300
scripting languages, VBScript and Tcl, 302
security
  register_globals function in PHP, 254
  sessions, 293–296
  superglobal variables in PHP, 57
SELECT command, 7, 183
  grouping results with GROUP BY, 191
  issuing SELECT * FROM statement using PHP, 241
  joining two tables in single SELECT, 193
  SELECT COUNT, 183
  SELECT DISTINCT, 184
  sorting results with ORDER BY, 191
  using LIKE qualifier, 186
  using LIMIT qualifier, 187
  WHERE keyword, 185
select tags in forms, 260
  using with multiple parameter, 261
self keyword (PHP), referencing constants, 107
servers, 1
  Apache web server, 8
  basic request/response procedure, 2
  dynamic request/response procedure, 3
  shared, session security and, 296
sessions, 289–296
  ending, 292

word (\w) character in regular expressions, 368
WordPress blogging platform, 86
World Wide Web, 1

X

XAMPP, 18
   downloading for Mac OS X, 25
   installing on Linux, 25
XHTML, 151
   benefits of, 151
   document types in XHTML 1.0, 153
   HTML 4.01 document types, 153
   rules differentiating it from HTML, 152
   validation, 154
   versions, 151
XML
   Ajax XML example using YUI, 399–400
   example XHTML 1.0 document, 152
   example XML document and DOM tree, 389
   fetching Yahoo! XML news feed via Ajax, 390
   reasons to use with Ajax, 391
   sending XML requests with XMLHttpRequest, 387
XMLHttpRequest object, 378–391
   cross-browser function for, 378
   example program (urlpost.html), 380–385
      readyState property, 382
      server half of Ajax process, 383
   example program using GET, 385–387
   properties and methods, 379
   sending XML requests, 387–391
xor (exclusive or) operator, 44
   precedence in PHP, 65
XOR operator, 69
XSS injections, 248

Y

Yahoo! User Interface (see YUI)
yahoo-min.js file, 396
YEAR data type, 172
YUI (Yahoo! User Interface), 394–403
   compressed versions, 396
   installing, 394
   other uses for, 400

sign-up page for social networking site project, 415–417
simple calendar, 400–403
using for Ajax, 396–400
   Ajax GET example using YUI, 397
   Ajax XML example using YUI, 399–400
   asyncRequest method, 397
   including framework files, 396

Z

Zend Server CE, 25
ZEROFILL qualifier, using with INT type, 171

About the Author

Robin Nixon has worked with and written about computers since the early 1980s (his first computer was a Tandy TRS 80 Model 1 with a massive 4 KB of RAM!). During this time he has written in excess of 500 articles for many of the UK's top computer magazines. *Learning PHP, MySQL, and JavaScript* is his third book.

Robin started his computing career in the Cheshire homes for disabled people, where he was responsible for setting up computer rooms in a number of residential homes, and for evaluating and tailoring hardware and software so that disabled people could use the new technology—sometimes by means of only a single switch operated by mouth or finger.

After writing articles for computer magazines about his work with disabled people, he eventually worked full time for one of the country's main IT magazine publishers, where he held several roles including editorial, promotions, and cover disc editing.

With the dawn of the Internet in the 1990s, Robin branched out into developing websites. One of these presented the world's first radio station licensed by the music copyright holders, and was featured in several news reports on TV and radio networks in the United Kingdom. In order to enable people to continue to surf while listening, Robin also developed the first known pop-up windows.

Robin lives on the southeast coast of England with his wife Julie, a trained nurse, and five children, where he also finds time to foster three disabled children, as well as working full time from home as a technical author.

Colophon

The animals on the cover of *Learning PHP, MySQL, and JavaScript* are sugar gliders (*Petaurus breviceps*). Sugar gliders are small, gray-furred creatures that grow to an adult length of six to seven-and-a-half inches. Their tails, which are distinguished by a black tip, are usually as long as their bodies. Membranes extend between their wrists and ankles and provide an aerodynamic surface that helps them glide between trees.

Sugar gliders are native to Australia and Tasmania. They prefer to live in the hollow parts of eucalyptus and other types of large trees with several other adult sugar gliders and their own children.

Though sugar gliders reside in groups and defend their territory together, they don't always live in harmony. One male will assert his dominance by marking the group's territory with his saliva and then by marking all group members with a distinctive scent produced from his forehead and chest glands. This ensures that members of the group will know when an outsider approaches; group members will fight off any sugar glider not bearing their scent. However, a sugar glider group will welcome and mark an outsider if one of their adult males dies (the group will typically replace a deceased adult female with their one of their own female offspring).

Sugar gliders make popular pets because of their inquisitive, playful natures, and because many think they are cute. But there are disadvantages to keeping sugar gliders as pets: as they are exotic animals, sugar gliders need specialized, complicated diets consisting of items such as crickets, a variety of fruits and vegetables, and mealworms; healthy housing requires a cage or space no less than the size of an aviary; their distinctive scents can be bothersome to humans; as they are nocturnal creatures, they will bark, hiss, run, and glide all night long; it's not uncommon for them to extricate their bowels while playing or eating; and in some states and countries, it is illegal to own sugar gliders as household pets.

The cover image is from *Dover's Animals*. The cover font is Adobe ITC Garamond. The text font is Linotype Birka; the heading font is Adobe Myriad Condensed; and the code font is LucasFont's TheSansMonoCondensed.

Try the online edition
free for 45 days

70502